TAX SHELTER
DESK BOOK

TAX SHELTER
DESK BOOK

Lewis G. Mosburg, Jr.

INSTITUTE FOR BUSINESS PLANNING, INC.
IBP PLAZA, ENGLEWOOD CLIFFS, N.J. 07632

© 1978 *by*

Institute for Business Planning, Inc.
IBP Plaza, Englewood Cliffs, N.J. 07632

Sixth Printing.....June, 1980

Library of Congress
Catalog Card Number
78-057937

"This publication is designed to provide accurate and authoritative information in regard to the subject matter covered. It is sold with the understanding that the publisher is not engaged in rendering legal, accounting or other professional service. If legal advice is required, the services of a competent professional person should be sought."

—From a Declaration of Principles jointly adopted by a Committee of the American Bar Association and a Committee of Publishers and Associations.

Printed in the United States of America

ISBN 87624-578-5

About the Author

Lewis G. Mosburg, Jr., author of the *Tax Shelter Desk Book,* is the former Vice-Chairman of the Board of the Oklahoma City law firm of Andrews Mosburg Davis Elam Legg & Bixler, Inc., and is now Senior Partner of a newly organized Oklahoma City law firm.

A frequent lecturer and prolific writer on tax-sheltered investments, as well as oil and gas and real estate transactions, Mr. Mosburg serves as Chairman of the Industry Advisory Committee to the North American Securities Administrators Associations's Oil and Gas Interests Committee, and is a member of the Oil and Gas and Real Estate Advisory Committees to the California Commissioner of Corporations, and the National Association of Securities Dealers, Inc.'s Committee on Direct Participation Programs (formerly the Committee on Tax-Sheltered Programs). Mr. Mosburg is also special counsel (and former general counsel) to the Oil Investment Institute and is an affiliated member (and a former member of the Board of Governors) of the Real Estate Securities and Syndication Institute.

Mr. Mosburg's numerous publications on oil and gas, real estate and tax-sheltered investments include *Real Estate Syndicate Offering Handbook* (Property Press, 3rd ed. 1976); *Financing Oil and Gas Ventures* (The Institute for Energy Development, Inc. 1978); *Financing Coal Ventures* (The Institute for Energy Development, Inc. 1977); and *Structuring Tax-Sheltered Investments Under the Tax Reform Act of 1976* (The Institute for

Energy Development, Inc. 1977); as well as cassettes on the structuring, analysis and securities aspects of tax-sheltered investments.

Mr. Mosburg is also the creator of *The Tax Shelter Coloring Book* (The Institute for Energy Development, Inc. 1977), an innovative introduction to tax shelters which has been hailed by a former Securities and Exchange Commissioner as "explaining tax-shelters in a way anyone can understand."

Mr. Mosburg's annual lecture series include full-day institutes for investors on "Understanding Tax-Sheltered Investments," for which *The Tax Shelter Coloring Book* was initially developed, and a two-day institute for investment professionals on "Structuring Tax-Sheltered Investments."

A member of Phi Beta Kappa and Order of the Coif, Mr. Mosburg also serves as Chairman of the Board and Academic Director of the Oklahoma City and Fort Worth-based Institute for Energy Development, Inc., President of IED Professional Center, Inc., and IED Publishing House, Inc., Director of IED Exploration, Inc., the industry leaders in the education of oil and gas explorationists, and as President of Ideamation, Inc., an Oklahoma City book distributor.

Acknowledgements

I abhor acknowledgements in books. It's not that any author isn't incredibly indebted to the numerous people that made possible the book for which he takes all the credit. It's just that few bother to read the "acknowledgement" section of a book. However, in connection with this undertaking, I feel compelled to express my appreciation for the yeoman efforts expended by *Jim Thielke* and *Marshall Snipes* of the Oklahoma City office of Peat, Marwick, Mitchell & Co. in providing expert advice in connection with this book. (To this I might add that they take no responsibility for *my* errors; that's my burden.)

In view of my strong feelings against this sort of thing, I have decided not to acknowledge the substantial debt of gratitude that I also owe to *Karen Wechsler* and *Olivia Goldenberg,* or how much I appreciate the incredible artwork of *Trey Aven* and *Steve Hill* which went into the author's *Tax Shelter Coloring Book* (The Institute for Energy Development: 1977), from whose pages the illustrations contained in this book are taken. Nor will I mention the debts I owe, on all levels, to *Peggy Durham.* They'll just have to go unrecognized.

Lewis G. Mosburg, Jr.
Oklahoma City, Oklahoma
August, 1978

From Mosburg, *The Tax Shelter Coloring Book.*© 1977, by The Institute for Energy Development, Inc. All rights reserved.

What This Book Will Do for You

Most Americans with high incomes work hard to earn that money. They'd like to be able to enjoy the rewards that such hard work should bring. But more and more, high-salaried individuals are discovering it next to impossible to retain any substantial portion of their income. This is because of a Federal income tax structure which penalizes those capable of earning substantial income.

Let's not debate the social merits or demerits of this system. Instead, let's realize that there are legitimate ways of avoiding its confiscatory results. You can keep a far larger portion of your hard-earned income by taking advantage of certain investment opportunities deliberately built into the tax code by Congress. This tax code encourages investment of capital in such nationally-vital industries as energy, housing, and food.

These "tax-sheltered investments" aren't "gimmicks" or "loopholes." They are legitimate opportunities to increase your "spendable" income, or your estate, by providing venture capital for industries which, in turn, benefit the country.

Sounds great, doesn't it? But consider this:

(1) Most of these tax-shelter opportunities are high risk. (Why would Congress have to provide the tax incentives if the investment was a "sure thing?") Even with the tax benefits, you can lose money as well as make it.

(2) Since tax shelters are a complicated investment area, far removed from the "traditional," and more familiar, investment areas of stocks, bonds, and debentures, there are many "questionable" tax shelters being offered. Even the experienced investor may find it hard to determine what is glitter, and what is gold. (Now you can *really* lose money.)

(3) Over the last ten years, Congress and the Internal Revenue Service have been consistently hacking away at many "traditional" tax benefits. You have to be more creative in today's tax climate to provide tax shelter. And you have to be better prepared to assess the *economics* of the investment, over and above the hoped-for tax benefits.

So what should this book do for you? It should do the following:

- **Explain** the basic principles upon which all tax-sheltered investments rest.
- **Examine** each type of tax-sheltered investment, and see what it offers or does not offer you in terms of your specific investment objectives.
- **Learn** how you can plan creatively to avoid the impact of recent tax law changes, and to protect against future change.
- **See** how you can tell a good tax-sheltered investment from a mediocre or bad one, and how to get yourself (and your money) out of those investments which go sour.

If you are a high-tax-bracket investor, this book should help you keep more of your earnings by paying the government less. If you are a lawyer, accountant, or investment advisor counseling such investors, it should aid you in better assisting your client. And if you put together tax-sheltered investments—or advise those who do—it should help you structure your investment opportunities. It should make them more appealing and more rewarding to your prospective investors—and thus to you.

Read on!

Introduction

This entire book is about "tax shelters," a form of investment which permits you—and even encourages you—to "hit back" against a confiscatory Federal income tax system. This sytem makes it virtually impossible for the hard and successful worker to save or enjoy any substantial portion of the income he has labored so hard to produce.

The tax-sheltered investment can defuse much of the tax time bomb which proves so discouraging to most successful Americans. However, a failure to understand:

☐ How tax-sheltered investments work
☐ When a tax-sheltered investment will benefit you—and when it won't
☐ Which tax shelter (or shelters) are right for you—and which aren't
☐ How to tell a good tax-sheltered investment from a mediocre, bad, or fraudulent one can lead to just as much—or more—grief than staying out of tax shelters entirely.

Part One of this book will "introduce" you to the tax-sheltered investment. It will show you how it works, its potential rewards and pitfalls, the effects of recent changes in Federal tax laws, and what to expect in the future. **Part Two** will guide you through the intricacies of the "traditional" tax-sheltered investments: Real Estate, Oil and Gas, Cattle, and Agriculture. **Part Three** will deal with the latest in the less traditional tax shelters—from movies to coal, record, and book syndications—which offer the very affluent investor a chance (but *not* the assurance) of very high initial tax deductions, with commensurate risks. **Part Four** will outline what few tax-shelter manuals cover, such as: how to select the right tax shelter for *you*; deciding how much to invest in what kind of tax-sheltered investments; and how to determine which particular investments offer an opportunity to make money, and which are destined primarily to channel your hard-earned dollars into the promoter's pocket. In **Part Five**, you'll find charts and checklists which you can use in analyzing prospective tax-sheltered investments. These aids will also help you in structuring a tax-shelter so that it should legitimately appeal to prospective tax-shelter investors.

Additional Sources of Information

It is not the purpose of this book to detail exhaustive citations for each of the points stressed. Instead, it seeks to provide an overview, to emphasize basic concepts, and to alert you to problem areas.

Following each major subdivision is a list of "Additional Readings" in each area. The following is a partial list of sources which publish various periodicals and provide a steady stream of data concerning tax shelters:

Brennan Reports
William G. Brennan, Inc.
P.O. Box 357
Johnstown, Pennsylvania
(814) 255-4151

IED Publishing House, Inc.
P.O. Box 11167
Oklahoma City, Oklahoma 73116
(405) 236-2453

The Institute for Energy Development, Inc.
P.O. Box 19243
Oklahoma City, Oklahoma 73144
(405) 631-7679

Questor Associates/Property Press
115 Sansome Street
San Francisco, California 94104
(415) 433-0302

Resource Programs, Inc.
521 Fifth Avenue
New York, New York 10017
(212) 986-7510

CONTENTS

PART THREE THE UNCONVENTIONAL TAX SHELTERS—HEREINAFTER OF THE "EXOTICS"

PART FOUR SELECTING THE RIGHT TAX SHELTER FOR YOU

APPENDIX

PART ONE
Introduction to the
"Tax Shelter" Concept

1.

The Tax-Sheltered Investment—What Is It, How It Works, and Why

WHY GOVERNMENT CREATES "TAX ADVANTAGED" INVESTMENTS

Tax shelters have come a long way in the 1970's. In the 1950's and 1960's, tax shelters were considered primarily a "toy" of the very wealthy. They were regarded as "investments" of questionable economic value either from the investor's or the public's standpoint, but something our tax system permitted to exist.

In the 1970's, tax-advantaged investments stand as a chief source of venture capital for the energy, housing, and food industries. These investments are a source of capital which, it has been estimated, is responsible for the discovery of as much as 60% of our new oil and gas reserves and as a bulwark of the housing industry. They are a critical factor in the beef industry's fight to survive. And in addition to the critical role played in energy, housing, and food, tax shelters have proved a key capital source for the motion picture industry, and the acquisition of various types of equipment.

You'll hear, time and time again, that by investing in these critical industries, you are somehow shirking your "duty" to pay your fair tax share. How many times have you heard that "the rich pay no taxes?"

You are in a relatively exclusive group. Less than 1½ percent of our taxpayers have over $50,000 in taxable income. And only one-third of one percent have taxable income of $100,000. But if you are in the $50,000 category, you are paying nearly 25 percent of the nation's total taxes. And at $100,000, you pay 10 percent of the total tax bill—some 30 times your per capita share!

So tax shelters aren't "gimmicks" or "loopholes." Instead, they result

1

from a conscious decision on the part of Congress that various key industries, vital to the economy, can best be financed by attracting capital through the technique of granting tax incentives for such investment, rather than by supporting such industries through direct government subsidies or government owned and operated companies. The wisdom of this policy, as compared with other approaches, is reflected in a popular bumper sticker reading: "If You Like Our Postal System, You'll Love Our National Oil Company!"

[¶101.1]   Tax Incentives Serve the Nation's Needs as Well as Your Needs

The Congressional decision to encourage investment in various critical industries also reflects the fact that the historic return on dollars invested in such industries is not high enough to attract sufficient capital to the industry without the encouragement of the tax incentives. (If sufficient venture capital were forthcoming for the industry to supply the nation's needs without the incentives, the tax advantages wouldn't be necessary.) The risk involved makes more traditional financing methods insufficient or totally unavailable for the needs of these industries.

This system of securing necessary capital through the tax-saving's "carrot" is constantly re-evaluated by the Congress. When it is determined that the tax advantages are excessive, or unnecessary, they are reduced or eliminated. (Thus, the Tax Reform Act of 1969 severely restricted tax benefits available for citrus and almond groves. (See Internal Revenue Code, §278(a)). However, a point to remember if you start to feel guilty about "avoiding" your just share of taxes is that Congress didn't enact these tax incentives with the benevolent purpose of reducing your tax bill. Instead, it is seeking to reduce the price of heating and transportation to the consumer, of making better quality housing available to low- and middle-income families, and providing cheaper beef, through what it considers the most effective means: in effect, giving you a tax break if you invest your excess dollars in these industries instead of taking an expensive vacation, buying a new home, or replacing your car. Thus, at the same time you are reducing your taxes, you are also furthering some social or economic Congressional objective that benefits the public at large.

(And, hopefully, if you invest wisely, you'll still be able to afford that vacation or car, with dollars to spare.)

Tax evader? No, you're a patriot!

[¶102]   HOW A "TAX SHELTER" WORKS

Most investors, including those who have invested in tax-sheltered investments in the past, are woefully ignorant of how a tax shelter actually works. This can be a disaster. If you don't understand your tax shelter, you may tragically misevaluate just what it can (and can't) do for you.

"Taxable income" is your *income from all sources,* including compensation for services, the gross profits of your business, rents, interest, and dividends which you receive, and gains from property transactions ("gross income"), *less deductions permitted by the tax code,* such as noncapital expenditures made to generate this income, and certain "itemized deductions" for interest and taxes paid by you, your charitable contributions, etc. Internal Revenue Code, §61.

If you are a single taxpayer with a taxable income of $34,000, at least 50 percent of every dollar you earn above this level will go to the Federal Government in taxes—you are in the 50 percent Federal income tax bracket. If you are a married taxpayer filing a joint return, you similarly find yourself in the 50 percent Federal income tax bracket when your taxable income reaches $47,000. "Gross income" less business deductions equals "adjusted gross income." (Internal Revenue Code, §62.) Adjusted gross income less itemized deductions gives you your "taxable income"—the figure against which the Government's tax rates will be applied to compute your income tax. You may then be permitted to apply certain "tax credits," such as the *investment tax credit* (see ¶201), to arrive at the amount you actually owe the Government in taxes.

Once your taxable income reaches $100,000, 70 percent of every additional dollar you earn goes to the Federal Government if you are single, unless you are saved by the maximum tax on personal service ("earned") income, or by "income averaging." (For married taxpayers filing joint returns, the 70% bracket is reached at the $200,000 taxable income level.)

This doesn't mean that as a 50 percent bracket taxpayer, you pay 50 percent of your income to the Federal Government, or 70 percent when you reach the 70 percent bracket. Our tax system has imposed a *graduated* income tax. Only those dollars above the level at which the higher tax bracket is reached are taxed at the higher rate. Thus, the tax on $47,200 of taxable income for the married taxpayer is $14,060, and is $110,980 on taxable income of $203,200, for *effective* tax rates of 30 percent and 55 percent, respectively.

For a graph of effective tax rates at various income levels, see Chart 102-1, in the Appendix. For tax bracket levels, see Chart 102-2.

Despite the difference between tax bracket and effective tax rate, the total tax bite if you stay at a high "taxable income" is staggering. You may not consider yourself a terribly "affluent" person. Inflationary factors are forcing more and more persons into the higher tax brackets, even though the buying power of their dollars stays constant. But your taxes *don't* stay constant as inflation ups your income, so that your buying power on the same "real" income is actually being reduced by those additional taxes. In any event, you find it becomes increasingly hard to keep dollars over and above your normal living expenses.

[¶102.1]   Inflation Increases Your Tax Bill

The interplay of the "graduated" Federal income tax and inflation, and its effects on you or your clients, is something to give anyone pause. For example, if in 1970 you were in the 30 percent Federal income tax bracket, it would take you $57,000 in pretax earnings to purchase a $40,000 house. (70 percent—the dollars you had left after the Federal Government's 30 percent income tax "bite"—of $57,000 would equal the $40,000 you needed to purchase your home.) But today, you will probably find that the same house would cost you $80,000. So what, you might say? My earnings have kept pace with this rising inflation: just as the cost of that house has doubled, so has my salary. However, if this is true, instead of your earnings being taxed at 30 percent, in all likelihood you now find yourself in the 50 percent income tax bracket (or even higher). This means that to buy that $80,000 house, you will now have to earn at least $160,000 in pretax earnings, or nearly *three times* the amount of money you would have had to make to purchase it in 1970. Thus, while your *pretax earnings* may have risen to keep pace with inflation, the graduated Federal income tax means that the *aftertax buying power* of those dollars has been seriously eroded.

[¶102.2]   The Double Tax Bite on Your Income

Even if "your" income is primarily generated through an incorporated business, you may face serious tax problems. If the corporate earnings are distributed to you in the form of dividends, you must pay a double tax "bite." This means the corporation's earnings are taxed first at the corporate level, and then again at your personal level when you receive the dividends. (And these dividends are *not* deductible by the corporation for Federal income tax purposes under present law.) Thus, if the corporation has $100,000 in taxable income, and distributes $50,000 to you, the Federal Government will take $24,000 in corporate taxes on that $50,000, and an additional $25,000 in personal taxes if you are a 50 percent bracket taxpayer—an amount equal to nearly the *entire dividend* goes to the Government, when you consider the combined corporate and individual taxes! (*More* than the entire dividend amount will go to the Government—directly or indirectly—if you are in the 70 percent bracket.)

So I'll just keep the earnings in the corporation to avoid the double tax, you say. Consider this:

• The dollars are not spendable by you, unless they can be justified as corporate "fringes" for your benefit. And at some stage, these "fringes" may become suspect.

- 48 percent of the dollars are still going to the Government in the form of corporate taxes.
- The corporation may be subjecting itself to the possibility of confiscatory "personal holding company" or "accumulated earnings" taxes. As to personal holding companies and the accumulated earnings tax, see Internal Revenue Code Sections 541-547 and Sections 531-537.

So tax-sheltered investments can make sense for corporations as well as individuals. And since the Tax Reform Act of 1976, *some* types of tax-sheltered investments may make *more* sense for corporate taxpayers than for the individual taxpayer. (See Chapter 5.)

[¶103]   HOW A TAX-SHELTERED
          INVESTMENT REDUCES YOUR TAXES

Here's how the tax-sheltered investment works to reduce your taxes, thus increasing the dollars you have to save or spend.

If, after meeting your normal living expenses, you have $10,000 left, $5,000 must be paid in taxes to the Federal Government if you are in the 50 percent Federal income tax bracket. (If you're in the 70 percent bracket, $7,000 must be paid to the Government). So, out of your $10,000 "surplus," you have only $5,000 (or $3,000) left to spend, invest, or build an estate.

However, the tax incentives legislated by Congress create certain deductions and other tax benefits for Federal income tax purposes. These tax incentives will serve, to the extent of these benefits:

- ☐ To *defer* taxes on the deductible portion of the investment
- ☐ To *shelter income* from the investment from further taxation
- ☐ In some instances, to *permanently shelter* the deductible portion of the investment. (This last benefit is referred to as "deep" shelter.)

The end result of this process is some very advantageous tax consequences to you. (See ¶201). To the extent you have gained "deep" shelter, the investment has created a permanent tax savings. Even if the result is only a deferral of tax, you will have the use of the money in the meantime—and money has a "time value". (See ¶402). And an 8 percent *tax-free* income from an investment is far more valuable to you than a 10 percent return, half or more of which must be paid to the Federal Government in taxes.

Even if tax-sheltered investments are normally not for you, a sale of your business or a substantially appreciated piece of property can trigger tremendous capital gains liability. While long-term capital gains are taxed more favorably under the tax code than "ordinary income" is taxed, even this more favorable taxation will eat up a substantial portion of your gain. (See ¶201.) When inflation is taken into account, which our tax code ignores, you may find that virtually all of your "real dollar" profit has been consumed by taxes. This may be a time for you to consider utilizing tax-sheltered investments to protect your long-term profit from "elimination by taxation."

[¶103.1]   How to Achieve Permanent Tax Shelter

So, however your tax problems arise, your objective will be *permanently to shelter* as much of your income as possible from any form of taxation. This can be done through *deep shelter deductions* and through *sheltering the income* from the investment. Also, you can have the *dollars taxed at a lower rate* by postponing taxes to years in which you will be in a *lower Federal income tax bracket*. You can *defer taxes* until later years so that the "time value" of the deduction reduces its impact. Or, you can *convert "ordinary income" dollars*—dollars taxed at the higher rates typically applicable to taxable income—*into "capital gains"* dollars. These are dollars taxable at the lower rates applicable to long-term capital gains.

A word about this ordinary income-capital gains "alchemy." For many years, the conversion of ordinary income into capital gains was one of the most effective planning tools for high-income investors. But various tax law changes have substantially reduced the benefits of this technique, especially for the 50 percent bracket investor. (See ¶201.)

Before deciding that the tax-sheltered investment approach has solved all your tax problems, let's consider two other points:

1. *You must look at the tax results over the life of the investment.* While you will receive tax benefits going in, there will be tax consequences coming out: today's tax savings may become tomorrow's tax liability.

   ☐ If you sell your business for a $1,000,000 profit, and you are in the 70 percent bracket, your long-term capital gains tax will be $350,000—leaving you $650,000 after taxes.

   ☐ Invest $500,000 in a series of 100 percent deductible oil and gas investments. You will still have $500,000 left—plus any production revenues. In other words, it has cost you only $150,000 for exposure to a half million dollars worth of drilling results!

   Thus, in an investment whose income (and capital) are not totally sheltered from taxation, taxes must be paid when the dollars come back to you. Since a part of the "return" to you from a tax-sheltered investment is the tax-savings component, this eventual taxation may represent an economic erosion of your capital. Thus, if you bought a stock for a dollar, then sold it for a dollar, there would be no taxable income, only a return of your original capital or "basis" in the investment: you'd still have the dollar left. But if you invested a dollar in a tax-shelter, taking a 100% deduction (and creating a tax savings), your "basis" in your investment is zero. If you resell that investment for a dollar, the entire return is taxable to you, and, after paying the tax on your "gain," you'll have something less than a dollar left.

Certain investments which augment your equity dollars with borrowings—*leverage*—create additional problems. You may be able to deduct an amount equal to both your equity investment and the borrowed dollars, receiving an *excess write-off* far greater than the cash you personally put up. (See ¶201.) But the dollars you later receive which must be used to pay off the borrowings are taxable to you, and the mortgage payments are non-deductible. So the price tag for your earlier excess write-off on dollars you never put up is a subsequent tax on dollars that the bank—not you—receive. Thus, you will be taxable on "Phantom Income", even though you are receiving no cash with which to pay those taxes. (See ¶¶202, 2601.)

2. *The tax savings only reduce, but do not eliminate, the risk.* Tax deductions reduce risk by letting you make part of your investment with dollars that otherwise would be paid in taxes. This portion of your investment is referred to as *"tax dollars"* or *"soft dollars."* However, since there can be no *permanent* tax savings in excess of the savings on your cash investment, even in the "excess write-off" programs that offer initial deductions of 200%, 300%, or 400% (see ¶2601), you will always have some of your money at stake that is not subject to being permanently offset by tax benefits. These "at risk" dollars are referred to as *"hard dollars."* And the risk that you will lose all or a part of these hard dollars is very real. (See Chapter 3.)

[¶104]   **BENEFITS TO THE INVESTOR—**
TAX-WISE AND OTHERWISE

By now, you have probably decided that tax-sheltered investments are something that you might like to look into further. However, for you to understand the risks that we have mentioned in tax-sheltered investments—they are not an automatic solution to all your problems—you will need to understand how a tax-sheltered investment works.

The tax-sheltered investment is a *direct participation investment.* This may be a new term to you. However, it's much more accurate than the

taxable portion of the income, "phantom" or otherwise, from your investment), *cash flow*, and *appreciation*, of 10 percent to 12 percent, depending upon your tax bracket.

This estimated rate of return has been computed on an "internal rate of return" or "discounted cash flow" basis. This means it takes into account the "time value" of money. (See ¶402.) But it also assumes that you have invested in a well-structured, well-selected, and well-managed investment. The assumption is that speculative factors have not combined to increase (or, as is more often the case, decrease) the return from your potentially profitable investment. And, also, that there have been no adverse changes in the tax laws.

Unfortunately, in today's political climate, you must face the reality that tax laws *will* change, and at an increasingly rapid pace. (See Chapters 5 and 6.) However, hopefully these problems can be dealt with as they arise by continued intelligent tax planning on your part and the part of your advisors.

Obviously, you may do better if you are in a tax-sheltered investment which proves of extremely high quality or which outruns the averages. But even in such "good" investments, if you properly diversify—a necessity to be discussed later—the law of averages usually will catch up with you. Equally significant, you can be assured that you can do much worse if you end up in a mediocre, poor, or fraudulent tax-sheltered investment. In this case, expect a zero return to a total "wipe-out" of your capital. Or, if your investment, though well-selected and well-managed, is affected in an adverse way by the ever-present and unavoidable speculative factors that mark all tax-sheltered ventures, you will do less well.

We have seen, then, that you may be benefited by a tax-sheltered investment in many ways. Let's take a moment to overview what tax-shelter opportunities may be available to you.

[¶105]   **THE MANY FORMS OF**
                         "TAX SHELTERS"

Tax-sheltered investments come in many forms. They have included such exotic investments as chinchilla breeding, oyster and catfish farming, and the raising of bees. (As a matter of fact, any business that has a need for venture capital will probably operate at a loss in its early years, and could be structured as a tax-sheltered investment.) However, the most popular tax-sheltered investments by far are real estate, oil and gas, and cattle. Likewise, in recent years, there has been increasing attention paid to motion pictures, equipment leasing, agriculture, timber, coal, and books and records as investment vehicles which can be structured to provide you with tax benefits in addition to their hoped-for economic potential.

For now, you should probably focus on real estate, oil and gas, and cattle as your primary area of investment interest. Why? Chiefly because there will be more of these investments readily available to you. You will normally find it easier to locate an investment in this group which can be checked out to determine if it truly has investment potential or is merely an attractively-packaged opportunity for losing money, despite its apparent (or real) tax benefits.

Each of the investments we have just mentioned has very different investment characteristics in the areas that should be highly important to you: tax benefits; cash flow; appreciation potential; liquidity; and risk. Also, within each investment area, there are kinds of investments that vary markedly as to which and how much of these investment benefits or detriments they provide. Thus, the investment characteristics of acquiring an interest in a government-assisted housing project vary dramatically from an investment in raw land, although both involve real estate. Similarly, the investment characteristics of participating in the drilling of exploratory oil and gas wells is totally different from what may be offered by the purchase of an interest in producing oil and gas properties—the so called "oil income" program. And cattle *feeding*—one form of livestock investment—offers you totally different potential benefits and risks than an investment in a cattle *breeding* program.

The investment characteristics of each form of investment that we have mentioned, plus various other investment opportunities, will be discussed in detail in the chapters dealing with that form of investment. Similarly, Chapter 28 will give you an overview of these investment characteristics by investment type to help you determine which investment area or areas are most appropriate for you. For now, it is enough for you to be aware that there are a number of investment opportunities available, some of which will be potentially right for you and some of which will not, and that your first consideration, unless you are an extremely knowledgeable tax-sheltered investor, or have available to you advice from an experienced professional in the area, will probably center around real estate, oil and gas, or cattle.

[¶106]   **POPULARITY OF VARIOUS
TAX SHELTERS**

It should help you, in determining which tax shelters you want to look at first, to see their relative popularity among investors. The fact that a given investment is, or is not, popular is not necessarily an indication of its investment merit. However, the popularity will give you some idea of how the investment community views the overall investment potential of various kinds of investments. Also, the number of investments available will give you some idea of how likely it is that you will be able to "pick and choose" among a number of investment opportunities in that area in trying to find one that is right for you. Unless you have large sums to invest, it will also help you to determine what kind of investment opportunities may in fact be coming your way, since the better informed sponsors of such investments are very alert to the fact that they are offering you a "security" under Federal and State securities laws.

Just as it is difficult to determine historical investment returns in the tax-shelter area, in the past it has proved impossible to accurately discover exactly how many dollars are being invested, and how many investment opportunities are being offered, in the tax-shelter area. This is expected to change in the near future as a result of studies being undertaken by various "securities" agencies. However, there are certain figures available which are kept by the National Association of Securities Dealers, Inc. (the "NASD"), the quasi-governmental agency which regulates the majority of the nation's securities brokerage firms. These figures, based upon those investments offered by NASD member firms which are required to be filed with the NASD, show that oil and gas and real estate are by far the most popular form of widely distributed tax-sheltered investments. At the present time, this by no means covers *all* tax-sheltered investments being offered by NASD broker-dealers. NASD members also offer you investment opportunities in cattle, agriculture, and the so-called "exotics." (Figures released by the NASD in mid-1978 indicate that the "exotics" may account for up to twenty-five percent of such "private" activities by its members, and that such private offerings far outweigh "public" offerings in number of investments offered.)

The NASD figures through December 31, 1977, both as to number of programs, and by dollar amounts, registered, are illustrated in the following chart:

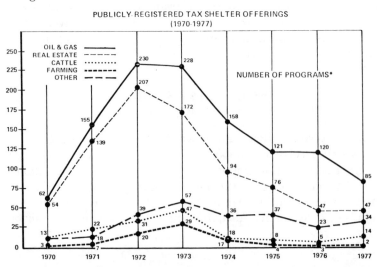

PUBLICLY-REGISTERED TAX SHELTER OFFERINGS
(1970-1977)

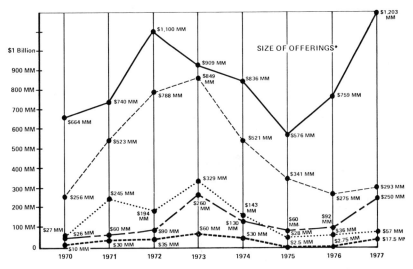

©1978, The Institute for Energy Development, Inc.   *Based on records of National Association of Securities Dealers, Inc.

NASD figures through June 30, 1978, show a continuing rapid increase in such offerings in the areas of oil and gas, real estate, and the "exotics," with the number and size of such offerings increasing by fifty percent or more in all three of these tax shelter investment areas over the comparable 1977 period, and the dollar amount of real estate offerings more than tripling over the 1977 level.

You have now looked at various concepts concerning the "tax-sheltered" investment—why they were created, how they work, what benefits they may provide for you, and the forms they take, as well as their relative popularity. Now, let's turn to the subject which made you pick up this book—tax deductions and other tax benefits—to get a better understanding of how the tax incentives provided by the government actually operate. For unless you understand how these tax consequences work, the likelihood of your investing in the right tax-sheltered investment will be severely reduced, and the likelihood of your being misled by a less scrupulous sponsor will be significantly increased.

2.

The Tax Consequences— How to Understand Them Better

[¶201]   **THE GENERAL CONCEPTS**

How does your investment in a tax shelter translate into benefits to you for Federal income tax purposes? The tax benefits find their foundation in three basic concepts under the Internal Revenue Code:

(1) Certain expenditures that are made in conducting your tax-sheltered activity are permitted to be *deducted* for Federal income tax purposes rather than being capitalized as would be moneys paid if you purchased a stock. (Remember, the use of an unconventional "flow-through" vehicle permits these deductions to be taken directly by you on your Federal income tax return rather than by the entity conducting the activity, which, in its tax bracket, should need the deduction much less than you do.) This is the reason that it is so critical to avoid the tax "pitfall" that your investment is treated as an "association taxable as a corporation". (See ¶302 and ¶2701.) Thus, dollars spent for intangible drilling and development costs in the conduct of oil and gas activities (see Chapter 11), for interest and property taxes in a real estate venture (see Chapter 8), and for feeding and raising cattle (see Chapters 15 and 16) can all be deducted when computing your tax liability to the government.

(2) Assets, other than land, are assumed to be constantly reducing in value over time as a result of the physical *depreciation* of buildings, equipment or cattle, or the *depletion* (using up) of "wasting" assets such as oil and gas or coal. Under the Internal Revenue Code, a deduction is allowed for this assumed deterioration or exhausting of the asset.

(3) In most forms of investment—oil and gas being a notable

exception—the amount of deductible items incurred in the conduct of the venture may be relatively small. However, whether the deductions are for direct expenditures of funds which fall in the "deductible" category, or are for assumed depreciation or depletion, these deductions can be greatly enhanced from the standpoint of the dollars you were required personally to expend by supplementing your equity contribution with borrowed dollars. This increase in deductibility through the use of borrowing, referred to as *leverage*, may be limited to your tax "basis" in the investment and has further been restricted by the "at risk" rules added to the tax code by the Tax Reform Act of 1976. (See ¶503.) However, leverage still remains a critical factor in most forms of tax-sheltered investment.

[¶201.1]   The Investment Tax Credit and Long-Term Capital Gains

There are a number of other concepts under the tax code which will affect the tax consequences of your tax-sheltered investment. For instance, the *investment tax credit* available as to certain types of investment permits you to offset a certain portion of your investment—including that portion augmented by leverage—against your tax liability. (See Internal Revenue Code, §38.) Thus, if you are in the 50 percent Federal income tax bracket, this tax credit is worth twice—in the minds of some commentators, even more than twice—the value of an equal deduction.

The investment tax credit may be taken so long as the property in question is "put in service" prior to the end of the taxable year. Thus, while most deductions, including depreciation, require that you invest substantially prior to December 31 in order to secure any significant tax benefits, an end-of-the-year investment may permit you to secure tax relief if the investment tax credit is available. Similarly, while the investment tax credit is subject to its own rules concerning "recapture," it is not subject to many of the limitations which apply to recapture of depreciation. Since the investment tax credit is not dependent upon the taxpayer having a sufficient "basis" in his investment to justify the deduction, it may also permit benefits in excess of the investor's cash contribution to the venture. In other words, an "excess write-off" may be available, even though the investment is subject to the "at risk" rules.

Another concept under the tax code—the special tax treatment afforded long-term *capital gains*—is also important in tax-sheltered investment.

Ordinarily, all income, including gains from the sale of property, is treated as "ordinary income" and taxed at the government's normal (or, you may feel, abnormal) tax rates. However, if you sell a *capital asset*—generally speaking, property other than property held primarily for sale to customers—and if you have owned the property for the required "holding period," only half of your long-term capital gain is subject to taxation at ordinary income tax rates.

The historic 6-month holding period for long-term capital gains was extended to one year by the Tax Reform Act of 1976 (9 months for the 1977 taxable year). And longer holding periods may apply to certain transactions, such as the sale of breeder cattle. (See Chapter 16.) (Internal Revenue Code, §1202.)

For the definition of "capital assets" subject to capital gains treatment, see Internal Revenue Code, §§1221 and 1231.

Under a second "alternate tax" method, a special tax rate of 25 percent is applied to your first $50,000 of net long-term capital gains, so that, depending upon the size of your capital gain and your tax bracket, the effective tax rate on your long-term capital gains will be between 25 percent and 35 percent. However, the tax impact may be increased by the inclusion of a part of the gain as an "item of tax preference." (See Chapter 5.)

Long-term capital gains, tax credits, deductions, and leverage are the pluses provided for you by the tax code. However, other code provisions may reduce these benefits, or provide more beneficial methods of tax reduction. These code provisions include:

(1) The 15 percent *minimum tax on "items of tax preference."* (See ¶504.)
(2) The 50 percent *maximum tax on "personal service" (earned) income*—a benefit which will be lost, dollar for dollar, for each dollar you take in "tax preference" deductions. (See ¶504.)
(3) The reduction in tax bite available through such techniques as *"income averaging,"* an *"installment sale"* or a contribution to a *profit-sharing plan.* (See Chapter 7.)

Depreciation, leverage, and capital gains are such an integral part of most tax-sheltered investments that a further discussion at this point should help you in understanding the later discussions of specific investments and their tax advantages.

[¶201.2] How Depreciation Affects Tax-Sheltered Investments

Depreciation is not merely a tax concept. Property, other than land, *does* decrease in value with age as a result of wear and tear, obsolescence, and other such factors. Accordingly, basic non-tax accounting rules recognize depreciation as an economic fact of life and require an offsetting entry to be charged against the original value of depreciable assets to reflect their deterioration in value. Similarly, for tax purposes, Congress permits a deduction for the assumed deterioration in the value of those assets which will depreciate with the passage of time and whose costs of acquisition were required to be capitalized for Federal income tax purposes.

To the extent the depreciation deduction reflects an actual reduction in the value of your property, it confers no tax benefits. It merely permits a tax-free return of the capital you originally invested. However, with good maintenance, the property acquired through your tax-sheltered investment may not be decreasing in value; instead, the value of the property may actually be increasing. Even if there is no appreciation in terms of "true" dollars, if you are only able to maintain the property so that it "holds its own," the effects of inflation will cause it to increase in terms of the dollars for which it can be sold. Thus, to the extent the Internal Revenue Code permits a tax deduction for depreciation which exceeds any economic deterioration in the value of the property, the depreciation deduction confers an actual tax benefit.

Accounting concepts do not always square with reality. Under Generally Accepted Accounting Principles (GAAP), property is normally assumed to depreciate at a level amount each year over the estimated life of the property. Anyone who has ever purchased a car realizes that this ratable or *"straight-line" depreciation* doesn't square with the economic facts of life: in the marketplace, property depreciates more rapidly in earlier years, and less rapidly in later years.

Congress, in providing for the depreciation deduction, has in some instances permitted this economic reality to be reflected on your tax return. Thus, as to certain kinds of property, greater depreciation deductions are allowed in earlier years, with reduced deductions as the property grows older. While the total depreciation that can be taken over the life of the property will not exceed its total cost, the Congressional sanction of this *"accelerated" depreciation* gives you greater tax benefits: the earlier a deduction can be taken, the more valuable it is to you due to the time value of money. (See ¶402.)

Historically, tax-sheltered investment areas which offer accelerated depreciation have been looked at as providing greater tax incentives than those in which only straight-line depreciation is permitted. This general rule must be looked at with greater care under current tax laws, however, since *"excess" depreciation* is usually subject to "recapture" as a result of various tax "reform" acts, and often constitutes an "item of tax preference." The amount by which the accelerated deductions exceed the ratable deduction under the "straight-line" method is referred to as "excess depreciation."

The concept of "recapture" is something we need to understand in seeing how deductions work.

Normally, when property is sold, the amount of any excess depreciation must be reported, and will be taxed, as ordinary income. Only gain in excess of the "recapture" amount (or allocable to non-depreciable assets, such as land) will qualify for beneficial long-term capital gains treatment. And in some investments, such as cattle breeding, *all* depreciation must be reported as ordinary income on sale.

The fact that excess depreciation is subject to recapture must be highlighted under Federal and State securities laws by any syndicator who seeks your investment. However, recapture is not the end of the world. You still have the use of the tax savings throughout this period; hopefully, you have put those dollars represented by the tax savings to work to earn further moneys for you. Furthermore, the longer your investment is held, the less "excess" depreciation remains to be recaptured. However, if you are unaware of the potential for recapture, and have "spent" your entire initial tax savings, recapture can create a potential tax disaster for you. Excess depreciation deductions are an interest-free *loan* from the Federal Government, not a permanent tax savings. (See ¶202.)

Recapture and additional "gain on sale" income can also be triggered by a sale of your tax-sheltered investment or by a foreclosure of the mortgage which permitted the leveraging. Upon foreclosure, there is assumed, for tax purposes, to be a constructive receipt of "income" equal to the amount of the outstanding debt. It was previously argued by tax practitioners that any such constructive receipt should be limited to the value of the property interest at the time of foreclosure, and not to the amount of debt. However, this hope now seems fairly forlorn. (See IRS Rev. Rul. 76-111; *Millar*, 67 T.C. 656 (1977).)

The irony of your situation may appeal to the Internal Revenue Service, but it certainly won't appeal to you. At the very time when your investment has been wiped out, you are treated for tax purposes as having sold your foreclosed asset at a huge profit—another instance of "phantom income."

[¶201.3]   The Effects of Leverage

Let's leave depreciation for the present, to talk about *leverage*—the key to the high deductions available in many tax-sheltered areas. In the typical tax-sheltered investment other than oil and gas, only a small portion of the expenditures incurred in connection with the venture are deductible for Federal income tax purposes. However, these ventures normally involve the purchase of an asset. In addition to the asset's depreciable nature, a major portion of the moneys used to acquire the asset often can be borrowed. Thus, the venture's deductible expenditures, and the depreciation available, *expressed as a percentage of the equity dollars which you are required to invest*, substantially increase.

For an example of the effects of leverage, let's turn to an investment in a cattle feeding program. As a general rule, approximately two-thirds of the expenditures in a cattle feeding venture are for the non-deductible costs of acquiring the cattle; only one-third of the venture's expenditures will be for deductible costs such as feed and the services required to take care of your cattle. However, look at the effects of leverage if, instead of funding the venture solely through equity investment, the venture borrows three dollars for every equity dollar that you put up:

| | Available Deductions | |
	Without Borrowing	With Bank Borrowing
(1). Equity Investment	$10,000	$10,000
(2). Borrowing at 3 to 1	—	30,000
(3). Funds Available	10,000	40,000
(4). Cattle purchased at ⅔ of "(3)"	6,600	26,400
(5). Deductible costs at ⅓ of "(3)"	3,400	13,600
(6). Deductible Costs as % of Equity Investment	34%	136%

Leveraging a small equity investment into substantial tax deductions is dependent upon an exception to the general rules established by the Internal Revenue Code concerning your tax *"basis."*

Generally speaking, your "basis" for tax purposes in property acquired by you is the price you paid for it. As charges or credits are made to your capital account, such as deductions for depreciation or other deductible expenses, or additions for capitalized expenditures to improve the property, your basis in the property will also be adjusted. This adjusted basis is used, under the tax code, in determining your gain or loss on the sale or exchange of the property, and in computing depreciation.

Under the general rules concerning the taxation of partnerships—and, remember, many tax-sheltered investments are structured as partnerships—partners can deduct partnership losses only to the extent of the "basis" of their partnership interests. When your aggregate loss equals your basis, no further losses will be permitted until additional basis is added.

The basis in your partnership investment will include your equity investment, your undistributed revenues, and a proportionate part of any partnership debts for which you are personally liable. However, as an added benefit, prior to the enactment of the Tax Reform Act of 1976, you could also claim as a part of your "basis" your share of any "non-recourse" borrowings—loans for which no partner was personally liable. Many tax-sheltered investments, including cattle programs, and equipment leasing, movie, and coal syndications, used such non-recourse borrowings to generate substantial excess deductions. However, as a result of the 1976 Reform Act, if your tax-sheltered investment takes the form of a partnership, your non-recourse borrowings generally can be used to create deductions in excess of your amount "at risk" only if the partnership is engaged in investment in real estate. (Internal Revenue Code, §704(b)). Non-partnership ventures in oil and gas, livestock and other farming activities (other than timber), equipment leasing, and films, are subject to analogous "at risk" limitations. (Internal Revenue Code §465.)

Note that the investment tax credit is not subject to these limitations. (See ¶503.)

Despite the "at risk" and "partnership borrowing" provisions of the Tax Reform Act of 1976, excess write-off offerings remain "alive and well" in livestock and the exotics, as well as in real estate. However, such investments are subject to particular economic and tax perils. (See ¶202, ¶203 and ¶2601.)

[¶201.4]   Pitfalls of Leverage

Just as the benefits of accelerated depreciation are partially offset by the eventual recapture of any excess deductions, leverage creates substantial deductions. Even repayments on the mortgage do not adversely affect such deductibility, and may even add to the benefits, since, in the early years, most of such "debt service" is going for the payment of deductible interest expense. However, certain restrictions apply to the deductibility of "investment" interest. (See Internal Revenue Code, § 163(d)). Repayments of the debt principal, while creating a call on venture revenues, are not deductible for Federal Income Tax purposes. Thus, as the venture progresses, the specter of "phantom income," dollars which you never see, because they have gone to repay borrowings, but which are treated, under the Internal Revenue Code, as taxable income to you, comes closer to reality. As your mortgage principal payments increase, and your interest payments decline, a point eventually will be reached where your taxable income—your net revenues before non-deductible debt service—will exceed the depreciation deductions which would otherwise shelter the cash distributed to you. This particularly becomes a problem where accelerated depreciation has been taken. At the very time that more and more of your debt service is being used for non-deductible repayments of debt principal, your depreciation deductions will have shrunk. Eventually, a point will be reached where taxable income will actually exceed the cash flow available for distribution to you. At this *"crossover point,"* your cash flow is not only taxable, a part of it must go to pay taxes on the phantom income that is going for the non-deductible portions of your debt service.

Finally, repayments on mortgage principal may reach the point where the *taxes* payable on this phantom income actually exceed the distributable cash flow. Since you are still being taxed on your share of the venture's net revenue prior to debt service, you have now reached a negative tax position—the Internal Revenue Code's opposite of "deep shelter."

Just as you can anticipate and provide for the eventual recapture of excess depreciation deductions, similar advance planning can help prepare you for the day on which the crossover point may be reached in your tax-sheltered investment. Crossover also can be, and often is, avoided by a sale of the property prior to the time the crossover point is reached. But remember—such a sale will trigger recapture of any excess deductions. Such sale may also result in a recapture of any investment tax credit previously taken. (See Internal Revenue Code, §47.)

Before leaving leverage, let's take a moment to look at the concept of the "excess write-off." Investors always have looked and always will look for some way of assuring the success of their investments through tax savings alone. The possibility of accomplishing this is slim. This year's excess deduction eventually becomes a future year's phantom income. However, the use of leverage can substantially increase the *initial* deductibility of your investment, expressed as a percentage of your equity dollars. While, as mentioned, the Tax Reform Act of 1976 has placed restrictions on the use of borrowings—particularly non-recourse borrowings—to create deductions in excess of 100 percent of your equity investment, it has by no means eliminated the excess deduction. (See ¶503.) Thus, the use of leverage can generate deductions that exceed the amount of your equity investment.

Despite high initial deductibility, the excess deduction does not create a permanent tax shelter which will leave only soft dollars at risk, returning a profit from the tax consequences alone. Even from the standpoint of the initial investment, some "hard dollar" investment exposure remains until the initial deductibility of your investment has risen to the 140 percent to 200 percent level, depending on your tax bracket. Furthermore, at some point you will be required to use taxable dollars to repay your earlier borrowings. This "day of reckoning" for the excess deduction cannot be avoided by making a gift of the property or permitting the loan to be foreclosed. For tax purposes, such an event will be treated as a "sale" for the balance of the debt. (The "phantom" sale proceeds may qualify for capital gains treatment, however; see IRS Rev. Rul. 76-311.) Thus, the effect of the excess deduction will be to grant you a "tax reprieve," a deferral, not a permanent elimination, of your tax liability. This is by no means "bad" but it does not represent the typical investor's expectation of what excess deductions offer. (See ¶202.)

[¶201.5]   The Importance of Understanding the
             Effects of Capital Gains

As a final lesson in this tax-shelter primer, take a deeper look at the "capital gains" concept.

Prior to the Tax Reform Acts of 1969 and 1976, conversion of "ordinary income" dollars to "capital gains" dollars was a key step in tax planning, since long-term capital gains were subject to a maximum "alternate tax" of 25 percent. Thus, if you invested $10,000 of 70 percent bracket income in a 100 percent deductible oil and gas venture, discovering reserves which could be sold for $10,000, the tax results were spectacular:

	Without Oil Investment	With Oil Investment
(1). Income	$10,000	$10,000
(2). Deduction for Investment	—0—	[10,000]
(3). Taxes Payable at 70%	[7,000]	—0—
(4). Proceeds from Sale of Reserves	—0—	10,000
(5). 25% Tax on Sale Proceeds	—0—	[2,500]
(6). Dollars Remaining After Tax	$ 3,000	$ 7,500

Of course, "Catch 22" was whether or not sufficient reserves would be discovered. If the well was a dry hole, the "dollars remaining after tax" would be zero!

The "magic" of converting ordinary income into capital gains has been dampened by the 1969 and 1976 tax legislation. The *effective* tax on even long-term capital gains may now equal 40 percent to 45 percent—close to the 50 percent maximum tax on personal service income—when the higher alternate tax rate, and the "tax preference" effects of long-term capital gains, are taken into account.

This does not mean that seeking capital gains treatment should no longer play a part in your tax strategy. It does mean that you should not be mesmerized by the long-term capital gains opportunity. Instead, be sure you understand how much economic effect such treatment will have under today's tax laws, and don't ignore alternate planning approaches.

[¶202]   **DEFERRAL VERSUS PERMANENT SHELTER**

It's highly important in understanding tax-sheltered investments to understand the distinction between *permanent tax shelter* and tax *deferral*.

Certain forms of tax-sheltered investment generate deductions which are "permanent" in nature. Thus, if you invest $10,000 in a 100 percent deductible oil and gas program, you can use the deductions so generated to offset $10,000 of otherwise taxable income. While any income from the oil and gas program will be partially taxable, if there is no income, there is no tax. (See ¶1101.) Similarly, the deductions for interest, property taxes, and depreciation (subject only to recapture of accelerated depreciation) in real estate also create a permanent shelter. (In real estate, depreciation may also permit you to receive income from your investment tax free.) However, "deferral" deductions, such as the deductions created in most livestock and agriculture investments, as well as the exotics, primarily serve to defer the payment of taxes.

Not that deferral isn't of substantial value. It permits the shifting of dollars into taxable years in which taxes may prove easier to pay. This use of "year shifting" for tax purposes is usually praised for permitting you to take deductions in the year in which you will be in a lower tax bracket. However, in this day of the 50 percent maximum tax on personal service income, you may rarely find yourself earning so little that your tax dollars are not taxed at 50 percent. But deferral may be used to "bunch" certain types of tax deductions, and certain types of income, in various years so as to minimize or avoid the effects of "tax preference" or other tax code pitfalls. (See ¶504.) Likewise, in some years you may be better prepared to pay your taxes than in others. The "cash flow" needs of many investors vary significantly from year to year. Accordingly, this ability to shift income or deductions from one taxable year into another is of real value. However, in addition to shifting income into a year in which you are in a better tax bracket, or better prepared to pay the taxes, tax deferral also permits more effective long-range tax planning and, if continued for a number of years, may indefinitely postpone the day of reckoning for tax purposes.

[¶202.1]   You Can Use the Government's Money
                Interest-Free

The foregoing benefits of tax deferral are the ones which will most often be cited to you as the advantages of tax deferral. However, a far more significant benefit of deferral is your ability to use the Government's money interest-free until you are eventually required to pay your taxes. Since, as mentioned, money has a "time value," this postponing of the tax obligation can prove highly important to you: if the tax can be postponed for a long enough period, its impact will be substantially reduced, and if you have put your money to use in the meantime, may, from a practical standpoint, be virtually eliminated. (See ¶402.)

The key problem with deferral, then, is not that it does not have value—it does—but the failure to recognize deferral for what it is: an interest-free loan from the Government. Just as in any other loan, the deferral will create a current positive cash flow, but must eventually be repaid. If you will establish a "sinking fund" or other plan for eventually repaying this "loan"—*i.e.,* paying taxes on the eventual taxable income—you will have the benefit of interest-free use of this money. However, if you treat these temporary tax benefits as permanent, without giving thought to, and providing for, your eventual tax liability, your initial tax advantages can result in disaster.

[¶203]   **HOW "SURE" ARE THE
                          TAX CONSEQUENCES?**

You may think that "a deduction is a deduction is a deduction." In tax-sheltered investment, this simply is not true. Certain deductions which you may claim on your Federal income tax return as a result of a tax-sheltered investment are clearly deductible for Federal income tax purposes, e.g., deductions for intangible drilling costs, interest, and property taxes. However, what about a deduction for an "abandonment loss" in an oil and gas drilling venture? A "covenant not to compete" in a real estate transaction? An advance annual minimum royalty or a prepayment of expenses in a coal transaction? These may fall in totally different categories.

Certain deductions and tax benefits are clearly granted you under the Internal Revenue Code. However, other tax benefits may fall into a less certain area. In certain circumstances this uncertainty may deepen substantially. So long as there is a basis on which to claim the deduction, so that you will not be subject to "fraud" or "negligence" penalties even if the IRS should disagree with you concerning the tax consequences of your investment, there is nothing wrong with claiming a grey area deduction, *so long as* you understood, when you made the investment, exactly what you were getting into.

There are sound business reasons why you may wish to invest in a given tax-sheltered investment even though some, or all, of the deductions are less than sure. Thus, even in the "exotics" area, where many of the deductions may be challenged on audit, the investment still may be worthwhile for a particular, and informed, investor (See ¶2601). However, you need to know whether the tax benefits which you are claiming are: (1) certain, (2) probable though not sure, or (3) risky. A grey area deduction may open your *entire* Federal income tax return to audit, leading to a possible disallowance of other tax benefits claimed by you which had nothing to do with your tax-sheltered investment. Furthermore, the less certain the deduction, the more important it is that provisional "sinking fund" arrangements or other methods of repayment be made by you in the event your deduction is disallowed. Also, in determining whether or not you wish to make a given tax-sheltered investment, the certainty of the deduction, and the expense of conducting even a successful litigation of your tax position is something you will wish to take into account.

So how do you determine the relative certainty of the hoped-for tax consequences of a particular tax-sheltered investment? A first step is an evaluation of the credibility of the firm responsible for the preparation of the tax opinion:

☐ Are the tax consequences based upon mere representations of the investment syndicator, unsubstantiated by an independent tax opinion?

☐ Is the tax opinion prepared by a firm with recognized expertise in the tax area?

☐ How reliable have this firm's opinions proved in the past?

[¶203.1]   The Three Types of Tax Opinions

Once the tax representations have passed the credibility test, you must study the opinion carefully to determine exactly what it says. There are three types of opinions issued by reputable tax experts which indicate, to the knowledgeable reader, the degree of certainty surrounding the conclusions reached in the opinion:

1. If the opinion states that certain items "are deductible" for Federal income tax purposes, and if the source is reliable, the deduction should stand in the "firm" area.

2. If, however, the deduction may be subject to question by the Internal Revenue Service, the opinion should state that, "in the opinion of counsel" (or the accounting firm), the items are deductible and will be sustained in the event of an attack.

   While this does not insure that your return will not be audited, or that you will not be put to some expense in defending the tax deduction, it does indicate that in the opinion of the writer, the deduction will eventually be sustained. (But remember, this is an "opinion" only, albeit an expert one. It is not a guarantee that the deduction will in fact be sustained; nor will the expert be liable if his opinion proves in error, so long as reasonable care was used in issuing the opinion.)

3. The final type of opinion, frequently issued in connection with investments in the exotics, will state that, in the opinion of the writer, "there is a basis on which to claim a deduction" for a given tax

benefit. You should be aware that this type of opinion does not say that such deductions will not be challenged upon audit, *or that such challenge may not be sustained.* It does indicate that you will not be acting fraudulently or negligently in claiming the deduction on your tax return.

Why would you wish to make an investment in a tax shelter where even the tax benefits fall in the "high risk" area? See ¶2601 for the answer.

3.

Deductions Aren't Enough

RISK—THE OTHER SIDE OF REWARD

The very aspect of the tax-sheltered investment which may make it most appealing to you—its beneficial tax consequences—also proves the major pitfall in the tax-sheltered investment. Far too often, an investor is so intrigued with reducing his Federal income taxes that he forgets that the tax consequences of these investments reduce, but do not eliminate, his loss exposure. There are *always* hard dollars at risk in a tax-sheltered investment. And the very reason Congress provided the tax incentives to encourage your investment is the *high degree of risk* in the industries in which you are being asked to invest, and the inadequacy of their historic return in attracting sufficient venture capital from conventional sources.

When you are asked to invest in a tax-sheltered investment, you should be provided information by the "syndicator" concerning the problems and pitfalls in the venture he is proposing: this is required by Federal and State securities laws. (See Chapter 31.) If you are not provided such information, you'd better watch out: either the syndicator is poorly informed concerning his obligations under the securities laws, or he is not worried about those obligations, because he doesn't expect to be around for very long. Normally, this "offering circular" or "prospectus", will contain a bold face caveat **"THESE ARE SPECULATIVE INVESTMENTS."** You'd better believe it!

This speculative nature of the tax-sheltered investment applies to good, mediocre, and bad tax-shelter ventures. In the mediocre, poorly-conceived tax shelter, you stand little chance of making money, and none in the bad or fraudulent one. But even in the best of tax-sheltered investments—the ones that are well conceived, well structured, and well managed—the risk of loss is ever present and very real.

This speculative nature of the tax-sheltered investment is emphasized by experience of tax-sheltered investors in cattle feeding in the 1970's. In the early 1970's, an approach referred to as "steer averaging" appeared to provide a relatively low-risk method of investing in what was inherently a highly speculative investment area. By the fall of 1973, astronomical profits were being realized, even by the "averagers." However, by late 1973, a freeze in beef prices and the rapid rise in the price of grain, coupled with the degree of leveraging then being used in cattle feeding, wiped out these profits along with most, if not all, of the investors' initial capital. These economically disastrous conditions continued for the longest period in the history of the cattle industry. While many investors continued to invest in cattle feeding, hoping for a change in industry economics, it continued to cost more to add a pound of beef in the feed lot than the per pound price which could be received by the investor. Only recently have these economic conditions started to change.

The experience suffered by cattle feeding investors in the mid 1970's was not unique to the cattle industry. In the 1960's, low oil prices and artificially depressed gas prices made it extremely difficult for investors to profit in oil and gas. The experience of investors in new multifamily residential construction and in Real Estate Investment Trusts in the 1970's was equally disastrous.

Does this mean that, despite the tax benefits, you should forget about tax-sheltered investment as an intelligent investment area, and simply pay your taxes? Hardly! By the use of diversification, and an informed analysis of industry economics and your own investment needs, you can develop an intelligent investment program which should compensate for most of these investment risks. These methods of "investigating before you invest" will be discussed in detail in Part Four. However, you must be aware that tax-sheltered investment is a risky business. Your hard dollars are subject to loss. Tax benefits alone are not enough. Only through an *intelligent, informed* investment strategy will you be able to profit in the tax-shelter area.

[¶302]   PITFALLS IN TAX-SHELTERED INVESTMENTS

The risks involved in tax-sheltered investment are of three types:

- ☐ Those *generic* to *all tax-sheltered investments;*
- ☐ Those *generic* to the *particular investment* area;
- ☐ The risks of investing in a *sub-standard investment* in that investment area.

Each tax-sheltered investment area has its own risks, which will be discussed in detail in the later portions of this book. But the risks may be classified as follows:

(1) *The Economic Risks.* Each of the industries for which Congress has offered tax incentives is speculative, as is each venture which you may undertake in

that industry. Wells can be dry, marginal, or unexpectedly costly. Buildings can have cost overruns or not rent up. Cattle can die. Market prices fluctuate. While each of these economic risks will be discussed in detail when we talk about the particular industry, it is far less important for you to know each particular economic risk of that industry than to know that the risks do exist and can affect even the best conceived venture. However, there are certain points concerning such economic risks that you must keep in mind.

(a) The risk increases if there is no diversification provided in the investment, or if you have not provided your own diversification by investing in several such ventures. This necessity for diversification applies not only to spreading your money over several projects at one time, but also requires that you plan to invest similarly for several years; in other words, a "time-line diversification."

(b) Your risk will be markedly heightened if the project is of dubious financial soundness or if the caliber of management, or management's prior performance for its investors, is poor.

(c) The risk can also be increased by compensation arrangements or conflicts of interest which encourage or permit the venture's sponsor to profit irrespective, or with too little reference, to the profitability of the venture to you.

(2) *The Passive Nature of the Investment.* Many of the tax-sheltered investments presented to you will be structured as limited partnerships. Under such an investment vehicle, you cannot participate in management decisions without losing the limited liability which the partnership was formed to provide you. Furthermore, even in a tax shelter which is not structured as a limited partnership, you will normally be totally at the mercy of the sponsor-selected management, both in selecting the projects to be undertaken by the venture and in their actual operation. Despite what your investment contract may say as to your rights of management, it is highly unlikely that you will have the knowledge of the industry required to play any significant managerial role. (If you did, you wouldn't need the sponsor.) Since your likelihood of profit is dependent upon the proper exercise of management's discretion in selecting and managing the project—a role which you are incapable of assuming—it is a must that you and your advisors properly and realistically assess management before making the investment.

(3) *The Tax Risks.* Taxes are certainly one of the major factors that have motivated you to make this investment. While, as we have seen, tax savings are not enough, there is little likelihood that you will profit unless the general economics of the venture are supplemented by the expected tax benefits. (If the tax incentives weren't necessary, they wouldn't be there.) Accordingly, you must make certain that these tax benefits are not inadvertently lost. This requires an assessment of:

(a) The degree of certainty that the deductions will be sustained. (See ¶203.) The fact that deductions are subject to dispute, or are even highly controversial, does not mean that the investment is necessarily wrong for you. However, you must understand, prior to making the investment, just how sure the deductions are. If you are moving into the area of controversial deductions, you must be sure that the benefits of the investment are sufficiently significant to you to make the increased tax risk acceptable.

(b) The key to securing tax benefits from a tax-sheltered investment is the "direct participation" nature of the investment, i.e., its structuring so that the investment consequences, including the tax results, will "flow-through" directly to you, rather than being taxed at the venture level. This "flow-through" character is essential. If the venture were taxed in the same manner as a corporation, the tax deductions would go only to the venture entity (which will be operating, in early years, at a loss and does not need deductions) and would not provide you the shelter which is your motivation for selecting a tax-sheltered investment over more conventional investment forms. Furthermore, any profits from the venture would be subject to a double tax. (See ¶201.)

Under Section 761 of the Internal Revenue Code, "flow-through" benefits are provided joint investment undertakings through an unusual definition of "partnership" which includes not only common-law partnerships, but also syndicates and joint ventures so long as they are not considered trusts, estates, or corporations under the Internal Revenue Code. However, Section 7701(a)(3) further defines the term "corporation" as any "*association taxable as a corporation*," an organization whose characteristics more closely resemble a corporation than a partnership or trust. Such an "association" characterization would be devastating from your standpoint as a tax-sheltered investor, as it would prevent the tax consequences of the investment from flowing through to you.

Until 1975, most tax practitioners felt relatively safe in being able to structure a joint venture, general partnership, or limited partnership in such a fashion that it would not be considered an "association taxable as a corporation." However, since 1975, a series of tax decisions and proposed regulation changes have turned the "association" problem into a far greyer area. (For more detailed discussions of the "association" question, see the sources cited under "Additional Readings" at the close of Part One.) While it is impossible to foresee what new court or administrative decisions may affect the flow-through characteristics of tax-sheltered investments in the future, this is a risk that most informed tax-sheltered investors and their advisors are willing to assume. However, in view of the highly critical nature of the "association" problem, it is of utmost importance that your investment not *unnecessarily* subject you to the risk that it will be classified as an association. Accordingly, you and your advisor must insure, prior to making an investment, that all reasonable steps have been taken to protect the "flow-through" nature of your investment.

(c) The possibility of changes in the tax law are an inherent, unavoidable risk in tax-sheltered investment. This risk, which includes not only future legislative changes in the tax code, but changes in its interpretation by the Internal Revenue Service and the courts, has always been a risk of tax-sheltered investment. However, in recent years, the risks have moved more and more out of the "possible" into the "probable" category. (See Chapter 6).

Nothing can be done to prevent some unexpected future tax law change which could affect today's tax-sheltered investment. However, you can be aware that such changes are possible, and take adequate steps to guard against them. One such step is to be wary of investments which are particularly apt to be subject to such changes; for example, investments which are under open attack. This would include most investments in the "exotics." (See Chapter 26.) Investment in such areas may still be worth it to you; however, you should be aware that such investments are subject to a heightened risk of being affected by changes in the tax law. A second precautionary step, made particularly significant as the probability of tax law change increases, is the close investigation of the economics of your investment. (See Part Four.)

(d) You should also be aware, that an investment in a tax shelter creates the risk of an audit of your entire Federal income tax return. This risk of audit may be heightened if your investment is in one of the "grey area" tax shelters, such as the exotics. However, in recent years, an increased audit policy has been put into effect by the Internal Revenue Service on all investments in tax-sheltered partnerships. Thus, an audit of your partnership investment can trigger disallowance of other tax positions asserted by you, even if your tax-sheltered deductions are eventually sustained.

(4) *The Difficulty of Evaluation.* Tax-sheltered investment is far more complicated than investment in the stock market or in other conventional securities. While most tax-sheltered syndicators are legitimate, the tax-sheltered area has had its share of "con games," many of which were played at the expense of highly sophisticated investors. When the risk of investing in mediocre or substandard projects is added, the chances that many of the tax-sheltered "opportunities" offered to you will not be sufficiently attractive to warrant *informed* attention skyrockets.

The methods of analyzing and evaluating a proposed tax-sheltered investment will be discussed in considerable detail in Part Four. However, here is the "bottom line:" you will be dealing with a highly complicated investment area where the "public" information which surrounds the market in listed stocks will not be available to you. You will be asked to analyze venture opportunities involving a high degree of risk which are outside your personal experience and expertise. Again, this does not mean that you should stay away from tax-sheltered investments. It does mean that unless you are willing to accept the significant risks involved in investing based upon blind faith alone, you will need to secure expert help in evaluating whether or not a given tax-shelter venture is right for you. Such sources of advice are available to you, and at a cost which you should be able, and willing, to pay. (See ¶2902.2.)

(5) *The Risks of Illiquidity.* For tax and other reasons, the transferability of your tax-sheltered investment normally will be restricted by your program agreement. Whether or not such restrictions exist, you will normally find that there is no "after-market" for your tax-sheltered investment, such as would exist in listed or over-the-counter stocks. This means that you are in a truly "frozen" investment: you will be locked into your tax-sheltered investment irrespective of emergency needs.

Part of the "frozen" nature of your investment will arise from economic and tax practicalities: it will normally take two to five years for your oil and gas venture properly to develop its "prospects;" for your apartment house to be constructed and leased up; or for your cattle breeding or agricultural syndication to get its activities well under way. A forced sale prior to this time would result in the forfeiture of the hoped-for economic benefits of the venture, assuming it is successful, and normally would trigger unpleasant recapture and other tax consequences. In any event, usually you will find that there is no market for your tax-sheltered interests at any price. Thus, unless the moneys you place in your investment can be left there for a substantial period of time, and you have other, more liquid assets to meet your emergency needs, you should give serious thought before entering into the tax-shelter area. (The risks of tax-shelter illiquidity are discussed in greater detail in Chapters 28 and 29.)

[¶303]   **HOW TO AVOID TAX "OVERKILL"**

Section ¶301 emphasized that the risks of tax-sheltered investment are only partially offset by the tax benefits: that "deductions aren't enough." This same warning should be considered in determining whether the ultimate profit potential of your proposed tax-sheltered investment has been unnecessarily reduced, or even eliminated, by going for tax "over-kill."

As seen in earlier chapters, the tax consequences of a tax-sheltered investment are an integral part of its economic soundness. An intelligent use of tax incentives can substantially increase your after-tax return. Thus, an oil and gas well which might prove unprofitable for an entity whose dollars were being taxed at 20 percent could prove highly profitable for an individual whose dollars were being taxed at 70 percent. However, you must constantly ask yourself the question: how much am I paying for the tax benefits?

The "return" from a tax-sheltered investment includes a multiplicity of benefits—benefits which are interdependent. (See ¶401.) An increase in tax benefits normally is "paid for" by reduction in the economic return which the investor will receive. Thus, in a "functional allocation" oil and gas program (see ¶1301), the deductibility of the investment is increased from the normal 70 percent to 80 percent deductibility of oil and gas investment to 100 percent by having the program's "general partner" bear all non-deductible costs. In return, however, the general partner receives a larger share of program revenues than he otherwise would have received. So long as the dollars lost in economic benefits are exceeded by the dollars gained through tax benefits, the trade has been a wise one. But if the share of program costs to be borne by the sponsor is in fact relatively small, and the share of revenues to be received are disproportionately out of line, the investor may find that the tax savings secured through increased deductibility are more than offset by the loss of economic potential. His *combined* benefits have thus been reduced by tax over-reaching.

[¶303.1]   Beware of Excessive Write-Offs

The "tax over-reach" problem rises to particularly serious proportions in excess write-off programs. Here, the degree of deductibility is primarily a function of the price paid by the investor for the asset being acquired. Even if, at the price paid, the project will still prove profitable, where the investor has paid more than necessary to increase deductibility from 200 percent to 400 percent, he usually will find that he had made a poor economic bargain, particularly in view of the eventual recapture of the "excess" tax benefits.

Tax over-reaching can also blind an investor in analyzing the appropriate type of tax shelter, or the particular program in which to invest. The lure of high tax benefits may entice you to invest in a project which, upon closer examination, has little if any economic potential. (With hard dollars at risk, this is a poor bargain, no matter what the initial tax savings.) Likewise, an investment which offers lower than normal tax benefits may be dismissed without giving careful consideration to its ultimate economic potential.

The higher tax benefits offered by new residential construction in real estate may be far outweighed in today's economy by the potentially sounder economics of existing properties, despite their lower tax benefits. Similar examples exist in every industry. Your need for immediate tax shelter may be such that the tax savings are sufficiently valuable to you to outweigh the other economic considerations. Even if you are giving up more in eventual economic recovery than you will save in terms of today's taxes, your current cash needs may make this an intelligent trade. (See ¶2601.) However, the choice should be *intelligently made:* far too many investors are lured into inappropriate tax-sheltered investments by a blinding drive for tax savings, without giving thought to the effect of these savings on their ultimate combined return.

For examples of when tax consequences cease to become tax savings and become tax overkill, see Appendix 303-1.

4.

"Return"—What Does It Mean and How Do You Figure It?

RETURN—A COMBINATION OF BENEFITS

Return expectations in tax-sheltered investment were discussed in Chapter 1. A word of caution—there is little empiric data available upon which to base a conclusion as to "average" returns from tax-sheltered investments. All you have is the sure knowledge that your return will unquestionably be substandard if the venture you choose is itself substandard. Also, as we have seen, the return expectations of most investors as to *all* their investments, not to mention returns from tax-sheltered investments in particular, are usually unrealistically high. For an excellent discussion of the return expectations of real estate investors versus the actual returns realized, see Roulac, *Modern Real Estate Investment* (Property Press: 1976), pp. 88-97.

Your return from a tax-sheltered investment will consist of *cash flow, tax benefits* and *appreciation* in equity value. *Cash flow* represents the dollars *actually distributed* to you. To this extent, it might be compared with the dividends on a common stock. However, such a comparison could be highly misleading, since dividends do not reflect a return of any portion of your capital. In many tax-sheltered investments, where the venture's assets are depreciating or depleting, a portion of the "cash flow" (and possibly all of it) will merely represent a return of your initial investment. In some instances, the cash being distributed to you by the syndicator represents unused portions of cash held in reserve and not used in operations. A required "guaranteed" return to you from the general partner may even be from profits he received by selling a project to you at an inflated price. Thus, the fact that you are receiving cash distributions from your investment does not necessarily mean that the venture is operating at a profit, or that you will ever receive back all of your invested capital.

The *tax benefits* that flow from your investment will include the *initial tax consequences,* such as the deductions generated by the drilling of an oil and gas well, the payment of interest or property taxes, or feeding and maintaining your cattle; depreciation and similar "paper loss" *deductions occuring over the life of the investment;* and any *special sheltering of investment income,* such as that provided by the depletion allowance. However, early year tax benefits are often partially offset by *later year tax detriments.*

Upon the sale of the assets of your venture, taxes will be payable, either at ordinary income or capital gains rates, on that portion of the sale proceeds which is considered "taxable gain." This "gain" may exceed what you normally would expect the "profit" portion of the sale proceeds to be. For tax purposes, gain will be based not upon what you paid for the asset, but upon the *adjusted basis* of the property—its original capitalized cost less subsequent tax deductions. Furthermore, as discussed earlier, the use of leverage may result in the recapture of prior depreciation or similar deductions, and other taxes on "phantom income." So, in determining your "return" on your investment from tax consequences, it is critical that you consider these tax consequences *over the life of the investment,* taking into account subsequent taxes payable and other adverse tax consequences as well as initial tax benefits.

[¶401.1]   Appreciation Versus Actual Dollars in Your Pocket

The increase in the value of your equity interest in the property referred to as *"appreciation"* can come about in various ways. If the venture has relied upon leverage in acquiring its assets, and these assets have not actually depreciated in value, payments on the mortgage principal will lead to "equity build-up." In addition, your property may be increasing in value due to the effects of inflation, or because of an appreciation in the value of your property in terms of "real" dollars. However, it is important to remember that this "appreciation" is not a "real" return until it is realized, i.e., until the property is actually sold and results in dollars distributable to you. Until that time, your "appreciation" merely represents someone's *estimate* of what the value of your property may be. This is particularly true if it is automatically assumed that the property is appreciating in an amount equal to the equity build-up, some inflation factor, or a combination of both.

Even if your property has truly appreciated in value, and this can be reflected in an impartial, reliable appraisal, there is still no assurance until the property is sold and the gain is "realized" that the estimated appreciation will be converted into dollars in your pocket. As anyone who has invested in the stock market knows, today's paper gains may become tomorrow's paper losses. Changes in economic conditions can drastically affect the value of real estate, just as changing "fads" in the purebred cattle breeding industry have resulted in drastic drops in the value of last year's "favored" exotic breed. Furthermore, when your property is sold, and the appreciation is realized, there will be commissions and other sales costs, as well as taxes to pay, all of which will reduce this appreciated gain.

[¶401.2]   Refinancing Your Property

One method of realizing upon appreciation without selling the property, and thus triggering tax consequences or losing the chance for additional future gains, is to *refinance* the property, distributing the excess moneys to yourself and your fellow investors. However, such refinancing creates additional debt against the property. If economic conditions should later change for the worse, that portion of the existing gain not reflected by the distributed refinancing proceeds will be lost to you. Furthermore, refinancing may substantially increase the amount of "phantom gain" on which you will have to pay taxes.

[¶401.3]   Structuring for Individual Needs

The three elements of return in tax-sheltered investment are normally interdependent. (See ¶103.) An investment can be structured to emphasize cash flow; to emphasize tax benefits; to emphasize appreciation potential; or to achieve a blend of all benefits. However, if tax consequences are to be increased, it will normally be at the expense of cash flow and appreciation potential; if either of these two benefits are enhanced, it will also be at the expense of the other return components.

A key means of increasing potential deductions from a tax-sheltered venture is to increase the purchase price or other incentives offered for acquiring the property, or to increase the degree of leverage. Obviously, however, if more money is paid for the property, there will be less appreciation potential when the property is eventually sold. Likewise, the greater the borrowings, the more of the cash flow which must be used for debt service, and the greater the amount of the eventual sale proceeds that must be used to satisfy the mortgage.

If deductibility is increased by a different method of structuring payments to the seller of the property so as to secure their tax deductibility, it may trigger adverse tax consequences for the seller. This normally means a higher purchase price. Similarly, where the seller is required to "guarantee" a given cash flow for a specified period of time, he will insist upon being paid more for his property, thus reducing its appreciation potential.

[¶402]   **THE TIME VALUE OF MONEY**

Money does have a time value. A dollar paid to you today is more valuable to you than a dollar which you will receive tomorrow. You can put today's dollar to work for you immediately, thus earning interest on your money and, eventually, interest on that interest. Similarly, if you can postpone an obligation to spend dollars—defer an obligation or liability—that obligation is less costly to you, since you can use that money, and benefit from that use, for a longer period of time.

How do we translate this time value of money into dollars and cents? We do so by expressing our right to receipt of money in the future, or of a similar obligation to make a future payment, in terms of its *"present value"*—an expression of the value in terms of today's dollars. Thus, the process of reducing the time value of money to present value is the reverse of compounding interest.

To express money in terms of its present value, we must first determine the rate at which we could put these dollars to work for you today. Once this "interest rate" has been determined, the future rights or obligations can be reduced to present-day values by the use of "discount factors." The following table reflects the discount factors used to state the present value of moneys to be received in the future at various future dates, applying various interest rates:

Discount Factors for Present Value of
One Dollar To Be Received at Various Future
Dates and Discounted at Various Interest Rates*

End of Year	Interest Rate			
	5%	**10%**	**15%**	**20%**
1	.952	.909	.870	.833
2	.907	.826	.756	.694
3	.864	.751	.658	.579
4	.823	.683	.572	.482
5	.784	.621	.497	.402
10	.614	.386	.247	.162
15	.481	.239	.123	.065
20	.377	.149	.061	.026
30	.231	.057	.015	.004

---

*Copyrighted by and reproduced with the permission of Roulac, *Modern Real Estate Investment* (Property Press: 1976). All rights reserved.

[¶402.1]   Putting Your Money to Work Over Time

As this table indicates, if you assume that you can put your money to work at 10 percent, a dollar to be received a year from now rather than today is worth only 91 cents. If the period of receipt is extended to the end of five years, the dollar is worth only 62 cents, and will be worth only 38 cents if it is not to be received until the end of ten years. If you assume that you can put your money to work for you at a 15 percent rate, those same figures would be 87ᶜ, 50ᶜ and 25ᶜ. Similarly, however, if you can put off the liability to pay a dollar for a year—such as a dollar in taxes—that dollar will cost you only 91 cents in terms of today's money at a 10 percent "time value" rate, and only 87 cents at a 15 percent rate. If the period of payment can be delayed for fifteen years, the dollars will cost you only 24 cents at a 10 percent time value figure and only 12 cents if you assume your money has been working at a 15 percent annual rate.

The time value of money is a critical factor in computing your "return" from a tax-sheltered investment. (See ¶403). A $10,000 investment may generate a two to one return; but the question is two to one *realized over how long a period,* and with what dollars being received *during which years?* Similarly, if you can "stage" your investment over a several-year period, that "two to one return" will be much more valuable to you.

The following examples illustrate just exactly how the time value of money can drastically affect a $10,000 investment yielding this hypothetical two to one return:

Present Value of "Two-to-One Return" Under Various Assumptions

Received at End of 5-Year Period:

	Amount	Present Value at 10%
1. Initial Investment	$10,000	($10,000)
2. 2 to 1 return at end of 5th year (discount factor: .621)	20,000	12,420
Total Profit (Loss)		$ 2,420

Received at End of 10-Year Period:

	Amount	Present Value at 10%
1. Initial Investment	$10,000	($10,000)
2. 2 to 1 return at end of 10th year (discount factor: .386)	20,000	7,720
Total Profit (Loss)		($ 2,280)

Received Evenly Over 5-Year Period:

	Amount	Present Value at 10%
1. Initial Investment	$10,000	($10,000)
2. 2 to 1 return received evenly over 5-year period:		
(a) First year at .909	4,000	3,636
(b) Second year at .826	4,000	3,304
(c) Third year at .751	4,000	3,004
(d) Fourth year at .683	4,000	2,732
(e) Fifth year at .621	4,000	2,484
Total Profit (Loss)		$ 5,160

Received Unevenly Over 5-Year Period:

	Amount	Present Value at 10%
1. Initial Investment	$10,000	($10,000)
2. Receipts Over 5 Years		
(a) First year at .909	1,000	909
(b) Second year at .826	3,000	2,478
(c) Third year at .751	9,000	6,759
(d) Fourth year at .683	5,000	3,415
(e) Fifth year at .621	2,000	1,242
Total Profit (Loss)		$ 4,803

Staged Contribution

	Amount	Present Value at 10%
1. Investment		
(a) Start of first year	$ 4,000	($ 4,000)
(b) End of second year at .826	3,000	(2,478)
(c) End of third year at .751	3,000	(2,253)
2. 2 to 1 receipt at end of 5th year (discount factor: .621)		12,420
Total Profit (Loss)		$ 3,689

These examples represent economic conditions that might exist under, respectively, a raw land investment, a cattle breeding investment, a real estate investment, an oil and gas investment, and an agricultural investment, if the eventual return were two for one.

These examples have not taken into account tax benefits, and subsequent tax liabilities. The following examples add these factors:

Present Value of "Two to One Return"
Considering Effect of Tax Rates
Assuming a 10 Percent Discount Factor*

	100% Write-Off	
Return Received at the End of 5th Year	*Amount*	*Present Value*
Initial Investment	[$10,000.00]	[$10,000.00]
Initial tax savings - 70% Bracket	7,000.00	7,000.00
Two to one return at the end of the 5th year (.621)	20,000.00	12,420.00
Tax costs at the end of 5th year 70% bracket (.621)	[14,000.00]	[8,694.00]
Return on investment	$ 3,000.00	$ 726.00
Return Received at the End of 10th Year		
Initial Investment	[$10,000.00]	[$10,000.00]
Initial tax savings - 70% Bracket	7,000.00	7,000.00
Two to one return at the end of the 10th year (.386)	20,000.00	7,720.00
Tax costs at the end of 10th year 70% bracket (.386)	[14,000.00]	[5,404.00]
Return on investment	$ 3,000.00	$ [684.00]
Return Received Evenly Over 5 Year Period		
Initial investment	[$10,000.00]	[$10,000.00]
Tax savings - 70% Bracket	7,000.00	7,000.00
Return over 5 years, net of tax		
1st year (4,000—2,800) @.909	1,200.00	1,090.80
2nd year (4,000—2,800) @.826	1,200.00	991.20
3rd year (4,000—2,800) @.751	1,200.00	901.20
4th year (4,000—2,800) @.683	1,200.00	819.60
5th year (4,000—2,800) @.621	1,200.00	745.20
Return on investment	$ 3,000.00	$ 1,548.00
Return Received Unevenly Over 5 Year Period		
Initial investment	[$10,000.00]	[$10,000.00]
Tax savings - 70% Bracket	7,000.00	7,000.00
Return over 5 years, net of tax		
1st year (1,000—700) @.909	300.00	272.70
2nd year (3,000—2,100) @.826	900.00	743.40
3rd year (4,000—2,300) @.751	2,700.00	2,027.70
4th year (5,000—3,500) @.683	1,500.00	1,024.50
5th year (2,000—1,400) @.621	600.00	372.60
Return on investment	$ 3,000.00	$ 1,440.90

Staged Contribution
Investment, net of tax cost

1st year (4,000—2,800) @ 1.00	[$ 1,200.00]	[$ 1,200.00]
2nd year (3,000—2,100) @.826	[900.00]	[743.00]
3rd year (3,000—2,100) @.751	[900.00]	[676.00]
Return, net of tax cost		
4th year (20,000—14,000) @0.621	6,000.00	3,726.00
Return on investment	$ 3,000.00	$ 1,107.00

[¶403]   **HOW TO FIGURE—AND MISFIGURE—RETURN**

Now that we have some of the principles of "return" firmly in hand, how do we calculate how well we have done on our tax-sheltered investment? This is frequently difficult to do, since return can be quite a "numbers game."

For example, consider a $10,000, 100 percent deductible, investment in oil and gas by a taxpayer in the 50 percent Federal income tax bracket. The well is completed as a producing well, and, at the end of the first year, the investor is advised by the syndicator that the reserves from the well can be sold "in place" for $10,000. Our first problem is, how do we calculate our investment? If we look at our investor's $10,000 cash investment versus his potential $10,000 cash return, we might state, ignoring the time value of money, that our return had been one for one. On the other hand, if we look at the investor's "after-tax investment" of $5,000 ($10,000 less the $5,000 tax savings), our return has magically jumped from one to one, to two to one, all by simply changing the basis on which our investment is calculated. But we have already seen that this "return" does not take into account the time value of the money.

We also should ask ourselves, does it take into account:

☐ The taxes payable on the sale proceeds?
☐ Any interest of the syndicator in those sale proceeds?
☐ Just how sure are we that the reserves, if sold, would actually bring $10,000?

As we can see, it is fairly easy to distort "return" to make it indicate anything that the person preparing the figures wishes it to show. The "investment" may be a gross dollar investment figure, or it may be net of tax benefits. "Return" will, of course, include cash generated from the investment, but it may also include equity build-up and estimated appreciation. Whatever definition of "investment" and "return" are used, you must be careful, if tax benefits have been used in defining either, that the taxes payable are also taken into account. You must also be sure, if the amount of the investment has been reduced by the tax benefits and is expressed on an "after-tax" basis, that these benefits have not additionally been computed as an aspect of "return," thus giving them double effect. Likewise, it is critical to be sure that cost of sale and the syndicator's participation, as well as the taxes payable on the sale, have been taken into account in computing any return based upon estimated asset value. (Estimates of "return" which include equity build-up and assume appreciation should be viewed with suspicion in any event. Even where such estimations are made in good faith and are currently accurate, there is no assurance that they will actually still be realizable when the property is sold.)

A number of approaches are commonly used to measure "return" on a tax-sheltered investment. Unfortunately, many of the most popular methods of calculating investment return are unduly simplistic; such "return" approaches accordingly can be highly misleading to you.

[¶403.1]   Accounting Return Ignores Time Value of Money

The most popular method of computing return is *"accounting return,"* which seeks to determine the average return over the entire holding period of the investment. This is done by deducting the initial investment from the total return received, and then dividing this "gain" by the number of years required to realize this return. The result is then divided by the amount of the initial investment to express the return as an annual percentage figure. Unfortunately, this most popular approach disregards the time value of money, and often includes return of capital as if it were a "profit" element. A far preferable approach is to determine the present value or "discounted cash flow" of the various items of income and liability. This can either be done by determining whether the present value of the return exceeds the present value of the investment and other obligations—the *"present value"* or *"profitability index"* approach—or by establishing the "internal rate of return" for the investment.

[¶403.2]   The Profitability Index

The profitability index or present value approach to calculating return requires that you initially determine the interest rate at which you assume your money could be put to use in order to discount the future flows to present values. Thus, the interest rate is fixed; and the unknown is whether the present value of your items of return will exceed the present value of your investment and future liabilities. Internal rate of return is calculated by determining the interest rate which will make the present value of the return equal the present value of the investment and other obligations. Thus, the "unknown" is the interest rate which you will be earning on your money. Since this is exactly what you should be seeking to determine in calculating "return," the internal rate of return approach and its variations are looked at as a highly effective approach. Internal rate of return also eliminates the problem of determining how tax consequences should be taken into account in determining rate of return.

Assume that you have made a $10,000, 100 percent deductible tax-sheltered investment. You are in the 50 percent Federal income tax bracket. At the end of five years, you sell your interest for $15,000.

Look at the difference that selecting a particular method of expressing "return" makes. (And remember: the "return," taxwise or otherwise, didn't vary; *only the method of expressing return changed):*

RATE OF RETURN COMPUTATION*

Accounting Rate of Return Method—Ignoring Tax Consequences

1. Initial Investment	[$10,000]
2. Sale Proceeds	15,000
3. Gain on Sale	$ 5,000
4. *Annual Return* (Gain divided by initial investment divided by number of years held)	**10%**

Accounting Rate of Return Method— Including Tax Consequences

1. Initial Investment	[$10,000]
2. Tax Savings on Investment	5,000
3. Sale Proceeds	$15,000
4. Taxes Payable on Long Term Capital Gain (25% of $15,000)*	[3,750]
5. After-Tax Gain on Sale	$ 6,250
6. *Annual Return* (After-tax gain divided by *pretax* investment divided by number of years held)	**12.5%**

---

*©1978, by The Institute for Energy Development, Inc. All rights reserved.

*Your "adjusted basis" in the asset is zero, due to your prior deduction of 100 percent of the cost.

*Accounting Rate of Return Method —Including
Tax Consequences (Another Method)*

1. Before-Tax Investment	[$10,000]
2. Tax Savings	5,000
3. After-Tax Investment	[5,000]
4. Sale Proceeds	15,000
5. Taxes Payable	[3,750]
6. After-Tax Gain on Sale	$ 6,250
7. Annual Return (After-tax gain divided by *after-tax* investment divided by number of years held)	**25%**

Discounted Cash Flow Method —10% Discount Rate

1. Present Value of Initial Investment	[$10,000]
2. Present Value of Initial Tax Savings	5,000
3. Present Value of $15,000 Return in 5-Years	9,315
4. Present Value of $3,750 Tax Cost	[2,329]
5. Total Discounted After-Tax Gain on Sale	$ 1,986
6. *Annual Return (Above Discount Rate)*	**13.97%** (or approximately 14%)

Internal Rate of Return Method

Present value of initial investment ($10,000) less the tax savings ($5,000) must equal the present value of the future sale proceeds ($15,000) less the tax cost of the sale ($3,750 or 25% of 15.000) at some interest rate. This interest rate is computed to be **17.61%**

Misleading Presentation of Rate of Return

An *intentionally misleading* way of "calculating" return by giving double effect to tax benefits, while ignoring taxes payable, is illustrated by the following recasting of our prior example:

1. Initial Investment	[$10,000]
2. Tax Savings	5,000
3. After-Tax Investment	[$ 5,000]
4. Tax Savings	5,000
5. Sale Proceeds	15,000
6. Gain on Sale	$15,000
7. Annual Return as % of *After-Tax* Investment	**60%**

5.

The Tax Reform Act of 1976 — A New Ball Game

[¶501]   **EROSION OF TAX-SHELTERED INCENTIVES**

Prior to the Tax Reform Act of 1976, most congressional changes in the tax laws were aimed at increasing the benefits available for "legitimate" tax-sheltered investment. The laws were also aimed at eliminating those provisions that were seen as "loopholes," tax incentives that were not accomplishing the congressional intent of funneling moneys into under-capitalized industries which directly affected the public interest. Thus, changes in the tax laws provided increased tax incentives for new residential construction and, in particular, for low and moderate income housing. Benefits available in the citrus area, which was looked at as having been overly favored, were reduced.

With the Tax Reform Act of 1969, a new congressional thrust became obvious. There had been too much publicity concerning how to "get rich" through tax-sheltered investments. There had been too many tax-sheltered "rip-offs" which benefited no one except the promoter of the scheme. Publicity concerning "millionaires who pay no taxes" likewise placed considerable political pressure on Congress to show that it was doing something in the area of tax shelter "abuse."

The Tax Reform Act of 1969 reflected this change in congressional attitude. As early as 1963, Congress had provided for recapture of excess depreciation in real estate for property sold within ten years, although such recapture would be phased out if the property had been held for more than twenty months. However, the Tax Reform Act of 1969 imposed further restrictions. These restrictions required a longer holding period for residential real property and full recapture of excess depreciation upon all nonresidential real estate, no matter how long it had been held. The availability of various methods of accelerated depreciation was also restricted, with new multifamily residential property being placed in the "most favored" position. The Tax Reform Act of 1969 likewise created substantial restrictions on tax-sheltered investments in cattle breeding and farming, creating a 24-month holding period in order to claim capital gain on the purchased portion of a breeding herd. The Act also required recapture of all depreciation taken in connection with the purchased animals and created the concept of an "Excess Deductions Account" for all types of agricultural syndications.

[¶501.1]   New Tax Concepts of the 1969 Act

The direct attack on real estate, cattle, and agriculture was not the only impact of the Tax Reform Act of 1969. The Act went further to create certain new tax concepts which would cut across all tax shelter areas, and which set the stage for the drastic reforms enacted by the Tax Reform Act of 1976. These 1969 tax law changes included:

(1) A substantial increase in capital gains tax benefits by restricting the automatic 25 percent alternate tax rate to $50,000 of gain;
(2) The introduction of a new "hobby loss" ("profit motive") rule (IRC,§183), *which would disallow deductions in activities not carried on for profit;*
(3) The creation of the concept of "items of tax preference," together with the imposition of a 10 percent minimum tax on all deductions taken for specified "items of tax preference" in excess of exemption levels specified in the act. It also created a 50 percent "maximum tax on earned income" aimed at discouraging investment in tax shelters;
(4) The disallowance of "excess investment interest" as a tax-deductible item.

[¶501.2]   Hostility to Tax Shelters Is Unwarranted

These changes enacted by Congress in 1969 showed not only a congressional desire to curb tax-sheltered "abuses" but a growing hostility toward the whole concept of tax-sheltered investment. Some moneys invested as a tax-sheltered investment do find their way into swindles that do not benefit the public, or into tax-favored industries where there may be question as to the public benefit to be derived from encouraging such investment. However, the vast amount of tax-sheltered dollars are funneled into various activities which do directly affect the public interest, with very beneficial results for the public consumer. There is no question but that our energy, housing, and food problems would be substantially greater than they are today if it had not been for the congressional policy encouraging tax-sheltered investments in these industries. The number of persons who have avoided the payment of any (or significant) taxes through the tax shelter route is small, and is primarily used as a propaganda item by those who, for reasons of their own, are opposed to the tax shelter concept. And those persons who have reduced or eliminated their taxes through the tax shelter route have done so only by pouring their money back into the economy in vital industries and by putting hard dollars at risk. In most businesses, this would be lauded as a boon to the economy. For some reason, in the tax shelter area, politics has turned this reinvestment of capital into some form of sinister "abuse."

Despite the fact that energy, housing, and food costs continue to skyrocket, the outcries for "curbing" tax shelters continue. For several years, new reform proposals were drafted and redrafted, with the issuance in 1975 of the potentially- disastrous "Schultz Proposals". This would have created a "Limitation on Artifical Accounting Losses" ("LAL"). The LAL concept would have had a disastrous effect on most publicly-beneficial tax-sheltered areas and on the economy. At the same time, as has been the case in most tax "reform" efforts, it failed to close most of the loopholes which did exist in the tax laws.

[¶501.3]   The Tax Reduction Act of 1975

The pressure for tax "reform" saw the enactment of the Tax Reduction Act of 1975. From the standpoint of the oil and gas producer, this terminology was highly misleading. The Act imposed substantial reduction, and in some instances elimination, of the benefits of percentage depletion, particularly for companies not falling within the "independent producers and royalty owners" exemption. Then, in 1976, the "reform" efforts culminated in the enactment of one of the most confusing and imprecise pieces of tax legislation in the history of this country—the Tax Reform Act of 1976.

[¶502]   HOW THE TAX REFORM ACT OF
1976 AFFECTS TAX SHELTERS

It is difficult to imagine how the extensive studies that led up to the Tax Reform Act of 1976 could have resulted in such confusing legislation. Frequently referred to as "The Accountants and Attorneys Civil Relief Act of 1976," the pressures on the Congress to enact some form of tax legislation led to last-minute decisions which in many instances were highly detrimental to the public interest and are often highly unclear as to their intended effect. While the act did resolve a number of prior grey areas in the tax laws, its interpretation will be the subject of numerous IRS administrative actions and undoubtedly considerable court litigation. However, it is the law of the land. You, as a potential tax-sheltered investor, must understand the effects of the Tax Reform Act intelligently to plan your tax-shelter strategy.

One thing that should be emphasized, the Tax Reform Act of 1976 did not deal a "death blow" to tax-sheltered investments. Instead, the interest in tax-sheltered investments, and the amount of dollars being invested in tax shelters, stands at an all time high. Even the supposed congressional goal of eliminating excess deductions was not accomplished by the Act. However, the Tax Reform Act of 1976 does require much more careful planning of your tax-sheltered investment strategy. Greater study of the economics of your proposed investment, aside from taxes, is needed if your tax-sheltered investment is to prove economically beneficial, rather than economically disastrous.

[¶502.1]   Three Basic Principles of 1976 Act

Three basic principles emerge from the Tax Reform Act of 1976:

(1) The requirement that a number of *items which were formerly* given a preferred status as *immediately deductible* expenditures *be capitalized and amortized* over the life of the investment, or a specified lesser life, *or*, if deductible, are *subject* to some form of *"recapture."* These provisions include such items as: construction period interest and taxes in real estate; prepaid interest; prepaid feed; and, in the "recapture" area, all excess depreciation deductions in real estate and productive-well intangible drilling and development cost expenditures in oil and gas.

(2) An attempted *limitation of tax-sheltered deductions to the amount of money the investor actually stands to lose if the venture fails.* This attempt to eliminate excess write-offs is found in two new provisions in the tax law: the *"at risk"* limitation imposed on investments in oil and gas, equipment leasing, films, and farming (other than timber); and the *"partnership borrowing"* restrictions imposed on all partnership activities not falling within the "at risk" category, other than partnerships engaged in "investment in real property."

(3) *Changed rules imposing increased burdens on "items of tax preference,"* both in the *size of the minimum tax* imposed on such items, their effect on *the availability of the maximum tax* on personal service (earned) income, and in the tax *deductions which are considered tax preference items.*

[¶502.2]   How the 1976 Act Affects
Tax-Sheltered Investments

Various provisions enacted by the Tax Reform Act of 1976 have general applicability to a number of tax-sheltered investment areas. These include:

☐ *Increased limitations on "investment interest"* (Internal Revenue Code, §163(d)). The limitation on the deductibility of interest on investment indebtedness does not apply to personal interest or business interest, and likewise is not applicable to corporations.

☐ *The deductibility of "management" and other such fees* as "guaranteed payments" under §707(c) of the Code. Section 707(c) has been amended to specify that the deductibility of a guaranteed payment depends upon its deductibility under §162 (ordinary and necessary business expense) and §263 (non-deductibility of capital expenditures). A new §709 has been added to the Internal Revenue Code, specifying that no deduction should be allowed for amounts paid in organizing a partnership or selling the partnership interests. The revision of §707(c) merely reflects the position taken by the Tax Court in *Jackson E. Cagle, Jr.,** and by the Internal Revenue Service in Rev. Rul. 75-214.** However, §709(b) does permit organization fees to be amortized ratably over a sixty-month period. The Tax Reform Act does not deal with the amortization of selling expense.

☐ *Elimination of the "retroactive allocation"* of expenses incurred early in the year to year-end investors. Section 706(c) of the Internal Revenue Code has been amended to specify that a partner's share of income and loss will be determined according to his varying interests throughout the year.

☐ *Limitations on the Code authority to make special allocation of partnership income or loss* so long as the principal purpose of the allocation was not to avoid Federal tax. Section 704(b) now provides that such allocations must have "substantial economic effect"—must actually affect the dollar amount of the partners' share of partnership income and loss, independent of tax consequences.

☐ *Elimination of the "stepped-up" basis for property acquired from a decendent.* Previously, heirs were permitted to carry over the decedent's basis. This eliminated the one method by which deductions in excess of basis could eventually escape taxation.

☐ *Increase in the holding period for long-term capital gains from six months to one year.* (A nine-month capital gains period was provided for taxable years beginning in 1977.)

Numerous other provisions of the Tax Reform Act relating to specific investment areas will be discussed later in this book in connection with the tax-sheltered investment in those industries. The balance of this chapter will deal with two of the most critical aspects of the Tax Reform Act: (1) the "at risk" and partnership borrowing restrictions (¶503), and (2) minimum and maximum taxes and items of tax preference (¶504).

---

*63 T.C. 86 (1974), affirmed 539 F. 2d 409 (5th Circuit 1976).
**1975-1 C.B. 185.

See Appendix 502-1 for a chart outlining the effects of the Tax Reform Act on various tax-sheltered investment areas.

[¶503]   **THE "AT RISK" CONCEPT**

In a report issued by the U.S. Congressional Joint Committee on Taxation on December 29, 1976, the Committee stated as a rationale for the development of the "at risk" (Internal Revenue Code, §465) and "partnership borrowing" (Internal Revenue Code, §704(d)) restrictions:

> "Non-recourse leveraging of the investment and other risk limiting devices which produce tax savings in excess of amounts placed at risk substantially alter the economic substance of the investments and distort the workings of the investment markets. Taxpayers, ignoring the possible tax consequences in later years, can be lead into investments which are otherwise economically unsound and which constitute an unproductive use of investment funds.
>
> "Congress believed that it was not equitable to allow individual investors to defer tax on income from other sources through losses generated by tax sheltering activities. One of the most significant problems in tax shelters is the use of non-recourse financing and other risk-limiting devices which enable investors in these activities to deduct losses from the activities in amounts which exceeded the total investment the investor actually placed at risk in the activity. The Act consequently provides an 'at risk' rule to deal directly with this abuse in tax shelters."

The original reaction of commentators to §§465 and 704(d) was that the "excess write-off" programs were dead. Motion picture, equipment leasing, and similar syndications which depended on excess write-offs for their investment appeal were now a thing of the past. However, a careful study of §§465 and 704(d) by tax practitioners showed that there were a number of ways in which excess write-offs still (or *arguably* still) could be obtained, despite the Tax Reform Act of 1976.

Neither §465 nor §704(d) imposes any limitation on the benefits which can be claimed by an investor under the investment tax credit, even though a substantial portion of the purchase price of the investment may have been financed through non-recourse borrowing. The investment tax credit likewise does not limit the amount at which a taxpayer is considered to be "at risk." However, §465 does provide that taxpayers cannot claim deductions in excess of their amounts "at risk" for investments in certain named activities (whether engaged in by the taxpayer directly or through a partnership). Further, §704(d) provides that partners in a partnership engaged in non-§465 activities (other than "investment in real property") cannot increase their adjusted basis in their partnership interest by borrowings for which they are not personally liable.

[¶503.1] At-Risk Concept Includes Cash Investment Plus Borrowings

The taxpayer is considered "at risk" to the extent of his cash invest-ment and also as to borrowings for which he is personally liable (or non-recourse borrowings secured by the taxpayer's personal property not related to the venture), so long as such borrowings are not from a related party or a person with an interest in the venture and are not limited by any "stop loss" or similar indemnification arrangement. (See Rev. Rul. 77-401.)*

"At risk" limitations in §465 apply to a taxpayer engaged in oil and gas, film or video tape, equipment leasing, or farming activities. Farming does not include timber activities. See Internal Revenue Code, §464(e). The restrictions of §465 apply, whether or not the tax payer is utilizing a partnership as his investment vehicle. However, the restrictions do not apply to investments by regular business corporations, i.e., corporations other than Subchapter S corporations or personal holding companies. The restrictions do not apply to activities in investment areas other than the four specifically named.

The partnership borrowing restrictions of §704(d) apply only to investments structured as partnership. Investments not structured as partnership are not covered by §704(d). However, its restrictions do apply to investments by corporations. Special provisions cover a partnership engaged in several activities, a part of which would be covered by §465 and a part of which would not, or where a corporation invests through a partnership.

[¶503.2] Techniques for Avoiding At-Risk Limitations

What techniques, then, have been developed to avoid these restric-tions? *Corporations* can still invest on a non-recourse basis in oil and gas, motion pictures, equipment leasing, and agricultural investment (includ-ing livestock). For this reason, the better quality motion picture and leasing syndications are primarily being financed through corporate in-vestors at this time. Since the corporate investor can include *professional corporations,* if you are a taxpayer such as a lawyer, accountant, or similar professional whose business is being conducted through a corporate format, you may wish to consider leaving certain dollars in your profes-sional corporation rather than distributing the dollars from the corpora-tion directly to you. Since the professional corporation, as to its income over $50,000 a year, is taxed at a 48 percent rate, the difference in taxes

*I.R.B. 1977-44, page 10.

between dollars invested through this corporate vehicle and directly through the taxpayer (whose compensation from the corporation presumably would be in the form of 50 percent "personal service" dollars) is relatively minor. However, this suggestion would apply only if, as a taxpayer, you are primarily interested in "exotic" excess write-off investments, despite their problems and pitfalls, rather than more conventional tax-sheltered investments in real estate, oil and gas, or livestock. Likewise, the suggestion would only apply if your professional corporation was presented with a motion picture or equipment leasing syndication which seemed to have exceptional economic, as well as tax, merit.

Even if you are an individual taxpayer, non-recourse borrowings can still be used in the following situations:

- *To bring the deductibility of your investment to the 100 percent level.* Such an approach is currently being used in cattle, racehorse, and coal syndications, and is available since the "at risk" rules do not affect your basis in your property.
- In all but the four named investment areas covered by §465, *direct ownership of the asset which is the subject of the tax-sheltered investment avoids the applicability of the "partnership borrowing" restrictions,* since no partnership is involved. This approach is primarily being used at the present time in "master record" and book syndications. However, it creates economic dangers where the likelihood of personal liability is present, such as in coal activities, and similarly creates problems that a "co-ownership" may be taxed as a partnership under the Internal Revenue Code, and thus be subject to §704(d), if the asset is owned by more than one person. (In certain syndications, such as coal, a co-ownership is possible if each co-owner is permitted to take his share of venture production in kind.)
- Where the venture is considered "low risk," or where it will acquire assets which have a high resale value and which would support a high degree of leverage, *straight recourse borrowing can be utilized.* This technique is currently being used in cattle breeding, and has likewise been used in coal syndications where a large part of the non-recourse proceeds are used to purchase equipment to be utilized in the coal operation. Other approaches have included the purchase of treasury bills on a "recourse" basis, with the bills then being pledged to secure the moneys for the conduct of the primary activities of the venture, or the packaging of "seasoned" projects, which could support recourse borrowing, with more speculative ventures. However, before investing on a recourse basis, you should give serious question as to how "low risk" the venture truly is.
- *Other recourse borrowing approaches* include: (a) guaranteeing that

portion of a loan which is considered relatively low risk; (b) guaranteeing the loan once it becomes obvious that the project will suceed (§465 only requires that the taxpayer be "at risk" at the end of the tax year for which the deduction is being claimed); (c) entering into a recourse loan which will convert to a non-recourse loan at some time in the future.

- *Distributing a portion of the non-recourse loan proceeds to the taxpayer* as a non-taxable return of capital. Since the "at risk" provisions are not restrictions on the taxpayer's basis in the property, such a distribution may reduce the amounts that the taxpayer actually has at risk, without currently resulting in taxable gain.

As just seen, the three principal approaches used to create excess deductions despite the Tax Reform Act of 1976 are the direct ownership vehicle in non-Section 465 activities; the use of part recourse borrowing, particularly where secured by the pledge of "solid" assets; and the conversion of recourse to non-recourse borrowing (or vice versa). While the Internal Revenue Service in 1977 issued a spate of rulings attempting to discredit these approaches, most of these should have little effect on the popularity of the "excess write-off" programs. As will be seen in ¶2601, most excess write-off investments involve a high risk of tax disallowance in any event. It is not expected that the latest series of rulings by the IRS, many of which seem somewhat questionable in their reasoning, will serve to make much greater the already "grey" area risks of these deductions. The more significant question that you should ask yourself before entering into a tax-sheltered investment involving excess write-offs is whether this is truly the type of tax-sheltered investment for you.

[¶503.3] Excess Write-Off Programs Offer High Tax Risks

Excess write-off programs offer a high degree of tax risk which is rarely offset by any strong economic potential of the venture. While, in some instances, the excess deduction may be worth this risk, it will always be subject to eventual recapture. And excess write-offs are obviously a clear target of further tax reform legislation. (See Chapter 6.) Therefore, unless strong reasons exist for seeking the excess write-off, you should seriously consider the potentially stronger economic benefits that may be available in other tax shelter areas before blindly turning to an "excess write-off" investment.

The verbatim text of §465 and §704(d) as revised are contained in Appendix 503-1.

[¶504]   MINI-¹AND MAXI-TAXES AND
           "ITEMS OF TAX PREFERENCE"
HOW DO THEY AFFECT YOUR PLANNED INVESTMENT?

The Tax Reform Act of 1969 created the concept of the "item of tax preference." Insofar as you, as a potential tax-sheltered investor, are concerned, the key tax preference items are the following:

☐ One-half of any amount allowable as a net *long-term capital gain.*
☐ *Excess accelerated depreciation* on real property and on leased personal property.
☐ *Percentage depletion.*
☐ The *excess* of *itemized deductions* (other than deductions for medical expenses and casualty losses) over 60 percent of adjusted gross income.
☐ *Productive well intangible drilling and development costs* to the extent such costs exceed the greater of the amortization of such costs over a ten-year period or the amount of the deduction allowable as cost depletion.

A number of these items of tax preference were contained in the Tax Reform Act of 1969. However, productive well IDC and excess itemized deductions were added to the list of tax preferences by the Tax Reform Act of 1976.

The characterization of a deduction as "an item of tax preference" can affect your tax return in two distinctly unpleasant ways. First, §56 of the Internal Revenue Code imposes a *"minimum tax"* of 15 percent of the total of your items of tax preference reduced by the greater of $10,000 or one-half of your income tax for the year. The minimum tax was increased from 10 percent to 15 percent by the Tax Reform Act of 1976, and the exemption figure reduced from $30,000 *plus* the taxpayer's regular tax liability to the $10,000 (*or* one-half your regular tax) by the Tax Reform Act of 1976.

The second unpleasant impact of the "tax preference" characterization is the loss of the protection afforded by the 50 percent *maximum tax* on "personal service" income. Prior to the Tax Reform Act of 1976, items of tax preference would reduce the amount of personal service income eligible for the 50 percent maximum tax rate under §1348 only to the extent the preference items exceeded $30,000. However, while the Tax Reform Act of 1976 extended the maximum tax protection to deferred compensation, such as compensation under employee pension plans, it also eliminated the $30,000 tax preference exemption in determining the amount of personal service income subject to the maximum 50 percent rate. Thus *for every dollar of tax preference which you claim on your Federal income tax return, a dollar of earned income which would otherwise be subject to tax at a maximum rate of 50 percent will now be subject to tax at your regular income tax rate.*

[¶504.1]   Choosing Tax-Sheltered Investments Without Items of Tax Preference

A number of tax-sheltered investments are available which do not include items of tax preference. These include investments in most "exotic" areas (other than equipment leasing), and investments in livestock. However, the two most popular tax-sheltered investment areas—oil and gas, and real estate—often will create items of tax preference.

In planning your tax-sheltered strategy, you must give careful consideration to the degree to which the tax benefits which you secure from the investment may be partially offset by a loss of earned income protection or the imposition of a minimum tax. Similarly, if you are sheltering "personal service" dollars, but those dollars will subsequently be taxed to you as unearned income, your consideration of potential investment profitability must include the possible increase in tax rate when the income from your investment is returned to you.

[¶504.2]   How A Tax Shelter Can Actually Increase Your Taxes

What do these mean to you in terms of dollars and cents. Consider the following:

☐ Your taxable income is $97,200, which will create a tax liability of $41,580. By use of tax shelters, you create $30,000 in deductions (all items of tax preference), thus reducing your taxable income to $67,200, and your tax liability to $24,420—an apparent tax savings of $17,160, secured by reducing both your taxable income and your tax bracket. However, *over $2,700 of this tax savings is eaten up by the "minimum tax" generated by your tax preference deductions:*

1. Total Tax Preference Items	$30,000
2. Exemption (50 percent of your regular tax)	(12,210)
3. Net Tax Preference Items	17,790
4. Minimum Tax @ 15 percent of "3"	$ 2,669

☐ Your earnings are "personal service" income, taxed at a maximum rate of 50 percent. To reduce your taxes, you go into tax shelters, creating an additional $10,000 in non-preference item deductions and a tax savings of $5,000. However, your $10,000 will come back as "unearned income," taxable at a possible 70 percent rate, so that *you* *actually have an eventual tax loss of $2,000.*

1. Tax Savings from $10,000
        investment (@ 50 percent) $5,000
2. Tax Cost of $10,000 of
        Unearned Income (@ 70 percent)   (7,000)
3. Tax Loss   ($2,000)

Item of tax preference characterization, despite its mini/maxi implications, does not mean that there are not good tax-shelter opportunities for you. It does mean, however, that before entering into the tax-sheltered investment, you must analyze the effects of tax preference items on the eventual tax consequences of the investment to you. It also again emphasizes the significance of analyzing the economic potential of the venture, over and above its tax consequences.

6.

More New Ball Games on the Horizon—Or Can You Stand Future Shock?

[¶601]   **TAX-SHELTERED INVESTMENTS
ARE NOT "ABUSES"**

As the proceeding chapter has stressed, the congressional and administrative attitudes toward tax-sheltered investments are tending to become more and more hostile. The present Commissioner of Internal Revenue, and his immediate predecessor, have both expressed extreme concern over tax-sheltered "abuses" and have emphasized their intention to press active audit policies where tax-sheltered investments are involved. Administrative actions have likewise involved the issuance of revenue rulings, proposed and enacted changes in regulations and policies on audit which have disallowed or changed what were considered long-established policies in the tax-shelter area. Many Congressmen are pressing for even more changes in the tax law to further curb what they consider tax shelter "excesses."

Unfortunately, what many persons seem to view as "abuses" in tax-sheltered investments are activities which in the minds of most of those intimately involved with tax shelters do not involve abuse, and in fact have proved beneficial to the American public. Despite this, further tax law change is not only possible, but is indeed almost a certainty. Also, recent changes in the tax law frequently have been applied so as to affect existing investments, and not merely ventures entered into after the effective date of the legislation.

As one commentator has stated, "the only thing that is 'sure' about the tax consequences of a proposed investment is that it will be taxed throughout its life under different tax laws than those which were in effect when the investment was entered into."

[¶601.1]   New Tax Legislation Seems Certain

So here you are. Additional tax legislation appears virtually a certainty. No one can state at this time what form this legislation will take, or which areas of tax-sheltered investment it will affect. In addition, the Tax Reform Act of 1976 is itself confusing and imprecise. Further administrative action, both in the interpretation of the TRA '76 and in other aspects of tax-sheltered investments, will clearly be forthcoming and undoubtedly will, in many instances, be unfavorable. Even the critical area of "flow-through" classification is not free from attack. Based upon this, can you still afford to go into a tax-sheltered investment?

For some, where certainty is a psychological necessity, the answer may be no. However, changes in the tax law have occurred in the past, just as they will in the future; and tax-sheltered investment now stands at an all-time high. This is because the alternative to tax-sheltered investment—Pay Your Taxes—is similarly unattractive. However, the likelihood of tax-law change emphasizes points made earlier in this book: it is critical that you:

• Do not invest more than you can afford to lose.
• Carefully analyze the economics of a proposed tax-sheltered investment.
• Do not go for tax overkill at the price of eventual return.

If you have not overreached, economically or tax-wise; if the use of the existing tax benefits permits you to invest in an economically sound project which otherwise might be unavailable for you; and if you are not carried away solely by tax considerations, tax-sheltered investment should prove a beneficial experience for you, despite future tax-law uncertainty. However, if taxes are such an overriding consideration that your personal economic situation must stand or fall based upon the continuance of what is now perceived to be "existing tax laws," you should give serious consideration to changing your tax-shelter strategy.

7.

Alternatives to the "Tax-Sheltered" Investment

[¶701] PAYING YOUR TAXES AND OTHER ALTERNATIVES

Before leaving this portion of our book—the introduction to the "tax-sheltered" concept—you should give consideration to the alternatives that are available to you in lieu of investing in tax-sheltered investments.

One alternative is simply to pay your taxes. Before dismissing this thought out of hand, give it some consideration. Even if you are in the 70 percent bracket, you will still have 30 cents out of every dollar remaining after paying your taxes. This figure moves to 50 cents out of every dollar, if, due to the "personal service" classification of your income, or your general income level, you find yourself in the 50 percent Federal income tax bracket as to most of your dollars.

While no one likes to give 50 to 70 percent of the top portion of his income to the Federal Government, such payments are preferable to losing 100 percent of those dollars through an ill-conceived tax-sheltered investment strategy. If the cash flow required to make tax-sheltered investments is not available to you due to other commitments; if you do not have sufficient "risk" dollars to afford tax-sheltered investment without risky personal borrowing; and if you cannot afford to follow the steps outlined in Part Four of this book as to the proper diversification and screening required before entering into a tax-sheltered investment program, tax shelters may not be the best solution to your problem. This is particularly true since the Tax Reform Act of 1976, with its changed rules concerning the loss of personal service income protection, as well as the possibilities that tax-sheltered investment may involve an eventual return of what was originally 50 percent "personal service" income in the eventual form of future 70 percent "unearned income" dollars.

[¶701.1]   Income-Averaging and Other Techniques May Benefit You More

Even if the payment of taxes does not seem a satisfactory solution to your personal economic situation, you should study other alternatives before deciding to make a tax-sheltered investment to solve your tax problems. If your income has only recently skyrocketed into the 50 percent bracket, you may find that the "income averaging" provisions of the Internal Revenue Code reach a more satisfactory result for you than would a tax-sheltered investment. The following is an example of how income averaging might prove a more satisfactory solution for the problem of the young business executive or professional whose income has only recently climbed than would a tax-sheltered investment.

Assume that for the last 4 years, your taxable income has been modest: $13,200; $14,200; $15,200; and $16,200, respectively. This year, your taxable income shoots to $90,000.

Your normal tax on $90,000 would be $37,284. However, with income averaging, that tax is reduced to $27,678—all without any risk on your part, or any diverting of your cash flow.

The use of tax-sheltered investment to protect against the dilution of the sales price through large capital gains taxes has been mentioned elsewhere. However, in certain instances, an "installment sale" of the property may make even more sense.

A final alternative—and one to be seriously considered—is the tax deferral offered by the various kinds of pension and profit sharing, or "retirement," plans.

In most situations, you will probably find that an intelligent tax-sheltered investment program will prove the best solution, in whole or in part, to your problem of keeping a greater share of your income. However, in view of the risks involved in even the best tax-sheltered investment, these alternate protective steps at least should be explored before embarking on the tax-shelter route.

Additional Readings: Part One
Chapters One and Two:

Chapters One and Two: Basic Concepts; Tax Consequences In General

DAUBER, *"How Tax Shelters Promote Our National Goals,"* from Reid (ed.), *Corporate and Executive Tax Sheltered Investments* (Presidents Publishing House, Inc.: 1972)

DROLLINGER, *Tax Shelters and Tax-Free Income for Everyone,* Introduction; Parts Two-Four (Epic Publications, Inc.: 3rd ed. 1977)

HAFT and FASS, *Tax Sheltered Investments,* Chapter 1 (Clark Boardman Co., Ltd.: 2d ed. 1974)

IRS Tax Shelter Training Manual (Internal Revenue Service: 1976*

MOSBURG, *The Tax Shelter Coloring Book* (The Institute for Energy Development, Inc.: 1977)

Tax Incentives—A Tool for Financing Business Growth and for Sheltering Income (Arthur Andersen & Co.: 2d ed. 1977)

Overview of Tax Shelteres (Joint Committee Staff: 1975*

Understanding Tax Shelters (E.F. Hutton & Co., Inc.: 1977)

Partnerships and Other Flow-Through Vehicles

CRANE and BROMBERG, *Law of Partnership (West Publishing Co.: 1968)*

DROLLINGER, *op. cit.,* Part Four

HAFT and FASS, *op. cit.,* §1.06

LEVINE, *Real Estate Tax Shelter Desk Book,* Chapter 12 (Institute for Business Planning, Inc.: 1978)

ROULAC, *Modern Real Estate Investment,* Chapter 14 (Property Press: 1976)

ROULAC, "Resolution of Limited Partnership Disputes," *Real Property, Probate and Trust Journal* (Summer, 1975)**

WILLIS, *Partnership Taxation* (McGraw-Hill Book Co.: 2d ed. 1976)

Chapter Three: Investment Pitfalls

MOSBURG, *The Tax Shelter Coloring Book, op. cit.*

MOSBURG, "How to Evaluate Tax Shelters," *Financial Observer (Oct. 1972/Nov. 1972)*

Tax Incentives—A Tool for Financing Business Growth and for Sheltering Income, op. cit.

---

*Reproduced in Mosburg (ed.), *Structuring Tax-Sheltered Investments under the Tax Reform Act of 1976* (The Institute for Energy Development, Inc.: 1977)

**Reproduced in *New Challenges in Real Estate: Integrating the Disciplines* (Property Press: 1977)

Chapter Four: Return

McNEELEY, "Money-Making in Real Estate Is a Numbers Game," *Real Estate Review* (Spring 1972)

PARISSE, "Fundamentals of Real Estate Investment Analysis," from Roulac (ed.), *Real Estate Securities and Syndication Workbook* (National Association of Realtors: 1973)

ROULAC, *Modern Real Estate Investment, op. cit.*, Chapters 4-6, 20

Chapters Five and Six: Tax Reform Legislation

DROLLINGER, *op. cit.*, Appendix D

HAFT and FASS, *op. cit.*, Introduction

MOSBURG (ed.), *Structuring Tax-Sheltered Investments under the Tax Reform Act of 1976* (The Institute for Energy Development, Inc.: 1977)

Real Estate Investment Under the New Tax Reform Act of 1976 (Property Press: 2d ed. 1977)

Tax Incentives—A Tool for Business Growth and for Sheltering Income, op. cit., Chapter 1

Chapter Seven: Tax Shelter Alternatives

DROLLINGER, *op. cit.*, Part One (Chapter 9), Parts Two-Three, Appendix D

REID (ed.), *op. cit.*

PART TWO

The "Traditional" Tax Shelters—Real Estate, Oil and Gas, and Cattle and Other Agricultural Investments

Section 1: Real Estate—Tax Shelter for Large and Small Investors

8.

When and How Can Real Estate Be A "Tax Shelter?"

THE DIFFERENT TYPES OF REAL ESTATE "SHELTERS"

Real estate is by far the most popular form of tax-sheltered investment. It is also the one most readily available to you when smaller "private" offerings are taken into account in addition to those "public offerings" registered with the Securities and Exchange Commission. These are available to you through your securities broker.

Real estate investment has had particular appeal to small as well as large investors due to the historic position of real estate as an inflation hedge and the popular view that land is "the source of all wealth." Real estate has likewise appealed to the investor since, unlike oil and gas, it is something with which the investor deals in his everyday life, and is also a tangible, visible investment property. For this reason, many investors have felt more comfortable with investment in real estate than they might in oil and gas, cattle, or the exotics.

The early 1970's saw a boom in large, publicly registered real estate syndications. However, the number of these offerings began to decline sharply in the mid 1970's. While several SEC-registered real estate offerings are firmly established as a source of real estate investment, the vast majority of real estate syndications are offered as much smaller "private" investments.

The significance of the private market to the real estate syndicator is reflected by the fact that while only 50 real estate syndications were registered in the year 1977 with the National Association of Securities Dealers for offerings totaling slightly under $300,000,000, nearly 600 real estate syndications were offered through NASD member firms in unregistered offerings with such offerings totaling in excess of $500,000,000.

Only a few of these offerings were SEC-registered offerings, the vast majority being "intrastate" and other offerings exempt from SEC but not State securities registration. (See Chapter 31). These figures are even more revealing when you realize that the vast majority of real estate syndications are sold directly by the syndicator without the intervention of any NASD brokerage firm.

**[¶801.1]   Real Estate Is Not an Automatic
            Road to Wealth**

Unfortunately, this familiarity with real estate has also proved the undoing of a number of investors. Purchase of real estate is not an automatic road to wealth; and real estate investment, just as every other investment area, has its definite pitfalls as well as its rewards. The investor who has blindly invested in real estate based upon the comforting theory that "land can never go down in value" has often found to his dismay that this statement is true only if he has picked an appropriate piece of land, devoted to a sensible use, and acquired at a reasonable price. Investors have also found that real estate investment requires staying power. (Unfortunately, many of the syndicates through which they invested were not equipped to deal with anything less than immediate success.)

Real estate syndication became popular in New York following the second world war. As the economy boomed, Eastern investors were offered an opportunity to share in this unending stream of profit opportunities by investing in real estate. Unfortunately, these offerings were characterized by unrealistic projections and promises of returns that were far in excess of those reasonably attainable. As a result, this bubble burst; and, even today, the securities laws of New York State treat real estate syndication in a far harsher manner than the offering of any other securities.

In the late 1960's, a new method for investing in real estate became popular—the Real Estate Investment Trust, or "REIT." Here again seemed to be an area which offered protection against loss, and an opportunity for securing tax benefits along with the unusually high return and inflation protection popularly associated with real estate. While real estate's inflation-hedge characteristics are a definite plus in real estate investment, the use of real estate as an inflation hedge depends upon the ability to acquire the property at a realistic price and to hold it for a sufficiently long period. Recent studies have also indicated that real estate's return is characterized more by predictability of return, assuming an appropriate investment has been selected, than by unusually high profit, and that investors in real estate are highly unrealistic in their return expectations. Roulac, *Modern Real Estate Investment* (Property Press: 1976), pages 57-98. In fact, Roulac concludes, there is no conclusive proof that real estate returns are significantly higher than those provided by the stock market.

While the REIT's were not characterized by the willfully fraudulent activities of the earlier New York real estate syndications, the performance of most REIT's proved to be extremely disappointing; and the "performance" (or lack thereof) of REIT's has been the subject of considerable comment in the financial press over the last several years.

While the REIT's were at the height of their popularity, a new investment vehicle in real estate arose: the publicly registered real estate limited partnership. By the early 1970's, the public real estate syndication was one of the most popular forms of tax-sheltered investment vehicles being offered through the nation's brokerage houses. This popularity, which was enhanced by the faltering of the public oil and gas drilling programs as a result of scandals in the late 1960's, was matched by a similar dramatic increase in activity in smaller, private real estate syndications.

The real estate syndications of the early 1970's primarily focused on new, multifamily residential construction, which offered significant first-year tax benefits, particularly when highly leveraged. Investors flocked to these offerings, feeling that they combined the safety which the average investor traditionally associated with real estate investment with the tax characteristics of oil and gas.

Unfortunately, a combination of skyrocketing construction costs, investment structure which favored tax benefits over economic reality, and high front-end loads, overpaying for properties, overleveraging, and inadequate reserves, saw many of these real estate limited partnerships fall into serious trouble. While investors could understand the risks associated in oil and gas investment, it was difficult for many of them to comprehend that analagous—albeit different—investment risks also apply to real estate. Accordingly, investment in real estate syndications dramatically plunged; and it is only recently that this steady decline in real estate investment has been reversed. For a comparison of the number and size of real estate offerings from 1970 to 1977 and the comparative popularity of real estate with other forms of tax-sheltered investment, see the chart at ¶105.

Today's real estate syndicator, and today's real estate investor, may be sadder; but he is also considerably wiser. The real estate syndication offerings of the late 1970's generally feature far more emphasis on the economic potential of the property and a more conservative tax policy. As a result, the real estate syndicators who have survived are for the most part a savvy lot with considerable staying power. While the publicly-registered syndication industry has declined to approximately seven companies, these syndicators raise approximately $200,000,000 a year in nationally-offered real estate syndications.

Real estate offers an unusual blend of potential investments which vary greatly in their characteristics as to tax benefits, cash flow, appreciation potential, and risk. The predictability of return from real estate, and its inflation-hedge characteristics, where appropriately selected, are very real. However, in deciding whether your tax-sheltered investment strategy calls for an investment in real estate, it is necessary for you carefully to consider the various types of real estate investment available to you, both as to each area's generic investment characteristics, and its desirability in today's financial climate.

The current economics of real estate investment will be discussed in Chapter Nine. Here, we will concern ourselves with the various forms of real estate investment available to you and their substantially varying investment characteristics.

Real estate investment comes in many forms including:

- Apartments under construction (new multifamily residential construction).
- Existing multifamily residential projects
- Commercial or industrial buildings, either new or planned
- Raw land
- Recreational real estate, such as ski resorts and condominiums
- Orchards, farms, and other agricultural syndications

A preliminary decision in determining which of these types of real estate investment is right for you is to determine your personal investment objectives in the area of tax shelter and cash flow needs, appreciation potential, and the degree of acceptable risk. Each of the forms of real estate investment varies dramatically as to which of these investment characteristics are present, and to what degree.

The following chart illustrates the investment characteristics of various kinds of real estate investment:

TYPE OF INVESTMENT	Tax Benefits	Cash Flow	Appreci- ation Potential	Risk
Real Estate				
(a) New Multi-Family Residential	High	Good	Good	Moderate to High
(b) Existing Multi- Family Residential	Moderate	Moderate	Moderate to Low	Low
(c) Commercial + Industrial	Moderate	Moderate	Moderate to Low	Low
(d) Raw Land	Low	Low	Good, but Speculative	High
(e) Gov't Assisted Housing	Very High	Low	Very Low	Moderate
(f) Agricultural	High	Moderate to Low- Delayed	Good, but Speculative	High

The investment characteristics outlined are general conclusions applying to the typical real estate project in these areas. As will be seen, a raw land syndication could be structured in such a fashion as to significantly increase the tax benefits that might be available. While government assisted housing is considered high in tax benefits, but low in other areas of investment potential, a given government assisted project in a particular area could offer a high appreciation potential. However, the foregoing general observation will assist you in making preliminary conclusions as to which forms of real estate investment you wish to investigate more closely and should also help you avoid real estate investment areas which would not meet your particular investment goals. And remember, comments as to risk refer to *relative risk:* all tax-sheltered investments, including existing properties in real estate, are speculative.

[¶802]   **WALKING THROUGH A TYPICAL
REAL ESTATE SYNDICATION**

Before a real estate syndicator presents a proposed real estate investment to you, he will have reviewed many projects to find one which in his opinion makes economic sense. Where a new construction project is involved, he will have studied construction plans, feasibility studies, and economic factors to determine the project's basic economics. He should also have carefully checked out the builder to determine his capabilities and bonafides.

This "screening" process or "acquisition" phase is just as important in real estate as the review of prospective drilling prospects is in oil and gas. A recent survey indicates that the typical real estate syndicator reviews nearly 50 projects for each property acquired, with over 100 man-days being involved in the screening process necessary to locate one economically-suitable property.

Caveat: Obviously, this means that there are a number of uneconomic real estate projects which are being presented to potential syndicators and potential investors. It is critical, therefore, that you carefully investigate to determine whether the property being offered to you involves one out of the fifty proposals which makes potential economic sense, rather than one of the remaining forty-nine. (See Chapter 10.)

Where an existing property is involved, the real estate syndicator will review the current income and expenses of the property and will consider methods of improving occupancy or reducing expense to arrive at a "capitalization rate" which he can afford to pay for the property in view of the return objectives he knows must be satisfied to attract potential investors. On raw land projects, this syndicator has two problems to resolve concerning the land: its cost in reference to anticipated construction prices; and the likelihood of its development, and for what purposes, and how quickly, in view of the nature of the surrounding area.

Once a "go" decision is reached to acquire a particular property, the syndicator will seek out investors to raise the necessary offering proceeds. In some instances, the syndicator will have already tied up the property through an option. In others, the syndicator may be the builder or developer of the property, or may be going through a real estate broker as syndicator/general partner who has agreed to find investors for the project. In any event, a substantial part of the moneys raised for acquisition of the project will go for various "front-end" fees, such as paying for organizational and offering expenses, a built-in profit to the builder-developer, and so-called "acquisition fees."

This substantial portion of your money invested in a real estate syndication which is taken "off the top" will normally represent at least one-third of the total equity proceeds of the offering. While this is a standard arrangement in real estate syndications, it is also the cause of a number of the problems in unprofitable real estate syndications. (See Chapter 10.)

The remaining offering proceeds, after deduction of these front-end fees, will be augmented by borrowings—from three to nine "mortgage" dollars for each remaining equity dollar, and these dollars will be used to acquire the land, to pay financing charges and costs of construction, and to establish a "reserve" for the property. (If an existing property is included, the proceeds will be used to pay for the property acquisition and possibly for a more advantageous refinancing of the property, for property improvement, and for the establishment of reserves.)

The percentage of dollars which are held back as a "reserve" limit the front-end tax deductions which can be offered to you in a real estate project. Likewise, increasing the degrees of leverage, and creating various deductible "front-end" fees, can increase the initial deductibility of the venture. However, a major problem surrounding the real estate syndications of the early 1970's was tax overreaching, brought on by the demands of potential investors for high initial write-offs, which often lead to overpaying for the property and inadequate staying power. Accordingly, both as a result of the Tax Reform Act of 1976 and due to the sad experiences previously realized, the typical real estate syndication now limits leveraging to two-thirds to eighty percent of the equity dollars and seeks to establish more reasonable reserves, even though such practices may lead to reduced first-year tax benefits. (See ¶805 for TRA'76 effects on real estate.)

After construction is completed on a new project, the syndicator will lease up the building, provide property management services and building maintenance, and collection of rents. The cash flow from operations will be used to make payments on the mortgage and establish, where needed, additional reserves; the remaining "cash flow available for distribution" will be distributed to the investors, less the syndicator's share.

(Where an existing property is involved, the process will be much the same, although greater emphasis will be placed upon improving occupancy rates, performing necessary maintenance, and taking all possible steps to improve net cash flow from the property.)

The syndicator will (or at least *should*) report to his investors concerning results of the property's operation and how "on target" with original projections the project is proceeding. If such reports are not provided for, and timely received, beware!

Eventually, the property will be sold or refinanced. A sale or foreclosure of the property will result in a taxable event. As mentioned earlier in this book, refinancing may not create immediate tax consequences to the investor; however, it will increase the amount of rents and eventual sale proceeds which will be unavailable for distribution to the investor, but which must be reported as taxable income. The mortgage will then be paid off, and the remaining proceeds distributed to the investors, again less the syndicator's share.

The process just outlined will create various potential benefits for you as an investor. The gross rentals from the lease of the property, after being reduced by expenses such as real estate taxes, property management fees, employee payroll, utilities, insurance, and building maintenance, will generate cash flow from operations which, after the payment of debt service, the syndicator's participation, and additional reserves, will generate *cash available for distribution* to you. The deductible expenditures incurred in connection with the property—interest, property taxes, and the like—and depreciation, all magnified by leverage—will create initial *"deep shelter,"* varying depending upon the type of property acquired and the manner in which the acquisition is structured, and will *shelter* much if not all of your *cash flow* from the property, as well as possibly creating additional deep shelter, for a number of years to come. (This sheltering effect will decline over the years, however, particularly if accelerated depreciation has been taken, leading to an eventual day of "cross-over.") Similarly, if the property was initially well selected, and has been well maintained, and if unexpected economic factors do not intervene, the eventual sale of the property should generate a cash, as well as a taxable, gain as a result of *appreciation* through equity build-up, inflationary factors, and true economic appreciation in the value of the property.

Normally, except in *"blind pool"* real estate syndicate offerings, usually registered with the Securities and Exchange Commission, you will be offered an opportunity to invest in one, or possibly several, *specified properties.* You will also be provided *"projections,"* showing the anticipated rentals, expenses, debt service, and distributable cash flow from the property. While the Securities and Exchange Commission in the past has discouraged the use of projections in real estate offerings, a number of the real estate investments presented to you are exempt from SEC registration. In such "private" or "intrastate" offerings, the providing of projections in a specified form may be required by local securities regulatory authorities. In certain SEC-registered offerings of specified properties, projections may also be required or permitted.

Projections are aimed at giving you an idea concerning the anticipated return on your investment. However, the only thing that can be said with certainty concerning a "projected" return is that it will normally prove either too low, or, as is more commonly the case, too high.

The major use of projections is as a part of your own "screening" process in determining whether or not you wish to invest in a particular real estate syndication and as an indication of the syndicator's "bona fides." (See also Chapter 10.) However, even in the best real estate syndication, projections should not be assumed to offer any guarantee as to return which you will actually receive from the property. Since the assumptions on which the projections are based involve estimates of many erratic factors, such as occupancy rates, future growth of expenses, and obtainable rental rates, and since most assumptions are "sequential"—are dependent upon the accuracy of the preceding assumption—the probabilities of a projection proving accurate to the penny are highly unlikely. To quote one authority: "The importance of timing cannot be overemphasized. Markets that are strong and fully capable of supporting a project when it is on the drawing boards may be soft and overrun with vacancies by the time it is ready to open. At a time when one developer perceives that a specific market will support 500 new apartment units and plans to be 'conservative' by building only 400, ten other developers may be doing the same thing." Roulac, *Modern Real Estate Investment* (Property Press: 1976), page 4.

Accordingly, such projections should not be taken as any "guarantee" as to the return which you will receive from even the best real estate syndication.

A sample projection of the anticipated expense requirements and cash flows for a typical real estate investment is contained in Appendix 802-1.

[¶803]   **TAX BENEFITS OF**
                          REAL ESTATE INVESTMENT

The expenditures incurred in connection with real estate acquisition fall into three categories:

(1) *Completely non-deductible costs* such as land costs;

(2) *Costs* that are *deductible as paid or accrued,* such as interest;

(3) *Costs* which *must be capitalized, but* which can be included in the cost of the building and other depreciable assets and *amortized* over their life.

The key to the initial deductibility of real estate investment, and particularly "new construction," was to increase the "soft dollar" deductible expenditures incurred during construction. During the construction period, many costs in addition to the capital expenditures for construction were incurred which, prior to the Tax Reform Act of 1976, were deductible for Federal income tax purposes. These included interest on the loan (including prepaid interest); fees paid to financing institutions for making the loan commitment, normally referred to as "points;" commitment ("standby") fees for agreeing to provide specified financing; and property taxes incurred during the construction period. To be deductible as interest, points were required to be paid prior to the loan rather than from the loan proceeds, could not relate to the providing any specific services, and could not come from funds initially provided by the lender. A "point" was equal to 1 percent of the principal amount of the loan. In addition, the taxpayer was permitted to depreciate the full cost of the building and its improvements even though most of the funds were provided through leverage, often without personal liability to the investor.

**[¶803.1]   Interest, Taxes, and Other
                    Deductible Expenditures**

Prior to the Tax Reform Act of 1976, the chief "soft dollar" expenditures in a real estate transaction involved projects in the construction phase, during which tax deductions, enhanced by leverage, would be created by payments for taxes and various financing expenditures, which would not be offset by any taxable rental income. Increasing the degree of leverage obviously would increase the degree of deductibility. Likewise, finding ways to characterize various payments as tax-deductible, rather than non-deductible, and particularly non-deductible/non-amortizable, expenditures would also increase the degree of deductibility.

Conventional lending institutions normally would have set rules as to the types of payments and the degree of leverage which they would extend in connection with a given project. To increase first year deductibility, "wrap-around" mortgages thus became quite popular in connection with real estate syndication. Another popular technique for increasing deductibility was the "sale/leaseback." See Levine, *Real Estate Tax Shelter Desk Book* (Institutes for Business Planning: 1978), Chapter 18.

Under the wrap-around mortgage—actually, a form of secondary

financing technique—a note would be issued to the seller of the property
equal to the amount of the existing first mortgage plus the amount of the
secondary financing from the seller. Often, such wrap-around mortgages
were highly inflated in amount, and reflected the "lending" of dollars,
usually on a non-recourse basis, which would immediately be repaid to the
seller in the form of prepaid and other interest, points and other financing charges, and various "guaranteed payments," all of which would
hopefully be deductible.

To the extent that the wrap-around mortgage technique reflected a
legitimate conversion of dollars that otherwise might have gone to the
seller as non-deductible cash down payments for the property, there is
nothing wrong in utilizing a different structuring technique to increase
tax deductibility. However, the payment of excessive rates of interest,
higher than normal financing charges, and various "management fees,"
which in most instances would not have been structured into the transaction except for their tax consequences, often resulted in the payment of an
excessive purchase price for the property, and a dangerously excessive
reliance on leverage. Investors were often lulled into a sense of false
security concerning the economic viability of their investment by the
"guaranteed return" that they would receive from the builder or the
general partner for the first few years of the project, not realizing that
they were simply receiving back a portion of the dollars which they had
overpaid for the property. In other words, two dollars of economic
benefit had been paid for a dollar of tax savings, often at the price of any
economic viability for the project.

[¶803.2]   New Techniques May Compensate for
              1976 Tax Reform Act

These structuring techniques used in "new construction" syndications have been seriously affected by the Tax Reform Act of 1976. However, new techniques are being developed to compensate for the effects of
the Tax Reform Act. (See ¶805.) To the extent that such techniques create
additional deductibility without reducing the eventual return to the investor from his *combined benefits* from the real estate investment, such structuring is merely wise tax planning. However, before gullibly accepting
such "creative structuring," you would be wise to heed the words of
respected real estate consultant Stephen E. Roulac:

> ... perhaps of more concern is the tendency, resulting from the reach
> for maximum front-end tax deductions, for the deal to be structured in ways
> that violate fundamentals of economic logic. Excessive prices are paid,
> 'supported' by inflated wrap-around mortgages, and the cash advance that
> is used primarily for 'deductible' payments with virtually nothing for equity.
> In such situations financial disaster is likely. Paying an expense before it is

otherwise due involves a 'present value' penalty. Such prepayments are justified only when the overall after-tax return in terms of the deal are enhanced. ***Frequently, the mortgage balance can so exceed the basis at sale that the investor must come cash-out-of-pocket to pay his tax liability. As such ventures often employ very high debt ratios, the breakeven point can approach or exceed 100% occupancy. The full implications of this precarious position are hidden and deferred by a short-term sale-leaseback where an investor pays a 'premium' for the 'security' of having debt service and expenses, as well as a specified cash distribution, guaranteed for several years. Such arrangements only temporarily forestall the inevitable problems.

'While tax factors are of paramount importance, they must not dominate basic economic considerations. Unless the deal has fundamental economic rationality, no amount of creative tax structuring will by itself make a venture viable. Many of the problems that have plagued real estate investment, particularly in recent years, are attributable to a distortion of priorities where the quest for tax shelter is placed above the iron rule of business that cash inflows must at least equal cash outflows. The preferred strategy is to verify the viability of the deal on basic economic grounds and then to investigate tax structuring as a means of enhancing the return to meet the investors' particular needs and objectives. (Roulac, *Modern Real Estate Investment* (Property Press: 1976), pages 257-58, 242.)

[¶803.3]   Depreciation Methods for Individual Needs

Depreciation is a vital factor in the sheltering of the income from real estate investment from taxation and in providing initial tax shelter in real estate ventures such as the purchase of existing properties which do not generate substantial amounts of first year "soft" costs. The use of "property management fees" payable to the syndicator or an affiliated property management company can also generate tax deductions. However, where such payments are in excess of normal property management rates, the tax advantages will be subject to the same economic disadvantages (discussed in ¶803.1) concerning excess interest and similar payments under wrap-around mortgages.

The depreciation deduction available in connection with a given real estate investment will depend upon the *method* of depreciation used; your *"depreciable basis"* in the property; the *"useful life"*; and the *degree of leverage* utilized.

The available methods of depreciation in connection with real estate include *straight-line depreciation; declining-balance depreciation* whether of the 200 percent, 150 percent, or 125 percent method; and *sum-of-the digits depreciation.*

These last two depreciation methods each give the investor the benefit of *accelerated depreciation:* depreciation at a rate faster than would be permitted under the straight-line method. While accelerated depreciation has the definite advantage of permitting you to take your deductions earlier—a real benefit to you due to the time value of money—this benefit has been substantially affected by the Tax Reform Act of 1976, which requires recapture of all excess depreciation without exception. Therefore, before electing to use an accelerated depreciation method, you should check with your tax planner to see whether other approaches may be more beneficial to you.

[¶803.4]   Accelerated Methods of Depreciation

Since the Tax Reform Act of 1969, the various depreciation methods are limited as to their availability, depending upon the type of real estate involved. Straight-line depreciation is available for all types of new and used property. However, the 125 percent declining-balance method of depreciation is the fastest depreciation method available for used residential real property (which must also have a useful life of 20 years or more); the 150 percent declining-balance method is the fastest available for new nonresidential rental properties; and the sum-of the years-digits and 200 percent declining balance methods of depreciation—the fastest methods—are only available as to new residential rental properties. No method of accelerated depreciation is available for used nonresidential property.

Straight-line depreciation is computed by reducing the cost (or other depreciable basis) of the property by its anticipated salvage value and dividing this amount by the remaining useful life to find the annual straight-line deduction. The declining balance method is determined by dividing the useful life by 100 and applying a factor of 2, 1.5, or 1.25 as applicable to determine the rate to be applied to the cost of the property. The second year this rate is applied to the cost less the depreciation taken in the first year, with the process being repeated each year. At some period the depreciation deduction given by the declining balance method will be less than a straight-line depreciation arrived at by dividing the remaining balance by the remaining useful life of the property. When this occurs, a shift is permitted, and should be made, to a straight-line method. Salvage value need not be considered in determining the depreciation deduction under the declining-balance method. However, depreciation cannot be taken below the salvage value of the property; and upon any switch to a straight-line method, salvage must be taken into account in computing the straight-line deduction.

The-sum-of-the-years-digits method of depreciation is computed by totaling the years that make up the useful life of the property and applying a somewhat complicated formula to arrive at the annual depreciation. (See Levine, *Real Estate Tax Shelter Desk Book* (Institute for Business Planning: 2d ed. 1978), ¶405.) However, when this method has been elected, you may not automatically switch to straight-line depreciation when this becomes more advantageous.

Your first-year depreciation deduction under the 200 percent-declining-balance method will be greater, where this method is available, than under the sum-of-the-digits method. (So will be your deductions for the first *two* years.) However, by the third year, the sum-of-the-digits method of depreciation will offer deductions which exceed the depreciation available under the 200 percent declining-balance method; and at the half way point in the life of the property, you will have recovered approximately three-quarters of your cost under the sum-of-the-digits methods, versus only two-thirds under the 200 percent declining-balance approach. However, remember that no automatic switch is permitted from the "sum-of-the-digits-method" to straight-line depreciation when this becomes more advantageous.

[¶803.5]   Advantages of Various Depreciation Methods Summarized

The following chart, from Mark Levine's *Real Estate Tax Shelter Desk Book*, summarizes the results of using various depreciation methods on a hypothetical property with a $10,000 cost, a ten-year life, and no salvage value:*

Year	Straight-Line	200% Declining-Balance	Sum-of-Digits	200% Declining Balance Switch to Straight-Line
1st	$ 1,000	$ 2,000	$ 1,818	$ 2,000
2nd	1,000	1,600	$1,636	1,600
3rd	1,000	1,280	1,455	1,280
4th	1,000	1,024	1,273	1,024
5th	1,000	819	1,091	819
6th	1,000	655	909	655
7th	1,000	524	727	655
8th	1,000	420	545	655
9th	1,000	336	364	655
10th	1,000	268	182	655
	$10,000	$ 8,926	$10,000	$ 9,998

In the past, as an investor you would normally automatically seek the most rapid depreciation methods available. However, in view of the tax law changes worked by TRA'76 (see ¶805) this is something to be discussed with your tax advisor.

Discussion of the useful life and the depreciable base for the property acquired by your real estate investment is beyond the scope of this book. However, as a real estate investor, you are not merely acquiring an

*See Levine *Real Estate Tax Shelter Desk Book,* Chapter Four (Institute for Business Planning: 2d Edition, 1978). The investment tax credit may also be available for qualifying personal property. See id., Chapter 8.

interest in a building; where rental property is concerned, you frequently are acquiring an interest in the tangible personal property which will be used in connection with that building. Special depreciation rules exist which permit first year "bonus" depreciation as to such tangible personal property (Internal Revenue Code, ¶179), and which may permit a more rapid depreciation through separately calculating the useful life of the various *components* of your building under "component" depreciation rather than by taking depreciation on the building as a whole (composite depreciation).

The degree of depreciation deduction generated, expressed as a percentage of your equity investment, will obviously also depend upon the degree of leverage which you utilize. However, extreme leverage also involves extreme risk. It likewise creates the definite possibility that, upon the sale of your real estate interest, your tax liability may exceed the sale proceeds available to you after satisfaction of the mortgage debt. Accordingly, great care should be taken to be sure that an increase in leverage to increase first and subsequent year deductions does not become tax over-kill.

[¶804]   **THE TAX PITFALLS—**
          CROSSOVER AND RECAPTURE

The effects of reaching a "cross-over" point, where nondeductible mortgage payments exceed available appreciation deductions, leaving the cash flow from your investment taxable (or even generating a negative tax position), and the potential for recapture of excess depreciation, are very present in real estate. If your real estate investment is held for a long period of time, at some point at least a portion of your income will become taxable. This is particularly true if you have selected an accelerated depreciation method. In addition, the potential for recapture of a portion of your depreciation deductions has been increased by the Tax Reform Act of 1976, which made all excess depreciation on real estate subject to recapture.

Crossover and recapture are not the end of the world. If your property is held for a sufficient period of time, your straight-line deduction will eventually "catch up" with the deductions taken under accelerated methods, so that there is no "excess" depreciation to be recaptured. Similarly, the property can be disposed of before the time that the crossover point is reached (though not without triggering possible depreciation recapture and "phantom" gain). Or, depending upon your particular needs, you may have foregone accelerated depreciation and thus prolonged the point at which "crossover" will be reached. In any event, you will have the use of your tax saving dollars and hopefully will put them to good use; the "recapture" has been an interest-free loan from the government and thus, even where inevitable, still represents a tax savings for you.

The key factors in dealing with crossover and recapture are:

☐ Be aware of their existence

☐ Do not be trapped, through tax overreaching, into unnecessarily stretching for tax benefits whose value is outweighed by economic considerations

☐ Be prepared through a sinking fund or other planning methods, to pay the eventual tax when it falls due, even if some tax on "phantom income" is involved.

With such advance planning, these tax "pitfalls" will be no more damaging than the fact that you must eventually pay a tax on the "gain" aspect of your property. However, if you have not prepared for the fact that some day your income may become taxable, and there may be taxes on phantom income reflecting deductions previously taken by you, this tax "surprise" will be highly unpleasant, to say the least.

[¶805]   **EFFECTS OF THE TAX REFORM ACT
OF 1976 ON REAL ESTATE INVESTMENT**

Initial reactions to the Tax Reform Act of 1976 were that real estate had emerged relatively unharmed from the tax "reform" efforts. However, a study of the Act showed that real estate had in fact been dealt with rather harshly, and in ways which would be much more difficult to avoid by restructuring than in cattle and the "exotics."

The general impact of the Tax Reform Act has been discussed in Chapter Five. Its specific impact on tax-sheltered investment in real estate is as follows:

(1) *"Construction period" interest and taxes* are now required to be *capitalized* and *amortized* over a ten-year period, rather than being immediately deductible. (Internal Revenue Code, §189). A "phase-in period" is provided both as to the effective date of the capitalization and amortization requirements and as to the amortization period, with separate rules being applied to nonresidential real estate, residential real estate, and government-subsidized housing. Since only interest and taxes *incurred during the construction period* are required to be capitalized, the question arises as to when the construction period commences and when it ends. Basically, this would seem to be determined by when site work is commenced, and when the property is ready for occupancy, i.e., to be "placed in service." This may occur when the project is completed, even though tenant improvements are not complete, so long as depreciation can be taken.

In some instances, capitalizing the construction period interest and taxes may make better sense for you than a ten-year amortization, as where there would be a high degree of "component depreciation" that could be taken in less than ten years.

The restrictions on the deductibility of construction period interest and taxes do not apply to corporations other than Subchapter S corporations and personal holding companies.

(2) All *excess depreciation* on real estate (other than government-assisted housing projects) is now *subject to recapture* (Internal Revenue Code, §1250), eliminating the special treatment formerly provided for residential real estate which had been held a specified period of time. TRA'76 also eliminated reducing recapture on foreclosure by litigation "delaying tactics": where the property is actually foreclosed, recapture will not be reduced by any holding period after the foreclosure proceedings were filed, even though the recapture will not be recognized until the foreclosure is complete.

(3) Many provisions of the Tax Reform Act of 1976 of "general applicability" to all tax shelter areas have a special impact on tax-sheltered investments in real estate as they were structured prior to the Tax Reform Act of 1976. (See ¶502.) These include:

☐ *Elimination of the deductibility of prepaid interest and "points"* (Internal Revenue Code, §461(g)). However, a true "commitment" or pre-loan fee is not directly affected. (But see *H.K. Francis,* T.C. Memo 1977-170, and *Lyndell E. Lay,* 69 T.C. No. 32 (1977).)

☐ *Restrictions on the deductibility of "syndication fees".*

☐ *Restrictions on "retroactive allocations."*

☐ *Restrictions on "special allocations" of partnership income and loss.*

☐ *Loss of "stepped-up" basis on death.*

Besides these changes, real estate investment has also been affected by the provisions of the Tax Reform Act concerning the increased and expanded *minimum tax* on items of tax preference, the more restrictive provisions concerning the availability of the *maximum tax* on personal service income, the increased restrictions on the deductibility of *investment interest,* and the increased long-term *capital gains holding period.* The availability of *bonus depreciation* on personal property held by a partnership was also limited by TRA'76.

Other aspects of investment in real estate not directly related to "tax shelters" were adversely affected by the Tax Reform Act of 1976. Of particular importance to the high-tax-bracket investors were the substantial restrictions imposed on the deductibility of expenses incurred in connection with vacation homes (Internal Revenue Code, §280A) or an office maintained in the taxpayer's home.

[¶805.1]   Real Estate Benefits in 1976 Tax Reform Act

Certain aspects of the Tax Reform Act of 1976 treated real estate in a more favorable method. For instance, the five-year amortization provision concerning costs incurred in rehabilitation of low-income housing projects was extended, special tax treatment was also given for historical ("landmark") structures and expenditures for improvements for the elderly and handicapped, and the allowable depreciation was increased. In addition, the competitive position of government-assisted housing in comparison with other tax-sheltered investment was substantially improved due to its more favorable amortization and phasing schedule on construction period interest and taxes and its more favorable position in relation to the recapture of excess depreciation. However, the Tax Reform Act, in substantially changing the rules concerning taxation of real estate ventures, has also significantly changed some basic assumptions as to what may be your best "bet" in real estate investment. (See Chapter 9.)

For a comparison of the effects of TRA '76 on a prior "typical" real estate syndication, see Appendix 805-1.

9.

Current Economics of Real Estate Investment

[¶901]   **REAL ESTATE IN
            TODAY'S ECONOMY**

While investment in real estate is the reason for the founding of our country, and the basis for many of the nation's great fortunes, real estate investment has in the past proved quite confusing to many "passive" investors. The investment process has also been affected by the fact that public information concerning real estate results, and trading markets in real estate interests, were nonexistent, a far cry from conditions existing in the stock market. Similarly, a number of the practices utilized by the real estate investment industry were highly oriented toward prior traditions, many of which have become substantially outmoded.

As inflation has skyrocketed, and investors view with dismay the returns available from the traditional investment vehicle most readily available to the passive investor—the common stock market—more and more investors have turned to real estate as a method of conserving and increasing capital. The structure of real estate as a tax-sheltered investment has intensified this interest.

Increased investor interest in real estate as an investment vehicle has led to a number of poorly conceived, if not fraudulent, schemes. However, this same pattern has also led to an increased involvement of Federal and State securities regulators in real estate investment. Protective rules have now been adopted for the real estate investor. Information concerning real estate investment and its results are becoming more readily available. As this disclosure of investment results and government involvement has increased, many of the past practices of the real estate profession must change to keep pace with the times. Accordingly, real

Pitfalls do exist even in government-assisted housing projects. While the Section 8 program, as contrasted with the formerly popular Section 236 projects, does permit the inflation-related automatic annual adjustment of the housing assistance payments, the subsidy program is limited to twenty years. If the program is not extended, or if Congress should cease to fund HUD, projects which are dependent upon longer financing could be placed in serious jeopardy. Also, unlike Section 236 projects, subsidies for vacant units under the Section 8 program cease after sixty days.

The primary pitfall in the government-assisted housing project is its historic lack of appreciation potential and the possibility that the tax advantages will become a tax disaster if the project proves economically unsuccessful. The rapid deterioration in value of certain government-assisted housing projects has received wide publicity. Since foreclosure would trigger recapture of many of the tax benefits previously taken, plus taxes on phantom income, it is critical that the potential investment be carefully analyzed as to its economic potential.

Many syndicators of government-assisted housing projects are convinced that a properly selected project in an appropriate location rather than deteriorating in value will in fact appreciate. Other commentators state that the opposite is more apt to be true. The one point on which all are in agreement is that the project must be carefully selected and provided with strong management if the venture is to prove a financial success, even with its admitted tax benefits.

[¶903]　　　　EXISTING PROPERTIES

Existing projects have the obvious disadvantage of providing significantly less "deep shelter" potential than new construction. While, just as in new construction, component depreciation and "interest only" structuring techniques are being used to reduce the impact of TRA'76— see ¶1001.3—the appeal of existing property investment is less tax oriented, with a major benefit being the ability to project with a substantially higher degree of certainty the anticipated return from the properties.

The present-day economy creates signficant "bargain" opportunities in existing properties. With a large number of newly constructed real estate projects "in trouble," many new construction projects were repossessed by banks and REIT's. Frequently, these lenders are interested in divesting their portfolio of such projects.

A prime candidate for "bargain" acquisition is the project which is well constructed and economically sound but which requires improved management or additional capital for improved maintenance or refinancing to turn the project around. However, if the project was not properly constructed, has fallen into such a degree of disrepair that "rehabilitation" would be highly expensive and difficult to estimate, or if the project was not economically sound in the first place, it provides no "bargain," whatever the price. Also, the promoter of such a venture may be unduly optimistic as to the benefits such as improved occupancy, better rentals, and reduced costs, that could be secured from additional capital, refinancing, or a change in management. However, with new construction costs (with the exception of the government-assisted housing projects) often proving virtually prohibitive in today's market, you may be well advised to give serious consideration to the acquisition of an existing property, despite its lack of "deep shelter" potential.

Where commercial or industrial projects are involved, you may at first be primarily tempted by the "quality" of the existing tenants. Tenant stability is a critical aspect in commercial and industrial properties. Just as overbuilding has occurred in the housing industry, many areas of the country are similarly faced with overly optimistic building policies by those constructing commercial and industrial projects. When tenants' leases prove less than reliable, or of a relatively "short-term" nature, it may prove difficult to place new leases for the available space, particularly if you are competing with a number of other projects, many of which may be newer and offer better tenant amenities. However, long-term "triple-A" leases frequently have been negotiated at such low rental rates, and with such inadequate escalation provisions, that they amount to little better than a mortgage, with no inflationary hedges. In such circumstances, you are receiving a relatively low return on your investment and are faced with all the risks of increasing costs and other such inflationary trends in the economy. Accordingly, in analyzing an investment in a commercial or industrial property, you may wish to pay more attention to the basic appeal of the project than to the "triple-A" quality of the long-term leases if such leases do not contain adequate inflationary protection.

[¶904]   **RAW LAND**

Raw land, historically, has been a key area for speculation in the value of real estate. While such an investment generally does not offer the type of "deep shelter" or cash flow discussed earlier in this chapter, it can offer a substantial potential for *appreciation in value*.

Land speculation does not require that you invest via a limited partnership or any other of the "syndication" approaches we have discussed elsewhere in this book. There is nothing to prevent you from an outright purchase of a tract of land which appears promising to you, or from your owning this land for your own account without the intervention of a "syndicator." However, to spread your dollars through diversification, or to secure the services of a real estate professional to manage your real estate investment and to try to arrange for the development of your land acquisition, you may decide to invest in raw land through a syndication approach.

Land investment has two potential areas of profit. First, you can acquire a tract of land which you hope will be developed within a reasonable period of time, and hold this land for resale to a developer, or for development by your own syndicate. Secondly, your syndicate may hold its land for resale to other speculators who are themselves interested in acquiring tracts of land for speculative purposes.

While there is no question that substantial amounts of money have been made by land speculators, the current economics of the real estate industry make raw land investment a dangerous game at this time unless you have substantial "staying power" and feel relatively certain you have acquired the tract at an attractive price. Land values in many parts of the country are extremely high at this time, even though, as we saw in ¶902, new construction is not particularly attractive. These prices have been driven up by the influx of foreign investors seeking a capital haven rather than immediate cash flow or resale profit. Since the ability to finance a new construction project must take into account land costs, the poor economics of new construction also affects the likelihood of finding a purchaser-developer who is willing to pay an attractive price for your tract, or whether you and your syndicate can directly develop the land. Likewise, the poor economics of new construction have affected the market for raw land *as raw land*. In other words, there are now fewer purchasers who are willing to acquire a tract from you simply to hold it in the hopes that its value will increase even further.

A final problem facing you as a raw land investor is the need to provide additional capital through what may prove to be a rather lengthy "holding period," during which there will be no cash flow. Taxes must be paid, and interest and debt service obligations met. So, unless you are willing to satisfy these obligations for an indefinite period, raw land may not be for you.

Undoubtedly, there are many good raw land "buys" available at this time. However, before you invest in a raw land syndication, you should ask yourself the following questions:

- ☐ Is the price that I am paying for the land such that it would be difficult to finance development of the land and still put together viable projects at rents that today's users of lands are willing to pay?
- ☐ How long will I have to hold my land investment before this property can be developed, or a new purchaser found at a higher price?
- ☐ And what will the "holding costs," the taxes, the interest, the debt service, and the fees to the promoter be on my land investment?
- ☐ How much additional moneys will I be required to invest each year

to hold on to my land investment until a developer or new purchaser can be found?

☐ How much must my land investment appreciate in value on an annual basis just to meet these holding costs, without reference to any real profit in my pocket?

In view of the factors we have just looked at, raw land investment at this time would only seem to be for you if you are willing to analyze the price at which the land is being offered to make sure that all potentials for profit—long-term as well as short-term—have not already been written into an inflated purchase price.

[¶905]   **RECREATIONAL REAL ESTATE**

Recreational real estate is often sold based upon dual motivations. An investor can acquire a condominium in a developed or to-be-developed recreational site primarily with the hopes that it will increase in value. He may never personally make use of the project that he has so purchased. However, if you are a skier, or are interested in taking your family to the mountains, the seashore, or for a golfing holiday, you will often be urged to purchase your "vacation home" on the basis that it will not only furnish a splendid recreational retreat, but will also offer you various economic and tax benefits.

In the past, purchasers of recreational sites have often been told that the tax and cash flow benefits that will be generated through their purchase may more than offset their cost of holding the property. Trips to the property with the family, so it is said, can be "written off" as business deductions to "check" on their investment. Cash flow from renting the property to others with similar recreational interests, when coupled with the deductions for depreciation, interest, and maintenance of the investment property, can be looked at as giving a cost-free second home. However, before entering into any such recreational real estate investment, you should ask yourself two questions. First, how likely is it that this investment will actually make money? Second, how sure am I that I will actually receive the tax benefits which I anticipate?

Even when your investment is entered into solely for profit motives, and you have no intention of using the property personally, many recreational ventures do not make money. If you are purchasing a unit in an established resort, you should ask to see the actual figures as to how your unit, or similar units, have performed in the past. Where the project is yet to be constructed, or where the resort is in its promotional phase, you must realize that you will be competing with a number of already established resort areas, and that many new projects never successfully get off the ground.

In many instances, Federal and state securities agencies require that you be furnished an offering document which contains specified projections. It is rare that the seller of such a property will encourage you carefully to study these figures to determine what they mean in dollars and cents. It is for this very reason that such figures must be given a careful review.

Insofar as tax benefits are concerned, even before the Tax Reform Act of 1976, the Internal Revenue Service was often attacking such "investments" as a mere "hobby loss"—an investment that you had entered into without any real expectation of economic profit. If it were found that there was no real profit motive in your investment, the tax benefits would be disallowed.

Certain deductions for Federal income tax purposes may be taken by you even though your use of the recreational second home is primarily personal in motivation. These include deductions for interest (Internal Revenue Code, §163), certain state and local property taxes (Internal Revenue Code, §164), and casualty losses (Internal Revenue Code, §165). However, to take the deductions for other key tax benefits, such as depreciation, maintenance, insurance, and utilities, you must be able to show that these expenditures were incurred as business expenses under §162 of the Internal Revenue Code, or for the management and maintenance of property held for the production of income under §212, and that you entered into the transaction with a reasonable expectation of profit as required under §183. However, even if it were held that there were no profit motives to the investment, deductions for such items as depreciation, insurance and maintenance could be taken to the extent that the non-personal use generated taxable income. (See Internal Revenue Code, §183.)

The question of whether or not your investment in recreational real estate was entered into with a profit motive is obviously a key determination from your standpoint. Treasury Regulations say that you may take into account any realistic expectation that your investment will appreciate in value, and thus generate a profit. However, until the Tax Reform Act of 1976, the key test provided for trying to solve this "profit motive" determination was a "presumption" which would arise in your favor if your investment actually generated a profit in two or more of five consecutive taxable years. However, even though your recreational real estate investment did not satisfy this test, this did not mean that the deductions were automatically disallowed.

To avoid the difficulties of determining whether or not your "second home" investment was in fact entered into with profit in mind, the Tax Reform Act of 1976 added a new §280A which would limit your deductions. They would be limited to an offset of your income from the property, less the interest and taxes already allowable irrespective of profit motive, if your personal use of the property exceeded fourteen days (or 10 percent of the number of days during the year that your unit was rented to third parties if this was greater). Your personal use would include not only the days on which you occupied the property, but use by family members as well.

If you are convinced that units or lot sites in a given recreational area offer substantial opportunities for appreciation, recreational real estate investment may still prove an excellent profit area for you. While rental income from such properties seldom, in itself, will generate a profit from the investment or even satisfy debt service and maintenance obligations, it will certainly offset a number of expenses incurred during your holding period. In addition, if you do not make personal use of the property in such a manner as to run afoul of the "profit motive" or new "personal use" tests contained in the Tax Code, the tax benefits generated from your investment will further offset these holding costs. However, it is critical that you make a totally objective analysis of the profit potential of your investment, not clouded by your personal recreational preferences, before undertaking such a purchase. Likewise, it is a good idea, from an economic and tax standpoint, to separate your personal use of property from the units which you acquire as an investment.

A chart showing the potential economics of a recreational real estate investment with and without the allowance of tax benefits is contained in Appendix 905-1.

[¶906]   OF TIMBER, RANCHING AND FARMING—
IS IT AN "AGRICULTURAL" OR A
REAL ESTATE INVESTMENT?

An "agricultural" or similar investment is often entered into where the primary motivation is not to profit from the immediate activity, but to rely upon the appreciation potential of the land as the primary profit source.

A raw land investment will often require that the property be held for a substantial period of time with relatively little tax or cash flow benefits to offset the debt service requirements of the property, taxes, and other expenditures required to hold the property. If use can be made of the land during this period, the cash flow or tax deductions generated by this use may be used to partially or totally offset these "holding period" cash requirements.

The use most often made of such raw land tracts during this speculative holding period is to use the land for timber, ranching, or agricultural purposes. If the tract has substantial appreciation potential due to the likelihood of its ultimate development for other real estate purposes, and if in the meantime it is suited to agricultural or similar use, this combining of investment approaches can prove wise planning. However, a potential pitfall exists that the assumed benefits from the agricultural use may blind you from analyzing the true development potential for the land. In other words, can this land actually be economically developed at the price being asked? Similarly, the hope for eventual profit when the land is developed can cause you to lose sight of whether or not the outlined agricultural or ranching scheme in fact makes economic sense.

Many pieces of raw real estate now command such a high purchase price that they have priced themselves out of the market of being available for further development under the current economics of new property construction. Similarly, other property simply may not be in line for development in the forseeable future, due to its location. Agricultural, timber, and ranching syndications are, in themselves, extremely high risk investments, which require a carefully thought out business plan, a highly realistic study of potential economics, and a need for truly experienced and hard working day-to-day management. Thus, while coupling a raw land investment with an interim use makes sense if both sides of the investment have been carefully analyzed as to their profit potential, such an investment makes no sense if one or both of the investment plans fail to make economic sense.

As an investor, you may be better prepared to analyze the profit potential of an existing apartment, office project, or new construction than you are to determine when a piece of raw land will likely be developed and what price can be demanded for the real estate at that time. Even that may be easier for you to determine than whether or not a ranching or agricultural syndication can be conducted on this property at a profit. Therefore, rather than entering into an "interim use" syndication with a raw land "kicker," you may wish to stay with more conventional tax-sheltered investments where the economic potential, and the present caliber and prior performance of management, may prove easier to analyze.

10.

What To Look For In Real Estate Investment

[¶1001]   **SEEK PROJECTS THAT MAKE ECONOMIC SENSE**

The preceding chapters in this section have analyzed the varying types of real estate tax shelters available to you. They have covered the organization of real estate syndications, their potential tax and economic benefits and pitfalls. They have given you a look at the current economics of various types of real estate investment. By now you should have reached some general conclusions as to whether or not real estate investment seems right for you, and what type of real estate investment might best suit your needs. This chapter will focus on determining whether or not a specific real estate investment offered to you actually offers the economic potential which is necessary if you are to profit from any tax-sheltered investment.

Many of the analytical steps which we will discuss in this chapter will be looked at in greater detail in Part Four of this book. It is highly important before entering into a real estate investment to determine whether or not the project was properly conceived and makes economic sense. It is also important to find out whether or not the management to be provided in supervising the construction of a proposed new project, or the refinancing and rehabilitation of an existing property, as well as the management for day-to-day operation of the property will be able to do its job. It is likewise necessary to determine whether or not the compensation to be received by this management, including the promoter's front-end and on-going charges, and his share of any proceeds from the sale of the property, will turn an otherwise economic venture into an economic disaster.

The economics of the proposed venture must be carefully screened to determine whether or not this project should in fact be built, or whether, if an existing property is being acquired, the property should operate at a profit. Such an economic analysis may be beyond your personal expertise. However, such evaluation is essential before you enter into a project. As will be seen in Part Four, if you cannot perform it for yourself, such services are available to you at a price which you can afford.

Even if you are not a real estate expert, and do not feel in a postion, at least at the preliminary stages, of hiring an expert to help you make this analysis, there are certain steps that you can take which will assist you in determining whether or not you wish to investigate further a prospective investment. A key part of this preliminary analysis is to carefully study the *projections* provided you by the syndicate sponsor.

[¶1001.1] How to Use Available Real Estate Projections

It is rare in real estate, whether the project be good or bad, that projections will not be available for your study. These projections invariably show that you will make a handsome profit by entering into this real estate investment. However, as we have seen, major real estate syndicators have found that less than one out of fifty of the projects presented to them are worth acquiring. The other projects still get built, normally through moneys supplied by investors who have not had the experience, or have not taken the time, to see whether the assumptions on which these glowing projections are based square with economic reality.

A first step in analyzing a projection concerning a real estate investment is to study the assumptions. Are these assumptions realistic? Do they contain any allowance for increase in the cost of operating the property? Do the assumptions concerning occupancy rates and the rentals that can be charged appear to make sense? A little inquiry on your part can help you determine whether the vacancy factors square with the experience of similar projects in the same area. A similar inquiry will determine whether or not the proposed rentals are in keeping with the rental rates for similar projects.

A second inquiry which you can make is to determine whether or not payments to the promoter for his share of project profits have been deducted from the figures presented you concerning anticipated economic results. Have costs of sale and the Federal income taxes payable when the property is sold been deducted? If not, you can reasonably assume that there are other "assumptions" built into these projections which only an expert can pick up, but which are undoubtedly equally unrealistic.

Once you have done your preliminary inquiry you can take further steps for review of the projections. State securities laws normally require that alternate projections be presented to you setting forth how your investment will fare if all does *not* go well. Many syndicators balk at furnishing such figures on the basis that they may prove virtually useless to the investor and overwhelm him in a sea of numbers. On the other hand, the failure to provide such figures, at least upon request, should be grounds for you to seek further information concerning the syndicator and how his investors have fared in the past.

[¶1001.2]   Study Performance of Past Syndications

A study of the performance of past syndications as compared with their projected performance will give you some idea of the likely accuracy of the present projections. Beware if these past performance figures are based upon assumed appreciation in the value of the past projects. While present value of a project—appreciated or depreciated—is the only way that a real estate expert may be able to analyze how well a property is doing, it is too easy to secure an optimistic appraisal for you to rely upon such figures as indicative that the investments will prove profitable ones. It is far better to determine whether projected occupancy rates have been obtained, whether projected rentals could in fact be collected, and whether estimations as to construction and operating costs and the inflationary factors built in to these expense assumptions have proved realistic. Have the projected tax benefits in fact materialized? And has cash flow—particularly, *distributed* cash flow—met the level set forth in the original projections? All of this information should give you some guidance as to how you may fare in your present project. Similarly, refusal on the part of the syndicator to provide you with this information may indicate that he is not overly proud of the results of his past projects.

Once you have determined that the project seems to make economic sense, both based upon the validity of its assumptions and the accuracy of prior projections, you need to get into a deeper study concerning the structure of the present proposal, both from the economic and a tax standpoint, and the caliber of management. You should insure that the syndication has been structured in such a way that you do not have extensive liability exposure in the event of cost overruns. Here, investment through a limited partnership vehicle may be called for. Does the proposed agreement provide for a free flow of information, including periodic reports, at least semi-annually, advising not only how well the project is doing, but whether the projected results concerning expenses, income, and tax benefits are on target? Do you have a right to replace the syndicator-general partner if his performance falls below standard? Is the general partner financially capable of performing his obligations under the syndication, and does he have sufficient financial staying power to be able to bail out a project which temporarily finds itself in trouble?

An analysis of whether or not the day-to-day management to be provided for the property is experienced in managing *this type* of project located in *this geographic area* is critical. Is there sufficient financial incentive for the management to stay with the property and manage it properly, without the deal being so "sweet" that the economics are wrecked? Is the compensation of the project's developer tied to the success of the project, and is the developer obligated to stay with the project?

Here, some discrete inquiry will help you. A visit to projects constructed by the same developer and managed by the same property management company is well worthwhile. A request for a list of investors in prior projects, and a few phone calls to these investors to see how satisfied they are with the syndicator, can likewise prove very enlightening.

[¶1001.3]   Consult Your Tax and Financial Counsel Before Investing

A review of the structure of the deal by your tax counsel is imperative to insure that the tax benefits which you are expecting will in fact be available to you. As we have seen, the Tax Reform Act of 1976 requires far more careful planning to secure significant front-end tax benefits. Likewise, it is critical that the syndication be structured in such a way that these tax benefits will flow through to you and not be stopped at the project level on the basis that the syndication was an "association taxable as a corporation."

Many analysts have concluded that it is quite difficult to offer high initial deductibility, particularly of the "excess write-off" variety, in real estate (other than government-assisted housing) since the Tax Reform Act. A number of "private" syndications continue to purport to provide such deductibility by utilizing such structuring technique as "interest only" notes and heavy reliance on component depreciation.

Whether such structuring devices will withstand audit and court tests remains to be determined.

A final step is an analysis of the compensation provisions structured into the deal, to insure that they motivate the developer, the syndicator, and the property manager—who may be one and the same person—to make the syndication profitable.

The problem of structuring a deal with excessively heavy "loads" —going in, during, and coming out—has already been mentioned. But if all the compensation to the syndicator is to be received "up front," or at some far off date in the future, he may have inadequate incentive or financial ability to make sure that the deal works.

The timing, as well as the amount, of the syndicator's profit can significantly affect the likelihood that you will profit. A real estate project goes through three basic stages—the origination of the project or "acqui-sition" phase; the operational or "management" phase; and the termina-tion or "winding up" phase. When the syndicator's profit is received mainly in the acquisition phase, there is less incentive to see to it that the property is properly managed. Instead, the syndicator must spend all of his efforts putting together new deals, and may spend insufficient time making sure that the projects previously syndicated are being operated at a profit. While the syndicator may point out that he is to share in the eventual profits upon the sale of the property, if the likelihood of those profits is slight, or if the receipt of this profit is too distant, his attention still may constantly be focused on projects being put together rather than those then in operation.

[¶1001.4]   Guidelines Exist to Aid Investors

As discussed in Chapter 31, guidelines have been adopted by various securities regulatory agencies concerning potential abuse areas in tax-sheltered investment. Among the most crucial guidelines are those adopted by the Midwest Securities Administrators Association and the National Association of Securities Dealers for publicly registered real estate syndications.

The Midwest and NASD guidelines detail requirements for compen-sation, conflicts of interest, sponsor net worth and experience, and other "structuring" aspects of *publicly registered* real estate offerings. These guidelines do not apply to real estate syndications which are not required to be registered under State or Federal securities laws, and in many instances will not be applicable to the "private" real estate syndications most often presented to you.

Many real estate syndicators complain that the Midwest and NASD guidelines are unrealistically restrictive. It is for this reason that so many real estate syndicators have "gone private;" and the fact that the Midwest-NASD guidelines are not strictly followed in structuring the syndication offered to you does not mean that the offering is necessarily unfair. However, the guidelines do reflect various past abuses in real estate syndications, and should serve to highlight potential problem areas even though the investment being offered to you is not required to register under these guidelines. Reviewing the proposed syndication against these guidelines should serve to highlight potential abuse areas. While minor variances from the guidelines may not require a "no go" decision, if the variances from the guidelines are substantial; if the abuse areas which the guidelines seem to close are left wide open in the pro-posed investment; or if the compensation to be received by the syndicator is substantially in excess of that which would be permitted in a registered offering, further investigation is a wise precaution.

The NASD and Midwest guidelines are contained in Appendix 3100-1.

Structure analysis, and an investigation of management, is a key to the analysis of any tax-sheltered investment. However, it is often difficult to determine whether an oil and gas operator, or a livestock syndicator, in fact knows his business. Where the investment is in real estate, the prior projects are living proof as to whether or not the syndicator has done his job. Likewise, since most real estate syndicators operate on a local basis, inquiries can determine the syndicator's reputation among other real estate professionals and in the financial community.

The steps outlined above may seem time consuming. However, of the millions of dollars invested in real estate each year by tax-sheltered investors, an unfortunate percentage goes into projects which make no economic sense, or whose economic potential will be destroyed by mediocre management. Following the steps outlined should help keep you from ending up among the list of sadder but wiser real estate investors who have found that tax benefits will never offset the potential loss from a poorly conceived or poorly managed real estate investment.

SECTION 2: Oil and Gas—Tax Shelter and Profit Potential for the High Tax Bracket Investor

11.

Oil and Gas: What Does it Offer to the Investor?

[¶1101]   **THE TAX BENEFITS—BEFORE,
DURING, AND AFTER PRODUCTION**

Oil and gas is the most popular, and readily available, form of tax shelter for the investor who wants to make a $5,000 to $10,000 investment, or who seeks to spread several such investments over several programs. While there are more real estate syndications being offered than any other type of tax-sheltered program, these syndications are often offered in very small units, or, in contrast, to very large investors. In the "public" area—tax shelter offerings registered with the Securities and Exchange Commission to permit a broad solicitation of numerous investors to bring together large pools of capital for a diversified group of projects—oil and gas definitely reigns supreme. (As to the relative popularity of oil and gas among tax-sheltered investments see ¶106.)

In addition to the "public" oil and gas programs offered to numerous smaller investors, private offers of one to several million dollars to a much smaller group of much larger investors are also quite common. These offerings, which vie with government-assisted housing syndications in their appeal, frequently involve the development of a single multiwell exploratory "prospect" and rely upon the "private offering" exemption under the Securities Act of 1933 to avoid SEC registration requirements. (See Chapter 31.)

The size of the public market for public oil and gas programs as compared with the private market is indicated by the fact that some 85 oil and gas sponsors registered programs with the National Association of Securities Dealers in the year 1977, seeking to raise in excess of 1.2 billion dollars. During approximately the same period, even more sponsors made offerings through NASD member firms in "private" offerings which were not required to be registered with State or Federal securities agencies. However, the dollars sought by these programs amounted to less than twenty-five percent of the amounts covered by the registered programs. (Oil and gas is the only type of tax-sheltered investment in which the SEC-registered offerings exceed the amounts sought through private placements.)

An indication of increasing popularity of oil and gas investment is the substantial rise posted in both the dollar amounts registered in the calendar year 1977, and in moneys raised. In 1976, 48 oil sponsors filed offerings with the Securities and Exchange Commission seeking to raise 590 million dollars. In 1977, this figure increased to filings by 59 companies for 951 million dollars. Similarly, the funds actually raised by publicly registered programs in 1977 was a record total of 539 million dollars, as compared with the 359 million dollars raised in 1976.

Undoubtedly, the energy crisis and rising oil and gas prices have played a major role. However, a key appeal of oil and gas investment has always been its tax benefits.

The wide publicity given the tax benefits available from oil and gas investment has placed oil high on the list of investments considered by investors who are seeking an offset to high Federal income tax. On the other hand, as in any tax-sheltered area, these tax benefits do not assure the profitability of the investment, and can even be lost if the investment is poorly structured, or reflects an outright fraud on the investors.

The key to the high initial tax benefits presented by oil and gas investment is the deductibility of *intangible drilling and development costs,* which represent a substantial portion of the expenses incurred in the initial conduct of oil and gas operations. These expenditures for items incurred in connection with preparing the surface of the land for drilling, for the conduct of the drilling, and for the preparation of the well for production, permit the taxpayer, under an option authorized by §263(c) of the Internal Revenue Code, to deduct expenditures for such items which have no salvage value, such as labor, fuel, and supplies.

Expenditures for *equipment* such as well casing and tanks are not immediately deductible, but must be capitalized and depreciated over the useful life of the property. (See Rev. Rul. 78-13.) These depreciation deductions are in addition to the deductions for depletion, to be discussed, and may also generate additional tax benefits through eligibility for the investment tax credit.

Expenditures for *lease acquisition costs* are also capital expenditures which are not currently deductible. Unlike equipment costs, costs of lease acquisition must be recovered through the *depletion* allowance. However, to the extent that a lease is proven worthless and is abandoned, its cost becomes immediately deductible as an *abandonment loss,* as will the cost of any non-salvageable equipment.

The initial deductibility of the expenditures incurred in connection with an oil and gas venture will depend upon the amount of money spent in acquiring leases; whether the well is productive, or a dry hole, which will affect the availability of the abandonment loss and the amount of equipment which must be installed in connection with the well; and the depth of the drilling (as a general rule, the deeper the well, the greater the percentage of IDC to tangible costs). However, as a general rule, the intangible expenditures in connection with a given oil well will run 50 percent to 80 percent of its total cost. (It should not be assumed from the foregoing that the purpose of drilling is to drill dry holes. Although such expenditures may be 100 percent deductible, they also result in a 100 percent loss of the investor's hard dollars!)

High initial deductibility is a key not only to motivating the tax-sheltered investor to put his money into oil, but to the economics of oil and gas investment. At current return rates, it would be nearly impossible for any diversified oil and gas operations to be conducted profitably, whether by tax-sheltered investors or oil and gas operators, if it were not for oil's tax benefits. (The truth in this statement is reflected in our current energy crisis.) Accordingly, to encourage the infusion of tax-oriented investor capital in the search for oil and gas, many oil and gas programs are structured under the "functional allocation" sharing arrangement, under which the sponsor of the oil program is charged with all expenditures for non-deductible items, and the investor is charged only with those expenditures which are made for currently deductible costs. Such an approach seeks to provide an investor with a deduction of 100 percent of his invested capital in the year of expenditure. (The functional allocation approach to oil and gas investment will be discussed in greater detail in ¶1301.)

The initially deductible expenditures in oil and gas investment include, in the "IDC" category, such items as location and surface damage, labor utilized in drilling wells, drilling mud and chemicals, drill stem tests and core analyses, footage and day-work drilling costs, engineering and well site geological expenses, and various deductible completion costs. In addition, amounts spent on "delay rentals"—the payments required from the oil operator to his oil and gas "lessor" to maintain the leases in effect—are also currently deductible, as are "abandonment loss costs," previously mentioned.

The tax advantages of oil and gas investment do not stop with these immediately deductible expenditures. In addition, §611 of the Internal Revenue Code permits the oil and gas investor to receive a portion of any oil and gas income which results from the drilling tax-free as a result of a deduction for *depletion*, which is the oil and gas equivalent of real estate's depreciation.

As in depreciation, the depletion deduction serves as a Tax Code recognition of the fact that the oil and gas reserves discovered by drilling are being exhausted as they are extracted from the ground. Thus, a certain portion of any revenue received by you from your oil and gas drilling will represent a return of your capital, since, unlike an investment in common stock, your oil and gas reserves are being exhausted as they are produced.

The depletion tax advantage to you as an oil and gas investor arises from your ability to deduct the *greater* of cost or percentage depletion in computing taxable revenues from oil and gas production. *Cost depletion* permits you to write off that portion of your oil and gas expenditures which you are required to capitalize over the life of the producing properties. You can do this by annually deducting that portion of your oil and gas revenues which represents the percentage of the total estimated recoverable reserves which you have produced that year. However, the Internal Revenue Code permits "small producers" alternatively to deduct a specified percentage of their oil and gas production as a statutorily-authorized *"percentage depletion,"* currently set at 22 percent of your annual gross income.

Under the Tax Reduction Act of 1975, this percentage will be reduced in future years. Percentage depletion will reduce to 20% in 1981 with additional drops until reaching a current floor of 15 percent in 1984 and subsequent years.

Unlike most deductions, "statutory" or "percentage" depletion may be taken without regard to your "adjusted tax basis"—your capitalized costs—in the property, so that your percentage depletion can and frequently does permit deductions in excess of 100 percent of your capitalized costs.

For this reason, the requirement that certain expenditures, such as lease acquisition costs, be capitalized and recovered through cost depletion normally confers no tax benefit on you. You would have been permitted such deductions in any event through percentage depletion, irrespective of capitalized costs.

Changes in the tax law enacted by the Tax Reduction Act of 1975 and the Tax Reform Act of 1976 have reduced to some extent the economic benefits available to you from statutory depletion. However, there is no question that this tax benefit available to you as an oil and gas investor is a highly valuable one. Furthermore, since the 22 percent figure applies to *gross* rather than net income, it will tend to shelter approximately one-third of your income from oil and gas operations from taxation.

In addition to the tax benefits provided for oil and gas investment when developing and producing the property, advantageous tax consequences also flow at the termination of the program. The sale of your interest in an oil and gas well, or of the program in which you invested to carry on this oil and gas exploration, is eligible for *long-term capital gains* treatment (subject to the recapture of certain productive-well IDC expenses as discussed in ¶1104). Furthermore, a number of oil and gas programs contain "stock exchange" features, either as a part of the program or as a result of periodic "exchange offers." These may permit you to *exchange* your drilling program interest *for* the *common stock* of the program sponsor or some other corporation. In many instances, this exchange may be on a *tax-free basis* Furthermore, the sale of the stock at a profit will normally also be eligible for a long-term capital gains treatment.

In the early and mid 1970's, "leveraged" oil and gas offerings were extremely popular with investors, particularly in the "private offering" market. Such offerings were at one time also conducted through publicly registered investment vehicles. However, the reluctance of the Securities and Exchange Commission to clear registration statements for such offerings shortly led to the demise of the public leveraged oil offering. Such offerings normally held out the hope of a 200 percent write-off by providing that investor funds would be matched by borrowings on a one-for-one basis, so that the investor who subscribed for a $10,000 program interest would receive a $20,000 write-off.

The leveraged oil program was looked at by most established oil and gas operators with a great degree of skepticism. Few traditional lending institutions will lend money on undrilled locations, even of the so-called "proven" nature. It was felt by many that such borrowings were being provided, directly or indirectly, by the sponsor or drilling contractor, and were normally compensated for by artifically inflated drilling or other costs.

In the *Bernuth* case,* the U.S. Tax Court held that a taxpayer would not be allowed a deduction for that portion of "turnkey" drilling costs—a fixed price to be paid irrespective of whether actual costs ran more or less—which were in excess of the usual and reasonable costs under such contracts. In Revenue Ruling 72-135, and in Revenue Ruling 72-350, the IRS further took the position that a non-recourse loan secured from the general partner of the oil program, or a loan which is convertible into an interest in the partnership, will be treated as a contribution to capital by the "lendor," and not a true debt which may be used to increase the "basis" of the taxpayer to generate excess deductions.

The nonrecourse leveraged oil program was dealt a virtual death blow by the Tax Reform Act of 1976, which included investments in oil and gas in its "at-risk" limitations. (See Chapter 5.) While the "basis" rules prior to the Tax Reform Act did not prohibit the use of *legitimate* leverage, such as using reserves developed by earlier drilling, which are a bankable

---

Charles N. Bernuth, 57 T.C. 225 (1971), affirmed 470 F. 2d 710 (2d Cir. 1972)

asset, the use of this leverage to secure loans for additional drilling, through "production loans" may have been adversely affected by the 1976 Act. Likewise, while a production loan will permit early deductions without additional capital contributions by the taxpayer, program revenues subsequently used to retire the loans will result in a subsequent tax liability to the taxpayer without additional offsetting deductions. The use of undistributed program revenues to conduct additional drilling will create additional IDC deductions for the taxpayer, but will be taxable to him even though not distributed.

In the past, legitimate uses of leverage have also arisen where advanced payments were received from gas pipelines to encourage the producer to develop gas reserves. Such advances were normally in the form of *recourse* borrowings. Similarily, even after the Tax Reform Act of 1976, recourse borrowing is a legitimate method of creating deductions in excess of your initial equity investment. However, before entering into any oil and gas arrangement involving "recourse" borrowing, you should be well aware of the risks involved. If the drilling does not establish sufficient production, you will be required to make sufficient additional capital contributions or payments to the lendor to satisfy the loans.

(As to the risks of recourse borrowing, see ¶2703.)

Deductibility going in, substantial sheltering of income during the program, and additional tax benefits on program termination—oil and gas investment offers all of these advantages. However, as in all forms of investment, these tax benefits do not eliminate, but only cushion the risk, for you will still have "at risk" the 30 percent to 50 percent of your investment which represents your "hard dollar" cost. Thus, understanding the potential economic benefits from oil and gas investment, aside from its tax consequences, and analyzing how likely such benefits are to flow from a particular proposed investment in oil and gas, is essential in making an intelligent investment decision.

Examples of the tax benefits which may flow from oil and gas investment, including the effects of the TRA'76, are contained in the Appendix.

[¶1102]   THE ECONOMIC BENEFITS—
CASH FLOW AND CAPITAL GAIN POTENTIAL

The mechanics of how an oil and gas investment will work for you in attempting to convert your risk capital dollars into oil and gas reserves in the ground will be discussed in Chapter 12. Basically, the oil operator will use your money to drill "prospects"—oil and gas leases which he believes lie upon a favorably situated geological "feature" which may be productive of oil and gas. A certain number of these wells will result in "dry holes"—wells which do not encounter commercial quantities of oil and gas. The oil and gas search is highly speculative, even for the expert professional, and the exact number of these dry holes will depend on a combination of how well the oil operator has done his job in "screening" the prospects and whether the prospects are "exploratory" or "developmental" in nature (see ¶1202.)To a great degree, success depends upon the "luck" factor which surrounds oil and gas exploration and development, despite over a hundred years of technical advances. However, with any luck, a certain number of the wells that you drill will discover commercial quantities of oil and gas. This "luck" factor is the reason diversification is so important in the oil and gas industry.

As the oil and gas reserves developed through your investment are produced, *cash flow* will be generated and eventually distributed to you. Approximately 30 percent of these net revenues will be sheltered from Federal income taxation by the depletion allowance. The exact amount of revenues so generated, and the period over which they will be recovered, will depend upon the success of the drilling program, how quickly the wells can be connected to a necessary pipeline if gas is discovered, and the producing characteristics of the oil and gas formation. In many instances, the amount of oil and gas discovered may not prove sufficient to return a profit to you on your overall investment, due to the number of dry holes also drilled or the size of the oil and gas reserves discovered. In other instances, even though all wells are productive, the length of time required to recover these reserves may mean that the investment still does not prove profitable, due to your long-term loss of the use of the money initially invested by you. (As to this "time value" of money, see ¶402.)

At a given point, the oil operator may determine that it would be more profitable to sell the oil and gas reserves discovered by your drilling "in place" to someone who has a need for these reserves than to continue to produce the wells until the reserves are depleted. No depletion allowance is available on the proceeds from such a sale. However, the money so distributed normally will be subject to long-term *capital gains* treatment, subject since TRA'76 to recapture of productive-well IDC costs. If the reserves discovered were substantial enough, you may thus secure a profit from your investment at a substantially earlier date than if the reserves were produced over the life of the well. Likewise, your program may contain a *"stock exchange"* feature or may contain a "buy-back" or "redemption" provision where the sponsor agrees, at your option, to purchase your reserves from you for cash, which would similarly offer long-term capital gains opportunities, or, in some stock exchanges, an opportunity to receive the stock tax-free. While the desirability of such redemptions was lessened by capital gains changes in the 1969 Tax Reform Act, and seriously hurt by the productive well IDC recapture requirement in the

1976 Act (see ¶1104), the redemption provision is still useful for estate tax valuation purposes, as well as providing a source of some cash in the event of an emergency.

The profitability of your investment, whether you hold your reserves to depletion or sell or exchange your interest in the reserves, will always depend on the amount of oil and gas discovered through the drilling. Even when a program contains either a cash or stock "redemption" feature, there is no assurance of the amount of money that you will receive—this depends entirely upon the results of the drilling. Since, if you hold your reserves to depletion, you will also have delayed your return, figures as to estimated recoverable reserves must always be discounted to "present value" to determine the true profitability of your investment by taking the time value of money into account. Likewise, any "buy-back" offer from the sponsor, whether for cash or stock, or any sale of the program reserves by the sponsor, will be subject to a similar discounting of the reserve value by the purchaser. In addition, there is a second discounting, which takes into account the risk that the estimated reserves are not in fact present, or cannot be produced either as rapidly as possible or at all. This second discounting or "hair cut" is standard in the oil and gas industry even when producers sell reserves to one another. However, it frequently may come as a surprise to you if you are not an experienced investor in oil and gas to discover that a dollar's worth of net recoverable reserves in the ground may only realize you 50 cents or less, in the event of sale.

A successful oil and gas exploratory effort can generate substantial revenues for you in the form of cash flow from production. This money may be received over a substantial period of time—often seven to twenty years or even longer—or through a distribution of the proceeds from the sale of such reserves after your properties have been fully developed. These economic benefits will also have certain advantageous tax aspects. However, it is difficult accurately to estimate the amount of reserves that have been discovered by drilling some 8,000 to 20,000 feet below the surface of the earth. It is also difficult to estimate the oil and gas reservoir conditions that affect how rapidly and how much of these reserves can be recovered. Consequently, it will be several years before an accurate estimation can be made as to the results of the drilling program. Likewise, as will be discussed in ¶1104, the profitability of any sale of reserves has been adversely affected by 1975 and 1976 tax legislation.

[¶1103]   **MISCELLANEOUS BENEFITS OF**
                   OIL AND GAS INVESTMENT

[¶1103.1]   Diversification For the Small Investor

The term "small investor" in the field of tax shelters bears a highly different meaning that in most investment areas. As a person earning $70,000 to $100,000 a year, it may be hard to visualize yourself as being in the "small" investment category. However, intelligent tax-sheltered investment usually requires a minimum investment of $5,000 to $10,000 per program. Since, as discussed in Part Four, you are normally better off to spread your tax shelter needs over more than one program, frequently in several tax-sheltered investment areas, it may be difficult for you to secure the necessary diversification in your tax-shelter investment plan that the speculative nature of all tax shelters dictates.

Even when investor moneys are being pooled, the tax shelter syndicator normally does not wish to deal with a large number of investors. A $5,000 to $10,000 minimum investment per investor normally represents the smallest amount which a syndicator will accept. Even if you need $20,000 to $25,000 worth of tax shelter, this means a relatively small amount of diversification for you if you were to invest in real estate, cattle, or agriculture. The problem intensifies if your tax shelter needs for a given year fall in the $5,000 to $10,000 tax category. Thus, you may find that your entire tax shelter funds have been tied up in one or two real estate, livestock, or agricultural projects, each one of which is subject to the speculative factors affecting that industry. A drop in cattle prices, a change in the economy of the area in which your apartment project is located, or local overbuilding, all can have serious adverse impact on your investment program.

Few tax-shelter sponsors go to the public market to raise substantial amounts of money for numerous projects through registered public offerings. (The securities implications of the public offering are discussed in Chapter 31.) The exception to this policy is the publicly registered oil and gas program, where smaller $5,000 to $10,000 investments from hundreds of investors are pooled to generate millions of dollars in a single program for oil and gas exploration and development. This raising of oil search capital from numerous investors means that you will own a proportionate interest in dozens of oil and gas "prospects," and in hundreds of wells. Since most sponsors of publicly registered oil and gas programs offer similar programs annually, you will be assured of a similar investment opportunity, year after year as your tax shelter needs continue. Likewise, since history has shown that investing over a several-year period is just as important in oil and gas as is investing in numerous oil and gas prospects within a single year, the public oil and gas program can offer such "time-line diversification." Oil and gas thus remains the single most available means of participating in numerous projects within a single year, or over a period of years, for the investor whose tax shelter needs fall within the $10,000 to $25,000 a year category.

[¶1103.2]   Oil and Gas as a "Seasoned"
             Investment Area

Despite the admitted advantages of tax-sheltered investment, the tax shelter investor frequently finds that he is plagued by two basic problems. The first is analyzing the *profit potential of the industry* in which he is to invest. The second is to find, either through his own resources or through competent advisors, professionals within that industry with a proven ability of investing investor dollars wisely and profitably, i.e., the *"proven" sponsor.*

In most tax shelter investment areas, it is difficult to find reliable data upon which to base a conclusion as to the reasonable return expectations which a passive investor can anticipate. Even in real estate, the most popular form of tax-sheltered investment, it is difficult to determine how investors have fared, on the average, over the years, and what reasonable return expectations may be. It is also difficult to determine exactly how well a given syndicator has performed for his particular investors, or to locate industry analysts who can recommend particular programs and program sponsors to a prospective investor. The one exception to both of these problems is tax-sheltered investment in oil and gas.

The oil and gas industry has been offering drilling programs to public investors since the 1960s. The results of these programs are required to be reported to these investors, and substantial amounts of information concerning such programs are required to be filed with State and Federal securities administrators. Thus, it is possible to draw certain conclusions concerning expected program results from such investment. The involvement, since the mid to late 1960s, of the securities broker in the sale of such programs, has likewise resulted in a greater awareness of probable program results on the part of the brokerage community.

In addition to the 10-plus years of history concerning the results of drilling in the public drilling program industry, this body of information permits information to be developed concerning the capabilities of various program sponsors. Since brokerage houses have a responsibility to their clients in recommending such programs—see Chapter 31—various industry analysts have now emerged who interpret the results of previous programs. The availability of information and the need for analysis has resulted in the development of various tests for analyzing program results.

The relatively "seasoned" nature of public oil and gas investment means that more realistic determinations can be made of reasonable return expectations from oil and gas investment, and which program sponsors are more (or less) apt to achieve such results. The results have been far less "spectacular" than is traditionally associated in the lay investor's mind with the search for oil and gas. The spectacular "finds" are historically offset by a large number of dry holes and less profitable discoveries. However, certain guideposts have emerged as to what is a "reasonable"return from an intelligently planned investment in oil and gas.

Does this mean that if you limit your tax-sheltered investments to oil and gas, you can be reasonably assured of a particular return? It most certainly does not. Oil and gas is highly speculative, and even when dealing with a qualified, capable program sponsor, there is no assurance that his current projects will achieve industry results or will even equal the results of his prior programs. Furthermore, the "results" of a given program reflect the particular leases, the particular area, and the particular exploration team responsible for such results. As new programs are developed, new leases must be acquired, often in different areas. Geologists and other specialists may leave one company to go with another, or to start their own businesses. However, the greater volume of information concerning oil and gas drilling program results makes it clear what *not* to expect from oil and gas exploration and development. Likewise, while past successes do not guarantee future profitability, a long standing history of poor results may be quite enlightening in attempting to determine whether a program sponsor's current efforts will meet with success.

The oil and gas search is highly speculative. Despite its scientific underpinnings, luck in addition to expertise always appears to play a role in oil and gas exploration. However, luck *in lieu of* expertise seldom will provide successful oil and gas results, particularly in view of today's expensive drilling requirements and greater program diversity. A highly qualified program sponsor may still have a string of unsuccessful program years, despite a careful selection of promising prospects. This "bad run" may suddenly be broken, and followed by years of successful results. However, verifiable information concerning a sponsor's past results on behalf of his investors gives the oil and gas investor a leg up in his attempt to select potentially profitable programs in which to invest—an advantage not present in other tax shelter areas.

[¶1104]   **EFFECTS OF THE TAX
                 REDUCTION AND TAX REFORM ACTS OF
                        1975 AND 1976**

Oil and gas investment emerged relatively unharmed from the Tax Reform Act of 1969. While percentage depletion was added as an item of tax preference by that legislation, substantial exemptions were available before this "tax preference" status required the imposition of a minimum tax or caused a loss of "maxi-tax" benefits. This meant that these changes had relatively little effect on the typical public oil and gas investor. The main effect of the Tax Reform Act of 1969 on oil and gas investment was to make less attractive the sale for redemption of an investor's program interest due to the changes in the laws concerning long-term capital gain. However, other than the reduction of the percentage depletion rate from 27½ percent to 22 percent, the key tax benefits of oil and gas investment—the deductibility of intangible drilling and development costs and the availability of percentage depletion—were not markedly changed by the Act.

In 1975, the rules of the game changed for oil and gas. The Tax Reduction Act of 1975 eliminated percentage depletion for the larger oil companies, though an "independent producers and royalty owners exemption" still left percentage depletion available to most tax-sheltered investors. However, rules providing that such exemption was not available upon the transfer of "proven" properties meant that less money could be paid for the sale of proven properties, or a program interest, since the purchaser would not receive the benefits of percentage depletion. Likewise, the Tax Reduction Act provided for an eventual reduction of the percentage depletion figure from 22 percent to 15 percent.

The Tax Reform Act of 1976 adversely affected oil and gas in several ways. The imposition of the "at risk" limitation on non-recourse borrowing severely curtailed the availability of "excess write-off" programs in oil and gas. While this was looked at by many in the oil and gas industry as a step forward rather than a step backward, two other changes in the Tax Reform Act had more far reaching consequences. These were the changes in the rules concerning minimum and maximum taxes, and the requirement that productive well IDC deductions were subject to recapture upon the sale of a program interest or a program property and would further serve as items of tax preference.

The Tax Reform Act of 1976 did not affect the initial deductibility of productive well IDC expenditures nor affect in any way moneys expended on dry hole IDCs. Thus, oil and gas still remains one of the few tax-sheltered investment areas that can generate a deduction approximating 100 percent of your investment under deductions clearly authorized by the tax code. (Note that this 100 percent deductibility assumes investment in a "functional allocation" program. In programs where nondeductible costs are also borne by the investor, normal deductibility will be in the neighborhood of 70 percent to 80 percent.) However, you will now find that, in the event of a sale or redemption of your program interest, or a sale of program reserves by the sponsor, a significant "recapture" of tax benefits may result. Equally signficant is the classification of productive well IDCs as items of tax preference.

Initially, it was concluded by most analysts that the changes imposed by the Tax Reform Act of 1976 on oil and gas investment would have relatively little effect on the tax consequences to the investor. Subsequent studies have shown that, while this is substantially true for the investor with $100,000 or less of annual taxable income, the impact is quite substantial on the investor with significantly greater income, particularly where such income would otherwise be taxed at the 50 percent maximum rate applicable to personal service (earned) income. For such investors, many of whom invest up to $100,000 or more a year in various "private" oil and gas programs, the elimination of the various "cushions" before the imposition of the minimum tax or the loss of "maxi-tax" benefits, has had significant adverse effect on the potential profitability of oil and gas investment.

Appendix 1101-1 illustrates the effects on such investors of the Tax Reform Act changes.

The changes worked by the Tax Reform Act of 1976 have not eliminated the benefits of oil and gas investment for the high tax bracket investor. If you are earning in the neighborhood of $100,000 a year and seek tax-sheltered investments of $10,000 to $25,000, the changes will have relatively little effect upon you. In any event, oil and gas programs can be structured in such a way as to eliminate the impact of the Tax Reform Act changes, even for those with high "personal service" income, by restructuring a modified functional allocation program which charges productive well IDC expenses to those who would not be significantly adversely affected by the loss of maxi-tax benefits. However, few such programs are currently being offered. Accordingly, if you are seeking to shelter $100,000 or more through oil and gas investment, and have large amounts of income which is currently subject to "maxi-tax" protection, you should consult your tax advisor in analyzing whether or not oil and gas in its typical form remains the best investment for you.

[¶1105]   THE PITFALLS OF OIL AND GAS INVESTMENT

A number of risks surround the drilling of oil and gas wells. Many of these risks are generic to the oil and gas industry and apply as much to a major oil company as they do to you. Key among these risks are the dangers that the moneys spent on your behalf in the oil and gas search will not find any oil and gas. In other words the wells will be *dry holes*. Or, the quantities of oil and gas discovered, when weighed against the amount spent, will be insufficient to return a profit on the investment. This is particularly a danger in oil and gas in view of the long period of time over which any reserves discovered will be produced and thus generate distributable cash flow to you. (And remember: each dollar distributed to you represents, at least in part, a return of your original invested capital. When the reserves are exhausted by production, there will be no remaining assets. This is what is meant by "depletion.")

In addition to the problems concerning how much oil and gas will be discovered and developed by the drilling effort, a number of *natural hazards* surround the drilling for oil and gas. You are looking for oil and gas thousands of feet below the surface of the earth. Even the best planned drilling project can run into problems underground. In addition to causing your drilling expenditures to run much higher than anticipated, "subsurface" problems can even cause the loss of the well or liability to third parties in the event of a "blow out" or damage to the environment. And many of these dangers are impractical or impossible to insure against.

To understand what these pitfalls mean to you as a potential investor in an oil and gas drilling program, you need to understand the following:

☐ *Even the best oil and gas drilling program results in the drilling of many dry holes.* Thus, theoretically, no matter how well the oil man has done his homework, your drilling expenditures might result in the discovery of *no* oil and gas. This "dry hole risk" is heightened to the extent you engage in "exploratory" drilling. However, even a so-called "development" program may be marked by 25 percent or more unproductive wells. (The relative risk-reward potential of exploratory versus development drilling is discussed in ¶1202.) However, the risks of total wipeout are usually reduced by investing in a diversified oil and gas drilling program. (See ¶¶1103.1 and 1202.)

☐ *The fact that a well is productive does not insure that it will be profitable.* Even with the admitted tax benefits, spending $10,000 to discover $5,000 worth of oil and gas will not prove beneficial from your standpoint as an investor. Most drilling programs are structured in such a way that the program sponsor can make money off such a well even though you do not. (See ¶1301.) You will normally find that these risks of *unprofitable*, as contrasted to *unproductive*, drilling, are a far greater danger to you than the dry hole risk. Even if you discover a dollar's worth of oil for every dollar that you spend, you may end up a loser, despite the tax benefits. The dollars distributed to you will still be subject to taxation (less the partially-offsetting depletion allowance). And since such dollars will be returned to you over a substantial period of time, the loss of the use of your money in the meantime is a significant consideration. Also, when the reserves are depleted, you will have no remaining asset value.

☐ *A number of conflicts of interest surround even the best structured oil and gas program.* These risks are discussed in greater detail in ¶1302. However, to the extent that the oilman is selling leases to your program at a "mark-up"—in other words, at more than he paid for the leases—or is performing drilling or other services for the program at a profit, he stands to make money whether you do or not. These profits to the sponsor for the *sale of services or materials* can eliminate the potential profitability of an otherwise sound drilling project. Likewise, as discussed in ¶1301, even in the best program, the program sponsor will receive a *"promotional interest"*—an interest in revenues either cost free, or at a smaller share of program costs than the share of revenues with which he is credited.

The fact that the sponsor is receiving a promotional interest does not mean that the program is a bad one. In some ways, this works to your benefit: because of the promotional interest, the professional oil man often turns to investors as the source of the drilling capital rather than drilling the wells "heads up" (solely at his own cost). Thus, through a tax-sheltered investment in oil and gas, you may be permitted to "partner" in the oil and gas search with some of the best talent the oil industry has to offer. However, the promotional interest also means that wells may be drilled which are profitable to the sponsor but not to you.

Unlike most forms of tax-sheltered investment, the oil and gas sponsor takes relatively little of his profit "up front." While some programs do feature heavy front-end loads to the oil sponsor, at the present time this is a relatively infrequent practice.

Avoiding such programs will be discussed in ¶1302. However, while front-end "loads" are normally less in oil and gas than in other tax-shelter areas, the program sponsor will take a greater percentage of program revenues. (See ¶1301.)

☐ *The chief pitfall to you as an oil and gas investor is how well the sponsor will perform in intelligently expending your moneys in the oil and gas search.* In real estate or livestock, it is relatively easy to determine whether or not the syndicate's projects are operating at a profit: if they are not, the bank loans are normally foreclosed. However, in oil and gas, it may be years before it is determined whether or not your program is financially successful. Since many dry holes or productive but unprofitable wells will be drilled in even the best program, your key concern must be: how likely am I to profit from this investment? The fact that your sponsor has been actively engaged in the oil business, drilling many wells for a number of years, is no assurance that he has been drilling such wells profitably. (Remember, these wells have been financed, normally at a profit to the sponsor, by numerous investors such as yourself.)

Whether or not you make money in the oil and gas business

partially is affected by factors which have nothing to do with your operator's ability. However, it is also directly affected by the operator's skill as an oil finder, and the degree to which he utilizes these skills for your benefit as well as his own. This analysis of your operator's "track record" (to be discussed in ¶1303), will prove the single most important factor in selecting a potentially profitable oil and gas investment.

There are other pitfalls that you should consider before getting into an oil and gas investment:

- The *need for additional capital* to fully develop program properties.
- The often *lengthy period between* the *investment and* the receipt of *cash flow.*
- The "blind investment" *risks of investing in a "blind pool."*
- The need for *limited liability.*

[¶1105.1]   How to Avoid Being Forced to Sell Out Promising Well Locations

Once the sponsor has competed the drilling of the program's exploratory wells, additional drilling will be required fully to develop those "prospects" which appear to be commercially productive. Additional capital may likewise be required to complete wells which prove more costly than anticipated. This additional capital requirement is usually a good sign for you. In most instances, it indicates that initial drilling has met with some degree of success. However, unlike the real estate investment, where capital requirements can normally be projected with a high degree of accuracy, there is no way to project in advance exactly how much money may be required fully to develop program properties.

A portion of the capital needs of the program can be satisfied through the reinvestment of program revenues or through borrowing against the reserves established by the initial drilling. However, a program sponsor frequently finds that he must "farm out" well opportunities to other oil men to drill due to the lack of sufficient development funds within the program. Often, these wells have a high degree of potential profitability. They are the very kind that the sponsor (and you) should want to drill with *your* money.

To avoid being forced to sell or "farm out" promising well locations due to the lack of development capital, oil and gas programs often include an "assessment" feature. This "assessment" feature is a provision where the sponsor can call on you for additional funds to complete the activities which the program has begun. While some program sponsors make quite an issue of the fact that their program is "non-assessable," an assessment feature is normally to your advantage, so long as it is limited to a specified percentage, 25 percent to 100 percent of your initial investment. If the program does not provide for an assessment, you may find that opportunities are lost due to the inadequacy of available financing sources to conduct desirable additional drilling.

[¶1105.2] Additional Oil and Gas Pitfalls

Oil and gas drilling is not for you if you require an *immediate cash flow* from your investment. The drilling phase of your program will normally last from months to several years. Until a sufficient number of wells have been drilled to interest a production purchaser, the wells will generate no revenues. Even after the wells have been put "on-stream," a significant portion of your revenues may be required to finance the additional development drilling discussed above, or to retire program borrowings which have been used to finance such additional drilling. Accordingly, it is often several years or more before the program sponsor is in a position to commence the distribution of revenues to his investors. And cash flow, once commenced, may be interrupted if deeper horizons prove productive, requiring (and permitting!) further drilling, or when wells must be "reworked."

Some private programs, normally offered to the more affluent investors, feature "specified" properties—the leases which the program will drill are described in the offering document. Likewise, single well offerings similarly describe the wells to be drilled. However, most "public" drilling programs are the *"blind pool"* or "blank check" variety: the wells to be drilled are not specified in the offering document but are chosen by the sponsor after the offering has closed.

Caveat: One bit of investor lore is that all "good" prospects end up in private programs. Don't believe it: there are good, mediocre, and bad private programs, and good, mediocre, and bad public programs. *You must be selective!* (See Chapter 29.)

As an investor in an unspecified property program, you will be at the mercy of the program sponsor as to the quality of the projects he selects. This is not as bad as it sounds: even if the drilling prospects were specified, it would probably be beyond your expertise to evaluate their potential for profit. However, if you are planning an extremely large investment in oil and gas, or are represented by an investment advisor who can retain a geologist to evaluate a sponsor's proposed package of properties on behalf of you and his other clients, you may prefer the "specified property" approach. (In the public drilling program, the brokerage house through which you purchase your interest should similarly have retained competent professionals to review the "inventory" of leases maintained by the sponsor from which a large number of the program's leases will normally be selected.) (See ¶1303.)

A final pitfall of oil and gas investment is the potential exposure to liability in the event of a well "blow out" or a similar disaster. While many real estate, agricultural and livestock offerings are structured as limited partnerships, your absolute need for limited partnership protection in such offerings may not be as great. Seldom does a building collapse or a cow run amuck, and, in any event, most of such risks can be insured against. However, the risks of damage to third persons and their property in oil and gas drilling are a significant risk factor, and it is normally impossible or impractical to insure against many of these risks. Accordingly, it is critical that your investment in oil and gas be through a *limited partnership vehicle* to protect you against unexpected liability in excess of your investment.

[¶1106]   **IS OIL AND GAS A SUITABLE INVESTMENT FOR YOU?**

There is no question that an investment in a well-selected oil and gas program can offer excellent opportunities for you, *if* you are the proper type of person to invest in oil and gas. However, due to the special risks and characteristics of oil and gas investment, it is not suitable for all investors. Therefore, even though you need tax shelter, you should ask yourself the following questions before investing in oil and gas:

☐ *Am I in a sufficiently high Federal income tax bracket?* Oil and gas does not make economic or other sense for the investor who is not in at least a 50 percent Federal income tax bracket.

☐ *Can I afford the risk of an investment which may result in a total loss* of my investment capital? While, as we have noted, investing in a diversified program substantially reduces this "wipe-out" risk, an occasional partnership may find little or no oil, even in programs organized by legitimate and capable sponsors.

☐ *Can I afford, and will I need, to make a similar investment for a several-year period?* As discussed above, "time line" diversification is necessary for an intelligent oil and gas investment strategy.

☐ *Am I in a position to make additional "assessment" payments in the event* further drilling is required?

☐ *Can I wait a substantial period of time for any cash flow?*

If the answer to even one of these questions is "no," then oil and gas is not an appropriate investment for you. If, however, you have answered each of these questions "yes," and if what you have read up to this point indicates that oil and gas is an investment you may wish to consider, it is time to look, in greater detail, at exactly how an oil and gas investment works.

12.

How Does An Oil and Gas Investment Work?

[¶1201]   **HOW THE OIL MAN FINDS OIL**

Before an oil well is drilled, the oil man's technical staff make a determination that a well should be drilled in a given location. If the well is "exploratory" in nature, that is, located in an area where there is no oil and gas production nearby, this means locating subsurface rock conditions indicating that oil and gas *could* have accumulated in a given "formation."

Only by drilling a well to the required depth can it be determined that commercial quantities of recoverable oil and gas reserves are in fact present. However, the technical staff's expertise will permit them to determine that the area is "prospective" for oil and gas—that oil and gas may be present.

Once a likely "prospect" has been identified, the oil man will secure oil and gas leases from the owners of the land and mineral rights in this prospect area. A number of such prospects are brought under lease, until the oil man has "inventory" of what he believes are attractive drilling locations. At this time, money will be raised from investors such as yourself, frequently from a "public" offering registered with the Securities and Exchange Commission and sold through securities brokerage houses.

A part of the moneys raised through this offering will go for such "front-end" costs such as sales commissions and the cost of the offering. These front-end charges are usually substantially lower than in other types of tax shelter offerings, and usually provide little if any profit to the sponsor. The remaining "net" proceeds are used to reimburse the sponsor for his costs of lease acquisition. (In the "functional allocation" program, the sponsor bears these costs of lease acquisition, at least as long as the well is productive.) The net proceeds are further used to drill one or more exploratory or "test" wells on each of the prospects committed to the program, and to operate those wells which appear to have commercial possibilities. A portion of the funds may also be used to further develop productive exploratory prospects, although, as mentioned, such additional development may require bank borrowings or assessments.

If the wells to be drilled by the sponsor are "developmental" in nature, the oil man will base his drilling decisions on an evaluation of how much oil and gas is likely to be developed by drilling this particular location, based upon the results of the "offsetting" wells. This evaluation will also take into account the fact that even drilling in a "proven" location does not assure that the well will not result in a dry hole.

The drilling of "development" wells on an exploratory prospect successfully developed by a program differs significantly from investment in development wells acquired from another oil man. When an exploratory well proves successful, it is normally surrounded by a number of equally lucrative drilling locations. The exploitation of the prospect then continues until the less profitable portions of the reservoir are all that remain to be drilled. A strict "development" program normally involves drilling on these less attractive locations, or on development opportunities surrounding exploratory wells which, though productive, have proved potentially less profitable than anticipated.

A portion of the funds invested in a drilling program, and a portion of the production revenues, will frequently go to reimburse the program sponsor for his general administrative overhead or "GAO"—items of expense necessary for the conduct of the oil and gas operations which do not relate to any particular drilling prospect. They will include such items as the expense of the sponsor's general office; of the employees, both technical and administrative, employed in the general office; and record keeping and reporting expenses.

Reimbursement for administrative overhead is a normal part of oil and gas operations, which applies in dealings between major oil companies as well as in arrangements between a program sponsor and his investors. "GAO" expense is a necessary part of the conduct of successful oil and gas operations. However, such reimbursement also offers a potential for abuse, since it can be a method of hiding salaries and elaborate expense reimbursements for the principals of the general partner, and in any event keeps the sponsor in business, whether his operations are successful or not. Likewise, since different companies use different methods of allocating such costs, it is difficult to evaluate merely by comparing cost levels from sponsor to sponsor whether or not the "GAO" reimbursement is being abused. (A high GAO may reflect that the sponsor has an effective, well-staffed operation, which may mean more productive drilling, and thus more money, for you.)

After drilling is completed, the sponsor will arrange for the marketing of the program's production, including securing any necessary pipeline connections where gas is involved. Investors are frequently unpleasantly surprised by the period of time that may elapse from the completion of a well until "run" checks are received. However, before a well can be put on production, it must be thoroughly tested, and often additional wells must be drilled to secure the necessary pipeline connection. Likewise, before accounting to the program for production proceeds, the production purchaser will require that title be verified to its satisfaction. Thus, a period of months or years may elapse before run proceeds are actually received by the program, and are available for distribution to you, particularly where your initial investment has been "leveraged" by borrowing to fund additional drilling. (See ¶1105.)

[¶1202]   **EXPLORATORY VERSUS DEVELOPMENT DRILLING**

A key decision for you as a prospective oil and gas investor is whether you wish to invest in a program which is primarily exploratory in nature, or whether you prefer a "development" program.

Exploratory drilling or "wildcatting" involves the drilling of wells that are not located near proven production. Exploratory programs involve a much greater risk of dry holes. However, the return potential from such wells, particularly when a number of such exploratory prospects have been packaged in a program to provide diversification are believed by many to offer a much greater opportunity for profitable return than the drilling of development wells near established production at "proven" locations in the same field.

While development drilling involves far less dry hole risk (though dry holes will definitely result even in development drilling), the development prospects which can be acquired from other parties involve wells which the person selling ("farming out") the prospect does not wish to drill. Thus, the return potential of such wells normally is significantly less than the return potential of a successful exploratory well, particularly when you consider that the exploratory well, if productive, should be surrounded by a number of equally attractive "development" locations. (See ¶1201.)

Whether or not exploratory drilling is in fact more profitable, for the last few years investors in public drilling programs have tended to prefer programs oriented toward exploration over development programs. Thus, of the 426 million dollars raised for drilling by public drilling programs in 1977, nearly 60 percent ($250 million) was invested in exploratory programs, 23 percent ($98 million) in development programs, and 17 percent ($78 million) in "balanced" or "combination" programs. See *RPI Newsletter* (Jan. 1978). The figures exclude amounts raised by "oil income" programs. (See ¶1203.)

The fact that a well is "exploratory" in nature does not mean that it will offer a high degree of return, even if it is productive. The return potential cannot be determined until the well is actually drilled. Likewise, a development well may prove to have surprising return characteristics and may actually result in a return more commensurate with that anticipated from exploratory drilling.

Many investors seek to balance the risks and benefits of exploratory and development drilling by entering into programs in which the high risks of exploratory drilling are offset by a lesser number of development prospects, or where the lower return potential of development wells is offset by some percentage of exploratory tests. Others invest in truly "balanced" offerings, in which drilling moneys are split equally between exploratory and development prospects.

The decision between exploratory and development drilling is one for you to make. Investing in a strictly exploratory program, particularly a program engaged in the drilling of "rank" wildcats ("hunting for elephants") requires a definite degree of "staying power" on your part, and should only be entered into if you are certain you can make such an investment for several years in a row. However, in today's economy, it would appear that a program which is substantially oriented toward exploration, with a minimum of 60 percent to 75 percent of its subscription proceeds so committed, may offer greater return potential than a program which is primarily oriented toward development drilling. This observation presumes, however, that you will follow the recommendations contained in Chapter 13 to insure that you have selected a program with superior performance potential.

[¶1203]   **OIL INCOME PROGRAMS**

Oil income or production purchase programs involve the acquistion of producing properties to provide a steady stream of partially tax-sheltered income to the investors. Since the costs of acquiring such properties are required to be capitalized for Federal income tax purposes, the oil income program offers relatively little front-end tax benefits. Since the oil income program is "cash flow" rather than "deep shelter" oriented, it possesses totally different investment characteristics than a drilling program, exploratory or developmental. Since no drilling is involved (though one type of oil program, the "combination" program, involves both production purchase and drilling) and "established" reserves are being purchased, it is considered as "lower risk" than "drilling" programs. (The risks are still there; they just differ in their nature.)

The purchase of producing properties involves the acquisition of the right to receive a volume of oil and gas which a petroleum engineer or geologist *estimates* will be recovered from presently producing oil and gas wells. Such properties are acquired from oil and gas operators who have completed their drilling, and prefer to sell their reserves "in place" rather than holding the properties for the life of the production.

Producing properties are evaluated by:

☐ Estimating the amount of recoverable oil and gas reserves remaining in the ground

☐ Discounting the estimated future net revenues from such reserves to their present worth

☐ Further discounting this present worth of the "income stream" to take into account various risk factors to arrive at a "fair market value" of the properties

If the appraiser has been accurate (and lucky) in his estimate, and no unexpected changes in producing conditions or price occur, the resulting income stream should provide an attractive return to the purchaser. However, if the estimates are inaccurate, or prices are reduced due to market or regulatory conditions, or subsequent difficulties are encountered in recovering the reserves, the investment may prove less than rewarding.

Oil income programs have proved extremely attractive to investors in the 1970's. In 1977, some $113 million—21 percent of the total moneys invested in SEC-registered oil and gas programs—was invested in such "production purchase" programs. (*RPI Newsletter* (Jan. 1978). An additional $18 million was invested in "combination" programs.) However, serious doubt exists on the part of many as to whether the anticipated levels and safety of the return from such investment has been overemphasized or misconstrued. While reserves can be estimated with some accuracy, even the best reserve "estimate" is nothing more than that, albeit an educated one. Accuracy increases as the period of actual production increases. If prices should change, the reserve estimates are too high, reserves cannot be recovered due to production slowdowns or problems in the operation of the well or market conditions change, the return to the investor may be significantly less than originally anticipated. While recent price increases have been of great assistance to many oil income programs, the sale price for producing properties often has taken potential price increases into account, creating additional risks under Federal price control policies.

A bank will loan money against reserves in the ground. Accordingly, many oil income programs engage in borrowing so that investor funds can be leveraged to provide a higher yield on equity, assuming that the reserve and price estimates on which the purchase price is based are accurate and the reserves are in fact produced and marketed on schedule. However, in the event of inaccurate reserve determinations or other developments which adversely affect the program's cash flow, the downside risks of leverage can substantially reduce or even eliminate the return on investment.

A high degree of competition exists in the oil and gas industry for the purchase of attractive producing properties. A significant danger exists that a sufficient number of attractive properties may not be available to the program, or that the sponsor may overpay for the reserves in order to acquire producing properties for his program. This is particularly a problem where large amounts of money have been raised which must be invested.

To avoid a "rush to invest," and still provide cash flow, some programs keep substantial amounts of money in reserve, and may even use a part of these reserves, or the sponsor's independent funds, to maintain a particular return level to the investor. However, to the extent that the amounts paid the investor represent other than cash flow from production, they cannot be looked at as accurately reflecting what should be anticipated as the eventual return rate on his production purchase.

Some programs contain a reinvestment feature through which the investor is permitted to reinvest that portion of his cash flow which represents the "return of capital" element of his depleting asset. This prevents the investor from inadvertently consuming his capital, a pitfall for the unwary who might otherwise erroneously view the return as being similar to non-depleting bond income.

Oil income programs are viewed by many as being a relatively safe yet high return investment which will substantially exceed return levels which can be expected from conventional money instruments without possessing the risks normally associated with oil and gas. However, there is a high danger that investors and their advisors may have misconstrued both the risk and the potential return involved in oil income programs. While production purchase does not involve the same *type* of risk as is involved in oil and gas drilling, as indicated above it definitely possesses risks of its own. Likewise, it is difficult at this time to analyze what reasonable return expectations may be in the oil income area, particularly if the rapid price rises experienced by the oil and gas industry in the mid-1970's do not continue at the same pace.

This is not to say that an oil income investment may not meet your needs as an investor. Prices can increase, and reserve estimates prove too low. It does point out the dangers, however, of assuming that such an investment can be safely compared with investments in high quality bonds, or that the 10 percent to 12 percent return rate assumed by many to be easily attainable on an oil income program is necessarily a realistic return expectation.

Several of the potential pitfalls of the oil income program are dealt with in the "Guidelines for the Registration of Publicly-Offered Oil and

Gas Programs" adopted by the North American Securities Administrators Association. Article VI. A.2. of the NASAA Guidelines prohibits the sponsor of a production purchase program from purchasing properties from another program of the sponsor (including the sponsor's own drilling programs) except at cost (as adjusted for intervening operations), unless the fair market value of the property, as determined by an appraisal by an independent petroleum reservoir engineer, is materially more or less than cost. Article V. B.2 of the NASAA Guidelines also limits the sponsor's compensation to a 3 percent working interest (unless the sponsor provides the management and operating responsibilities for the program, in which event a 15 percent working interest may be retained.) This may be increased to a 5 percent working interest after investors have received a return from production of 100 percent of their capital contribution, computed on a "total program" basis.

As to the conflicts which such restrictions seek to limit, and the effectiveness of the restrictions, see Chapter 13.

The attitude of investors toward the oil income program is reflected by comparing the $113 million raised by SEC-registered oil income programs in 1977 with the $39 million raised in 1976. However, while five companies were engaged in sponsoring publicly registered income programs in 1974, this figure by 1977 had dropped to two, with the vast majority of the funds—over 98 percent—being raised by a single company. Since some 48 companies successfully offered publicly registered oil and gas programs in 1977, this figure is some indication of the view of much of the industry as to the availability of attractively priced producing properties.

13.

Analyzing An Oil and Gas Investment

[¶1301]   **IMPORTANCE OF THE
                              SHARING ARRANGEMENT**

Oil and gas programs are normally not characterized by the heavy "front-end" loads which mark most tax-sheltered investments. However, the sponsor receives a significant "promotional interest," which can create a real danger for the unwary investor.

The investor is offered some protection against entering into a totally unrealistic venture in most tax shelter areas by the fact that such projects require financing through the use of leverage in addition to the investors' capital contribution. To the extent that such borrowings represent funds provided through a "wrap-around" mortgage, or other sponsor-provided borrowings, the protection is significantly less. Even in the case of borrowings from established financial institutions, the investor is not protected against the loss of his equity interest. However, in the oil and gas program, the investor has no such protection.

To the extent that the sponsor's promotional interest is cost-free, the sharing arrangement offers no protection against the drilling of costly wells which will never prove profitable. There is no pressure on the sponsor realistically to evaluate profitability. He will receive his share of cash flow even if the wells never pay out. Even in the program where a portion of costs are to borne by the sponsor, if the promotional "spread" is too high, it is possible for the well to prove profitable to the sponsor even though it never results in a profit to the investor. This means that a prospect which is potentially rewarding when *overall* costs are compared with *overall* revenues can be converted to a windfall to the sponsor and an economic loss to the investor due to the disproportionate sharing of costs and revenues.

Contrary to popular belief, it is not difficult to find oil and gas; it is merely difficult to find oil and gas *profitably*. Many areas in the United States can be drilled by an oil man with productive wells resulting in almost every case. However, many of such fields are characterized by drilling which will never result in a profit. Such fields are a bonanza for the unscrupulous oil promoter, who can impress an investor with his marvelous productive-well "track record," and even provide a quick distribution of cash flow, while knowing that such wells will never pay out. It is for this reason that the "box score" charts included in an SEC-registered prospectus, showing the total number of wells drilled by the sponsor and the characterization of such wells as oil, gas, or "dry", is informative not as an indication of the success of such drilling, but merely to provide information concerning the scope of the sponsor's prior operations. It is for this reason that the SEC requires that such wells be labeled "productive" rather than "successful." (See ¶1303.) As an investor, you may assume that, with the tax benefits available to you from oil and gas drilling, relatively little income is required for a successful investment. However, as the following charts show, when the taxes payable on your income are taken into account, along with any reasonable allowance for the time value of money (a 10 percent time value has been assumed), a well which does not "pay out", cash on cash, within approximately 5 years, or which does not generate reserves with a present value of at least 75 percent to 100 percent of your initial investment is of doubtful "profit" to you.

The profitability of your investment cannot be measured by comparing the results of the productive wells alone. Revenues from productive wells must return not only their own costs, but also the costs of any dry holes. Accordingly, in analyzing the potential profitability of an oil and gas investment, the *total costs*, including the cost of dry holes, must be compared against the anticipated program revenues, utilizing the profitability tests outlined above. Thus, unless you will recover your overall *pre-tax cash investment* in all wells, dry and productive, within the specified period, your investment has not been profitable.

In the 1960's, oil and gas syndications were often marked by front-end loading in the form of guaranteed profits from sales or services to be provided by the program similar to that which is found in other tax shelter syndication areas. The oil and gas operator would sell leases to the investors at a substantial mark up over actual cost, or would perform drilling services for the partnership at inflated "turnkey" prices. (See ¶1302.) However, this form of "loading" no longer marks the typical oil and gas offering, except in those instances where undivided interests in a single "deal" are sold, usually to investors who are quite experienced in oil and gas transactions and can evaluate the merits of the proposed well and the reasonableness of the mark ups, or to highly inexperienced and unsuspecting investors, such as those who acquired interests in 1976 in the highly publicized "bucket-shop" marketing of "Reg B" offerings.

The effects of the sponsor's promotional "spread" on the potential profitability of an oil and gas investment are indicated by the following example:

Effects of Promotional Spread*
Assumption: Well costing $100,000 discovers reserves with present value of $130,000. Tax consequences are ignored.

	Costs and Revenues Divided 50%-50% Between Sponsor and Investors (No Promotional Spread		Sponsor Bears 35% of Costs and Re- ceives 50% of Revenues (15-Point Spread)		Sponsor Bears 25% of Costs and Receives 50% of Revenues (25-Point Spread)	
	Sponsor	Investors	Sponsor	Investors	Sponsor	Investors
1. Costs	$50,000	$50,000	$35,000	$65,000	$25,000	$75,000
2. Revenues	65,000	65,000	65,000	65,000	65,000	65,000
3. Profit (Loss)	15,000	15,000	30,000	-0-	40,000	(10,000)

While the front-end profit has now been eliminated from most of the oil and gas offerings to which you will be exposed, it is highly important that you be aware of the effects the "sharing arrangement" (method of allocating costs and revenues) selected by your proposed sponsor may have on the likelihood of your profiting from the investment. Since, in the oil and gas offering, the sponsor will receive his major compensation through the sharing arrangement, much is made of the fact that the sponsor will "profit along with" you and your fellow investors. While this is true, and the *size* of the sponsor's profit will increase as the return to the investors increases, this does not insure that the sponsor cannot make a profit even though the investors do not. Accordingly, a brief review of the various types of sharing arrangements should help you in preliminarily evaluating whether or not to consider a proposed oil and gas investment.

The typical sharing arrangements are:

☐ The *overriding royalty interest,* in which the sponsor bears no part of program costs, but shares in revenues from the first through a cost-free interest in production;

☐ The *reversionary ("subordinated") working interest,* in which the sponsor bears no costs, but similarly does not share in production revenues until the investor has recouped his costs;

☐ The *disproportionate sharing arrangement,* in which the sponsor agrees

---

to bear a certain portion of *all* costs (frequently, 25 percent), in return for a specified share of program revenues (often 50 percent);

☐ The *"functional allocation"* program, in which only deductible ("non-capital" or "intangible" costs) are borne by the investor, with all non-deductible ("capital" or "tangible") costs being borne by the program sponsor.

The *overriding royalty interest* is a share of production delivered, free of any costs other than taxes on production, to the program sponsor. It is normally a relatively small interest in production—usually between 1/16 and 1/8 of the gross production from the well, or of the program's interest in revenues from the well. However, since the overriding royalty interest: (a) shares immediately in revenues, and (b) bears no part of well costs, not even the costs of operating the well, the arrangement encourages the drilling of wells without regard to their profitability. (A variation of the overriding royalty interest is the *net profits interest.* The net profits interest is measured by the revenues of the program from a given well or prospect (or, in some instances, from the revenues as a whole), determined after deducting certain specified costs, which can be limited to the costs of well operation, or can include additional costs, such as drilling costs. However, unlike the subordinated working interest, the holder of a net profits interest is never required to put up his share of additional costs incurred after a well has paid out, even though the well may cease, temporarily, to operate at a profit. Instead, the net profits interest holder's interest in production is simply suspended until the deficit position is eliminated.)

In the 1960's, unsophisticated investors were frequently attracted to overriding royalty interest arrangements due to the smaller interest in production being reserved by the promoter as compared with other sharing arrangements. (Such overrides were frequently coupled with "turnkey" drilling arrangements, where the investor paid a specified cost for the drilling of the well, without regard to actual drilling costs. Frequently, the investor did not realize that the promoter was receiving a healthy profit from his "mark up" on the costs of drilling, in addition to his "small" interest in production: see ¶1302.) The overriding royalty interest approach, by permitting the promoter to share in revenues from first production, involved no consideration of the time value of money—how long would it be until the investor's interest was "paid out." The abuses that arose from the drilling of numerous productive but unprofitable wells under such an arrangement led to a general discrediting of this approach by the 1970's; and such arrangements are "looked upon with disfavor" under the NASAA oil and gas rules (NASAA Guidelines for the Registration of Oil and Gas Programs, Art. V.B.)

For guidelines concerning the deductibility of prepaid turnkey drilling costs, see IRS Revenue Ruling 71-252 (1971-1 C.B. 146), and *Pauley vs. U.S.,* 11 AFTR 2nd 955.

The *reversionary interest* approach has been quite popular in oil and gas programs, particularly in the area of "private offerings." Under this sharing arrangement, a program sponsor does not share in revenues from a given well or prospect until the revenues credited to the investor's account (or in some instances, *distributed* to the investor) equal all costs charged to the investor in connection with the well or prospect.

At first glance, it may seem that this is a "no lose" situation for the investor. While it does not guarantee that he will make money, it seems to indicate that, unless he does, the sponsor cannot. And who would spend the time to put together a drilling program if he did not anticipate profiting from it?

While the reversionary interest approach does increase the pressure on the sponsor to perform, it does not equate to "no investor profit/no sponsor profit." First, the formula does not take into account the time value of money. Since the sponsor has nothing at risk, and since all of his expenses of operation, including his administrative overhead, will be reimbursed, he has nothing to lose. If a well eventually pays out, he will back in for a share of the revenues after pay-out. However, "pay-out" does not in fact make the investor whole, since he has lost the use of his money in the meantime.

To take into account this "time value" factor, in one variation of the reversionary interest program, the sponsor bears his proportionate part of development well costs, putting his own money at risk. In another, the sponsor backs in only after the investor recovers 120 percent of his costs.

A more significant factor in analyzing the reversionary interest approach is that the reversion is normally figured on a *well-by-well* or *prospect-by-prospect*, not a whole-program basis. (One public program does compute the sponsor's reversion on a "whole-program-payout" basis.) Thus, for a program which has drilled 10 wells, seven of which are dry, but three of which would return three times their original investment, the sponsor will have received a significant profit even though the investor has never been made whole. (See the Appendix.)

Under the *disproportionate sharing* arrangement, the sponsor will normally put up 25 percent of *all* costs in return for 50 percent of program revenues. This has the advantage of putting the sponsor at risk as to a portion of program expenditures, so that he, as well as the investor is affected by the time value of money. It has the further advantage, not found in most functional allocation programs, that he also shares in dry hole costs. However, it requires that the investor share in non-deductible, as well as deductible, costs. More importantly, if the spread between the sponsor's share of costs and his shares of revenues exceeds 10 to 15 points, it is unlikely that the investor will come out, except on an unusually successful program. (See the chart earlier in this ¶1301.)

Functional allocation involves the charge of only deductible program expenditures to the investor, with all non-deductible costs being borne by the sponsor. Under this approach, also referred to as the "tangible/intangible" or "capital/noncapital" formula, the investor's expenditures will be 100 percent tax deductible. This does not always mean that, as an investor, you will receive a 100 percent deduction *in the year of investment,* since it is not the *investment* of the moneys, but their *expenditure* on deductible items, that gives rise to the tax deductions.

The vast majority of all public oil and gas drilling programs utilize the "functional allocation" formula. This is primarily due to the sales appeal of the "100 percent deductibility" feature.

Functional allocation has been criticized on the grounds that the large share of revenues received by the program sponsor—normally 40 percent to 50 percent—may over-compensate him for the share of cost that he is bearing, particularly since most functional allocation programs do not require that the sponsor bear any part of "dry-hole" risk.

The criticisms leveled against the functional allocation program—the bearing of all dry hole costs by the investor; the spread that may exist between sponsor and investor costs; and the "casing point conflict" created when a decision must be made as to whether or not to complete a well which might prove profitable to the investor but not to the sponsor, who must now bear the vast majority of completion costs—are all valid. However, functional allocation has definite advantages to the investor in addition to its 100 percent deductibility:

(1) While the sponsor bears no portion of dry hole costs, he does share in the costs of all productive wells. His money is thus at stake from a "time value" standpoint, and he also must share in the risks of a well proving productive but not profitable—the major problem in oil and gas drilling programs.

(2) The key problem area in the functional allocation program—the spread between the sponsor's share of costs and revenues—can be lessened by requiring that the sponsor, in any event, agree to bear a specified minimum portion of the program costs. This requirement has been included in the present version of the NASAA oil and gas guidelines. It is also important that the sponsor bear *all* capital costs, and not merely capital costs incurred to a given point.

From the standpoint of the investor, the approaches which would place maximum pressure to perform on a program sponsor would be a reversionary interest on a *total program* basis, or a functional allocation program with an adequate sponsor "minimum investment" requirement, particularly if this were coupled with the requirement that the sponsor bear some portion of dry-hole costs. However, it is easy to place too much emphasis on "structure analysis"—the evaluation of the preferability of the program sharing arrangement, conflicts of interest, and other such features. While a given sharing arrangement may create so little sponsor pressure, or be so out of line with the economic realities of the oil and gas search, as to eliminate a program from consideration, it is far more important from your standpoint to evaluate a sponsor's track record than it is to dwell excessively on the structure of the program. (See Chapter 29.)

This is not to say that structure analysis is not important. Appendix 3100-1 contains the NASAA Guidelines of the Registration of Oil and Gas programs. While these guidelines are considered by many sponsors to unnecessarily restrict the oil man's flexibility, thus adversely affecting investor return, the guides concerning appropriate compensation levels, unreasonable conflicts of interest, and other potentially abusive practices are well worth review, even in a private program. While the guidelines need not be complied with in private offerings, a review of their provisions will indicate a potential area of abuse which may cause you to reevaluate and investigate further.

[¶1302]   **CONFLICTS OF INTEREST—**
                          HOW SERIOUS ARE THEY?

All tax-sheltered investments are marked by conflicts of interest. The fact that under any tax shelter syndication, the syndicator can profit even though the investor does not, is in itself a conflict. Likewise, any form of self-dealing creates conflicts. The analysis of a proposed oil and gas offering in the "conflicts" area thus should primarily be aimed at determining how *serious* is the potential for abuse, and whether or not the conflicts have in the past resulted in unprofitable returns to the investor.

Conflicts of interest normally involve self-dealing with program by the sponsor or its affiliates which creates the potential for profit irrespective of the profitability of the program, or the conduct of operations in such a fashion that there is an unnecessary potential for loss to the investor. This latter situation need not necessarily involve any potential profit to the sponsor and as such may not be a true "conflict." Likewise, the fact that services are to be provided to the program, or sales made, at "cost", or "competitive rates" is not an assurance that conflicts have been eliminated, since the mere providing of a market for the sponsor's properties or services, or utilization of idle personnel, can be of benefit to him.

The NASAA oil and gas guidelines, contained in the Appendix outline the key conflict areas in oil and gas programs. These include:

(1) The *sale of leases or producing properties* to or from the program, particularly when such sales are not supported by independent

appraisal. The sale of leases at a "mark up" to a program should likewise be looked at with some suspicion, even where such mark up is substantiated by an independent appraisal.

(2) The *transfer of less than all drilling locations* on a "prospect," which may result in the investors' funds being used to "prove up" the surrounding drilling locations for the sponsor.

(3) The *performance of services* for the program for compensation other than at cost.

(4) The *farming out of undrilled locations* of the program, even to third parties, where the effect of such a farm-out will be to reduce the sponsor's obligations.

(5) The *comingling of program funds* with the general funds of the sponsor or the *use of funds* of the program *as compensating balances* for the sponsor.

(6) *Loans* by the program *to the sponsor*, permitting the sponsor to *use program funds* for his *own account,* or the *loan* of moneys *by the sponsor* to the program at *unreasonable interest rates.*

(7) The *redemption of investor program interests,* except where based upon appraisals by qualified independent petroleum experts.

Certain conflicts of interest are inherent in oil and gas operations. (The fact that certain practices are permitted under the NASAA Guidelines subject to specified restrictions such as the sale of leases at mark up when supported by an independent appraisal, does not mean that the practices as restricted do not involve any conflict. It means only that the potential abuse is not so great as to warrant absolute prohibition.) The conflicts and other conduct prohibited or restricted by the NASAA Guidelines apply only to registered programs, and are not binding on the sponsors of private oil and gas offerings. Likewise, as in the case of the sharing arrangement, a review of the sponsor's "track record" is a far better indication of whether conflicts are being unreasonably resolved than is a mechanical following of any conflict "checklist." (See ¶1301.) However, each of the conflicts restricted or banned by the NASAA Guidelines is based upon a past abuse area. Thus, even a private offering should be reviewed against the NASAA Guidelines to determine whether or not further inquiry is advisable: see Chapter 31.

[¶1303]   **TRACK RECORD AND LEASE
INVENTORY OR PROSPECT ANALYSIS**

The most significant step in analyzing a prospective oil and gas investment is to determine how well the sponsor has performed for his past investors, and the quality of the "prospects" presently available to him for drilling.

While good past performance is not an assurance that similar results will be attained by the particular program in which you are considering investing, or by any of the sponsor's future programs, it is hardly wise to invest without some idea of the sponsor's prior results.

The SEC prospectus in a publicly-registered drilling program contains substantial information which can be used as a point of departure in analyzing past performance. The *"box score" tables*—indicating the sponsor's prior mix of exploratory and development drilling, and the number of his wells which have resulted in oil production, gas production, or have been dry holes—is no indication of the *success* of these wells. However, that is not the reason such information is required by the SEC to be provided you. Instead, the tables permit you to judge how extensive the sponsor's past operations have been and the type of drilling in which he has engaged. This will aid you in determining whether his present program falls within his past experience.

The most useful tables in the SEC prospectus are the *"net cash"* and *"payout" tables,* which indicate dollars expended and revenues received by investors in past programs, as well as similar information as to the sponsor. Since such tables contain this information both on a cumulative and a "last-three-months" basis, it is possible to make rough computations concerning potential program payout. From this, you can gain some idea concerning the likely profitability of past programs, both to the investors and, equally important, to the sponsor.

Payout and similar tables are frequently criticized as not reflecting reserves discovered as a result of past operations. While reserve information is critical to a determination of program profitability, it is often difficult accurately to estimate reserves until sufficient "producing history" is available. Reserve estimates based on "volumetric" methods, which do not reflect actual production history, are standard within the oil and gas industry but are recognized as being subject to substantial revision. Early estimates of *gas* reserves are particularly subject to revision.

Despite these problems, the SEC now permits, but does not require, the presentation of certain reserve data in the prospectus. To date, few sponsors have availed themselves of this opportunity.

Information similar to the "track record" history required in SEC-registered prospectuses should also be contained in the offering documents furnished to you in connection with private offerings. However, this does not always prove to be the case. When this information is not included in the private offering circular, you should request that it be provided you. You also might ask yourself (or the program sponsor) why it was not included originally.

Review of the information contained in the offering document will serve as a preliminary point of departure in your search for information concerning the sponsor's past performance (see Chapter 29). If, historically, a sponsor has performed poorly for his investors, the odds are against his suddenly reversing his record. However, offering circulars prepared for non-oil men such as yourself do not contain the information that a professional would deem necessary adequately to evaluate a sponsor's track record. Likewise, they do not provide the information necessary to determine the potential of the present projects to be undertaken.

This further evaluation requires going outside the offering circular, and securing the services of competent oil professionals, further to investigate exactly how past investors have fared and to determine whether the present prospects which the sponsor intends to drill are of similar quality.

The further steps necessary to evaluate past performance and future potential involve a review, by an independent petroleum engineer selected by *you* or your representative, of the reserves discovered to the investors' interest in prior programs, and a geological review of the leases which the sponsor intends to commit to the present program or which are contained in his lease inventory as potential drilling prospects.

The review of prior reserves must be performed on your behalf by an engineer who has only your interests at stake. This does not mean that the reserve estimates prepared by the sponsor, whether "in house" or by an independent engineering firm, have been prepared in bad faith. However, engineering estimates can vary widely, and the sponsor obviously will not have selected an engineering firm which is unsympathetic to its exploratory approach. A hard look by an equally qualified professional who is beholden only to you is the best means to verify exactly how well prior investors have done.

Even though review of past performance will not offer any assurance that the present program will meet with equal success—we are assuming that you have already eliminated those sponsors who have historically performed poorly—it is useful in determining the general oil finding abilities of the sponsor and his attitude toward performing for his investors. (See ¶1304.) However, if the sponsor is now moving in new directions in the oil and gas search—due to a switch in his emphasis from developmental to exploratory drilling, from the oil to the gas search, or to drilling in new areas—his past performance may be most misleading as to future prospects. Likewise, oil men frequently are extremely experienced in a given area: if the majority of the high quality prospects have now been exhausted, the present inventory of leases may be of lesser quality than those drilled in the past.

In the private program, the wells to be drilled will normally be designated by the sponsor in the offering document. Thus, it is an easy step to send in your representatives to review the quality of these prospects.

In the public oil and gas drilling program, the Securities and Exchange Commission puts limitations on the right of prospective investors to review information not contained in the SEC-registered prospectus as to past results or the sponsor's inventory of leases. Any indication by the sponsor that certain leases *may* be committed to a program would be contrary to the required representations in his typically "unspecified property" offering. However, the SEC does permit the broker-dealers who will be participating in the offering as selling agents to review such information as a part of their "due diligence" investigation. The broker-dealer's obligation to conduct this investigation on your behalf will be discussed in Chapter 31. While the broker-dealer is not permitted to furnish the results of this investigation to prospective investors, you can and should determine whether such review *has* been made by him. If not, you should avoid the offering. You can also ascertain through inquiry whether or not, historically, the broker-dealer has conducted such investigations in an effective manner. By limiting your purchase of publicly-registered drilling programs to those offered by broker-dealers who themselves have a track record of performing effective due diligence, you can substantially increase the likelihood that your oil and gas investment will be a "producer."

[¶1304]   SIZING UP MANAGEMENT

The key to a successful evaluation of any proposed tax-sheltered investment is an analysis of the syndicator's capabilities. This involves sizing up his *professional expertise,* including the adequacy of his staff and facilities; his *integrity*; and his *attitude toward his investors.* While these qualities are critical to the success of any investment, it is of particular importance in analyzing an oil and gas offering, since the oil and gas search is particularly management sensitive.

The *integrity* of your sponsor is an absolute must. No matter how good his staff, and no matter how high quality the leases which he intends to drill, no investor has ever made money when dealing with a questionable sponsor.

The quality just mentioned—integrity—also ties in with the sponsor's *attitude toward your money.* Obviously, if the sponsor lacks integrity, his attitude toward his investors will be unsatisfactory. However, many legitimate oil and gas finders may look at their investors as simply another source of financing. Since it is difficult to find oil and gas profitably, this may mean that they will unnecessarily resolve conflicts of interest against you; in any event, they will not have that essential drive toward making sure that *you* make money in the oil and gas search.

The sizing up of *management skills,* and particularly the caliber of the sponsor's staff, is a final and essential step in management review. Past performance may have been the result of the efforts of a particular exploration team. If this team has now been broken up, or key persons now have left, management, despite its integrity and desire, may be unable to perform adequately on your behalf. In any event, if there have been such changes, you need to know it. Further investigation will obviously be called for before deciding to invest.

The following steps should be taken when choosing an oil and gas investment:

☐ Review the proposed offering structure (including the sharing arrangement and conflicts of interest.)
☐ Review the past performance and the potential of present drilling prospects.
☐ Review management capabilities.

These steps are necessary if you are to make money in oil and gas. Such a review will eliminate at least potential frauds and clearly substandard offerings. More importantly, however, it should eliminate the mediocre performers who can find oil and gas and stay in business due to their promotional interest, but historically have not made money for their investors.

While such a review does not insure that a particular program will make money for you, it is the key to the formulation of an intelligent investment program in oil and gas.

Section 3: Cattle and Other Agricultural Investments

14.

The Many Facets of the Cattle Industry

INVESTORS AND CATTLE

As in real estate, agricultural investments come in many forms. However, by far the most popular form of agricultural investment has been *investment in cattle.* In fact, cattle is looked at as such a separate investment area that you may be surprised to find that the changes in the taxation of "farming syndicates" under the Tax Reform Act of 1976 apply to cattle investment.

Cattle investment itself comes in various forms, each of which has greatly varying economic and tax characteristics. The key forms of cattle investment are *cattle feeding, cattle breeding* and *ranching.*

[¶1401.1] The Cattle Industry

You can't understand cattle investment of any type without understanding how the cattle industry functions—how the various segments operate together from the raising of cattle to providing beef for your table.

The starting link in the cattle industry is the *seed stock breeder,* who operates a herd of registered purebred or hybrid cattle. The purpose of this herd is to provide cattle of superior genetic qualities for sale to other breeders who wish to upgrade their commercial herds. This upgrading is highly important, for as the tastes and needs of the American people change, our cattle herds must change to meet these objectives. Thus, when the economy permitted the raising of grain-fed beef, cattle herds sought to produce calves that were best suited to this form of nutrition. When prices of grain drove this form of beef out of the reach of the average American, it was necessary to "rebreed" our cattle herds toward cattle which could best function on grasslands.

Commercial breeders maintain large herds which seek to produce calves for slaughter, and to increase the size of the commercial herds, thus producing more and more cattle that can eventually be converted into beef.

A large part of the calves born to the breeding herd—the males and females of inferior quality—are marked for slaughter. These "culls" are "backgrounded" by grazing on grasslands until they reach "feeder" weight of 400 to 700 pounds. These feeder cattle are then sold to *cattle feeders* who place the cattle in feed lots for "fattening" to their slaughter weight of 1,000 to 1,100 pounds. However, at today's cost of grain, many cattle are pastured on grassland for the entire fattening process.

"Fat" cattle are then sold to *meat packers* for slaughter and processing. The packing house then sells the beef to *retailers* for sale to the consumer.

[¶1401.2]   Types of Cattle Investment

Cattle feeding programs seek to convert grain (or grass) into beef, at the same time offering *tax deferral* and an opportunity for *substantial profit or loss.* If the cost of converting feed to beef is less than the per-pound cost of the beef added, the cattle feeding program results in a profit to you as an investor. If the cost of feeding the cattle is more than the price of beef, you lose.

Cattle breeding seeks to increase herd size. Here, the economic name of the game is eventual *long-term capital gains.* In the meantime, the cattle breeding program offers substantial tax deductions of a *long-range "deferral"* nature. (Cattle feeding, as we will see, normally offers a short-term deferral).

Ranching seeks to combine the *benefits of cattle investment* with a long term *speculation in land value.* During the period of holding the land, the tax deductions generated by the ranching operation add tax benefits which raw land investment normally does not possess. (See ¶904 and ¶906.) Eventually, it is hoped that the ranching syndication will operate at a profit. (Whether or not this is a realistic expectation will be discussed further in Chapter 22.)

15.

Cattle Feeding—The "Go-Go" Investment

[¶1501]   **HOW A CATTLE FEEDING PROGRAM OPERATES**

As in real estate, the cattle feeding program depends upon *leverage*. Dollars put up by the investor are augmented by borrowing from a bank, with $2.00 to $4.00 normally being borrowed for every dollar of equity investment. Approximately two-thirds of these dollars are spent on the purchase of the feeder cattle—a nondeductible expenditure. However, the balance of the moneys available to the program are then spent on feed, services provided by the feed lot, and interest on the bank debt, all deductible items.

[¶1502]   **TAX BENEFITS OF CATTLE FEEDING**

As a *cash basis farmer*, so long as you are engaged in the business of farming "for profit," you can currently deduct all expenditure for the care and maintenance of your cattle, including feed, veterinary costs, and fees for services, as well as interest on your debt. This taxation of "farmers," including passive investors in cattle and crop farming, is discussed in Chapter 21.

As a result of leverage, your cattle investment will have generated a *deduction of 70 percent to 130 percent* or more of your equity investment, depending upon the degree of leverage used. While the Tax Reform Act of 1976 has affected the availability of deductions in excess of 100 percent, structuring methods still remain through which excess deductions can be secured. (See ¶1504.)

On the *sale* of your cattle, five to six months later, the proceeds are taxed as *ordinary income*. Thus, a one-time investment in cattle feeding from a tax standpoint provides *deferral only*. However, the use of a long-range program, in which the proceeds from the sale of your cattle are "rolled over" into a new cattle feeding program, can provide a deferral which can last just as long as you desire.

The effects of enhancing the deductible of your investment in the cattle feeding program through the use of leverage are illustrated elsewhere in this book. Some cattle feeding programs engage in leverage substantially in excess of the one-to-three or one-to-four equity to debt ratio discussed above. In some programs, as little as $5.00 of your equity money may be required for each $100 being made available for expenditure by the program. However, such excess leverage, while creating highly enticing first-year deductions, creates an unacceptable risk of "wipe-out" in the event of any significant fluctuation in profit margins.

[¶1502.1] Two Types of Cattle Feeding Programs

The cattle feeding program normally takes one of two forms. Under the *"agency arrangement,"* cattle purchased for and in the name of the investor are managed on his behalf by the cattleman as "agent" for his investor "principal." The other form of cattle feeding arrangement—the *syndicate*—involves the acquisition of the cattle by a limited partnership in which the investors serve as limited partners and the cattleman as the general partner. (Or, as in real estate, the general partner might be a "syndicator" who has put together the limited partnership, serving as a middleman between one or more feedlot operators and the investors.) Here, the limited partnership, rather than the individual investors, will contract with the feedlot operators for the fattening of the cattle.

An "agency" relationship normally creates less risk of audit of your tax return and reduced cost of administration. In addition, conventional financing may prove easier to secure under the agency arrangement. There is significantly less spreading of the risk than under the partnership approach, which provides more diversification plus limited liability. However, tax risks may be increased by the limited partnership approach due to increased danger of audit and the risks of being characterized as an "association taxable as a corporation."

Cattle investments other than ranching are also engaged in on a "one-on-one" basis, in which a single investor enters into a *"custom feeding" contract* with a feedlot operator or ranch owner. For the sophisticated and experienced investor, particularly one with sufficient funds to provide his own monitoring of the activities, this can avoid some of the inherent costs in a more broadly syndicated program. However, it can also offer an opportunity for disaster. Thus, unless you are in a position to assure yourself that the person maintaining your cattle knows his business and is performing his functions, and at a proper price, your "custom feeding" may cost you far more than the price you would have paid a professional syndicator to monitor your investment for you.

[¶1502.2]   Cattle Feeding Provides Flexibility in
             Your Tax Planning

Cattle feeding may prove of particular interest to you because of the *flexibility* it provides in your tax planning. Even if your eventual goals are to invest in some other area, a September or October cattle feeding investment can permit you to defer income taxation to a subsequent year, at which time a higher quality of investment opportunity may be available to you in other tax-sheltered investment areas. Through use of the "revolving" long-term investment program, or investment in a series of short-term cattle feeding investments, you can set your own timetable as to when, and what portion, of your investment dollars will be subject to taxation. However, investment in cattle feeding, short- or long-term, creates its own problems due to the leveraged nature of the investment and the high fluctuations in cattle and grain prices. A disastrous downturn in the profit margin of a particular lot of cattle can result in wiping out a substantial part of your equity investment, thus leaving insufficient or no moneys to reinvest to continue your tax deferral.

[¶1502.3]   Year-end Cattle Feeding Program
             Ended by 1976 Act

Prior to the Tax Reform Act of 1976, as a cattle investor on the *cash basis,* you were entitled to take current deductions for all your cash expenditures of feed, the care and maintenance of your cattle, and interest on your debts. While, under Section 183 of the Internal Revenue Code, this required that you be engaged in the business of *farming for profit,* this "profit motive" ("hobby loss") requirement primarily affected certain investors in exotic cattle breeds. As a result, a cattle feeding program could be formed late in the year—often on December 31—and still result in 100 percent deduction of your equity investment due to large prepayments for feed. While the IRS attempted to impose various restrictions on feed prepayments (see Rev. Rul. 75-152), the cattle feeding program remained as the most popular form of year-end deferral. However, the year-end cattle feeding program is now an interesting historical note, not a current planning technique, as a result of the Tax Reform Act of 1976: see ¶1504.

[¶1503]   **CATTLE FEEDING OFFERS SPECTACULAR
           OPPORTUNITIES FOR PROFIT—OR LOSS**

At one time, folklore told you that a key attribute of cattle feeding was its relatively low risk: "You may not make much money in cattle feeding, but at least you won't lose much."

Nothing could be further from the truth than the idea that cattle feeding is a relatively conservative investment opportunity. Instead, cattle feeding, due to the substantial fluctuations in the price of grain and beef, offers spectacular opportunities for profit—and spectacular opportunities for loss.

The price paid for beef varies widely even on a day-to-day basis. Grain prices similarly are subject to substantial fluctuations. When coupled with the leverage involved in a cattle feeding investment, your entire equity investment in a lot of cattle can be wiped out by the fluctuation in these two commodity prices. As a result, even though formerly the one-time, year-end investment in cattle feeding offered highly valuable deferral, it often, from an economic standpoint, could bear more similarity to gambling than to investment.

What then is the answer? Fat cattle cannot be *withheld from the market* to wait for a better price. Besides the increased cost of feeding and maintaining the cattle (which, after the cattle are properly fattened, does not result in additional weight gain), the quality of the beef will actually begin to deteriorate within a few days.

[¶1503.1]   The Stop-Loss Provision

One solution to the price fluctuation aspects of cattle feeding was the *stop-loss provision.* Under such a feature, the syndicator or feedlot operator would guarantee that the investor's loss per head would not exceed a certain figure. In return, the investor would agree that if the cattle were sold at a profit, a percentage of those profits—usually 50 percent—would be paid to the guarantor.

While the stop-loss provision might seem a solution to the speculative nature of this type of investment, in fact it seldom served the purpose. The loss figure was usually set at such a point that the guarantor would profit in any normal market. When markets remained in an adverse condition for substantial periods of time, as was the case in the mid 1970's, the guarantor frequently suffered financial collapse. As a result, his guarantee proved worthless to the investor. The stop-loss provisions also increased the risks that the taxpayer might be held not to have engaged in an activity "for profit," and thus might lose the majority of his deduction under §183 of the Internal Revenue Code.

[¶1503.2]   The Long-Term Approach to Cattle
Feeding Price Fluctuations

The basic solution to the speculative nature of cattle feeding has been to enter into a *longer-term "revolving" program,* so that the highs and lows would tend to balance out. For years, this approach, particularly when coupled with the "steer averaging" proved a satisfactory solution to the cattle feeding problem. Investors who would agree to reinvest the proceeds of their initial cattle feeding investment for up to three years seldom suffered any loss. Furthermore, an investment for up to five years almost guaranteed a significant profit.

Unfortunately, the disastrous economic circumstances which struck the beef industry in the mid 1970's proved that long-term investment, standing alone, was not enough to guarantee a successful cattle investment program. While it appears that the beef industry may be pulling out of its several-year slump, the experience of this earlier period shows that long-term investment, standing alone, is not enough to eliminate the spectacular profit/loss alternatives which traditionally have been more often (and equally erroneously) associated with oil and gas investment.

[¶1503.3]   Use of "Steer-Averaging"

Long-term investment in cattle feeding is itself a form of *"steer averaging."* This term—coined to compare the similarity of the approach with "dollar-averaging" in the stock market—means the effort to eliminate the risk of price fluctuation by investing a fixed amount of dollars in cattle over a period of time in "staged" amounts. Since the dollars will buy more head of cattle when beef prices are down, and fewer when beef prices are high, the "averaging" goal is attained.

In the true "steer averaging" approach, the investor's initial subscription would be paid in stages over a five-month period. At the end of the sixth month, the proceeds from the sale of the first lot of cattle would be received and would be automatically reinvested, ad infinitum. Thus, over several years, you would be investing money monthly in cattle feeding.

The steer averaging approach likewise had the effect of *indefinitely postponing* the day of reckoning as to *taxes*, until you decided to "come out" of your cattle feeding investment.

For a long time, steer averaging seemed the ideal approach to cattle feeding investment. Unfortunately, the drastic disparity between beef and grain prices experienced in the mid 1970's saw many investors wiped out in their cattle feeding investments despite steer averaging. While this does not mean that steer averaging is a bad investment policy, it does mean that, as in the case of simple long-term investment, it does not offer surefire protection.

[¶1503.4]   Systematic Hedging—A Current Technique

A current technique used at the present time by most cattle feeding syndicators is to engage on a regular basis in *systematic "hedging"* in the purchase and sale of cattle on the commodities market to offset price fluctuations. While cattle programs have normally given the syndicator the right to hedge, in the past the technique was used more sparingly. The current game plan, however, is to use hedging on a regular basis, as a definite part of the program's investment strategy.

The hedging utilized by most syndicators at the present time involves locking-in profit of $10 to $30 a head, and similarly limiting loss, by "futures" transactions. However, while this practice to date has proved relatively successful, it also creates substantial risks of its own. The potential for substantial per head profit in a rising market is eliminated by the approach. Additionally, the substantial margin reliance used in connection with "futures" trading, and the commissions charged on each "futures" transaction, can create significant risks.

Current experience would indicate that the systematic hedging approach has proven relatively successful in eliminating many of the problems previously faced by the cattle feeding investor. However, any investment in the "commodities" market has extreme risks of its own. It is far too early to say whether or not hedging will prove the answer to eliminating the present extreme speculative nature of a cattle feeding investment. And until it becomes more certain that the economy of the cattle industry has emerged from its long downhill slide, *cattle feeding remains a highly speculative investment!* (See Chapter 18.)

[¶1504]   NEGATIVE EFFECTS OF THE
TAX REFORM ACT OF 1976

At the very time that the cattle industry, and particularly cattle feeding, were suffering their worst experience in recorded history, the Tax Reform Act of 1976 dealt substantial blows to the tax benefits of cattle investment. The *"at risk" limitations* were applied to investments in farming, including livestock. While leverage can still be used to bring a cattle feeding investment to the 100 percent deductible level, excess deductions can be secured, as a general rule, only through *recourse* borrowing. The more sophisticated means of avoiding the "at risk" limitations are more difficult to apply to cattle feeding. (See ¶503.) And, in view of the speculative nature of cattle feeding, you should be very hesitant to borrow on a recourse basis for this type of investment unless you are fully prepared to pay the additional moneys represented by your recourse note.

A special portion of the "at risk" limitation provides that the taxpayer will not be considered "at risk" as to amounts protected by stop-loss and similar indemnification provisions. However, since, as noted in ¶1503.1, the stop-loss provision has proved of little benefit to investors, this change in the Tax Reform Act, while creating pitfalls for the unwary, has not significantly affected the desirability of cattle feeding investment.

[¶1504.1]   A Technique for Excess Deductions
             While Limiting Your Losses

Another technique being attempted to limit loss while still providing excess deductions is to provide that a first specified dollar amount per head loss is borne by the investor; the next amount by the sponsor; and all amounts above that limit again by the investor. In fact, hedging will be utilized to protect against any serious likelihood of investor loss. However, the question remains unresolved as to whether this "hedging," or the arrangement in general, will avoid the prohibition against "guarantees" contained in the "at risk" provisions, and will satisfy the "substantial economic effect" required for partnership allocations.

[¶1504.2]   Cattle Feeding—An Excellent High Risk Investment

The elimination of prepaid fee transactions has not removed cattle feeding as a means of tax deferral. While the year-end cattle feeding program is no longer available to the investor as a deferral vehicle, an *earlier investment in cattle feeding,* timed so that the vast majority of the syndicate's feed will have been consumed prior to the end of the year, still permits deferral, so long as the cattle will not have reached their slaughter weight until after December 31.

In one way, the effect of the Tax Reform Act of 1976 is to focus attention on the true attributes of cattle feeding—an excellent investment vehicle, under proper economic circumstances, for the investor who is willing to take a risk, and who is able partially to offset this risk by proper time-line diversification.

The prior year-end cattle feeding investments frequently were made by investors without an understanding of their potential for loss. Thus, subject to the economic considerations discussed in Chapter 18, cattle feeding may still be for you if you are willing to enter into your investment at an earlier period in the year (at which time you may be better prepared to analyze its true economic effects), thus providing yourself with tax deferral to the following year and a potential for economic gain—or economic loss.

Problems are created for the corporate investor, or for partnerships possessing a corporate partner, by another provision of the Tax Reform Act of 1976 which requires most large corporations which engage in the business of farming to use the accrual method of accounting and to capitalize certain "preproductive" period expenses. (Internal Revenue Code, §447.)

A tax advantage of cattle feeding is that it creates no "items of tax preference," and thus does not, in the year of investment, create the potential for minimum tax liability, or a dollar-for-dollar loss of "maxi-tax" benefits. However, personal-service dollars invested in cattle feeding at a 50 percent tax-bracket saving will be subject to tax as unearned income when the cattle are sold.

The Tax Reform Act of 1976 also created the concept of the *"farming syndicate."* (Internal Revenue Code, §464.) A farming syndicate is any form of enterprise in which more than 35 percent of the losses are allocated to limited partners or "limited entrepreneurs"—individuals who do not actively participate in the management of the farming activity. Similarly, any agricultural offering required to be registered with any Federal or State securities agency is a "farming syndicate," whether or not the offering was in fact registered.

The effect of the "farming syndicate" classification on cattle feeding investments is that deductions for feed or other farm supplies are allowable only in the taxable year in which the items are actually used or consumed—*"prepaid feed" deductions* are *eliminated.*

16.

Cattle Breeding—
The Unknown Quantity

[¶1601] **PUREBRED VERSUS
COMMERCIAL BREEDING**

The object of cattle feeding is weight gain. However, cattle *breeding* seeks to *produce calves*, either for sale to breeders to improve the quality of their herds—*purebred breeding*—or for sale to feedlots or meat-packers—*commercial breeding*.

The decision as to whether to invest in purebred or commercial breeding is a very significant one. Historically, the primary American cattle breeds have been the Angus and the Hereford. However, it has been customary to create other purebred herds by importation of "exotic" foreign cattle breeds to improve the weight gain or calving characteristics of commercial breeding herds.

If an "exotic" can ever be looked upon as "common," the names that usually come to mind are the Charolais, the Limousin, and the Simmental. However numerous other breeds have been imported into the United States, or created by crossbreeding. These include such names as the Brangus, the Chianina, the Gelbvieh, the Maine Anjou, and the Santa Gertrudis, to name only a few.

[¶1601.1] Premium Prices Paid for Exotic Animals

Premium prices are paid for "exotic" animals. Where prices paid normally range between $300 to $400 per cow, or $500 to $1,000 per bull, in commercial herds, purebreds may sell for $1,000 to $3,000 per cow, and up to $10,000 to $1,000,000 for bulls. Likewise, annual maintenance fees charged by the syndicator for purebred animals are normally at least twice the amount that would be paid for maintenance of your animal in a commercial breeding program

The rarity of the purebred has led to substantial investment at very high prices in such animals. However, a change in beef preferences, in thinking as to what exotics are in fact most desirable in improving herd quality, or merely in the current "fads" concerning breeding, can cause the value of high priced animals to tumble. Since both purebred and commercial animals will bring approximately the same amount at the slaughter house, investment in purebred breeding presents substantially greater financial risks than commercial breeding programs. The success ratio in actually generating profit dollars from purebred breeding is quite spotty, and a number of purebred investors have seen their "premium" animals plummet in value, or even be sold at slaughter house prices, when breeding preferences changed.

[¶1601.2]   Purebred Cattle Investments Less Liquid

Liquidity is substantially more restricted in purebred breeding operations. While annual sales are held in most of the exotic breeds, any effort to liquidate an entire herd of such animals would unquestionably depress the market price, thus destroying the very "premium" price benefits the program seeks to achieve. Accordingly, the purebred program may offer fewer benefits, both in flexibility in tax planning and in the opportunity for recovering your investment in times of financial need, than would be present in other forms of cattle investment.

There is heated debate as to the profitability of *any* breeding program. (See ¶1604.) However, in most instances, an investment in a properly structured and well-thought-out breeding program hopefully would not lead to a severe loss. The same cannot be said of purebred breeding. Where "wildcatting" in oil and gas presents extreme risks on a well-by-well basis, much of this risk can be protected against by proper diversification. Purebred breeding seldom offers this alternative. Accordingly, before throwing your hat into the purebred ring, you should thoroughly understand that you are entering into a highly speculative investment.

[¶1602]   MECHANICS OF THE CATTLE BREEDING PROGRAM

An investor in a cattle breeding program will normally acquire either an existing herd or sufficient cows and bulls to build a herd. As in the case of cattle feeding, a large degree of leverage, usually from commercial banks, is used to acquire the animals. Frequently, the animals are purchased from the syndicator or an affiliate at prices in excess of the normal market value of the animals. While this is a typical structuring technique in cattle programs, similar "mark ups" are often structured into the purchase of "feeder" animals in cattle feeding programs. (Prices can easily become so excessive that any possibility of profit from the program is effectively eliminated: see Chapter 17.)

Once the breeding herd is acquired, the cattle are bred and the offspring used to build the size of the herd, to sell to feed lots as feeder cattle, or are "backgrounded" and fattened by the program and sold directly to slaughter houses.

[¶1603]   TAX BENEFITS OF CATTLE BREEDING

While the costs of the *acquired cattle* must be *capitalized,* leverage insures a deduction which, subject to the restrictions of the Tax Reform Act of 1976, can be substantially in excess of your cash investment. The *costs of care and maintenance* of the cattle, such as feed, veterinary services, and general maintenance, including the annual fees paid to the syndicator for animal maintenance, are all currently *deductible. Interest* on the cattle loan is also deductible. In addition, *depreciation* plays a key role in the tax effects of cattle breeding.

Under the Tax Code, depreciation can be taken on the *purchased portion* of the breeding herd, though not on the resulting "calf crop." The cattle are normally depreciated over a seven-year period with *accelerated depreciation* methods being available. (If the program is the "first user" of a cattle, i.e., if the animals are first "placed in service" for breeding purposes by the program, the 200 percent declining balance method of depreciation may be used. "Second users" are limited, however, to the 150 percent declining balance method.) The 20 percent *"bonus" depreciation* and *investment tax credit* may also be claimed where applicable.

Since cattle held for breeding purposes qualify as Section 1231 assets, the *gain* from the sale of such cattle, subject to certain key rules concerning recapture of depreciation and excessive farm losses, will be treated as *capital gains.* However, as a result of the Tax Reform Act of 1969, the *holding period* for *long-term* capital gains on cattle held for breeding purposes is *24 months.*

As a result of the Tax Reform Act of 1969, upon the sale of any portion of the breeding herd, *all depreciation* previously claimed on the animals sold (not merely excess depreciation as in real estate), is *subject to full recapture* as ordinary income. Similarly, if the animals have been held for less than the specified period, any investment tax credit previously taken will be subject to recapture.

The Tax Reform Act of 1969 created the concept of an *"Excess Deductions Account"* (Internal Revenue Code, §1251) where the taxpayer's non-farm adjusted gross income in any one year exceeded $50,000, and his net losses from farming exceeded $25,000 in the same year. Farm losses taken by the taxpayer were then required to be charged against the account, which could also be credited with net farm income. Thereafter, *proceeds* from the sale of breeding cattle which would otherwise be taxable as capital gains would be *taxed as ordinary income* to the extent of prior losses. The taxpayer was not required to increase his "EDA" in years in which his net farm losses did not exceed $25,000.

The provisions of §1251 apply to any farming transaction, not merely to cattle breeding.

As a result of the Tax Reform Act of 1976, no further additions need be made to your Excess Deductions Account after December 31, 1975. Likewise, just as there is no depreciation permitted on your herd's calf crop, no depreciation recapture is required when that portion of the herd is sold. However, since even commercial breeding lies in the "question mark" area as to its ultimate profitability (see Chapter 18), the adverse tax changes imposed by the Tax Reform Acts of 1969 and now by the Tax Reform Act of 1976 have increased the risks of investing in cattle breeding programs. (See ¶1603.)

It is usual to cull a certain portion of the cattle breeding herd each year. Male animals are normally sold for slaughter. Likewise, inferior females, including those that are no longer capable of breeding, will also be culled. To the extent that these animals represent a portion of the purchased herd, the adverse tax consequences just discussed will be triggered.

If you are a first-time investor in farming, the recapture of excess farm losses under the "EDA" provisions of the tax code will thus have no effect on you. However, if you have previously invested in any type of farming operation and have incurred excess losses, requiring you to establish an excess deductions account, proceeds from the sale of your subsequent investment in cattle breeding will still be treated as ordinary income to the extent of the balance in your "EDA" resulting from your early farming ventures.

As in cattle feeding, cattle breeding creates no initial items of tax preference. Sales proceeds will create tax preferences to the extent long-term capital gains are created. But our key worry in cattle breeding seems to be not how profits will be taxed, but will there by any profits?

[¶1603.1]   Cattle Breeding Offers Tax Planning Flexibility

One very real advantage of cattle breeding is the *flexibility* which it permits you in your tax planning. Just as you can defer the recognition of income in a cattle feeding program by continuing to reinvest the proceeds of the sale of your cattle, you can pick the date on which you wish to realize the majority of the income from the sale of your breeding herd. Similarly, depreciation on your purchased cattle, and the costs of their maintenance, and interest on your debt, will create additional deductions until the herd is sold. However, this flexibility, while useful in your tax planning, does not insure that when the herd is eventually sold, it will be sold at a profit. And investment in a multi-investor "syndicate"—the normal vehicle for cattle breeding—leaves the "flexibility" in the hands of the syndicate manager.

All gain on the "raised" portion of your herd which has been held for more than 24 months, and any gain on purchased animals in excess of prior depreciation, will receive long-term capital gain treatment, except to the extent of any prior "EDA" excess farm losses. However, cattle breeding is a *long-term investment,* and you can expect *little,* if any, *cash flow* from your breeding venture for a substantial period of time.

[¶1604]   **EFFECTS OF THE TAX**
                           REFORM ACT OF 1976

The effects of the Tax Reform Act of 1969 had been severe indeed on the tax consequences of investing in breeding programs. Due to the uncertain economics of cattle breeding, the loss of these tax benefits raised severe question marks as to the desirability of investment in such programs. The Tax Reform Act of 1976 further adversely affected the tax consequences of such an investment.

The 1976 Tax Reform Act did eliminate the necessity for further additions, after December 31, 1975, to the investor's Excess Deductions Account. However, the elimination of deductions for prepaid feed affected the first-year deductions available for cattle breeding just as it affected cattle feeding. (See ¶1503.) Even more significantly, in view of the substantial excess write-offs that could be generated by cattle feeding prior to 1976, the imposition of *"at risk" restrictions* to farming investments, including livestock, significantly affected the critical tax "deferral" benefits of cattle breeding.

Most current cattle breeding programs do provide excess deductions, normally through the use of *recourse financing.* So long as the debt is truly "recourse," this is a legitimate method of providing deductions in excess of your initial cash investment. (Without such write-offs, it is doubtful that cattle breeding programs would appeal to many investors.) In addition to borrowing through conventional banking sources, efforts have been made to avoid "at risk" limitations by providing for a "staged" contribution of your agreed subscription, with the substantial portion of the subscription being payable several years in the future, often on the program's termination.

Assuming that you have invested in a carefully thought out program, your risks of being called upon personally to satisfy this recourse debt are substantially less than in the "go-go" area of cattle feeding. However, all recourse debt creates potential for liability in excess of your initial investment. Accordingly, no matter how "safe" your cattle program appears to be, you should not enter into recourse financing, despite the tax advantages, if you would not be financially capable of satisfying the debt should the program meet with unexpected reversals.

[¶1604.1]   How to Realize Write-Offs in Excess of 100 Percent

"At risk" limitations do not apply to the benefits provided by the investment tax credit. Accordingly, non-recourse borrowing can be used to bring deductibility to the 100 percent level, with benefits in excess of 100 percent being provided by the investment tax credit. Since most banks are currently willing to finance the purchase of cattle so long as the equity investment equals at least $75 per head, it is not too difficult to structure a cattle investment offering a write-off at least modestly in excess of 100 percent without resorting to recourse borrowing.

[¶1605]   HOW PROFITABLE IS CATTLE BREEDING?

The most serious question concerning an investment in cattle breeding has been the *ultimate profitability of the investment.* While cattle breeding does provide attractive long-term deferral and, if recourse financing is used, an excess write-off that is much more "assured" than that offered by most "exotic" investments, these tax benefits will not offset the downside risk if the activities are not conducted profitably. (See Chapter 26.)

Unlike oil and gas, information concerning the historical profitability of investment in cattle breeding programs is virtually nonexistent. However, it would not seem unrealistic to speculate that relatively few investors, particularly those investing in multi-investor "programs," have profited in purebred breeding operations. While given animals can certainly be sold at significant profits as the popularity of a breed is increasing, a purebred investment must clearly be looked at as a very high risk speculation.

The same lack of information affects any attempt to analyze the historic profitability of investment in a commercial breeding program. Certainly, the risks are less than in a purebred operation. However, since it will normally be five to ten years before your cattle herd is liquidated, and in view of the relatively few cattle breeding programs being offered, any conclusions concerning the general profitability of commercial breeding are difficult to draw.

Information concerning returns to real estate investors are likewise less easy to come by than figures concerning oil and gas. However, there is no doubt that while much money has been lost in real estate syndications, that substantial returns have also been realized in real estate by other investors. Similarly, while large sums of money have been lost in cattle feeding, large amounts have also been made. No such general conclusions can be drawn toward cattle breeding, either pro or con. This does not mean that you should dismiss cattle breeding, particularly of the "commercial" variety, from your tax-shelter consideration. It does mean that you should realize that you are entering into an uncertain investment area, and should take this into account in budgeting how much of your tax-shelter investment capital should be channeled into this form of investment.

17.

Pitfalls in Cattle Investment

[¶1701]   CATTLE BREEDING AND
                         CATTLE FEEDING

Both cattle breeding and cattle feeding possess definite pitfalls of which you should be aware before investing in these areas. Certain of these investment risks have a stronger impact on a particular aspect of cattle investment. For example, fluctuation in beef prices hits cattle feeding much more heavily than breeding. Due to the long-term nature of the cattle breeding investment, it is more directly affected by certain other aspects of cattle investment than is cattle feeding. However, many of the risks in cattle investment are applicable both to cattle feeding and cattle breeding.

A question to be answered in cattle breeding is whether to rely on breeding through the herd's own bulls, including the question of whether or not certain very expensive animals should be purchased. Or, should the investor rely, where necessary, on prize animals of other herds, or to use artificial insemination techniques?

The problems of acquiring extremely expensive animals have been touched upon in the purebred discussion. Normally, the herd will rely upon its own bull stock, or upon artificial insemination, rather than purchasing such "premium" animals. However, the decision to make in this regard, including the conduct of artificial insemination, is not a simple matter, and emphasizes the necessity for expert and highly skilled management and technical personnel. (See ¶1702.)

Any cattle investment is affected by factors such as weather, and calving and mortality rates. Adverse weather conditions can affect weight gain, the overall health and value of the cattle, and the rate at which cattle may die. The danger of disease is also ever present in the cattle industry. A carefully planned program of preventive health care can lessen these risks, but it will never eliminate them.

To have any hope of profitability, death losses should be held below the 2 percent industry average, and the 85 percent calving rates needed to equal or exceed the 85 percent historic industry average. Even here, however, the average calf crop figure does not tell the whole story of potential profitability. The "mix" of calves between male and female is extremely important in a breeding program, since males must be culled for slaughter, and will bring less money than a female, which can be added to the breeding herd. Likewise, if an animal must be culled from the breeding herd for slaughter, it will bring less money than was paid for the animal as breeding stock.

[¶1701.1]   Death Loss Insurance: Does It Protect Cattle Investors?

Death loss insurance can be secured for a feeder or breeder herd. Normally, however, the cost of such insurance is excessive, considering the degree to which mortality rates can be held at satisfactory levels by careful maintenance practices. However, here both the syndicator and the investor may be caught on the horns of the dilemma. If death loss insurance is provided, its cost adversely affects the potential profitability of the program. However, if such insurance is not provided, and an unexpected disaster strikes, the results could be disastrous to the investor.

Many cattle syndicators will agree to indemnify the program against excess death losses, and a guarantee against death losses in excess of 4 percent is required under the *Guidelines for the Registration of Publicly-Offered Cattle-Feeding Programs,* adopted by the Midwest Securities Commissioners Association in 1973. However, as an investor you must be sure that the syndicator possesses a sufficient net worth to render its guarantee meaningful, and that the guarantee has not been offset by excessive charges to the program in other areas. You should likewise make sure that the sponsor's net worth is reflected in reasonably liquid assets, and is not tied up primarily in feed lot and other facilities which are both illiquid and subject to loss if the cattle economy suffers disastrous setbacks.

[¶1701.2]   Other Considerations

Another key consideration in analyzing a cattle feeding investment is the degree to which the program engages in *geographic dispersion.* Weather and feeding conditions vary throughout the United States, and no firm conclusions can be made concerning the desirability of one location over another. Accordingly, many analysts feel that it is far preferable to spread the program's cattle among various feedlots located in a number of locations than to place all animals in a single feedlot or locale.

Just as in oil and gas, *expert management* is essential in any cattle operation. The careful planning and implementation of health care programs, the care with which your cattle are maintained, including the proper planning and implementation of the feeding and health care program, are essential to the profitability of your cattle investment, even in times of sound industry economics. Profit margins are quite small in the cattle industry, and the high degree of leverage utilized means that these low margins can result in a total wipe-out of your investment if the syndicator and his employees are not constantly diligent. Likewise, the industry is marked by constant changes in scientific technology concerning such matters as proper methods of artificial insemination, the use of ova transplants, and the development of a proper feeding program utilizing the most effective "mix" of high nutritive ingredients.

[¶1702] SEEK OUT EXPERT AND HONEST MANAGEMENT IN CATTLE PROGRAMS

Agriculture is a highly speculative industry. The cliche', "I always laugh at the farmer who says he doesn't believe in gambling," applies to your investment in cattle, as well as to the grass-roots farmer. And the farmer strikes of 1978 emphasize just how serious are the problems of agricultural economics during this period. When you add to this picture the acknowledged fact that, even in the best structured cattle program, you will be paying a "promotion" for your right to participate, as a passive investor, in the agricultural industry, it is obvious that you can hope to profit only if your investment is guided by expert and diligent management.

The risks discussed apply to any agricultural program, irrespective of the basic honesty of the syndicator and the cattle operator. Integrity is not enough: it must be coupled with ability on the part of management and a compulsion to see that *you* make money, as well as the syndicator and the feedlot or ranch operator.

Expert management of the type just outlined is not easy to come by in the cattle industry. Due to the legendary "independence" of the farmer, many agricultural professionals do not wish to have nonindustry investors looking over their shoulder, or to deal with the red tape that is historically associated with both public and private tax-sheltered investments. These problems are increased by the fact that, at this time, few feedlot operators find their facilities operating at full capacity (or even near full capacity) because of beef economics. For this reason, there is a temptation even on the part of the best operator to accept your investment simply to provide use for his facilities. In periods of poor economics, this can mean money loss for you even if services are provided at "cost."

Despite the historic honesty of the American farmer, cattle programs have been marked by more than their share of less reputable operators. There are numerous ways in which you, as an investor, can be gouged in a cattle investment.

[¶1702.1]   Pitfalls You Should Avoid

The following checklist outlines pitfalls to be avoided in cattle investment—pitfalls involving the reaping of excess profits by the operator which can "remove" the "speculative" nature of your investment by *insuring* that you will not profit:

- ☐ Markups
- ☐ Self Dealing
- ☐ Chicanery.

[¶1702.2]   Keep an Eye on Syndicator Markups

It is frequent practice in cattle breeding for the syndicator to sell animals owned by him to the program at a substantial markup. This guaranteed profit insures that the syndicator will benefit from forming the program. However, while increasing the depreciable base of the acquired herd, it also creates tax risks. Furthermore, if the "markup" is too high, it creates significant risks that the costs of the initial herd will never be recovered, despite an increase in herd size.

It is quite common in both cattle breeding and cattle feeding programs for services to be provided to the program by the syndicator or cattle operator, normally at a profit. Nutritionists, veterinarians, and ranch men may be made available to the program; or the syndicator's feedlot utilized in feeding the cattle. Where such services are provided on a cost-plus or "annual maintenance fee" basis, the fees, if too high, can again create a severe potential for loss. Where the fees reach such a point that a study of industry economics would show that, on a per-head basis, the cumulative effect will exceed the sale price that can reasonably be expected for the animals, a risk of tax disallowance is also created.

Finally, a number of cattle offerings have been marked by outright *chicanery*. In some instances, the program has purchased "premium" cattle at premium prices, but the animals actually delivered have been substantially inferior to those represented. Where the syndicator or cattle operator is feeding or maintaining his own animals along with those of the investor, deaths have mysteriously occurred only among the investor's animals. Weighing of animals on purchase and on sale can be marked with interesting games played with the weighing scales. And in some instances, there has been outright theft of investor cattle.

**[¶1702.3]   Investigate Monitoring of
                   Cattle Transactions**

These risks emphasize the problems involved in making a decision as to whether to invest directly with the feedlot or herd operator or to go through a syndicator "middleman." An investment made directly with the cattle man will eliminate the fees which would otherwise be paid to the independent syndicator. However, in most instances it will leave no one to serve as a watchdog for the investor in monitoring transactions to insure that cattle are in fact being properly cared for, and that the risks of excessive profiteering or outright fraud do not become a reality. However this also emphasizes the necessity that the syndicator in fact *properly* be performing his monitoring services. Ideally, transactions between the program and those providing services should be with recognized members of the cattle industry who are totally independent of the general partner and whose bonafides can be readily verified. Similarly, there should be an *independent monitoring agent* who will monitor both these cattle operators and the syndicator himself, serving solely as an agent for the investor. However, in this instance, it will be necessary to investigate the monitoring agent to insure that he is truly "independent" and possesses the expertise necessary properly to perform his functions.

"Must" reading for an intelligent evaluation of a proposed cattle investment is "How to Analyze a Cattle Deal," a chapter from Harold L. Oppenheimer's *Cowboy Arithmetic* (Interstate Printers and Publishers, Inc.: 3rd ed 1976). General Oppenheimer's book is an exhaustive review of all aspects of cattle investment and should be carefully studied before entering into any cattle program. While you cannot be expected to conduct all the analytical steps outlined, it should serve as an excellent point of departure in ascertaining whether or not the brokerage firm or monitoring service associated with the offering is properly performing its role.

[¶1702.4]   Other Cattle Investment Risks

In addition to the risks of syndicator profiteering, there are other pitfalls which can affect your cattle investment. The *hedging* which most feeding programs are currently utilizing to compensate for the speculative aspects of cattle investment creates risks of its own in view of the "margin" practices and commissions payable in connection with hedging arrangements. Likewise, there are a number of *tax risks* associated with cattle investment.

The *"hobby loss" (profit motive)* provisions of §183 of the Internal Revenue Code provide for disallowance of most of your deductions if your transaction was not entered into for profit. While this provision has primarily been used to strike down deductions taken by "gentlemen farmers" or for "model" farms or herds, it is possible that "stop loss" and "hedging" arrangements, or even the paying of fees so excessive that they destroy potential program profitability, could lead to a disallowance of deductions.

Some syndicators are attempting to avoid the *"farming syndicate"* provisions of the Tax Reform Act of 1976 by giving the investor a "voice in management." Under this approach, investor meetings are conducted periodically, at which time the investor is permitted to voice his opinion as to how his cattle operations should be run. Since the likelihood of you or your fellow investors being able to make intelligent decisions concerning cattle management are minimal, it is not anticipated that this tax "wrinkle" will be effective in avoiding the "farming syndicate" restrictions.

[¶1702.5]   Tax and Protective Techniques Useful to Investors

Numerous steps are also being taken to avoid the *"at risk" provisions* of the code. True recourse borrowing, while possessed of the economic risks previously discussed, should be effective in permitting your deductions to be increased over your initial equity contribution. However, the various steps taken to lessen risks of loss may be claimed by the IRS to serve as a form of "guarantee" or otherwise to reduce your "at risk" investment.

A tax risk of cattle programs which purchase animals at a markup is a possible position on the part of the Internal Revenue Service which would limit the depreciable base of the property acquired by you to the syndicator's *cost* and would exclude any markup from such computations. Where the animals are sold to the program at an independently established and verifiable fair market value, the IRS's position would seem untenable. However, if the markup brings the price of your purchased cattle to far above that which could be realized in arm's length industry transactions, your depreciation deductions may be threatened.

Appendix 3100-1 contains the 1973 guidelines for registration of publicly offered cattle feeding programs, adopted by the Midwest Securities Commissioners Association. The sudden drop in registered cattle offerings has resulted in little revision of these guidelines during the ensuing years. For this reason, certain of the limitations, and even certain of the requirements, may no longer be applicable in today's economic climate. However, the guidelines clearly serve as a point of departure for evaluating potential danger areas in cattle offerings, and can indicate potential pitfalls in cattle breeding as well as cattle feeding programs.

18.

Current Economics of The Cattle Industry

CATTLE SUBJECT TO CURRENT ECONOMIC TRENDS

While the profitability of investment in real estate and oil and gas are certainly affected by current economic conditions, the cattle industry is particularly subject to industry economic trends. Therefore, irrespective of how cattle investment may suit you from the standpoint of its tax consequences, it is necessary to review the economic state of the industry at the time of a proposed investment to determine whether or not cattle feeding or cattle breeding is for you—*at this time.*

Industry economic conditions have their greatest effect on investment in cattle feeding, since it is such a short-term investment. Even though a long-term "revolving" investment plan in cattle feeding is both available and sensible, the degree of leverage necessary to secure favorable front-end deductibility and the spectacular fluctuations in cattle and grain prices make it susceptible in a continuing bad market to a "wipe out" of your entire equity investment.

Commercial cattle breeding, being a longer-term investment, is not as susceptible to economic trends in the beef industry as is cattle feeding. However, due to the necessity of "culling" animals in the course of maintaining the herd, current economic trends still have a substantial economic impact on the commercial breeding program.

[¶1801.1]   Purebred and Dairy Operations
Least Affected by Trends

Purebred and dairy operations are the least affected by economic trends in the beef industry. However, as we have seen, purebred breeding is affected by economics all its own: due to the high premium which must be paid for the "in favor" purebred breeds, a falling out of favor can destroy the potential profitability of a purebred operation.

While, until recently, America's consumption has tended steadily to increase, the cattle industry has always been marked by cyclical overproduction. As prices rise, breeders tend to hold their calf crops off the market wherever possible to create greater demand. This increased demand causes an increase in beef prices. However, when the consumer "resistance point" is reached and demand and prices begin to fall, the breeder, burdened with the costs of a highly leveraged herd, has tended to rush to the market, liquidating a substantial portion of his cattle. This creates additional oversupplies, resulting in further downward pressures on price. Until this "liquidation phase" is ended, prices will continue to drop. However, as the liquidation phase ends the shortened supply of beef causes prices again to rise, starting the cycle all over again.

The beef industry faced serious overproduction and depressed economic conditions as parts of this cycle in 1952-1953 and 1963-1964. However, the period from 1974 thru 1977 represents the worst economic period for the beef industry in its history. Commencing with the 1973 consumer boycott, massive oversupply developed in the beef market, reaching an all-time high production point in 1976. The problems in the beef industry were aggravated by high grain prices due to the Russian grain sale and crop failures which created a grain shortage and resulted in high grain prices.

The effect of this crisis in the beef industry was reflected in a roller coaster decline in cattle syndications, as such offerings dipped from their high of 47 offerings for nearly 330 million dollars in 1973 to 5 offerings for 36 million dollars in 1976.* Preliminary figures gathered by the NASD in 1978 also indicate that unregistered private placements in cattle in 1977 also lagged far behind real estate, oil and gas, and even mining and other "exotics" in number of programs and the dollar amount of the offerings.

[¶1801.2]   Today's Investors Should Consider
             Cattle Syndications

Hopefully for the cattle industry and you as a potential cattle investor, 1978 and following years will see a continuation of the late 1977 improvement in beef economics. As grain prices dipped and termination of the liquidation phase created significantly shorter beef supplies, beef economics substantially improved. The economics of cattle investment were also substantially aided by the systematic hedging engaged in by those syndicators and cattle operators who were able to survive the 1974-1977 period.

---

* Based upon figures of the National Association of Securities Dealers, Inc., for offerings registered with the NASD.

The potential improvement in the current economics of the cattle industry indicates that cattle syndications are worth your investigation. However, the difficulty of securing reliable information concerning how cattle investors have actually fared, particularly in breeding offerings, suggests that care be used in determining whether or not to invest in this area. While another cyclical downturn should not be experienced by the industry for a number of years, there is no assurance that this is the case. In addition, the sensitivity of cattle investment to cattle economics clearly emphasizes the absolute necessity for assuring the program in which you invest is among the better structured and better managed of today's cattle offerings.

19.

Horse Racing Syndications

[¶1901]   **RACE HORSES AS AN**
            ALTERNATIVE TO CATTLE

The syndication of a single "prize" race horse has been common in the racing industry. However, recently the formation of horse racing syndicates on a much broader scale has gained substantially in popularity among investors. While such syndications do not approach in any way the degree of interest in real estate and oil and gas as tax shelter areas, and while they are far less common than more conventional livestock syndications, the publicity surrounding the syndication of certain "great" race horses in the recent past, the declining investor interest in cattle syndication due to fears concerning the economics of the cattle industry and the general excitement surrounding the racing industry have caused a surge of interest in utilizing the breeding of race horses as an alternative to cattle breeding for the tax shelter investor.

While cattle breeding offers excess write-offs and a long-term deferral, the degree of front-end deductibility seldom approaches the 300 to 400 percent level often associated with the "exotics" (see Chapter 26.) (The availability of the deductions offered by a cattle breeding program are relatively assured, however, subject only to the risks outlined in Chapter 17.) The race horse syndication, while based upon the rules applying to the syndication of cattle, in many ways is closer to the "exotic" syndications in the extent of its front-end deductibility, its structure, and the potentially serious economic and tax risks which surround these investments as currently structured.

Current race horse syndications primarily involve the acquisition of a group of brood mares, and possibly one or more stallion "shares," for the purpose of breeding and the sale of the "yearlings" produced from the breeding. In some instances, the training and racing of a select portion of the offspring may also be involved. And, as in other agricultural syndication areas, the race horse syndication may also involve the acquisition of a farm for ranching, the raising of crops, and potential real estate development (see Chapter 22.)

**[¶1901.1]   Race Horse Syndicates: Long-Term Tax
Deferrals, Excess Deductions, or Both?**

A race horse syndication may be structured along the lines of a cattle breeding program, generating substantial *long term tax deferral* with a *limited excess write-off* through the deduction of such items as the maintenance of the horses, interest payments on the debt incurred in connection with their purchase, and *depreciation* on the purchased animals. (The investment tax credit is not available in the race horse syndication.) However, often the horses are purchased from the syndicator or an affiliated company at a *substantial markup* over the cost of the animals to the syndicator, the purchase price being paid on an installment basis with a recourse "balloon" upon program termination. While hopefully this approach increases substantially the front-end write-offs, it also creates various tax and business risks.

The program, in addition to purchasing horses from the syndicator, will also engage the syndicator or its affiliates to perform various services, such as boarding and caring for the animals, training them, providing veterinary services, and arranging for the sale of the yearlings or of any animals not suitable for breeding purposes. The animals need not be purchased from the syndicator or an affiliate. However, the current syndication structure often provides for such purchases, thereby generating the out-of-the-ordinary initial deductions, not to mention a substantial profit to the syndicator.

The syndicator is compensated for providing the services by the payment of annual maintenance fees, boarding fees, training fees, stud fees, brokerage fees, insurance premiums, and numerous other payments. "At risk" limitations are avoided by recourse borrowings secured by chattel mortgages on the purchased animals. These mortgages may involve borrowings from conventional lending institutions engaged in the financing of livestock purchase and may also involve a "staged" subscription to the program, with a relatively small initial equity investment, the balance being payable at some date in the future, often the date of program dissolution.

**[¶1901.2]   Long-Term Capital Gain Possible
from Sale of Horses**

A horse racing syndication customarily involves the same basic tax consequences as in cattle breeding programs: long-term *tax deferral*, coupled with a hoped-for long-term *capital gain* upon the sale of the animals. *Accelerated depreciation,* customarily by the 150 percent declining balance method, can be claimed on the purchased animals (but not on the resulting foals), subject to recapture as ordinary income of all the depreciation so taken. Current deductions are provided for the fees paid the syndicator for the maintenance of the animals, for interest on the debt and for other current expenses. However, deductions for feed and other farm supplies are limited under the *"farming syndicate" rules* to deductions for items actually consumed during the taxable year.

Upon the sale of the animals, the proceeds on animals "placed in service" for not less than 24 months may be treated as long-term capital gains to the extent proceeds exceed the depreciation previously taken on such animals and any balance in the investor's Excess Deductions Account. As a result of the Tax Reform Act of 1976, an investor no longer is required to make additions to his "EDA" for excess farm losses incurred after December 31, 1975. However, to the extent the investor had incurred such losses prior to 1976 in other agricultural activities, the balance in his "EDA" is subject to recapture from the proceeds of this post TRA'76 agricultural investment.

As in other livestock investments, investment in a race horse syndication creates no items of tax preference other than the tax preference treatment of one half of any long-term capital gain upon the eventual sale of his animals at a profit. Ordinary income will also be subject to tax as unearned income.

[¶1902] **EXPERT MANAGEMENT ESSENTIAL
WITH PRIZE HORSES**

The risks of investing in a race horse syndication include those present in any livestock breeding activity, compounded with many of the same problems which apply to "purebred" cattle breeding, plus a few risks of its own. The same risks of disease, weather, accident, and death loss apply to the race horse syndication; these problems are compounded by the delicate nature of the animals involved. And while expert management is required in cattle, it is even more essential, and less easy to obtain, in the raising of prize horses.

Proper selection of the breeding stock, and their mating to appropriate stallions, is crucial. Even when the breeding stock has been properly selected, the question remains as to whether they will breed and produce outstanding progeny. The value of the progeny will also be a question mark. Moreover, all of these problems are intensified by the extreme competition in the horse breeding industry and the need to compete with established stables in the purchase of superior breeding stock, in securing the service of desirable stallions, and the sale of the herd's offspring.

The conflicts of interest created by the fee structure of the typical race horse syndication, particularly the system of fees for service and markup on the sale of animals to the program, create the same threat to the eventual profitability of the program as are present in cattle breeding. The problem is heightened by the fact that it will be most difficult for you, as an investor, to determine whether the animals being acquired for your herd are in fact appropriate breeding stock, and whether the price being paid for such animals, and the fees being paid for their maintenance and training, are reasonable. It will likewise be difficult for you to secure reliable information concerning the likelihood of the program being conducted at a profit. Often, it will prove equally difficult to evaluate the capabilities of the proposed management.

The economics of race horse syndication are even more difficult to evaluate than those of cattle breeding, even of the "purebred" variety. Furthermore, you should realize that, as in purebred cattle breeding, you are being locked into a long-term investment, like it or not. As in cattle breeding, an early liquidation of your interest will trigger highly undesirable tax consequences. At any time that you wish to sell your interest, tax liabilities will accrue. Whereas in cattle feeding or commerical breeding, a market will always exist for your animals, it will be much more difficult to liquidate a substantial herd of purebred racers.

[¶1902.1]   Race Horse Syndicates—Are They a Viable Alternative?

Race horse syndications may prove an alternative to the problems which have recently surrounded investments in cattle. However, until more experience is available concerning the economics of investment in this industry for the passive investor and until the industry matures as an investment vehicle, such investments must be reviewed with caution as being of extremely high risk.

The risks just mentioned also create various tax risks. While most of these risks have been discussed in connection with cattle investment (see Chapter 17), the "profit motive" requirements of §183 create particular problems for the investor in a race horse syndication. As in cattle breeding, if your venture is structured in such a way that there would have been no possibility for you to profit, the IRS may argue that the "profit motive" was not present. Similarly, if you are investing primarily for the "status" of being the owner of a race horse or race horses, your activity could be looked at as a "hobby" rather than as a true business venture. (A general presumption of profit motive arises concerning most business ventures if your venture operates at a profit for two out of five taxable years. However, more favorable treatment is provided by §183(d) of the Internal Revenue Code for the breeding, training, showing, or racing of horses: the activity is presumed to be engaged in for profit if gross income exceeds deductions for two out of seven consecutive taxable years.

20.

Other Forms of Livestock Investment

[¶2001]   SPECIAL TAX BENEFITS
                      OF LIVESTOCK INVESTMENT

The principles concerning tax-sheltered investment in cattle and race horses are equally applicable to most other forms of livestock. While poultry is expressly excluded from the §1231 asset category (Internal Revenue Code, §1231(b)(3)) and thus is not entitled to capital gains treatment on sale, other forms of livestock are afforded §1231 treatment. Furthermore, livestock other than cattle and horses is entitled to "long-term" treatment after the customary 12-month holding period, rather than the 24 months which apply to cattle and horses. (Internal Revenue Code, §1231(b)(3)(B).)

The same rules concerning initial tax deductions, depreciation, and the investment tax credit which apply to cattle apply generally to syndications of other livestock. Only horses are excluded from the investment tax credit. (Internal Revenue Code, §48(a)(6).) However, under §1245(a) of the Internal Revenue Code, all depreciation deductions on the acquired animals are subject to taxation as ordinary income when the animals are sold. Similarly, upon sale, any balance in your Excess Deductions Account resulting from pre-1976 farm losses would also be subject to recapture as ordinary income. As a result of the Tax Reform Act of 1976, no further additions for "excess farm losses" need be added to your EDA. And, again as a result of the 1976 Tax Reform Act, any investment in livestock is subject to the "at risk" limitations.

[¶2001.1]   Advantages of Poultry Syndicates

One form of "livestock" farming syndication which has found some use among investors has been the purchase of hens for commercial egg production. Prior to the Tax Reform Act of 1976, the purchase price of these hens could be deducted as an expense, subject to the limitations noted above. Often, a substantial portion of this purchase price could be borrowed, thus generating excess deductions. However, the "farming syndicate" restrictions imposed a special limitation on the deductibility of poultry expenses, requiring that the cost of poultry be capitalized and deducted ratably over a 12-month period (or the poultry's useful life if less than 12 months) where the poultry was purchased for use in trade or business. Internal Revenue Code, §464(b). The cost of poultry purchased for sale can be deducted only in the taxable year in which it is disposed of.

Other than the poultry syndications, there has been no effort made by tax shelter syndicators to make widespread use of these other forms of livestock as a form of tax-sheltered investment in farming. This does not mean that it would not be possible to structure such livestock investments, or that it has not been done in the past and will not continue to be done in the future. However, from your standpoint as a potential tax-sheltered investor in agriculture, the difficulties of analyzing industry economics, the appropriateness of the fees being charged as compared with normal industry standards, and the likelihood that you, *as an investor,* will profit from the syndication, should cause you to prefer other agricultural syndication areas unless you are particularly knowledgeable, or particularly attracted, to investment in this type of livestock.

21.

Agricultural Syndications

**FARM INVESTMENTS OTHER
THAN CATTLE**

While investment in cattle is a form of agricultural syndication, for years the cattle "tail" has wagged the dog. Agricultural syndications other than cattle have lagged significantly behind cattle. Thus, of the 16 agricultural syndications filed as "offerings to the public" with the National Association of Securities Dealers in 1977, only two were "farming" as contrasted with "cattle" syndications. The amount of "public" cattle offerings registered with the NASD in 1977 was over 57 million dollars, versus 17.5 million dollars in "farming" syndications.

For years, a number of commentators have suggested the potential profitability of agricultural syndications in areas other than livestock. A number of substantial offerings have been made in the agricultural area, notably in the California "intrastate" market and in several large SEC-registered offerings. To date, however, the farming industry has not turned to tax-sheltered investors as a source of industry capital in any degree comparable to that which the oil and gas operator, the real estate developer, or the cattle man has used you as a capital source.

In the view of the fact that constantly increasing farm costs and the uncertainties of the farming economy are creating pressures on agriculture to find new financing sources, it is well for you to understand the potential rewards and pitfalls of this area of investment in the event you are approached to become a "passive farmer."

[¶2101.1] Cash Method of Accounting a Key Advantage

Even though you are a passive investor in the farming industry, you will generally be permitted to take the same tax advantage as the farming professional, so long as you meet the requirements of §183 of the Internal Revenue Code that you have engaged in your farming activity "for a profit." A key advantage to you as a farming investor is your ability to make use of the *cash method of accounting*. Under this accounting method, and subject to the "farming syndicate" restrictions discussed below, you will be permitted to currently deduct your expenditures for such items as feed, seed, fertilizer and other similar farming supplies, which in other businesses would be required to be capitalized. However, until any gain from your farming activity is "realized" by the sale of your farmland, livestock, or crops, you need not report any unrealized appreciation for tax purposes. Frequently, such gain will be granted desirable capital gains treatment as a §1231 asset, subject to recapture as ordinary income of an amount equal to any balance in your excess deductions account resulting from any pre-TRA'76 excess farm losses.

While the Tax Return Act of 1976 made no effort to change your right as a passive farming investor to currently deduct all expenses other than those affected by the "farming syndicate" rules, *corporations* were not dealt with so charitably. Thus, with certain exceptions for small business and family corporations, or corporations having gross receipts of $1,000,000 or less, the *accrual method of accounting* must be used, and expenses incurred prior to the disposition of the first marketable crop (*"preproductive period expenses"*) must be *capitalized*. The same rule applies to partnerships engaged in the trade of business of farming if a corporation is a partner of the partnership. Neither of the rules applies to timber activities, other than those involving fruit or nut trees. (Internal Revenue Code, §447)

What do these differences in *accounting method* mean to you as an agricultural investor? Look at the difference in how various expenditures are treated for tax purposes to the *fulltime farmer*, to you as an investor in a *"farming syndicate"* (see Internal Revenue Code, §§464 and 278(b)), and to a *corporation* required to utilize the *accrual method of accounting* under §447:

Initial Deductibility*

Type of Expenditure	Total Amount	Fulltime Farmer	Farming Syndicate	Corporate Farmer
1. Partially consumed farm supplies (25%) no crop sales	$10,000	$10,000	$ 2,500	$ -0-
2. Reproductive crop expense—no crop sales	10,000	10,000	10,000	-0-
3. Reproductive grove or vineyard expense	10,000	10,000	-0-	-0-
4. Harvested but unsold crops	10,000 cost	-0-	-0-	(10,000)
5. Crops sold, but revenue uncollected	10,000 selling price	-0-	-0-	(10,000)

Non-livestock farming activities consist of the development of farm-land as an orchard or vineyard, or the development of potential farmland for the raising and sale of various vegetable crops. Another form of farming—the timber syndication—will be discussed in Chapter 23. In some instances, you will be engaged in a "roll-over" operation, where mature farmlands which produce short-term crops ranging from flowers to "row" vegetables offer short-term tax deferral, similar to cattle feeding. However, in many instances, your agricultural investment will be aimed at developing lands which were not previously used, or were only partially used for farming, into producers of vegetables, fruits or nuts. Since it will take a number of years for the trees or vines so planted to reach maturity and thus begin generating substantial income, or for the lands to be developed into mature farmlands, the intervening costs of development, when coupled with depreciation and interest deductions, will create sig-nificant losses for tax purposes, thus generating (subject to the "at risk" limitations) deductions substantially in excess of your equity investment. Considerable depreciation deductions will also be created by capital ex-penditures for fences, buildings, farming equipment, and trees and grapevines. The level of such deductions normally are in the 130 percent to 170 percent level associated with cattle breeding, rather than reaching the 200 percent to 400 percent deductions associated with the "exotics" (see Chapter 26).

But deductions, as we know, aren't enough. If your farming venture will always operate at a loss, you will end up losing your hard dollars. So where is the opportunity for profit in agricultural investment?

[¶2101.2]   How Investors Profit From
             Agricultural Syndicates

The investor in an agricultural syndicate hopes to profit in one of several ways. First, at the end of the "loss cycle," after his crop land, groves or vineyards have reached maturity, he hopes that his farming operations can be conducted at a profit through the *sale of the agricultural products.* However, in view of the uncertainties surrounding farming profits, this might not be enough to attract you to agricultural investment.

A second form of potential profit is the expectation of *appreciation in* the value of the land as *farmland.* Historically, agricultural land, which is in increasingly short supply, has tended to increase in value as productivity per acre improves and the population expands. Finally, again as a result of expanding population, the potential for *sale of the land as* a development site for *commercial, industrial, or residential real estate* is seen as a source of profit.

[¶2102] ## THE BENEFITS OF
AGRICULTURAL INVESTMENT

Even after the changes imposed by the Tax Reform Act of 1976, the tax benefits of agricultural investment are substantial. Where crop farming is involved, current expenses, including the "preproductive" period expenses of developing the land for agricultural use, are currently deductible. In addition, the Code specifically authorizes deductions (subject to specified limitations) for expenditures for clearing land to make it suitable for farming use (Internal Revenue Code, §182), for fertilizing or conditioning the farmland (Internal Revenue Code, §180), or for leveling or grading the land, constructing drainage ditches or earthen dams, or other expenditures for soil or water conservation or to prevent erosion. Expenditures for conservation purposes or land clearance taken pursuant to §§175 or 182 are subject to recapture as ordinary income, in whole or in part, if the farmer disposes of such farmland within ten years of its acquisition. (Internal Revenue Code, §1252) However, as a result of the addition of §464 to the Internal Revenue Code by the Tax Reform Act, deductions may no longer be taken by a "farming syndicate" for "prepayments" for feed, seed, fertilizer, or other farm supplies; expenditures for such items are now subject to deduction only in the year in which they are used or consumed.

Prior to the Tax Reform Act of 1976, expenditures in planting, cultivating and maintaining fruit or nut groves, orchards or vineyards could be taken as current deductions even though a period of several years might elapse before the lands would bear crops. The only exception to this rule—imposed by the Tax Reform Act of 1969—was the requirement that such expenses incurred in connection with citrus or almond groves be capitalized. However, as a result of an amendment to §278 of the Internal Revenue Code, expenditures by "farming syndicates" to develop any fruit or nut crops are now required to be capitalized.

The profitability of an agricultural investment, aside from its "land speculation" potential, is affected by risk factors analogous to those which apply to the cattle industry. Weather is obviously of critical concern, as is the availability of water—a constantly increasing problem. Insects and disease can wreck an otherwise profitable crop. Market conditions are critical; and, as in cattle, prices for agricultural products are highly unstable. Furthermore, in recent years, labor problems have intensified, leading not only to labor strikes but to nationwide boycotts of certain farm products.

The risks just mentioned apply to the career farmer as well as to you as a potential passive farm investor. However, certain additional risks apply to passive investments in the farming industry:

(1) The *need for competent management* is just as critical in crop syndications as it is in cattle and other livestock investments. Here, again, such management is difficult to find or replace; and the caliber of the proposed management may be difficult for you to evaluate.

(2) The *fee structure and conflicts of interest* in a proposed agricultural syndication may create many of the same problems as in cattle investment. However, while dealing with an affiliated company is common in agricultural investment, services are frequently provided for in the form of a share of farm income or a fee based upon productivity of the land. While this does not mean that the fee structure may not be so high as to destroy the economics of your investment, it at least may be easier to analyze than the multicharge structure which frequently plagues the cattle investment.

The substantial period between the initial development of the land and the production of commercial crops is a key to the availability of early year tax losses. However, this also creates problems which may affect the financial return from your agricultural investment. The period of delay creates an increased exposure to rising costs and changes in the tax laws. Similarly, this can mean that the investment capital and loan proceeds secured by the syndicator may not prove adequate for the development of your farmlands and the conduct of the farm operations until such time as the farming operations become self-sustaining. And it goes without saying that agricultural investment is not for you if early cash flow is one of your investment objectives.

[¶2102.1] Look for Crop Profits Plus Land Appreciation

As a potential investor in agriculture, it will normally prove extremely difficult for you to analyze the potential profitability of your investment insofar as the proposed farm operations are concerned. How do you analyze management? And aside from the questions of general market conditions and price stability as they apply to the agricultural industry in general, how do you determine whether the particular farmland on which your operations will be conducted is appropriately situated, is of high quality, and whether the one or more crops to be planted thereon are appropriate for the area and are among those that offer the maximum opportunity for profit (and a minimum opportunity for loss) in today's farm economy.

Agricultural syndications may involve various relatively small tracts of farming land or may offer you an interest in tens of thousands of acres to be developed for multiple crops and other agricultural purposes. Under the economic conditions that have historically faced the farming industry, it would not seem wise for the profitability of your investment to rise or fall based upon profit from the agricultural operations alone. Thus, in analyzing the profit potential of an agricultural syndication, you should give careful consideration to the likelihood that the land will appreciate in value, either for agricultural use, or as the potential site for urban real estate development.

22.

Ranching

**BENEFITS OF RANCHING
AS A TAX SHELTER**

Ranching seeks to provide you with the same investment benefits as are present in a "crop" agricultural syndication, using cattle or other livestock as the source of interim tax deduction and eventual profit from operations rather than vegetables, fruits, or nuts. As in the agricultural syndication, expenditures for the current maintenance of your livestock are currently deductible (see Chapter 16), as are expenditures for land clearance, fertilization and conditioning, and for soil and water conservation and erosion prevention. (See Chapter 21.)

Expenditures for fences, buildings and ranching equipment create substantial depreciation deductions, and similar deductions are available, for the "purchased" portion of your livestock herd. Likewise, except for expenditures for the acquisition of horses, the investment tax credit is also available.

The tax benefits of ranching create the potential for significant initial write-offs for long-term tax deferral. As in the case of cattle breeding and other "crop" agricultural activities, however, these deductions can be lost if it is determined that your activity was not engaged in for profit. (Internal Revenue Code, §183). Likewise, sale proceeds from the sale of purchased livestock will be subject to the recapture of all depreciation previously taken on the animals and to a potential recapture of the investment tax credit if the animals have not been held a sufficient period of time. The proceeds from the sale of your land are also subject to the same recapture of land "enrichment" and land clearance and soil and water conservation expenditures where the land has been held for less than 10 years as applies to agricultural syndications. And sale proceeds are further subject to recapture of any balance in your Excess Deductions Account.

As in any other farming syndicate, as a result of the Tax Reform Act of 1976, expenditures for fertilizer and feed can no longer be prepaid, but can be deducted only as consumed or used. (Internal Revenue Code, §464.)

[¶2201.1]   Sale of Land a Source of Profit

The risks surrounding the economics of the cattle industry and the pitfalls of cattle investment apply equally to ranching. However, as in the agricultural syndication, a key motivation for your entering into a ranching venture frequently will be your desire to profit through an eventual sale of the land.

Analyzing the potential economics of a ranching activity, while not easy, may prove easier than trying to determine whether avocados, pistachio nuts, or a given wine grape can be raised at a profit. Cattle industry economics seem to be improving, particularly where cattle feeding or commercial breeding activities are involved. However, it is still difficult to point to a significant number of widely held ranching programs which have gone from investment to liquidation stage, with a resulting profit to the investor.

While ranching offers a dual opportunity for profit, it also offers a triple opportunity for loss. An *unprofitable cattle operation* can wipe out the profits you might otherwise receive from the resale of your ranch land. If the land has been acquired at an *unrealistically high price,* a loss on its sale could destroy the profitability of a successful cattle operation. And if *both phases* of your activity *result in a loss,* your outlook will be doubly bleak. Accordingly, it is critical to carefully analyze a proposed ranching investment both as to the economics of its cattle and land speculation aspects to determing the potential profitability of the investment.

23.

Timber Syndications

[¶2301]   **TIMBER OFFERS TAX ADVANTAGES**

For years, you have probably heard that there are tax advantages in investing in timber. Your interest in this investment area may have been heightened by hearing that the Tax Reform Act of 1976 treated timber most kindly. And indeed it did. Not only does the definition of "farming" for purposes of applying the "at risk" limitations of §465 of the Internal Revenue Code exclude trees (other than fruit or nut trees) from its coverage (see Internal Revenue Code, §464(e)); this same definition avoids the requirement under §464(a) that amounts paid for farm supplies may be deducted only in the year in which they are used or consumed. By a similar definition, an exception is also provided to the requirement that corporations engaged in the business of farming (or farming partnerships which have a corporation as a partner) must compute their taxable income on the accrual method of accounting and capitalize "preproductive period expenses." (Internal Revenue Code, §447(a)). Excluding timber activities from the definition of "farming syndicate" under §464(c) likewise avoids the requirement that expenses incurred in maintaining or developing the tree growth must be capitalized if incurred before the first taxable year in which the grove will bear a yield in commercial quantities. (Internal Revenue Code, §278(b))

Despite these tax advantages, timber syndicates have not been widely offered to other than a very special group of private investors. Unlike agricultural syndications, where the failure of the syndicates to assume a greater share of the tax-shelter market has primarily been a result of uncertainty as to profitability, the lack of widespread popularity of the timber syndicate has primarily arisen due to the *nature* of the tax benefits provided.

When you think of the term "tax-sheltered investment," you are probably thinking of a "shelter" which provides a substantial degree of initial write-off. However, in studying the timber syndication, you will discover that very little initial "tax shelter" is provided. (Efforts to apply the same "advance royalty" approaches used in coal syndications (see ¶2605) were discouraged by the Internal Revenue Service in one of its "Halloween massacre" revenue rulings, which held that timber is not a "mineral property" entitled to the advance royalty benefits formerly provided under Treasury Regulations. See Rev. Rul. 77-400. For this reason, one SEC-registered tax shelter offering bore, in bold faced type on its cover: **"THIS PARTNERSHIP DOES NOT OFFER THE TAX BENEFITS COMMONLY ASSOCIATED WITH TAX SHELTERED INVESTMENT."**

While high initial tax benefits could arise from timber syndications involving young trees, few investments of this type have been generally available.

[¶2301.1]   Long-Term Appreciation and Special Depletion Allowances

The objectives of a tax-sheltered investment in timber are *long-term appreciation,* permitting you to *defer any realization of gain* resulting not only from inflationary factors but from the growth of your timber "stand," plus the ability to partially *shelter the proceeds* from the sale of your timber through *long-term capital gains* and a very special form of *"depletion allowance."* As do ranching and agriculture, timber may also offer a *"land speculation"* feature.

Despite the lack of initial tax benefits, you still may be interested in further exploring the possibility of a timber investment. If you can live without "deep shelter," the tax and economic benefits of *holding* a timber investment can be quite attractive. (They can also be quite risky, economically.) Also, if your deep-shelter needs have been satisfied by investment in a "excess write-off" program, you may wish to *blend* that investment *with an investment in timber.* (See ¶2802.)

[¶2302]   HOW TIMBER INVESTMENTS WORK

So how does a timber investment work? First, to secure the depletion and capital-gain benefits which are critical to the investment, you must have acquired an "economic interest" in the timber. One way of accomplishing this is to purchase timberland. This is what you may well do, particularly if the land appreciation aspect of a timber investment is attractive to you. However, you can also secure an opportunity for capital gains by purchasing "cutting rights" in the timber. (To secure the tax benefits associated with acquisition of a "cutting contract," a contract permitting you to cut timber for your own account, you must be sure that the contract has been prepared in such a way that you will be considered to have an "economic interest" in the timber rather than merely being compensated for performing a service in cutting the timber. See *Weyerhaeuser Co. vs. U.S.*, 402 F. 2d 620 (9th Cir. 1968).)

In acquiring your timber property, the syndicator will cause the value of the marketable standing timber to be evaluated by a forester, the process being referred to as *"cruising."* A substantial portion of the purchase price of your timber lands can be financed through borrowing. Often, these borrowed amounts may be arranged so that they can be paid as timber is cut, based on a minimum annual obligation. The costs of the acquisition of your timberland must be capitalized, and payments on the mortgage principal are non-deductible. However, cruising costs and other costs of maintaining your timberland, such as burning underbrush and "thinning" undesirable trees, are currently deductible. Also currently deductible are the carrying costs of your land acquisition, such as interest payments on the mortgage and ad valorem taxes.

Natural perils aside, a timber investment creates an almost sure "growth" in value. Unlike oil and gas and other natural resource investments, your trees will be increasing in size until they reach full maturity. However, this "appreciation" does not create any tax liability until the timber is cut or sold. And a great deal of flexibility exists as to when you realize this increase in value, both in your timing of the disposition of the timber, and your election under several options available to you as to methods of selling the timber.

If you sell your timber outright, and have held it for a period of one year, you're entitled to §1231 treatment, so that *gains* can be treated as *long-term capital gains*, and any *loss* on the sale as an *"ordinary"* rather than "capital" loss. However, whether you are a holder of timberlands or merely have a contract to cut the timber, you may elect under §631(a) of the Internal Revenue Code to treat your own cutting of the timber as a sale of the timber cut during that year, irrespective of whether the timber is disposed of in that year. If so, your tax is computed by deducting your adjusted basis for depletion purposes in the timber cut (see below) from the *fair market value* of the timber as of *the first day of the taxable year in which the timber was cut.* So long as you have held the timber for 12 months prior to the *first day of that taxable year,* the cutting will be considered a long-term capital gain. Note that the end of the 12 month period is measured not from the date on which the cutting occurs, but from *the first day of the taxable year* in which the cutting is conducted.

A third method of securing long-term capital gains on the sale of timber is a sale where you retain an *"economic interest,"* such as a portion of the proceeds from the sale of the timber. Where you do sell timber, retaining an economic interest, you *must* report the income as provided in §631(b); unlike §631(a), the method is not elective. Under §631(b) of the

Internal Revenue Code, such a sale is taxed in the same manner as a §631(a) sale, with the 12-month period being measured from the date of acquisition to the date the timber is cut (rather than the first day of the taxable year as in the case of §631(a)).If you receive payment under the contract before the timber is cut, you can elect to treat that as the date of disposition of the timber rather than the date it is cut.

Under either of these §631 methods, when you later sell the logs, your gain or loss will be based upon the difference between your sale proceeds and the fair market value on which you paid your earlier tax, with either being treated as "ordinary" income or loss for tax purposes.

In determining the amount of your capital gain on the sale of your timber, you will also secure the benefit of a *special depletion allowance* provided for in §611(a) of the Internal Revenue Code. This is somewhat unusual, since timber, unlike other natural resource assets, is not necessarily exhausted as it is sold: the amount of timber disposed of may be more than offset by past growth.

No "percentage" depletion is permitted on sale of timber as is the case of oil and gas or other minerals. However, a form of "cost" or *"unit" depletion* is permitted. Section 611(a) merely says that, in the case of timber, a "reasonable allowance for depletion" will be permitted. The "unit" method of depletion for timber is a result of IRS regulations. This depletion is computed by multiplying the number of "timber units" cut (i.e., the number of thousand board feet) by a "depletion unit," arrived at by dividing the adjusted basis of your standing timber—the cost of the standing timber less prior depletion—by the number of thousand board feet of "timber units" on hand.

In determining the depletable basis for depletion purposes, the "cost" of your acquisition must exclude any portion of the purchase price reasonably allocable to the land.

[¶2303]   **TIMBERLANDS CAN GENERATE EARLY CASH FLOW**

The type of timberlands purchased by you will determine whether your investment will generate cash flow at a reasonably early date, or should be looked to only as a long-deferred source of income. If your land includes some relatively mature trees along with those of lesser maturity (an "uneven stand"), your forestry consultant will undoubtedly recommend periodic harvestings, with the resulting income. Frequently, good forestry practices involve acquiring such tracts of land which will then be reseeded, with new trees grown to constitute a constantly regenerating timber asset. In other instances, you may acquire timberlands that will require years before the trees have reached sufficient maturity to permit harvesting.

As in most agricultural and natural resource areas, it is anticipated that the demand for timber will substantially increase in future years. While over half of our country's timber is used for lumber, a substantial portion goes into paper-related products, and some for firewood. However, the timber market is also marked by substantial cyclical changes in the prices paid for the timber products, with resulting economic risks to you. (Unlike most agricultural areas, these risks are at least in part offset by the fact that your asset is literally "growing" in value, and that you may further hold your "product" off the market rather than being forced to sell it when crops are ripe.)

Besides the economic factors affecting the timber industry, there are other significant risks to a timber investment. Forest fires, weather conditions, insects and disease, all can be a threat to your timber stand. Likewise, on relatively unattended timber properties, there is a threat of actual theft. Environmental factors are also becoming significantly more important, including such problems as regulation concerning erosion, wildlife, and ecology in general.

As a passive investor, you will find that the same problems that plague agricultural and cattle investment—a difficulty in securing reliable information concerning the economics of the industry, a fair amount to pay for your timber property, and a reasonable compensation to the forestry experts who are managing your investment—will be a concern. Affiliate dealings can be expected. However, to date, possibly due to the nature of those investing in timber, the extreme abuse of affiliate dealings do not appear to have been as significant a problem. (This offers no assurance that these problems would not exist in a particular program offered to you.)

The more serious problems from your standpoint would appear to be questions as to the economics of timber investment which, due to the lack of experience in this investment area, remains largely an unknown. The difficulty in evaluating the reasonableness of the proposed acquisition price; and the lack of any front-end deep shelter are also factors. However, to the extent that deep shelter is not an investment necessity for you, or can be secured through other investments, timber remains an interesting source of possible capital appreciation and tax-favored treatment on sale.

Additional Readings: Part Two

Chapters 8-10: Real Estate

DROLLINGER, *Tax Shelters and Tax-Free Income for Everyone*, Part One (Chapter 1) (Epic Publications, Inc.: 3rd ed. 1977)

FRESHMAN, *Principles of Real Estate Syndication* (Parker & Son, Inc.: 2d ed. 1973)

HAFT and FASS, *Tax Sheltered Investments*, Chapter 1 and 3 (Clark Boardman Co., Ltd.: 2d ed. 1974)

KANTER, "Real Estate Tax Shelters: Everything You Wanted To Know but Did Not Know What to Ask," *Taxes—The Tax Magazine.* (Dec. 1973)

LEVINE, *Real Estate Tax Shelter Desk Book* (Institute for Business Planning, Inc.: 2d ed. 1978)

New Challenges in Real Estate: Integrating the Disciplines (Property Press: 1977)

Real Estate Investment under the New Tax Reform Act of 1976 (Property Press: 2d ed. 1977)

ROULAC, *Modern Real Estate Investment* (Property Press: 1976)

ROULAC (ed.), *Real Estate Securities and Syndication Workbook* (National Association of Realtors: 1973)

ROULAC, *Real Estate Syndication: Principles & Applications* (RESD, Inc.: 1972)

Tax Incentives—A Tool for Financing Business Growth and for Sheltering Income (Arthur Andersen & Co.: 2d ed. 1977)

Chapters 11-13: Oil and Gas

ANDERSON, *Oil Program Investment* (Petroleum Publishing Co.: 1972)

BURKE and BOWHAY, *Income Taxation of Natural Resources* (Prentice-Hall, Inc.: 1978)

DROLLINGER, *op. cit.,* Part One (Chapter 2)

GRACER, *Now That You Have Invested in Oil and Gas* (Investment Dealers' Digest: 1972)

GRACER, *What Every Investor Should Know About Oil and Gas Investments* (Investment Dealers' Digest: 1972)

HAFT and FASS, *op. cit.,* Chapter 5

LOMASNEY, "The Importance of Assessments in Oil & Gas Drilling Programs," *Investment Dealers' Digest* (April 3, 1973)*

MOSBURG, "Evaluating Drilling Program Performance," *Financial Planner* (Dec. 1972/Jan. 1973)

MOSBURG (ed.), *Financing Oil & Gas Ventures* (The Institute for Energy Development, Inc.: (1977)

MOSBURG, "The 'New Look' in Oil and Gas Investment," *Investment Dealers' Digest* (Mar. 25, 1977)*

SHOCKEN, "Cash In vs. Cash Out—The Real Question in Evaluating Oil and Gas Drilling Programs," *Investment Dealers' Digest* (Sept. 3, 1974)*

STEWART, "Evaluating Investment Merits of Oil and Gas Drilling Programs," *The Commercial and Financial Chronicle* (Sept. 24, 1970)

Tax Incentives—A Tool for Financing Business Growth and for Sheltering Income, op. cit., Chapter 3

WHEELER and WHITED, *Oil—From Prospect to Pipeline* (Gulf Publishing Co.: 1958)

Chapters 14-18: Cattle

DROLLINGER, *op. cit.,* Part One (Chapter 4)

FELDMAN, "Cattle Feeding from A to Z," *Investment Dealers' Digest* (Mar. 27, 1973)*

HAFT and FASS, *op. cit.,* Chapter 6

OPPENHEIMER, *Cowboy Arithmetic* (Interstate Printers & Publishers, Inc.: 3rd ed. 1976)

REID (ed.), *Corporate and Executive Tax Sheltered Investments,* Chapters 18-19 (Presidents Publishing House, Inc.: 1972)

Tax Incentives—A Tool for Financing Business Growth and for Sheltering Income, op. cit., Chapter 5.

Chapters 19-23: Other Agricultural Investments

BURKE and BOWKAY, *Income Taxation of Natural Resources,* Chapter 22 (Prentice-Hall, Inc.: 1978)

DROLLINGER, *op. cit.,* Part One (Chapter 4 and 5)

HAFT and FASS, *op. cit.,* Chapter 7

LEVINE, op. cit., Chapter 22

---

* Reproduced in Mosburg (ed.), *Structuring Tax-Sheltered Investments under the Tax Reform Act of 1976* (The Institute for Energy Development, Inc.: 1977)

LOWENHAUPT, "Tax Advantages of Investing in Timber," *Tax Ideas* (Prentice-Hall, Inc.: 1969)

REID (ed.), *Corporate and Executive Tax Sheltered Investments,* Chapters 20-21 (Presidents Publishing House, Inc.: 1972)

Tax Incentives—A Tool for Financing Business Growth and for Sheltering Income, op. cit., Chapter 5

PART THREE
The Unconventional Tax Shelters— Hereinafter of the "Exotics"

24.

What Can Become A "Tax Shelter?"

[¶2401]   **ANY VENTURE CAN BE A TAX SHELTER**

While the typical investor usually thinks of oil and gas, real estate, cattle, or possibly motion pictures when he thinks of a "tax shelter," any venture can be converted into a "tax shelter" if the project will be marked by a high level of initial losses due to start-up costs. The "tax loss" characteristics are particularly apt to be present where the affected industry relies heavily on leverage and has a high level of depreciable assets. In addition, Congress has provided express tax incentives for a number of industries in addition to real estate, oil and gas, and cattle.

Investors have been offered tax shelters in such diverse areas as chinchillas, oyster, salmon, and catfish farming, and bees, to mention only a few. However, the likelihood that you will be given an opportunity of being "stung" in a bee venture is relatively remote. However, there are a number of tax shelter areas that, while lagging significantly behind real estate and oil and gas in popularity, still represent a significant portion of the venture capital expended in the search for tax shelter and profits each year.

For instance, over four times as many coal and other mining ventures were offered investors in 1977 as livestock and farming offerings. Furthermore, in such areas as motion pictures, equipment leasing, and books and master records, the number of offerings during 1977 probably e-qualled the number of "private" oil and gas offerings.

[¶2401.1]   Excitement Plus Extremely
            High Tax Deductions

The intrigue in these unusual tax shelters is that they normally combine extremely high initial tax deductions, often in the 300 percent to 400 percent or higher range, with the excitement of an industry such as motion pictures or the recording industry. The major pitfalls are the tenuous legal grounds on which many of these deductions lie, the eventual date of reckoning when "phantom income" strikes, and the shaky economic basis for many of the investments. This last pitfall is heightened by the virtual impossibility of securing reliable information concerning the profitability of both the proposed venture or of the industry in general, and the absence of any "track record" concerning results to prior participants.

As an investor, you may know little concerning the oil and gas industry, or how to evaluate the potential profitability of a new apartment project or a proposed cattle investment. However, you will now walk through areas even more foreign to your day-to-day experience: motion pictures, equipment leasing, records and books, coal, and Broadway plays. For this reason, we have chosen to label these as the "exotic" investments.

The following chapters will attempt to guide you in two ways. First, we will explore the common threads that run through many of the exotic areas. New "exotics" are constantly being conceived. Coal syndication, the "hottest thing going" in the excess write-off investment area in 1976, was virtually unheard of before that year. Likewise, the profusion of book and master record syndications presented to investors in 1977 represented an investment area that had barely been dreamed of the preceding year.

With the help of the guidelines presented in these chapters concerning the "exotic" shelters, you and your advisor can determine whether or not you wish to consider an investment in *any* type of exotic, whatever form future tax preferences may take. Following this general discussion, we will focus on some of the more currently popular forms for the "exotic," so that if this investment area does seem to be for you, you can understand its benefits and pitfalls.

25.

Investing in the "Rarities"

GOLD, GEMS, ART, WINE, ANTIQUES, ETC.

Some "exotics" are not true tax-sheltered investments, but primarily appeal to your desire to profit through the appreciation in value of a rare or scarce commodity such as gold or silver, paintings, gems, coins, commemorative medals, or antiques. In some instances, such as certain offerings involving wine, fine art, and lithographs, these investments are structured in such a way as to provide the possibility of considerable front-end tax benefits. (See ¶2604). However, normally such investments appeal to the investor's desire to own an asset which he believes offers a substantial hedge against inflation. The investor is also attracted by the expected substantial profit due to the scarcity or rarity of the asset, and the intrigue of dabbling in coins, gems, or fine art.

Undoubtedly, if you are fortunate or wise enough, and if you secure expert advice, an intelligent and long-range investment program in the rarities may yield rewards in both financial and emotional areas. However, far too many investment "opportunities" that are presented to you in the rarities will grossly overestimate the degree, and the likelihood of profit. Since such offerings rarely attempt to comply with any of the "full disclosure" or other requirements of Federal and State securities laws, the discussion of their investment potential will be anything but evenhanded.

[¶2501.1] Investing in Rare Commodities
Requires Rare Skills

Before investing in a rare commodity, you need to be aware of the following potential problems in such an investment:

1. *Most "rarity" investments will be highly illiquid.* While some investments in gold, silver, or foreign coins may be characterized by a market in the event you find it necessary to liquidate your investment, you should seldom expect that the appreciation in value which moti-

vated your investment can be realized during the immediate future. A rarity investment, even a good one, should thus be undertaken only if you are prepared to hold your acquisition for a substantial period of time.

2. *Many "rarities" are overpriced already.* In some instances, you may be acquiring an asset which has a definite, established value. This would be the case where precious metals, gems, antiques, or paintings by established artists were involved. However, often the "rarity" of the item will have been taken into account in the current price. The asset may have reached the limits of its appreciation, at least for the forseeable future. In other instances, the asset may be offered to you at substantially in excess of what a discerning purchaser would pay for the article. And it may be quite difficult for you to determine the degree to which the asset is likely to appreciate in value, or has reached the upper limits of its appreciation potential.

3. *Many "rarities" may not be all that rare.* It seems highly unlikely that future investors and collectors will be standing in line to acquire the plethora of commemorative coins and plates which are currently flooding the market. This does not mean that an attractive piece may not be something which you wish to acquire for your personal pleasure. However, before being stampeded into making the acquisition for investment purposes, you should seek competent advice as to the likelihood of any future market among collectors for such an item.

4. Even in the case of true rarities, *such items are frequently offered based upon a substantial markup to the seller.* In many instances, this will also be coupled with fees for a subsequent sale of the item. Your asset therefore, must appreciate a sufficient amount to cover these incoming and outgoing fees before you will even "break even" on your investment. Furthermore, the appreciation must cover the "time value" involved in having your money tied up for the substantial period of time which will normally be required before that appreciation takes place.

Unless you are an extremely discerning connoisseur or an expert in the value of precious commodities, a rarity investment normally seems called for only if you will also receive substantial pleasure from owning your "investment" acquisitions. Advice from a professional in the particular area also is a must to insure that the price and quality of your proposed purchase are in keeping with industry values.

26.

The "Exotic" Shelters

[¶2601] THE DESIRE FOR EXCESS DEDUCTIONS — BENEFITS AND PITFALLS

Some of the basic problems of the "excess write-off" programs were discussed in Part One of this book. These included the need to understand that the substantial initial write-offs offered by such programs offer deferral only and are subject to subsequent recapture, crossover, and taxes on phantom income. Also covered was the distinction between the relatively assured deductions offered by oil and gas, real estate, and cattle and the "gray area" risks of many deductions in the "exotic" area. Discussed, too, was the need for providing for your "day of reckoning" when taxes must be paid on "phantom income."

The "exotics" primary appeal is the potential for a *high initial write-off*, usually in the 200 percent-plus area, generated through *heavy reliance on leverage*.

The risks of investment in the "exotics" are easy to detail, and are ones with which you must be completely familiar before you decide to make an investment in this area. A full understanding of these risks is extremely important to you, because, unlike the "risks" of investing in oil and gas, real estate or cattle, the pitfalls of the "exotic" investment are almost certain to occur.

Not every oil well is dry, not every real estate project fails to lease up, and not every cattle feeding cycle sees beef prices plummet while grain prices rise. However, the following dangers in the "exotic" area typically occur in practice, not merely in theory:

1. *The venture frequently does not make money.* This does not mean that you will lack a "profit motive," even though there is always the possibility that the IRS may disagree. However, when the risks of the investment area and the degree of success which the venture must attain to be profitable are balanced against the likelihood of success, the dangers outweigh what would normally motivate an investor if it

were not for the extreme initial tax benefits.

The economic dangers vary significantly with the type of "exotic" investment undertaken, and also vary depending upon the amount of initial deductibility provided. Thus, the likelihood that you will profit from an investment in equipment leasing differs greatly from the similar likelihood of profit from a "master record" (so does the initial deductibility).

The higher the initial write-off, the more successful your venture will have to be in order for you to come out on your hard dollars. Similarly, the higher the initial deductibility, the less likely that this profit will occur.

2. *With certain exceptions, the high initial deductibility will invariably be challenged on audit if the auditing agent understands the investment and the tax principles involved.* With the possible exception of equipment leasing, deductions are normally based upon positions rarely approved, and often directly contrary to, the public pronouncements of the Internal Revenue Service, or are dependent upon extreme extensions of those pronouncements. There is also a substantial likelihood that, if challenged, the contentions of the IRS will be sustained.

3. *It will be extremely difficult for you to evaluate the investment merit of the proposed investment.* There is usually little available information concerning the profitability of such investments in general, of any historic return level, or of any "track record" concerning prior investments (with the possible exception of the initial deductions claimed). You will also find it difficult to secure the services of an independent technical analyst (see ¶2902.2) to give you an objective evaluation of the likelihood of profit from such an investment or the soundness of the proposed project. (But why should you worry: the syndicator will normally provide you such an analysis from an "independent" source selected by him.)

[¶2601.1]   Initial Deductions from Write-Offs Are Only Tax Deferrals

What motivates an investor to take the admitted risks involved in an excess write-off syndication? Unfortunately, many invest simply because of the size of the initial deductions. They may not understand the risks of disallowance and that the deductions offer deferral only with taxes eventually payable on the phantom income. However, tax overreaching leads many investors to seek two-to-one and higher initial write-offs without regard to the eventual tax liabilities, their hard dollars at risk, and the economics of the project.

Most investors seem absolutely unwilling to deal realistically with the fact that there will be a day of reckoning for their earlier excess deductions. The intrigue of having the negative drain of "taxes payable" converted into a positive current cash flow is well-nigh overwhelming. Taxes payable at some "far distant" day seem of little importance. And excess write-off syndicators often play up to this attitude by emphasizing that "extensions" can be granted on the nonrecourse note, that a "balloon" subscription payment can easily be satisfied out of proceeds on dissolution, or that such notes or balloon payments may well be ignored on program termination. Other investors seek to "avoid" ("evade") taxes due on phantom income by simply "forgetting" to report such income on their tax returns.

The notes necessary to provide the leverage for excess write-off investment, whether recourse or nonrecourse, will create future tax liability whether satisfied out of proceeds generated by the venture or the eventual foreclosure of the notes. At least a partially successful venture may generate some revenues from which a part of the taxes can be paid. However, "evasive" tactics such as neglecting to pay taxes when due can lead directly to the serious potential of "tax fraud."

Strangely enough, in certain "excess write-off" areas, and among certain investors, the investment was not considered a "success" unless it was relatively certain to be a failure! For instance, while many motion pictures have been syndicated to investors who were seeking a film that would have a substantial chance of being at least a "box office" success (see ¶2602), other investors primarily sought movies which they were sure would not "go," for nothing can prove a greater disaster to the investors seeking excess write-off than a project which produces merely enough revenue to pay off the nonrecourse note. If the project is to be that much of an economic success, the income normally will be realized in the very early years of its exploitation. Since most of the revenues from the project will be used to pay off the nonrecourse obligation, a nondeductible expenditure, but will still be taxed to the investor, this means that phantom income will almost immediately offset the previous year's excess deductions. On the other hand, if the project generated little if any revenue, the phantom income hopefully would not fall due until foreclosure of the note, which would occur a number of years in the future. Thus, the adverse tax consequences could be postponed for a significant period of time, giving the investor the "time value" of his earlier tax benefits in the meantime. This practice of investment in projects of little economic merit obviously frustrates the objectives of the tax incentives, and is a major and understandable basis for Congressional and IRS hostility toward such syndications.

Taxes on "phantom income" may come due far earlier than one would expect. An audit may lead to an early disallowance of claimed tax benefits and a loss of the "time value" advantages that an excess write-off investment may legitimately offer. Accordingly, any investment in an excess write-off program entered into without a clear and realistic understanding of the potential effects of disallowance of the deductions and of the certain recapture of the excess tax benefits is an open invitation to tax disaster.

[¶2601.2]   Excess Write-Offs Offer Definite Benefits to Some Investors

Despite the admitted risks of an investment in the "exotics," if you are an affluent investor with particular need for immediate tax shelter and if the need for improvement in your present cash flow position outweighs the future cash requirements that will be thrust on you when the tax on phantom income comes due, you may wish to give consideration to an investment in the exotics for an excess write-off investment does offer the following benefits:

1. *The deduction may not be picked up on audit or, if disallowed, may be sustained* by the courts. (You should not go into an exotic investment, however, if you are not willing to fight any IRS challenge.)
2. *The deduction will serve as an interest-free* (if unchallenged or sustained) *or low-interest loan from the government,* so long as the tax opinion on which it is based was sufficiently well reasoned that it does not subject you to fraud or negligence penalties. Since you will have the use of the government's money until your return is audited (three to five years in most instances), or hopefully until the phantom income falls due, either on the proceeds from the venture or upon the eventual foreclosure of the notes, the time value of your initial tax savings may offset to a great extent the eventual tax liability and possible hard dollar loss. In any event, it will permit you to do some long-range tax planning to take advantage of more economic tax shelter areas which you may not be able to afford in the absence of an immediate, more substantial sheltering, or which currently may be unavailable to you due to the scarcity of high quality tax-sheltered investments at year end.

Unfortunately, the savings generated by the time value of money from your interest-free or low-interest "loan" from the government frequently do not offset the loss of your hard dollars if your exotic investment proves an economic failure. Where no other tax shelter opportunities are available, or if current cash needs, off-set by an assured future improvement in your financial liquidity, dictate, an investment in the exotics may prove beneficial. However, any intelligent use of the write-off proved by the exotics requires the following protective steps:

1. *The economics of the venture should be carefully analyzed.* While any investment in the exotics will be of high risk, some offer no economic potential whatsoever. The greater the economic potential, the more the tax risks will be offset.

2. *You must set up a "sinking fund" or make other financial arrangements, so that you can satisfy your subsequent tax liabilities when they fall due.* This is the pitfall that traps most investors, who immediately "spend" their tax savings without realizing that the benefits were of deferral only and to a great extent will not be offset by future cash returns: the investment did not provide a permanent "deep shelter." This "sinking fund" requirement is wise even where you feel your investment does make economic sense and will result in some or even a substantial economic return, as well as in the cases where the economic return potential is far more risky.

But what of the investment that is relatively sure to generate early year revenues and "phantom income," such as the production service company (see ¶2602) or the equipment leasing syndicate (see 2603.) And are there other ways of dealing with the eventual adverse tax consequences?

Other than the "sinking fund" and similar approaches, the typical advice to the investor has been to continue to invest in excess write-off investments. However, this approach creates a vicious circle for you as a taxpayer. Such future investments, rather than providing shelter for your normal sources of income, may now merely provide a "holding action" for your phantom income obligations. Thus, your tax problems pyramid. Furthermore, in view of the present administrative and Congressional hostility to excess write-offs, it is highly dangerous to assume that deductions in the 300 percent to 400 percent level will be available indefinitely into the future.

For all the reasons discussed above, it is less than wise, even if you are in search of excess deductions, to invest in any form of "exotic" syndication if the underlying project does not have some economic potential. If you do invest in an "exotic" where some substantial cash return is realized on your investment, then the time value of your excess deductions will compensate to a great extent for many of the risks of the investment and may convert what would otherwise be a rather modest "cash on cash" return, or even a moderate loss, into a profitable investment. However, the time value of money will not compensate with a loss of the substantial part of your hard dollar investment.

Few "exotics" will be presented to you as sure money losers. Instead, the syndicator will assure you that this project is good and will "go." He will be believable (that's his business: he probably fools even himself), and you will *want* to believe him. (Everyone would like a 400 percent write-off from a "sure thing.")

To avoid losing money in the exotics, you must *force yourself to be realistic*. How likely is this movie to outstrip *Jaws* at the box office (see ¶2602), for the record to outsell a *Beatles* album (see ¶2604), for your play to outrun *Fiddler on the Roof*, for that is what most exotics must do to break even.

The Appendix contains an analysis of the economics of an exotic investment, using a hypothetical book purchase as an example (see ¶2604):

1. *Increasing leverage, and increasing the purchase price, increases initial deductibility.*
2. *Excessive increases can jeopardize eventual profitability to you.*
3. *A high degree of project success is necessary for you to "break even," even taking into account the time value of your deductions.*

Money can be made in a Broadway play, a motion picture, or the syndication of a "hit" record. However, as noted in ¶¶2602, 2604, and 2606, the *likelihood* of profit in such an investment, even where the venture possesses economic potential, is less strong than in many of the other investment areas we have looked at.

Many "hit" movies and plays never return a profit to their investors when the high costs of the "name" stars and directors are deducted, along with the heavy cost of production. As a matter of fact, some analysts feel that your chance of profit may be less in such "name" productions than when you gamble with a talented "unknown" (of course, your risk of total loss will likewise be less in a "name" venture).

Before an oil man drills, he prepares a "risk/reward" analysis of his drilling prospect, which involves dividing the estimated return *if* the well is productive by the estimated chances of productivity. Thus, a well which offers a potential 4 to 1 return with a 50 percent chance of producing (risk/reward ratio: 2 to 1) is looked at as a better risk than a well which should produce 10 times its cost if productive, but stands less than a 1 in 20 chance of producing (risk/reward ratio: 0.5 to 1). While the "risk/reward" estimation is by no means an exact science, it is a definite planning tool in the oil and gas industry.

A study of industry statistics undoubtedly would show that the risk to reward in most "exotic" areas would cause an oil man to run.

[¶2601.3]   The Higher the Write-Off the
             Greater the Trade-Off

The economic potential of an investment in the exotics can almost be measured by the degree of write-off provided. While there is no assurance as to upside economic potential, the down-side risk is often a direct corollary of the amount of write-off offered. Thus, while excess write-offs of 130 percent to 150 percent can often be secured in potentially economic ventures, write-offs of 200 percent to 400 percent are definite danger signals; and higher 800 percent to 900 percent write-offs usually indicate an almost assured economic failure. Why? Because the higher the write-off, the greater the "trade off" between cash flow/appreciation potential and initial deductibility. (This is particularly unfortunate, since the amount of hard dollars at risk remain constant irrespective of the degree of the excess write-off.) Also, the amount of the initial deductibility offered by the syndicator is also a function of how hard it would be to raise the venture capital in the absence of such a write-off. (A 200 percent deduction will attract most investors interested in excess write-offs, so long as the investment possesses some economic potential.)

The following paragraphs will cover those "exotic" investments most apt to be presented to you—motion pictures, equipment leasing, coal, books and "master" records and artworks, and Broadway plays. However, as the tax laws constantly change, so does the creative structure of tax-sheltered investments.

Today's exotic "fads" may mature into tomorrow's solid investment areas, financed with greater emphasis on economics and less on high initial deductibility, or may fade from the scene. If so, they will be replaced by new investment "opportunities." The principles outlined in this part of the book will serve as a guideline for analyzing the pitfalls of tomorrow's new breed of exotics.

[¶2602]   **MOVIE SYNDICATIONS**

Prior to 1976, the motion picture syndication was the most popular form of investment for the taxpayer who sought particularly large front-end deductions (300 percent to 400 percent or even greater), and who was not particularly concerned with the economics of his investment. This meant that many legitimate movie properties were not financed through the "syndication" approach. However, many low-budget foreign and "porno" movies were financed through syndications, with the tax benefits often depending upon a definitely nonspoken assumption that the movie would be a failure at the box office. By the mid-1970's, the movie syndication was also being used to finance a large number of movies featuring "name" stars, directors, and studios. However, fears that the Tax Reform Act of 1976 would deal harshly with movie syndications (and it did), and that such provisions might be applied retroactively (they were), led to the replacement of the movie syndication with the coal syndicate in 1976. On

January 1, 1977, when the "partnership borrowing" provisions of the Tax Reform Act affected investment in coal (see ¶2605), investor interest shifted to book and master record syndications.

Despite the effects of the Tax Reform Act of 1976, motion picture syndications are still in existence, although their tax benefits are of greater value to corporate investors than to individuals. So, you may wish to consider a possible movie investment, *if*:

☐ You are the owner of a corporation with tax problems, particularly one with a dangerous level of accumulated earnings, or a professional corporation.

☐ You are intrigued with this form of investment and satisfied with an initial write-off only slightly in excess of 100 percent.

☐ You are willing to take certain tax risks.

[¶2602.1]   Types of Movie Syndications

Prior to the Tax Reform Act of 1976, the two primary forms of investment in motion pictures were the *negative pickup (amortization) syndication* and the *production service company*. While both the negative pickup and production service company approaches were subjected to the "at risk" provisions of the Tax Reform Act, the production service company was hit with additional tax restrictions and a highly unfavorable 1977 ruling from the Internal Revenue Service. Accordingly, while you need to be familiar with both these syndication approaches, our discussion will center primarily on the negative pickup syndication.

[¶2602.2]   How the Amortization
("Negative Pickup") Syndication Works

In the *negative pickup,* the syndicate (usually a limited partnership) will purchase a completed film, the purchase price consisting in part of a cash down payment and in part of a nonrecourse note, due in seven to ten years, and payable out of the specified percentage of the receipts from the movie. The syndicate enters into an arrangement for distribution of the movie with an established distributor who arranges for exploitation of the movie through theater bookings and possible foreign exhibition, television showings, etc. For this, the distributor will receive from 40 percent to 50 percent of the net receipts of the movie, after deduction of distribution costs. The balance of the receipts are paid to the syndicate, with a large percentage of these receipts being applied to the nonrecourse note.

The arrangement just discussed hopefully will generate a substantial excess write-off in the year the movie is acquired through *depreciation* and the *investment tax credit* applied to the *entire leveraged purchase price*. Frequently, an extremely accelerated amount of depreciation is attempted using a "low ball" estimate of future revenues under the "income forecast" method. But see IRS Rev. Rul. 78-28. And use of the income forecast method can affect the availability of the investment tax credit, as well as leave very little depreciation shelter for the "phantom income" arising when the syndicate's share of distribution receipts are applied to payment of the nonrecourse note.

Book, master record, and master art work syndications rely on basically the same principles utilized in the negative pickup syndication. See ¶2604.

As indicated, while the negative pickup syndication creates extremely high deductions in the year in which the movie is acquired by the syndicate, there is substantial "phantom income" in future years as net receipts are paid to the syndicate, thus creating taxable income, but are then applied to satisfy the nonrecourse note, a nondeductible expenditure. Interest payments on the note will be deductible, subject to a possible "investment interest" limitation. If the receipts are sufficient eventually to retire the nonrecourse note, the purchase will result in a profit to you as an investor. However, as has more often proved the case, if receipts only equal or are less than the amount of the note, you will have secured a deferral only and will end up losing all or part of your "hard dollar" investment. And if the nonrecourse note has not been satisfied by its due date, which should not extend beyond the useful life of the movie, foreclosure of the note will result in additional phantom income in an amount equal to the unpaid balance.

[¶2602.3]   How the Production Service Company Works

The *production service company* approach involves the formation of a syndicate to "produce" a film for a motion picture studio or someone else who owns the property rights to a particular movie. The production service company (*a partnership*) pays for production of the movie by putting up a certain amount of dollars in cash, and borrowing the balance on a nonrecourse basis, with the loan frequently being guaranteed by the movie studio or the anticipated distributor of the movie. Normally, three or more dollars are borrowed on a nonrecourse basis for each dollar invested in the production service company by its partners to provide its equity capital. The studio agrees to pay the production service company a specified fee, payable in installments. Part of the fee—a lesser amount than the estimated cost of producing the movie—will be payable irrespective of movie receipts. However, a portion will depend upon the performance of the movie at the box office.

It was the hope of investors in a production service company that, as a cash basis taxpayer, the use of nonrecourse borrowings to pay for deductible production costs would create substantial excess write-offs as the movie was produced. Subsequent installment payments of its fee would of course create ordinary income. And the fact that much of these revenues had to be applied to the repayment of the nonrecourse borrowings created a "phantom income" tax obligation in these later years. Also, a serious problem would arise for the taxpayer who had invested dollars entitled to the "earned" income protection in the syndicate, since it was unlikely that the dollars received would be entitled to similar protection.

[¶2602.4]   How the Tax Reform Act of 1976 Affects Negative Pickup and Production Service Company Syndications

As indicated the Tax Reform Act of 1976 substantially affected the popularity of both negative pickup and production service company syndications, particularly for the individual investor. Since the "at risk" limitations apply to such investments, it has become particularly difficult for an individual investor to secure the 300 percent to 400 percent write-offs which lead many to invest in motion picture syndications. Furthermore, §280 of the Internal Revenue Code now provides, as a result of the Tax Reform Act, that a production service company must capitalize its production costs as to all noncorporate partners. A relatively disastrous 1977 IRS Revenue Ruling further held that the nonrecourse borrowings did not constitute an indebtedness of the production service company where the loan was guaranteed by the producer. IRS Rev. Rul. 77-125. The Revenue Ruling also suggested a disastrous method of tax treatment for the limited partners' hard dollar expenditures. As a result, the production service company approach is currently in disfavor.

[¶2602.5]   Today's Approach to Movie Syndication

For the investor interested primarily in excess write-offs and less interested in investment economics, other types of "exotic" syndications are proving far more popular at this time. (Whether *any* investor should go into an excess write-off without consideration of the economics has been discussed at ¶2601.) However, excess write-off potential still remains in movie syndications for corporations, which are not subject to the "at risk" restrictions of the Tax Reform Act of 1976. (See ¶503. The restrictions do apply to Subchapter S corporations and personal holding companies.) Similarly, an individual, despite the "at risk" rules, can utilize nonrecourse leverage to raise his deductions to 100 percent of his equity dollar investment, additionally claiming the benefits of the investment tax credit, which are not subject to the "at risk" restrictions. By *recourse borrowing*, the deductibility can be raised to its pre-TRA'76 levels. However, the recourse borrowing approach is highly dangerous in view of the speculative nature of motion picture production. And any efforts to provide guarantees or "take out" arrangements for the recourse loan will lead to a loss of the excess deductions. See IRS Rev. Rul. 77-398.

A current "at risk" technique is to utilize a loan which provides for *initial recourse liability* for a specified period, converting to nonrecourse status in a subsequent year so long as scheduled payments have been made to that date.

In view of the admitted excitement of involvement in the motion picture business, you may want to investigate the possibility of movie investment, so long as the film is an intriguing one with economic potential. If you are still considering an investment in motion pictures, however, you should fully appreciate the risks involved. In addition to the provisions of the Tax Reform Act there have always been numerous grey areas concerning the deductions available in connection with a negative pickup syndication. (We will assume that you are not considering investment in a production service company.) If the investment is not structured properly, it can be treated as a loan by you to the producer rather than a purchase of the film, or the IRS may take the position that you entered into a joint venture or a mere licensing arrangement. (If the arrangement were so treated, the syndicate would lose its depreciable base in the negative and its entitlement to the investment tax credit.) These dangers are heightened if the person to whom the nonrecourse obligations are owed also participates in profits from the film, as distributor or otherwise, over and above his security interest in film receipts. Dangers are also increased if you acquire only limited territorial rights to the movie, television rights are not included, or where the seller maintains a degree of control over exploitation of the movie greater than normally would be reserved by a creditor.

[¶2602.6]   Tax and Economic Risks

If the price at which the movie is sold to you is excessive, and does not represent a reasonable "fair market value" of the movie, you will lose the right to take depreciation or the investment tax credit on any portion of the nonrecourse debt. See Rev. Rul. 77-110, 1977-16 I.R.B. 7, and *Estate of Franklin*, 544 F. 2d 1045 (9th Cir. 1976). Having the purchase price substantiated by appraisals from recognized independent industry sources is thus a basic protection. And if you do not play the normal role of an owner, you stand a serious chance of the loss of your deductions. This does not mean that you cannot make arrangements with an experienced distribution company for the distribution of your movie. However, if you do not demand appropriate accountings, etc., your chance of deduction disallowance is significantly increased.

The rules concerning claiming the investment tax credit on motion pictures have always been highly complicated, particularly where foreign films are involved. The Tax Reform Act of 1976 clarified but restricted the availability of the investment tax credit for motion pictures (see Internal Revenue Code, §48(k)), and added various complicated limitations.

A key risk in motion picture investment, aside from the tax risks just discussed, is the extreme difficulty in analyzing which movies will make money and which will not. As one commentator has noted,

> "There are fewer less exact sciences than determining the fair market value of an unreleased film. The calibre and past box office success of the cast and director may be helpful, as well as the final negative costs, but otherwise the value is pure speculation." (Tax Management Memorandum: Tax Shelters—Current Developments Motion Picture Tax Shelters (BNA: TMM 75-07, March 31, 1975).)

Besides the general uncertainties as to results at the box office, the normal distribution arrangements for syndicated movies heighten the economic risks. Frequently, the distributor's arrangement with the exhibitor will call for the distributor to receive a percentage of box office receipts. Exhibitors have been known to take extreme liberties in reporting such receipts to the distributor.

Furthermore, the distributor then deducts his distribution costs from these "gross" receipts to arrive at net receipts from distribution. As much as half of these net receipts may go to the distributor for his services before any distribution is made to you. And the more you have paid for your movie to heighten the tax benefits, the longer the lion's share of your receipts will go to the seller of the movie before you see any profit from your investment.

The excess reliance on leverage to increase initial deductibility is highly unfortunate in movie syndication. As we have seen, it is very unwise to acquire an interest in any movie which you do not believe has real potential for economic success. Since your excess deductions are all subject to eventual recapture in the form of taxes on phantom income, it would seem far better, if you are intrigued by movie investment, to structure your investment on a far less aggressive tax position, settling for 100 percent deductibility, thus permitting you to take a greater share of the revenues from the movie. (Since the distributor of a syndicated movie is frequently related to the producer/seller of the picture, this will probably permit you to negotiate more favorable distribution terms.) However, before entering into a motion picture, you should realize that you have entered into a high risk venture indeed, where the risks are far greater than in the most speculative exploratory oil and gas venture.

[¶2603]   ADVANTAGES OF EQUIPMENT LEASING

Equipment leasing offers far less front-end deductibility and overall excess write-off potential than most "exotic" tax-sheltered investments. However, the potential for economic profit from an intelligently planned equipment leasing venture is substantially greater than in most of the "exotics," due to the predictable cash flow (assuming a financially stable lessee), the reduced significance of "speculative" factors, and the potential "residual value" of the equipment upon the termination of the lease. Unfortunately, if you are an individual taxpayer, the tax benefits of equipment leasing are substantially reduced for you as compared with those available to corporations. The same restrictions which apply to individuals also apply to Subchapter S corporations and personal holding companies.

The high cost of purchasing major items of equipment, plus the impact on the equipment user's financial statement, have made the leasing of such equipment by the end user far more attractive in many instances than its outright purchase. Where an airplane, a computer, railroad rolling stock, ships, oil drilling rigs, or even an entire industrial plant is involved, the corporation may find that purchase of the equipment would require substantial investment of its working capital, high loan payments, and the generation of tax benefits which actually exceed the equipment user's needs. Furthermore, the user stands a risk of being stuck with obsolete equipment. By entering into a leasing arrangement in lieu of an outright purchase, and permitting the lessor of the equipment to receive the tax benefits, the equipment user normally incurs lower costs in the form of rentals than it would be required to make on the bank debt which financed the acquisition, and can effectively achieve 100 percent financing and an improvement in its working capital. Furthermore, the "financing" available to it through the leasing route to some extent will be "off balance sheet" in nature, and may permit it to acquire equipment which could not have been purchased otherwise.

The lessor of the equipment, if the lease is properly structured, will receive *significant tax benefits* with substantially less risk than is normally associated with many tax-sheltered investments, and, subject to the risks of equipment obsolescence and overestimation of residual value, should have entered into an *economic transaction* as well.

[¶2603.1]   Mechanics of Equipment Leasing

In the typical equipment leasing transaction, the equipment manufacturer will sell the equipment to a syndicate (or corporate lessor) for cash. The syndicate then leases this equipment to the lessee-user in return for a fixed rental. The syndicate will secure the capital necessary to acquire the equipment both through the investors' equity contribution to the syndicate, and through borrowings (often at a 4 to 1 ratio) from a conventional lending institution. The lending institution normally will require both a security interest in the equipment and a pledge of the lessor's rights under the lease.

The rental payments to the lessor will permit it to meet its loan obligations to the lending institution and will provide some amount of cash flow. The level of these payments is normally less than the combined principal and interest payments which the lessee would have made to the bank if it had purchased the asset outright.

At the end of the lease, the lessor will be left with residual value in the equipment. However, frequently the lease will be for a period which is not only less than the useful life of the property, but may also be less than the period necessary to retire the mortgage. And both the residual value, and the possible earlier obsolescence of the equipment, are the "unknowns" that create a substantial part of the risk in equipment leasing.

[¶2603.2]   Tax Benefits and Economics

Taxwise, the lessor can take *depreciation* at an accelerated rate (double declining balance and often "bonus" depreciation) and can deduct its interest payments on the loan. In addition, if it is a corporate lessor, or if the lease is an "operating" lease (which requires that the lease be for less than half of the depreciable life of the equipment among other tests), *investment tax credit* can be claimed. This will provide some substantial deductions in the initial year, often reaching the 100 percent level, with such deductions rising substantially in excess of 100 percent (often to the 200 percent to 300 percent level) by the end of the second to third year as a result of the depreciation deductions.

As rental income continues, but must be applied to a great extent to amortize the mortgage, and as depreciation and interest deductions reduce, a *"crossover" point* will be reached where income is no longer sheltered from taxation and where a negative tax position is actually created. As a result, approximately halfway through the life of the lease, the overall deductibility of the investment will begin to decrease, finally leveling out at an approximate 130 percent to 150 percent rate. Furthermore, *all depreciation* (not merely excess depreciation) will be subject to *recapture* as ordinary income to the extent of any gain over the adjusted basis of the property if it is sold, given away, or the mortgage foreclosed.

Tax planners have tried numerous techniques to permit investors to avoid the effects of crossover by disposing of property in such a manner as to avoid these recapture problems. However, no truly satisfactory method as yet has been developed.

The rental payments are normally structured in such a manner that, cash on cash, relatively little if any profit is made on the lease. It is thus from the residual value that economic profits will come, ignoring the tax benefits. However, as a result of the *time value* of the early deductions, an investment that yields little if any profit from a strictly nontax standpoint may still generate a significant return.

In some instances, where the end user in fact would like to acquire the property on a permanent basis, the so called "lease" is nothing more than a financing technique, with the end user either indefinitely continuing to renew his lease or purchasing the property at the end of the lease period. However, if it is found that the transaction is in fact a conditional sale, the "lessor" will be denied the depreciation and (where available) investment tax credit benefits. Accordingly, it is critical that the transaction be structured so that it is in fact a valid lease and not a conditional sale.

Present Internal Revenue Service guidelines exist for such structuring. (See Rev. Proc. 75-21, 1975-18 I.R.B. 15; Rev. Proc. 75-28, 1975-21 I.R.B. 19.) While these rules are complicated, basically they require a minimum equity investment by the lessor of at least 20 percent of the total acquisition cost of the property, a residual value at the end of the lease term and its renewal periods of at least 20 percent of the original cost of the property, and a limitation that any option to purchase by the lessee must be based on the fair market value at the end of the lease term. The IRS guidelines also require that neither the lessee nor any related party guarantee any of the lessor's indebtedness for the purchase of the equipment.

The benefits to a *corporation* in serving as the lessor in an equipment leasing transaction (or member of the leasing syndicate) are substantial. As a general rule, the "at risk" limitations of the Tax Reform Act of 1976 apply to individual lessors, but not to corporations. (This can be avoided, of course, by recourse borrowing in connection with the purchase of the equipment.) The investment tax credit is not available to the individual lessor except under highly restricted circumstances. And accelerated depreciation on a net lease on personal property is an item of tax preference for individuals but not for corporations.

If you are an individual, equipment leasing definitely has its tax pitfalls. The "investment interest" limitations of the Internal Revenue Code, including the increased limitations under the Tax Reform Act of 1976, will apply to you as an individual taxpayer even though they would not apply to a corporate lessor. Under the technical definition of "net lease", the interest paid on most equipment leases would be treated as "investment interest." In addition to the "at risk," investment tax credit, and tax preference problems listed above, there is also a substantial chance that the "tax preference" treatment of your accelerated depreciation will cause a loss of "maxi-tax" benefits; and your income from the lease transaction will be "unearned" income subject to taxation without reference to the 50 percent maxi-tax protection. While some of these problems can be avoided by entering into an "operating lease," such short-term leases not only impose requirements of maintaining the leased property, but also create significant dangers of being unable to re-lease the property in the event of its obsolescence and thus threaten you with a possible loss of your interest in the property through foreclosure, with its resultant recapture "horrors."

As mentioned, economically speaking, an equipment leasing transaction involves significantly less risk and speculative aspects than does an investment in a motion picture, Broadway play, or a number of other tax shelter areas. If your lessee is clearly financially responsible—and this is a crucial "if"—you should be able to look to a steady income stream throughout the period of the lease. However, if the lessee should default on its obligations—and many substantial corporate lessees have suddenly found themselves in serious financial plight—you will find yourself saddled with an expensive piece of equipment which must be re-leased as rapidly as possible. If the equipment is now obsolete (a particular problem in the leasing of computers), this will create significant problems on how to satisfy your loan obligations. In any event, at the end of the original lease period, if you are not able to renew the lease with the original lessee, you are again faced with, at best, a loss of income (but no loss of mortgage payment obligations) until a new lessee can be secured; at worst, you may see your mortgage foreclosed with the resulting economic and tax unpleasantness.

An intelligent equipment leasing investment requires an ability to estimate the profitability of the particular industry and the financial stability of your particular lessee. It also involves your ability to determine the likelihood that your equipment will become obsolete, making its re-lease or sale extremely difficult if not impossible. Finally, you must be able to look into your crystal ball to attempt to determine what the residual value of your property will be at the end of the lease period.

Equipment leasing can be an attractive arrangement, tax-wise and economically, for an investor in need of tax shelter, particularly where that investor is a corporation. However, despite the *relative* financial stability of equipment leasing syndications, it should by no means be assumed that such transactions are without risk. And in today's sophisticated leasing market—dominated by leasing "packages" prepared by highly sophisticated investment bankers, manufacturers, and lending institutions—it is questionable whether the game is one for anyone to play other than the sophisticated corporate investor.

[¶2604]   RECORD, BOOK AND ARTWORK INVESTMENTS

Since 1976, the purchase of books, "master" records, and "master" artworks has been the most popular form of excess write-off investment for the individual taxpayer. While there are no reliable figures concerning how much money has been invested in such purchase, or how these amounts compare with investment in movie or coal syndications, the effect of the Tax Reform Act of 1976 was to make this type of investment the most attractive form for the investor seeking "a basis on which to claim" deductions of 300 percent to 400 percent (or in some instances 800 percent to 900 percent).

To understand why book, record, and artwork investments have eclipsed motion picture and coal syndicates in individual investor popularity, one only need look at the effects of the Tax Reform Act of 1976. The "at risk" limitation of the Tax Reform Act not only applied to the movie syndication; it was obvious by late 1975 that substantial restrictions would be placed on claiming excess deductions through motion picture investment and that such restrictions probably would be applied retroactively.

For the year 1976, the coal syndicate (see ¶2605) proved quite popular, since at that time it appeared to have considerable economic potential. Furthermore, the "partnership borrowing" restrictions, which would apply to coal syndicates as then structured, were not to take effect until January 1, 1977. (As to the "at risk" and "partnership borrowing" restrictions, see Chapter 5.)

After December 31, 1976, the investor seeking excess write-offs had the choice of settling for substantially less than the very high initial write-offs to which he had become accustomed; to seek new structures for motion picture or coal investment; or to find a new investment vehicle.

Obviously, the typical investor seeking excess write-offs, particularly of the 300 percent plus variety, does not wish to take a less aggressive tax position. While certain methods exist for claiming such a deduction in a movie syndicate (see ¶2602), the risk involved and the relative ease with which corporations could invest in the higher quality motion picture syndications substantially reduced film syndicate popularity among individual investors. Coal suffered a similar fate: affirmative action taken by the Internal Revenue Service in threatening to amend its regulations (a threat that was eventually acted upon) and the probable necessity of eliminating the "limited partnership" arrangement (a real necessity for limiting liability in coal operations—see ¶2605), saw a tremendous loss in popularity for the coal syndicate. At the same time, the development of books, artworks, and records as an investment vehicle by utilizing the same techniques previously applied in motion pictures quickly caught the investors' fancy.

The four-activity "at risk" limitations clearly appeared inapplicable to the investments. (The IRS has taken the position in its Rev. Rul. 77-297 that the "at risk" limitations would be applicable. However, the IRS position is based on very tenuous grounds and has generally been ignored.) Since unlike a motion picture or coal property, book, record, and artwork rights could be packaged in small enough increments to permit an entire work to be purchased by a single purchaser and did not create significant liability hazards, there is no need to form a "partnership." The partnership borrowing restrictions were thus inapplicable. (Under certain theories, the IRS might take the position that the typical arrangement utilized in such investments did result in the formation of a partnership. Here, again, it would appear that such a position would not be sound.) Thus, the "new breed" of excess write-off provided by the book, record, or artwork investment seemed of significantly less tax risk than other "exotics," and further offered what invariably has appealed to the "excess write-off" investor, a new and intriguing form of investment.

[¶2604.1]   How to Invest in Books, Records, and Art

What are the mechanics of a book, or master record, or artwork investment? Under the typical arrangement, you will purchase the rights of ownership and exploitation to the "master"from which records can be reproduced, the book "plates" or the silk screen or photo screen negative from which various graphics, including signed "limited editions," prints, or ancillary products (such as postcards or greeting cards, tapestries, ceramics, or even T-shirts) can be made. Your purchase will also include the related copyright.

As in the case of the "negative pickup" motion picture acquisition, the purchase price will be payable through a cash down payment (normally in the amount necessary to satisfy the costs of producing the plates or "masters," including the initial fees to the artist and the promoter's markup), with the balance being paid by a nonrecourse note due in a specified number of years (usually tied in with the requirements of securing the desired investment tax credit) and secured by a first lien on the plates or masters, plus an assignment of a specified percentage of the proceeds received by the purchaser from the sale of the books or similar products. This arrangement hopefully will permit the purchaser to take accelerated depreciation and the investment tax credit (together with any interest paid on the nonrecourse note) on the entire purchase price.

But how are these sales proceeds to be realized? In the syndication of legitimate motion pictures, arrangements normally will have been made (and insisted upon by the seller) for distribution by an established distributer. Frequently, however, the book or record being syndicated is by a virtual "unknown." Some master record syndications feature records by well known recording stars. Similarly, many master artwork syndications also feature "name" artists, since it would be difficult to substantiate healthy anticipated sales for artworks by an "unknown." Invariably, the seller must "point the way" to the purchaser through which his products can be distributed.

In the case of artworks by established artists, the purchaser may be furnished a list of galleries which have been contacted and would be interested, for a fee, in distributing the prints to be made from the artwork master. However, in the case of books and records, it is a frequent practice for an affiliate of the seller to be "available" to the purchaser to take on the distribution chores. This distribution contract will normally call for the distributor to receive a specified percentage of sale proceeds in return for his efforts, with the purchaser being paid a "royalty" on all products sold.

The IRS has already attempted to take the position that a master record purchase is subject to the "at risk" limitations as a "lease." (See Rev. Rul. 77-397, I.R.B. 1977-44.) However, the broad interpretation of the work "lease" relied upon by the IRS has no support in either prior judicial or IRS interpretations. (Compare Thomas R. Meagler, 31 t.C.M. 1091 (1977); Rev. Proc. 75-21; Rev. Proc. 75-28.)

If the IRS is unsuccessful in asserting that the "at risk" provisions of the Tax Reform Act of 1976 apply to book, record, and artwork investments, it may assert that the arrangement has resulted in a "partnership" arrangement which would be subject to the similar "partnership borrowing" restrictions of §704(d) of the Internal Revenue Code. Grounds for taking this position might arise from the fact that this type of investment is normally offered through an "Information Memorandum" through which a number of books or masters are offered for individual purchase. (The term "informational memorandum" or "confidential memorandum" is normally used in an attempt to avoid admitting that the transaction is a "security" subject to State and Federal securities laws. See Chapter 31.) However, since each investor will be the sole owner of the products which he purchases, and will not share in the profits from any other investors' products, the multiple sale aspects clearly would not create a partnership. Similarly, so long as there is a reasonable possiblity that the nonrecourse note may pay out, and since the seller will not share in any losses, no partnership would seem to exist with the seller. And no partnership appears to exist with the distributor.

[¶2604.2]   Tax Benefits Through Investment Tax Credit

Investment in books and masters hopefully provides important tax benefits through the availability of the investment tax credit. Court decisions and the express provision of the Tax Reform Act of 1976 normally allow such tax benefits for negative pick-up acquisitions (see ¶2602); and similar treatment should be available for this type of investment as "tangible personal property" under §48(a)(1) of the Internal Revenue Code. (See *Texas Instruments Inc. vs. U.S.,* 551 F. 2d 599 (5th Cir. 1977).) However, the IRS is expected to take a contrary position.

It is important that the product not have been "put in service" prior to your purchase to secure maximum tax benefits.

It would appear that an investment in a book, record, or artwork creates no items of tax preference. However, if the Internal Revenue Service should be sustained in its argument that such transactions are in fact leases, "excess" depreciation could create a tax preference item. (See Rev. Rul. 77-397, discussed above.)

The economic and tax risks of the investments just discussed are staggering. Where works of "name" artists are involved, the purchase price and interest in proceeds payable will be quite large. Furthermore, the purchase price normally is set at such a level that it is highly unlikely that sales necessary to recover the purchaser's hard dollar costs, much less to pay off the nonrecourse note, will ever be attained. For instance, in one recent "master record" offering, it was assumed that a long playing album of established "classics" by unknown moonlighting European musicians would sell nearly a million copies. And seldom is it revealed to you as a prospective purchaser just exactly how many copies of the book, record or artwork must be sold to attain these economic goals.

As in the case of the motion picture syndication, it is clear that if the purchase price being paid by you exceeds the fair market value of the rights you are acquiring, a substantial portion of your deductions will be disallowed. (See ¶2602; see also Rev. Rul. 77-111.) The possibility of sales at an economic profit is also necessary for the "profit motive" requirement of §183 of the Internal Revenue Code. Recent cases indicate that the *entire* nonrecourse loan may be excluded from your basis, and not merely that portion which represents the excessive portion of the purchase price (including the nonrecourse portion). While you normally will be presented with at least two appraisals from "recognized" experts in the industry concerning the reasonableness of the purchase price, if the sales projections necessary to support such appraisals are clearly unrealistic, you stand in serious peril of disallowance of your deductions.

**[¶2604.3]   Guidelines for Investment in
              "Exotic" Tax Shelters**

Appendix 2601-1 contains a sample book investment, showing the effects of varying degrees of leverage. By now, you may have determined that the type of investments being discussed are not for you. However, if your investment objectives require extremely high initial write-offs, a properly structured purchase of a plate or master to a book, record, or artwork with true economic potential remains "the only (or at least the best) game in town." If so, you should be careful to follow the following guidelines:

1. *The transaction must be structured in such a manner that it will be treated as a true purchase,* and not merely a loan, license, or joint venture. This will require that the product have economic merit and not be an established "dud" (see *Marvin M. May,* 31 T.C.M. 279 (1972)); that the price of the product is not unrealistically high so that the non-recourse note does not represent bona fide debt; and the rights acquired by the purchaser should not be limited in time or contain any territorial limits as to where the product can be exploited.

2. *The right to enter into any distribution contract should be optional with the purchaser,* who should remain free to contract with any distributor he wishes, or to distribute the product himself. The distribution contract should be customary in form to the type generally used in the particular industry, and the purchaser should retain, and exercise, the rights and control that would be expected of a person who has entered into a distribution arrangement with the third party; and the distribution agreement should be subject to termination after a specified period at the option of the purchaser.

See ¶2602 as to the general protective steps that should be taken in structuring this type of purchase.

An illustration of the effect of increased leverage on the deductibility and economic potential of a book syndication, and the importance of product sales levels on eventual profitability, is contained in the Appendix.

[¶2605]   **INVESTMENT IN COAL**

1976 saw the development of an overnight phenomenon, the coal syndication, which took the investor community by storm. This surging interest in coal investment on the part of investors seeking substantial excess write-offs was caused by the expectation, which proved to be true, that retroactive adverse tax treatment would be applied to movie syndications. (See ¶2602.) It was also brought about by creative tax planning which made use of a "lump sum advanced royalty" approach to acquire coal properties. Through use of this technique, it was possible for an investor to claim a possible 300 percent to 400 percent first year write-off with the economic "carrot" of profitable coal production.

Initially, it appeared to many that the coal "acquisition" syndicate combined the best features of earlier motion picture and equipment leasing syndications. The tax benefits were as large as those previously offered by the "negative pickup" approach. The possibility for economic profit offered the benefits attributed to a quality equipment leasing syndication. As a result, throughout 1976, coal held a virtual monopoly as "the" exotic investment opportunity for the individual taxpayer.

Coal particularly lent itself to syndication as an excess write-off "exotic." Coal offers substantially less immediate deductibility for its expenditures than does oil and gas, and has nothing comparable to oil's "IDC" deductions. Low coal prices and lack of "straight-forward" tax deductions had left coal virtually ignored as an industry whose activities could be financed through tax-oriented venture capital. Furthermore, the coal industry has been referred to as a "tack" characterized by a limited number of industry giants—the point of the tack—with a large base of very small "family" coal operations. These smaller coal operators were not oriented towards seeking innovative, nonconventional financing for development of their coal properties.

The development by tax practitioners of the lump sum advance royalty approach primarily paid, as in movie and similar syndications, through nonrecourse notes, made tax-sheltered financing of the acquisition of coal properties a reality. There were and are substantial risks as to whether such deductions would be challenged on audit, even as to investments entered into prior to recent tax regulation changes. However, the craze over this new syndication form, which was heightened by publicity concerning the energy crisis, lead to an incredible level of investment.

No one knows exactly how dollars were raised through the 1976 coal syndications. It has been estimated—hopefully facetiously—that such syndicates "acquired" properties whose represented coal content totalled three times our country's proven coal reserves. Unfortunately, many of these dollars were invested by the $5,000 to $10,000 investor who, in the past, had rarely participated in the sophisticated and high risk "exotic" offerings, and who rarely understood the significant tax and economic risks.

The circumstances surrounding coal investment in 1976 were an invitation toward the creative professional syndicator. Unfortunately, coal offerings were frequently sold by emphasizing tax benefits far over economics. Furthermore, many of the coal syndicators had very little knowledge of the industry in which their investors' moneys were to be expended.

[¶2605.1]   The "Acquisition" Syndicates of 1976

The typical 1976 "coal acquisition" syndicate operated along the following lines. A limited partnership would be formed to lease (or sub-lease) a coal property from the mineral owner or coal lessee. In addition to customary annual royalties on production, the syndicate would also agree to pay a substantial lump sum advance royalty, to be recouped out of subsequent production royalties. The coal was then to be mined pursuant to agreements entered into with a "contract miner" (usually an affiliate of the general partner) for additional fees. Since the large part of the lump sum advance royalty (and certain other expenses of the syndicate) were paid through the issuance of nonrecourse notes, the investor was entitled to claim first-year deductions which normally fell in the 300 percent to 400 percent range. However, the current deductibility of the lump sum advance royalty payments were based upon two IRS Revenue Rulings—Rev. Rul. 70-20 and Rev. Rul 74-214— neither of which involved payment through the issuance of nonrecourse promissory notes. Furthermore, on October 29, 1976, alarmed by the coal syndicate buying stampede, the Internal Revenue Service suspended these key revenue rulings, and announced a proposed amendment to its regulations to deny current deductibility for lump sum advance royalties. See Internal Revenue Release # 1687 (October 29, 1976). Yet, despite this IRS action, which included a proposed retroactive application of the amended regulations once adopted, investors continued to rush to the coal syndication.

[¶2605.2]   Advantages of Coal Investment

An advantage of coal investment *should be* that it is substantially easier to determine the amount of coal "in place" by core drilling than to estimate the amount of oil and gas, if any, that may be discovered by either exploratory or development drilling. Thus, it appeared that the prime risks involved in the coal syndicate, other than the admitted tax risks, were whether the syndicator had properly done his homework in determining the amount of coal reserves present and the quality of such coal; whether coal prices would increase or decrease; and whether contracts could be entered into to sell the coal produced. It was not anticipated that long-term contracts could be arranged to dispose of the minable coal; the syndicates were forced to rely upon the "spot sale" market. And a failure to mine specified annual minimum coal volumes would lead to a loss of the coal leases through foreclosure of the nonrecourse notes and thus would trigger disastrous tax consequences.

1977 saw most earlier coal syndicates turn to disaster. In many instances, through good faith error due to lack of experience in the industry or outright fraud, coal reserves had been substantially over-estimated, or were less easily extractible than originally assumed. In addition, the "contract miners" generally proved unable to perform their mining obligations. And—an unexpected "minus"—it was discovered that little consideration had been given by the syndicator or the contract miner as to how the extremely expensive equipment necessary to mine the coal would be secured.

As a result, the tax shelter industry was rocked in 1977 with numerous scandals concerning coal syndications. And few of these syndicates proved capable of mining coal in amounts even vaguely approaching the projected coal production on which economic assumptions had been based.

[¶2605.3]   How the Tax Reform Act of 1976
             Affected Coal Syndications

1977 saw a marked change in the popularity of coal syndication. On January 1, 1977, the "partnership borrowing" restrictions of the Tax Reform Act of 1976 became applicable to coal limited partnerships. Furthermore, as book and master record syndications grew in popularity, investors became less willing to take the risks that the lump sum advance royalties could in fact be deducted. Coal syndicates thus turned to new structuring techniques involving prepaid minimum annual royalties, prepaid mining costs, and start-up or mine preparation expense, which, if sustained, could generate deductions at an approximate 130 percent level, but which by no means provided the 300 percent to 400 percent initial deductibility previously associated with coal.

The coal syndicate as a "go-go" generator of extrodinarily high front-end deductions was dealt a death blow by the adoption by the IRS, in December, 1977, of the formerly proposed amendment to its regulations. As amended, any deduction for the payment of advance royalties was deferred until the year in which the minerals were actually sold. However, an advance deduction was still permitted for a one-year prepayment of annual minimum royalties payable uniformly over the life of the lease or for a period of at least 20 years. (See Treasury Regulation §1.612-3(b)(3); IRS Rev. Rul. 77-489.)

There is no question but that the coal industry needs venture capital, and that the nation needs coal. It is now possible to structure coal investment as a legitimate venture operation with substantial tax shelter. However, the question remains as to whether such structuring should still attempt to secure excess write-offs comparable to what might be secured in cattle breeding or equipment leasing, with an unfortunate loss of economics, or whether smaller deductions but greater economic potential should be emphasized.

Assuming that advance annual minimum royalty transactions are structured to comply with the amended IRS regulations, and that the prepaid deductions for mining costs and "start up" and mine preparation expense are allowed, or at least not challenged on audit, excess deductions can still be generated by a coal mining syndication. These deductions can be increased where equipment is also acquired by the syndicate, as discussed below.

[¶2605.4]   New Approaches to Coal Syndication

There are several approaches that you can use to claim deductions in excess of your cash investment in the syndicate. One method is to continue to utilize a partnership, but to become *personally liabile* on some or all of the partnership debt. A guarantee of all partnership indebtedness would create substantial risks in view of possible uncertainties as to the amount and quality of syndicate reserves, and certain "uncertainty" as to future coal prices and the availability of a market for your coal. However, assuming personal liability on a *first mortgage indebtedness secured by salvage-able equipment* sufficient to cover your excess losses, with a nonrecourse second mortgage being used for the balance of the debt, would not appear to create unacceptable hazards. Use of *recourse liability for a limited period of time,* with the debt converting to nonrecourse status at the end of the period, could also be used, as suggested in connection with motion picture syndications, so long as significant payments are required and made during the recourse period of the loan. Such a debt guarantee should be structured as a required "contribution" to the partnership.

If you are concerned over the possibility of recourse borrowing, you and the other syndicate investors could each acquire *undivided fractional interests* in the coal lease, electing to be excluded from the provisions of Subchapter K, the partnership income tax portion of the Code which contains the "partnership borrowing" restrictions. (See Internal Revenue Code, §761.) So long as you are the legal or beneficial owner of your fractional interest in the lease, and have the right to take in kind or separately dispose of your share of coal production, the co-ownership would neither be taxable as a partnership so as to be subject to the restrictions of §704(d) nor suffer even greater tax detriment by being classified as an "association taxable as a corporation." (See I.T. 3930, 1948-2 C.B. 126; I.T. 3948, 1949-1 C.B. 161; but see *U.S. vs. Steirwalt,* 287 F. 2d 855 (10th Cir. 1961).) However, the "co-ownership" structuring of your coal investment will subject you to the risk of *unlimited liability* to third parties—a high risk indeed in coal operations.

The "excess write-off" approach to coal syndications can generate initial deductions in the area of 130 percent, or even higher. However, the claiming of such excess deductions often leads to coal purchase arrangements which may not be economically favorable to the syndicate. If you will be satisfied with deductions in the 70 percent to 80 percent level (or possibly as high as 100 percent), you will probably find that your coal mining experience will prove much more economically beneficial to you than would have the value of the excess tax benefits. The experience of the coal syndicates formed in 1976 has shown that the problems encountered in mining and marketing coal acquired by the syndicate are an even more serious problem than the acquisition of the coal reserves. Accordingly, many coal syndicates are now being structured not only to acquire coal properties, but also to acquire the equipment necessary for mining the coal. Since the syndicate actually purchases or leases the necessary equipment, rather than merely serving as a lessor, the restrictions of the Tax Reform Act and prior tax legislation applicable to equipment leasing (see ¶2603) do not apply to such transactions. The equipment can normally be financed with a high degree of leverage, thus generating additional tax deductions through accelerated depreciation and the investment tax credit.

The experience of 1976 has also proved that coal investment has extreme risks. While qualified mining engineers can estimate recoverable coal reserves with a much higher degree of accuracy than is possible in oil and gas, the expertise level of coal syndicators in understanding the syndicated industry in most instances has not reached the level which investors have come to expect in oil and gas or real estate programs. Accordingly, before you invest in the acquisition and development of a coal property, you should ask yourself the following questions:

☐ Has the *price* to be paid for the coal properties been arrived at by a precise *geological and engineering analysis* of the property, including verification by drilling? Does it include a laboratory analysis of a sufficient number of coal samples? Does the syndicate have a carefully detailed and properly thought out mining plan? Is the contract miner truly experienced and properly equipped to perform his mining function? Will he "stay with" this venture? Do the syndicate contracts require the contract miner to produce established minimum production requirements necessary to comply with lease obligations and to produce volumes of coal sufficient to attain the economic objectives of the program? And is the contract miner in fact ready and able to satisfy these obligations?

☐ Have adequate long term "end user" contracts been entered into with responsible purchasers for a large percentage of the coal? If not, does it appear likely that adequate "spot markets" for the coal will exist?

It is too early at this stage to say whether the coal syndication will go the way of the citrus investments of the 1960's, or will take its place as a legitimate method of financing energy development through the use of tax-oriented venture capital. To a large extent, this will be determined by the degree of expertise which coal syndicators develop concerning the coal industry, and whether or not coal investors are willing to turn to a greater extent to economic, in addition to tax, considerations.

[¶2606]   **BROADWAY PLAYS BRING HUGE PROFITS—SOMETIMES**

You may have heard stories about the hugh profits made by investors in Broadway plays. *My Fair Lady, Fiddler on the Roof, Hair,* and *Godspell* all have generated incredible profits for their investors, not merely from Broadway box office sales, but through profits from subsidiary rights such as motion picture rights and "national" and foreign tours. However, Broadway plays for most investors do not in fact represent an "investment", but an opportunity to share in an exciting experience, and, if lightning strikes, possibly to make money.

The vast majority of Broadway plays do not make money. Costs of producing a play in Broadway are skyrocketing. And, even when a play is a Broadway success, the salaries to name stars, to the director and the author, and the producer's participation, often mean that an investor is still losing money even for a show that has run several years on Broadway.

In addition to the amounts paid the cast, the director will normally receive both a fee and a percentage of *gross* box office receipts. The producer-general partners, in addition to their share of net profits, will also receive a "management fee" payable out of a percentage of gross box office receipts plus reimbursement of various administrative overhead expenses. And a percentage of gross receipts will be payable to the author and the theatre. These percentage often may, in the aggregate, run as much as 40 percent of box office receipts or even higher.

While the amounts you spend will be tax deductible, the large calls on gross revenues mean that you will have to recover your investment out of a relatively small proportion of box office receipts. As a result, not only do the vast majority of plays currently being produced on Broadway lose money for their investors; the vast majority of plays produced by "successful" producers also prove a financial loss to their backers.

Many noneconomic benefits acrue to an investor in a play. While some of the glittering "extras" that were formerly used to entice investors have now been eliminated in view of increasing costs, the excitement of being involved in the theatrical industry is similar to the excitement that leads many investors to invest in motion picture syndications. Furthermore, the play investor may be permitted to secure even greater involvement in the thrills of the production than is true in the movies. However, do not look at a Broadway play as an investment: look at it as a speculation that is in fact a gamble—and a gamble that, under any "risk/reward" analysis (see ¶2602) is unlikely to pay off.

Additional Readings: Part Three

Chapters 24-26: "Exotic" Investments

Motion Pictures

DROLLINGER, *Tax Shelters and Tax-Free Income for Everyone,* Introduction; Part One (Chapter Six); Parts Two-Four (Epic Publications, Inc.: 3rd ed. 1977)

HAFT and FASS, *Tax Sheltered Investments,* Chapters Nine and Nine-A (Clark Boardman Co., Ltd.: 2d ed. 1974)

"Tax Shelters—Current Developments Motion Picture Tax Shelters," *Tax Management Memorandum* (TMM75-07: Mar. 31, 1975)

Equipment Leasing

DROLLINGER, *op. cit.,* Part One (Chapter 3)

HAFT and FASS, *op. cit.,* Chapter 8

REID (ed.), *Corporate and Executive Tax Sheltered Investments* (Chapter 23), (Presidents Publishing House, Inc.: 1972)

Tax Incentives—A Tool for Financing Business Growth and for Sheltering Income Chapter 4 (*Arthur Andersen & Co.: 2d ed. 1977*)

Other Exotics

BURKE and BOWHAY, *Income Taxation of Natural Resources,* Ch. 18 (Prentice-Hall, Inc.: 1978)

DROLLINGER, *op. cit.,* Part One (Chapters 7-8), Appendix D

JANEWAY, "Trick or Treat in Today's Treasure Market?," *Architectural Digest* (March/April 1974)

MOSBURG and NICHOLS (ed.), *Financing Coal Ventures* (The Institute for Energy Development, Inc.: 1977)

WEIL, "Bankrolling Broadway," *TWA Ambassador* (Sept. 1977)*

---

*Reproduced in Mosburg (ed.), *Structuring Tax-Sheltered Investments under the Tax Reform Act of 1976* (The Institute for Energy Development, Inc.: 1977)

PART FOUR

Selecting the Right
Tax Shelter For You

27.

Preliminary Investment Decisions

[¶2701]   **TAX SHELTER PITFALLS**

Throughout this book, we have seen that tax shelters, like any investment opportunity, are a "mixed bag." While an opportunity for profit is present there is also an opportunity for loss. We have also seen that investing in an inappropriate or poorly planned tax-sheltered investment will raise this "opportunity" to a certainty, and may even create tax *detriments* for you. The purpose of this portion of the book is to help you decide whether or not you wish to invest in tax shelters at *all*; how you determine *which type* of tax-sheltered investment is right for you; and, finally, how to pick the *particular tax-sheltered program* that is least apt to lose you money, and most apt to work to your economic benefit.

Without question, there are many potentially profitable tax-sheltered investment opportunities available to you. However, before deciding to invest, you must reach certain general decisions.

The first question which you must answer is *whether or not you should invest in tax shelters at all*. To your financial advisor, this may seem a strange question. If you are in a high Federal income tax bracket, and are not taking advantage of tax-sheltering opportunities, you are unnecessarily increasing the amount of money that you pay the government.

However, just as tax-sheltered investments have many "plus" attributes, they have certain characteristics that may be unacceptable to you.

[¶2701.1]   Analyze Your Tax-Shelter Needs

1. *Tax shelters are speculative and difficult to evaluate.* As we have noted in our discussion of agricultural investments and the exotics, it is difficult to determine just how much profit potential, if any, is present in a given industry, particularly in view of the compensation that the syndicator has a right (and will) demand. Bringing this

evaluation down to the level of a particular tax shelter project is even more difficult. As we will see in ¶2904, professional assistance will normally be a "must" for intelligent investment. And no matter how profitable the industry, or how well selected and managed the particular investment, the speculative nature of the industries which you are supporting means that your investment may result in a loss. So if a substantial loss of money would mean significant financial hardship for you, paying your taxes may be the wiser decision.

2. *Tax-sheltered investments are illiquid.* For securities law (see Chapter 31) and tax reasons, the right to transfer your interest normally will be severely restricted. But far more important than this "legal" restriction is the fact that a "secondary market" seldom exists in the tax shelter area: it is normally difficult to find a purchaser for your interest, particularly at a fair price, even if you were perfectly free to sell it. Furthermore, a premature sale of your interest will normally trigger adverse tax consequences with possibilities of loss of capital gains benefits, recapture of depreciation and the investment tax credit, substantial tax liability on the proceeds of the sale (including any "phantom income" portion), and possible adverse consequences in the minimum and maxi-tax areas. So if you do not have other liquid assets with which to satisfy emergency and other "living expense" needs, tying up your liquidity in illiquid tax shelter interests may be a mistake, despite the tax and potential economic benefits.

3. For intelligent investment in the tax shelter area, a *several year commitment* is a practical necessity. Due to the speculative aspects of tax-sheltered investment, you can expect certain projects to prove economically successful and others to turn out less favorably, no matter how well you have planned and implemented your tax shelter investment program. These "peaks and valleys" normally will level out, so long as you are able to continue your tax-sheltered investment program for a period of several years. However, if your tax problems are unique to a single year, or if you are not prepared to make such investments for several years running, your lack of diversification increases the speculative risks to unreasonable proportions. Furthermore, a multiyear tax-sheltered investment program will permit you to offset some of the "coming out" tax consequences of your investment by carefully selecting new tax-sheltered investment opportunities. Tax-sheltered investments have a snowball effect. Since the initial tax savings will, to some degree, be offset by future tax detriments, thus compounding your tax problems in subsequent years, you may find it difficult "to get off the runaway train." This is not inherently bad, so long as you have prepared for it. However "planning" your initial tax shelter strategy without

taking this into account can lead to unpleasant surprises.

4. There are *alternatives* to tax-sheltered investment which may equally or better serve your tax problems. Income averaging, installment sale, reliance on the maximum tax on personal service income, or contributions to a pension and profit sharing plan, all have their tax advantages. (See Chapter 7.) While investment in other tax-favored securities such as annuities or tax free municipals may not offer initial shelter, the tax treatment of the income from such investments can have pleasant results. Furthermore, the "phantom income," tax preference, and nonpersonal service income consequences of investment in many tax shelter areas can complicate your tax situation, and in some instances worsen, rather than improve, your overall tax picture. So unless you have consulted your tax adviser to consider these alternatives—with one being simply to pay your taxes—your entry into the tax shelter area has been commenced with less than thorough consideration.

All investments possess these same problems to a greater or lesser extent. Anyone who has seen his "blue chip" stock decline in a "down" market knows that even the best investment is speculative and difficult to evaluate, creates psychological pressures (compare your feelings when a review of the closing stock quotes shows that the "smart tip" which you acted on has just dropped another three points), and that a listed stock, though "liquid," is difficult to part with when its price is unrealistically depressed. However, General Motors is less speculative, less difficult to evaluate, and less illiquid than an interest in an oil well, a real estate project, or a breeding herd.

By now, you may have decided to stop here, or you may say, "I am willing to accept this side of tax-sheltered investment." If so, you need to make a *"suitability"* determination concerning which tax-sheltered investments are appropriate for you, and at what level of investment.

Chapter 28 will deal with matching your investment objectives to the characteristics of a particular type of tax-sheltered investment. However, certain "appropriateness" decisions are lumped under the heading of "suitability." These deal with your *tax bracket,* your overall *net worth,* and your *liquid net worth.*

As a general rule, you should not consider any form of tax-sheltered investment unless you are in not less than a *50 percent Federal income tax bracket,* possess a *net worth of at least $50,000,* and possess *sufficient liquid assets* so that any foreseeable financial needs can be met by you despite the fact that a portion of your capital is tied up in tax shelters and other relatively "frozen" investments.

**[¶2701.2]   The 50% Tax Bracket as a Guide to
                 Tax Shelter Needs**

Certain tax-sheltered investments, particularly investment in the less tax-oriented forms of real estate, are appropriate for investors in less than a 50 percent Federal income tax bracket. Normally, however, the 50 percent bracket requirement is an intelligent guideline, since the tax benefits tend to offset at least half the risk of the investment. Also, based upon normal return expectations in the particular tax shelter area, the economics will simply not "work out" if the tax benefits have less than a 50 percent value to you.

This "economics" aspect of the tax bracket requirement is often overlooked. However, as we have seen, the tax savings are a definite increment of the return that you can expect from your investment; without them, the cash flow and appreciation potential normally are not high enough to make the investment attractive. (See ¶¶101 and 201). Similarly, no matter how attractive a tax shelter opportunity may appear, if you invest so many dollars in it that you have reduced your taxable income for the particular year below the 40 percent to 50 percent level, the investment will cease to make economic sense.

**[¶2701.3]   Limit Investment to Ten Percent
                 of Your Net Worth**

The necessity for a sufficient overall and liquid net worth are equally important in determining the appropriateness of tax-sheltered investments and the amount of money which you should invest in them. While diversification, both within a single year and from year to year, may offset much of the speculative aspects of tax-sheltered investment, lightning does strike. To risk your entire economic future merely to reduce a particular year's taxes is not smart planning. Accordingly, as a general guideline, usually not more than 10 percent of your overall net worth should be tied up in tax-sheltered investments.

Your determination as to net worth must also be supplemented by a consideration of the sufficiency of your personal income to meet your anticipated living needs, including a consideration of the stability of your income sources.

The need for other liquid assets arises both from the "frozen" nature of your tax-sheltered investment, and the fact that, in most tax-sheltered areas, cash flow from the investment may be delayed for a substantial period of time, even several years.

Some of the investment programs offered to you may possess a *"liquidity" feature* that will permit you to liquidate your program interest through a "repurchase" or "redemption" feature. While in many instances such a feature is a valuable "plus," it may be subject to suspension or restrictions under certain circumstances and normally will trigger tax consequences that are less favorable than holding your investment through its normal liquidation phase. This is particularly true in view of the less favorable capital gains treatment now contained in the Internal Revenue Code. (And, remember, most of your "basis" in your program interest for capital gains purposes has been eaten up by those attractive initial tax deductions.) Furthermore, a "liquidity" feature only insures that you can sell your program interest for *something;* it does not mean that you can recover your initial investment. While the stock market is subject to its ups and downs, your asset value in a particular tax shelter venture will be based on what your interest in the investment is worth. Due to the speculative nature of the project, this may be only a fraction of your initial investment. Furthermore, under normal valuation techniques, your redemption price will have been arrived at by a substantial discounting of the expected revenues from the project. While this is partially compensated for by the "time value" of receiving your revenues now, traditional industry discounting practices normally go substantially beyond a mere "present value" discounting of revenues.

[¶2702]   HOW MUCH SHOULD YOU INVEST

It is seldom possible to shelter all of your income from taxation, particularly without delving into the "exotics," which, as we saw in Chapter 26, have pitfalls of their own. While, theoretically, your tax shelter strategy should be to invest sufficient moneys in tax shelters to reduce your taxable income to approximately the $40,000 level, this is an unrealistic goal for most investors.

If you are earning a substantial income, you normally might find it difficult to live on $40,000, particularly if this requires diverting $25,000 or more from your income. To maintain a satisfying life style is worth paying a certain amount of taxes, particularly if the alternative is to reduce your taxes only through the reduction of your own personal happiness. And aside from personal living conditions, a very real fact of life is that, to invest in a tax shelter, you must have dollars to fund that investment. (The use of borrowing, other than the "leverage"features contained in the program, to provide those dollars will be discussed in ¶2703.)

[¶2702.1]   You Must Consider "Hard" and
"Soft" Dollar Risk

The portion of your cash flow which you are investing in tax shelters definitely involves "risk" dollars. One guide to the amount of your investment can be found in the "suitability" considerations discussed in ¶2701. But another problem is that you must be able to divert from your present cash flow sufficient "risk" moneys to cover both the "hard" and "soft" dollar portions of your investment. While the "soft" dollars will, in effect, be returned to you in the future in the form of tax savings, the hard dollars are definitely at risk.

Here may lie the dilemma for you as a potential tax-sheltered investor. Often, a compelling reason for seeking tax shelter is a lack of the cash needed to pay your taxes. (In other words, you have overspent your after-tax income.) However, to enter into a tax-sheltered investment, you normally will need to find up to twice that amount of current income, even assuming 100 percent deductible, to gain the necessary tax shelter. Thus the popularity of the excess write-off investment. So your decision as to how much to invest in tax-sheltered investments will be affected not only by the dollars that you could afford *financially* to place "at risk," but also by the amount of money that you can divert from your personal income without *impairing your personal happiness.*

The amount which you can invest in any particular program will also be affected by your investment strategy as to *dividing your investment* between particular types of investments (see ¶2802), and subdividing such investments between the programs of several sponsors within such an investment area to provide greater diversification.

Normally, a detailed review of the particular investments available in a given tax shelter area will indicate that there are several which merit your consideration. While one of these may appear to be "superior" to the other acceptable investments, the uneven success experienced by most sponsors in any particular program normally indicates that investing in several high quality programs each year, as well as in each program offered throughout the year by a particular sponsor, is a wise investment practice.

Unfortunately, the practice just outlined could require considerable capital. thus, to invest $5,000 per partnership in each of the programs offered by three separate oil and gas sponsors could involve an overall commitment of $30,000 or more. (If the program minimum were $10,000, this figure would double.) Such an investment may be beyond your means. However, to the extent you do have substantial funds to commit, a spreading of your investments should be given serious consideration.

[¶2703]   TO BORROW OR NOT TO BORROW?

The problems of available cash to make your desired tax shelter investments raise the question of whether or not you should borrow to provide your equity investment.

There is nothing wrong with borrowing to invest if this is simply a matter of convenience. That is, if the money sources are and will be available to you to repay the loan if the venture does not prove successful. For instance, if, rather than selling a stock that is presently depressed in order to raise the funds for your tax-sheltered investment, you determine to wait to see if the market rises, or to repay the loan later in the year when a dependable source of excess income will be available to you, you have not taken an unacceptable risk even if the venture proves unsuccessful.

However, often investors are enticed into securing loans to finance a tax-sheltered investment on the basis that due to the "safety" of the investment, or the tax savings, this is a "no-lose" situation. This temptation is particularly compelling due to the fact that a tax-sheltered investment financed through borrowing will lead to a present increase in your spendable cash as a result of the tax savings. However, if you will not have the funds available to repay the loan, to meet subsequent tax liabilities resulting from the investment, and to replace any "impairment" of capital resulting from "prespending" your tax benefits, you will find that borrowing can create a nightmare far more serious than your present tax problems.

There is no such thing as a "sure fire" tax-sheltered investment. As emphasized throughout this book, hard dollars are always at risk, even in the relatively safer tax-sheltered areas such as a well established and reasonably priced existing real estate project. To borrow dollars that could not be repaid in the event the project is not successful, and to fail to take into account subsequent tax consequences, is to endanger your entire financial position unnecessarily and unwisely. And the greater the degree of initial tax savings, the more serious the problems created by borrowing can become. Thus, borrowing to enter into an excess write-off investment is both particularly enticing and particularly dangerous.

The points just mentioned apply not only to a bank borrowing to finance your equity investment but also extend to any tax shelter investment which involves the pledging of your credit on a recourse basis, either to a lending institution or through an agreement to pay portions of your subscription on a recourse basis at the time of program termination. While it is often represented that this day of reckoning will never come, recourse borrowing and agreed contributions involve a commitment of your assets. If you could not financially bear the burden of honoring those commitments, don't invest.

Another form of "borrowing" is to treat the tax savings which are generated by your investment as a "windfall," instead of realizing that these represent a significant part of the return from your tax-sheltered investment, including dollars necessary to replace your capital invested in the program to the extent the tax savings exceed the "profit" element of such return. Wherever possible, the initial tax savings should be used to replace the cash invested or to repay any borrowings. Since you will not know for a substantial period of time whether or not the venture in fact will prove economic, the dollars first received by you, whether in the form of tax savings or initial cash flow, should be treated as a return of capital, not as profit. If, instead, you "squander" the dollars generated by the tax benefits, you do so at the risk of an eventual reduction (rather than improvement) in your net worth.

28.

How To Select The Appropriate Type of Investment

[¶2801]   **WHAT ARE YOUR OBJECTIVES?**

As discussed earlier, tax-sheltered investments vary greatly in their investment characteristics. Just as each tax-sheltered investment area presents greater or lesser opportunities for *tax shelter*, these benefits will range from sheltering the income from the investment to long- or short-term deferral or the possibility of actual permanent "deep shelter."

The potential for *cash flow*, and the "spendable" amount of the cash flow after taxes, will vary significantly, both in amount, likelihood of the cash flow objectives being attained, steadiness of the flow, and whether cash distributions can be expected immediately or only after a substantial period of time. The length of time over which the cash flow will continue will likewise vary, as will the question of whether or not the cash flow partially represents a "return of capital" element.

There is also considerable variance in the degree and likelihood that your asset will *appreciate in value*. In some instances, the likelihood and extent of appreciation will be affected by the cash flow generated by the investment. In other areas, it may be possible to secure a blend of good cash flow without losing appreciation potential.

While no tax-sheltered investment is truly *"liquid,"* (see Chapter 27) certain investments are more liquid than others, particularly when you consider the presence or absence of a "liquidity" feature, the tax consequences on the sale of the investment, the length of time expected to be required for the venture to reach its "liquidation" stage, and the length of time required for the venture to "mature" sufficiently so that your interest can be sold without forfeiting possible or probable future revenue potential.

Similarly, while all tax-sheltered investments involve *risk*, some tax shelter areas are clearly more risky than others.

Selecting the appropriate type of tax-sheltered investment for you thus requires that you analyze *your own investment objectives,* and your personal needs, in the often competing areas of:

1. *Tax shelter*
2. *Cash flow*
3. *Appreciation*
4. *Liquidity*
5. *Acceptable degree of risk.*

A chart summarizing the investment characteristics of various types of tax-sheltered investment is contained in Appendix 15.

[¶2801.1]   High Initial Deductibility A Necessity

As a general guideline, if a *very high degree of tax savings* is absolutely necessary, *government assisted housing* investment should be given serious consideration. *Breeding* programs and the *exotics* should also be considered, but are subject to the economic, tax, and other risks discussed in connection with those investments.

[¶2801.2]   100% Deductibility Required

Where *100 percent deductibility,* or close to it, is of high importance to you, *oil and gas* should be considered. *Cattle feeding* and the more highly *tax-oriented* forms of *real estate* investment may also prove appropriate, but again are subject to the current economic problems affecting the "new construction" and cattle industries.

[¶2801.3]   Blend of Investment Objectives

Where you seek a more moderate *blend* of tax savings, cash flow, and appreciation, investment in *existing real estate* projects offers more moderate, but potentially more predictable, returns in each of these "return" areas.

[¶2801.4]   High Risk/High Reward Investments

Where a more aggressive posture can be taken concerning potential risks, *exploratory oil and gas* and, subject to industry economic problems, *new residential construction, raw land,* and *cattle feeding* investment offers a more speculative, but potentially higher reward—economic return.

The guidelines just mentioned assume that you will take the steps outlined in Chapter 29 to select a particular investment in the tax shelter area selected by you which has true economic potential. A blind investment, without careful evaluation of the bona fides and economic potential of the particular project, means that your overall investment objective, to make money, will certainly suffer.

[¶2802]   **BLENDING INVESTMENTS
FOR A BALANCED PROGRAM**

Often you may find that a *blend of different types of tax-sheltered investments* will best suit your particular investment objectives. For instance, rather than entering into a "balanced" oil and gas drilling program to offset the risks of the exploratory drilling, you might consider coupling an investment in exploratory oil with a more conservative investment in existing real estate projects. Such investment strategy might similarly fit your investment needs if immediate cash flow were an objective, along with eventual appreciation potential, since the real estate provides current income which would eventually be augmented as successful oil and gas wells came "on stream." (Here, again, we are assuming that the drilling program proved successful.)

If need existed for immediate tax shelter, but the programs which you reviewed in the "permanent" shelter area seemed substandard, an investment in cattle feeding could give short-term deferral until better investment opportunities in "permanent shelter" areas became available. (But remember the risk that your cattle feeding investment might prove unsuccessful, thus wiping out all or a substantial part of your investment capital.)

If you wished to invest in an oil and gas, real estate, or cattle feeding project, but did not have the funds to do so, investment in an "exotic" could provide an increase in your currently available spendable cash. While tax liabilities would accrue in the future, distributions from your oil, real estate or cattle investment could then satisfy the subsequent "phantom income" tax liabilities. (Again, however, remember if none of these programs were economically successful, you would have to find other sources of funds to pay the "phantom income" tax. And you should thoroughly evaluate the tax and economic risks associated with investment in the exotics before being lured by the apparent initial tax savings into making this a part of your tax shelter investment strategy.)

If adequate funds are available to permit you to diversify your tax-sheltered investment over several investment areas, a blending may give you a "package" far more tailored to your needs than investment in any single tax shelter offering. Thus, a careful review of your own investment objectives and the investment characteristics of various types of tax-sheltered investments, can lead to a highly personalized, and thus particularly potentially rewarding, investment program.

29.

How To Select
The Particular Program

[¶2901] SELECTIVITY—THE KEY TO
PROFITABLE TAX-SHELTERED INVESTMENT

Once you have selected the kind, or kinds, of tax-sheltered investment programs whose investment characteristics coincide with your particular objectives, you must select the particular program or programs in which to invest. This decision, which is far more difficult than the determination of the *kinds* of tax shelter you need, is the key to whether your tax-sheltered investment experience will be a pleasant one or a nightmare. Unfortunately, it is often the most neglected consideration in your tax-sheltered investment strategy.

Just as in the stock market, tax-sheltered investment offers good, mediocre, and bad investment opportunities. (It also offers its share of outright frauds.) If you are not willing to take the time properly to evaluate the particular investment opportunities presented to you, your romance with tax shelters will be short lived; and you will frequently find that "divorcing" yourself from your tax shelter is a difficult and expensive process. (As to getting out of the tax-sheltered investment that has gone sour, see Chapter 30.) Unfortunately, selecting the right tax-sheltered investment is a complicated process.

It is quite a temptation to disregard the numerous steps that need to be taken to insure that you have selected a tax shelter which presents a reasonable opportunity for profit. (Remember, this is an *opportunity* only: even the best tax-sheltered investment may prove financially unrewarding due to economic and other factors beyond your control or the control of your program management.) However, attempts at oversimplifying the selection process will almost always result in a poor investment choice.

The less scrupulous promoter usually sounds just as sincere as the sponsor offering an excellent investment opportunity. As a matter of fact, his story will usually be much more appealing; investment returns at which he "hints" will be far greater; and the risks will be downplayed. However, if you succumb to this "siren song", (see ¶2902) you will pay a significant price tag in loss of your hard dollar investment and in unexpected tax consequences that may worsen, rather than improve, your tax picture.

You would never consider making an investment in the stock market without a careful analysis of the outlook for the industry in question and the probability (or lack thereof) that the company whose stock you are considering will outperform the industry. However, in a rising stock market, a number of stocks perform well because of general market reaction, even though the company may be doing rather poorly. In a "direct participation" investment, you cannot depend on profiting through marketplace reaction. The only way to profit through a tax shelter program thus is to apply the same selectivity in choosing your tax-sheltered investments that you would apply in analyzing a prospective investment program in common stocks.

[¶2902]   AVOIDING THE SIREN SONG

It is an incredible but true fact that a large number of the tax shelter scandals publicized in the financial press involved huge investments by knowledgeable businessmen or by affluent investors who have available to them expert financial counsel. In most instances, the very factors that caused their investments to crater would have been readily apparent with even minimal investigation.

Why do otherwise intelligent business people invest in a tax shelter which is doomed from the first to failure? Why have recognized investment counselors poured so much of their clients' money into such investments? The answer usually can be found in the inherent unwillingness of investors and their advisors to abide by the maxim that "there is no free lunch"—the refusal to look behind an offering which is "too good to be true."

[¶2902.1]   Beware of the Tax-Shelter Fraud

The tax-shelter fraud almost invariably involves a promise of higher-than-usual tax benefits and high-than-usual return. It is normally sponsored by a promoter who has little operational experience in the industry in question. Usually, investors will be assured that their dollars are being invested with industry operators who have been unwilling, in the past, to "permit" investors to share in their highly lucrative operations;

and that the promoter's superior financial abilities have permitted him to strike a particularly advantageous arrangement with these industry members. However, when the returns being offered are significantly higher than legitimate operators in the industry have historically provided, or think they can provide, it is time to ask yourself, "Why can this program, sponsored by persons not directly involved in the industry, offer me returns that legitimate industry sources can not."

"Financial expertise" is seldom a satisfactory answer.

What steps should you take, then, to avoid being added to the ranks of disillusioned investors?

A preliminary decision in selecting your particular tax-sheltered investment is whether you wish to invest in public programs registered with the Securities and Exchange Commission or with your State securities agency, or whether your investments will be limited to "private placements." (The legal distinctions under the securities laws between public and private offerings are discussed in Chapter 31.)

One bit of investment folklore is that public programs are invariably inferior to private ones. Another misconception—that the "registered" nature of a program insures its economic soundness—is equally fallacious. Regulatory agencies do everything they can to see that the risks of the offering have been fully disclosed and that obvious sponsor overreaching in the form of excess compensation, blatant conflicts of interest, and other "structuring" considerations have been restricted. However, Federal and State securities agencies are not in the position to review the economic soundness of the underlying projects, and, due to budgetary and other limitations, are in no position to "guarantee" that the promoter will not defraud you. (See Chapter 31.)

The private placement can be structured in such a way that the admittedly *heavy cost of "going public,"* which, with sales costs, may eat up as much as 15 percent to 25 percent of the offering proceeds, can be avoided. This is particularly important where a relatively small amount of money (under $500,000) is needed for the venture. In any event, dollars spent in "going public" are dollars that are not available for investment in your program's projects. (On the other hand, when these dollars result in more complete disclosure, fairer investment structuring, and independent investigation by a broker-dealer of the economic soundness of the program, they may still be very valuable to you.)

While a number of very legitimate syndicators are unable, or unwilling, to take on the burdens of "going public," there are numerous good investment opportunities in public programs, and numerous bad investment opportunities in private ones—and vice versa.

[¶2902.2]   Advantages and Disadvantages of
             Public Registration

In addition to the reduction of venture capital available for the projects, many syndicators who could easily afford the costs of a public registration are unwilling to put up with the time delays, loss of flexibility in deciding how to manage your money, and the general *"hassle" of the public program.* If their superior performance records (or the "appearance" of such records) have generated a substantial investor following, they see no need to incur the burdens of public registration. However, you should be aware that many private offerings are just as "loaded," and in some instances more so, than public offerings.

If you have significant amounts of money to invest in a single project (or are represented by an investment advisor whose "pooling" of his clients' capital gives him a similar bargaining position), negotiations with the sponsor of the private program may also permit you to secure a more favorable investment structure or a *tailoring* of the proposed investment *to your particular investment needs.* As seen, an investment can be structured to emphasize tax benefits, cash flow, appreciation potential, or a combination of these benefits. Since the legitimate syndicator is primarily interested in securing venture capital for a project which he believes can economically be undertaken, he may be quite flexible in tailoring the investment to your particular investment objectives, so long as the investment structure still provides him the necessary capital.

Public programs present the disadvantages of the high costs of public registration, and the discouraging effects of regulatory constraints on the legitimate sponsor. Also, it is an economic fact of life that unless a syndicator requires several million dollars in equity capital to fund his project, public registration is impractical. However, for larger fund-raising efforts, the public program offers the advantages of *enforced full disclosure* and *review of the fairness of the structure* of the program by the regulatory agencies, together with the advantages that the *employment of larger amounts of capital* in diversified projects can also provide. Sometimes this "larger capital" can prove a disadvantage. A syndicator who has done quite well in managing projects involving smaller amounts of money may founder when attempting greatly to increase the size of his operation overnight. Accordingly, a significant part of your review will be to determine whether the syndicator has experience in putting this amount of capital to use.

Another advantage of the public program is the availability of *independent "rating" services,* particularly in "public" oil, and the obligation imposed on the broker-dealer firm selling the investment to have conducted a *"due diligence"* of the program's *investigation* of its economic soundness. The extent of the broker-dealer's "due diligence" and "know your customer" obligations are discussed in Chapter 31. However, as noted in ¶2904, some broker-dealers give only lip service to honoring these obligations. Since public programs normally involve the more established types of tax-sheltered investment, you may also find it *easier to secure* the *information* necessary to evaluate the potential profitability of both the industry and the particular projects, and the syndicator's capabilities and prior track record.

[¶2902.3]   Type of Shelter You Need May Determine Your Choice

The decision as to public or private investment may well be answered for you by your earlier determinations as to the *type* of tax shelter in which you wish to invest (see Chapter 28), and the amount of money reasonably available to you to invest in tax shelters (see ¶2702). Private offerings usually involve either very small or very large minimum investments. If your investment capital is limited, or you wish to spread it over multiple investments, you may find that the $5,000 to $10,000 "units" of the public program best fit your particular investment program. Similarly, unless your overall investment program is large enough to permit you to retain experts to analyze proposed investment economics or to retain an investment advisor who performs such an analysis on behalf of you and his other clients (see ¶2904), a properly selected public program may be your only means of intelligent investment selection.

The *public market* primarily centers around investments in *oil and gas, real estate,* and, to a lesser extent, *cattle.* Occasionally, other types of syndications—including equipment leasing, horse racing, and agricultural programs—will be the subject of SEC registrations. However, this is far less common. Without question, oil and gas has found a permanent source of needed investment capital through publicly-registered drilling programs, many of which offer excellent investment opportunities.

The public drilling program industry has formed its own trade association—the Oil Investment Institute—which attempts to upgrade investment opportunities in "public" oil.

While the popularity of public real estate programs has substantially declined from its mid-1970 high, the handful of public syndicators who remain are raising substantial public dollars each year. The Real Estate Securities and Syndication Institute, established by the National Association of Realtors, performs a function similar to the Oil Investment Institute in both the public and private real estate syndication areas. In addition, there are a large number of "intrastate" real estate and agricultural syndications offered to residents of a single state, with such programs being particularly prevalent in the State of California. And while public cattle programs are far less in vogue at the present time due to the economic woes of the cattle industry, the apparent improvement in cattle economics should see an increase in the availability of such programs. However, if your investment is to be in tax shelter areas other than oil and gas, real estate or cattle, you may find that your investment opportunities are limited to the private market.

[¶2902.4]   Blind Pools Versus Specified Projects

Another factor which may influence your choice between public and private programs is your desire to be able to look at the specific projects in which your program will invest. Due to the size of public programs and the time delays involved in clearing them through securities agencies, the projects in SEC-registered offerings are normally not specified in the registration or offering document, but are left to the selection of the sponsor. For this reason, such offerings are frequently referred to as *"blind pools"* or "blank check" programs. On the other hand, the private offering normally involves specified projects.

The specified/unspecified nature of public and private offerings should not play as key a role in your investment decision as you might think. In most instances, even where the projects are specified, it will be quite difficult for you, whether you are an investor or an investment advisor, personally to analyze the economic soundness of the projects. For the $5,000 to $25,000 investment which you are planning to make in the public program, securing expert assistance to perform such an evaluation solely on your behalf would be impractical; you will instead rely on a "pooled" evaluation of such projects by your broker-dealer or similar screening source. In the private program, the larger size of your investment (or of the group of investors represented by your investment advisor) will permit such an economic evaluation.

Your "public versus private" decision should be dictated more by your overall investment objectives than by any automatic exclusion of public programs. Even for the investor with huge amounts of money to shelter each year, the higher quality public programs, such as the better "public oil" offerings, should receive serious consideration. And in the final analysis, a careful review of the economics of the underlying projects, is far more important than any generalized conclusion concerning the pros and cons of public versus private investment.

[¶2902.5]   How Bad Investments Are
             Made to Look Good

A critical requirement when choosing among competing proposals for your tax-sheltered dollars is to be *realistic concerning the return* from the investment you can reasonably expect. You certainly need to have a return objective. However, if you are not realistic in setting this objective, you will automatically eliminate the legitimate investment proposals offered to you, and be a target for the promoter who is far less concerned about with the likelihood of obtaining the projected results he hints are available. The level of realistic return objectives is discussed elsewhere. (As to computing return, see Chapter 4.)

Your evaluation of the potential "return" from an investment requires a review of the points made in Chapter 4. A program with far less investment merit can be made more attractive on paper than a legitimate investment opportunity. This is done by varying the "base" on which the return is to be computed and by ignoring the fact that in many tax shelter investment areas the cash flow also includes a "return of capital" element from a depleting asset. Tax benefits "going in" will be offset by tax obligations "coming out," including crossover, recapture, and "phantom income" problems.

As a rule of thumb:

☐ Projected returns in excess of 15 percent to 20 percent should be viewed with suspicion. Even these returns are difficult to attain.

☐ Initial tax deductions in excess of 130 percent to 150 percent have usually been "purchased" at the expense of eventual economic return.

☐ Deductions in excess of 200 percent to 400 percent are signals of very shaky economics.

☐ Projections which do not illustrate taxes payable on sale, and tax effects of payments on prior borrowings or nonrecourse purchase obligations, don't give the full—or even a balanced—picture.

☐ Have the syndicator, or your accountant, also show you figures showing the effect of:
  • Performance at less than projected levels
  • Sales necessary for you to "break even."
  • Sales necessary to pay non-recourse or recourse borrowings or required contributions.
  • Effects of foreclosure.

The return computations also must not ignore the time value of your money, or that a portion of cash flow and any proceeds from the sale of the program properties will go to the syndicator. Likewise, you should be very suspicious of profitability based upon an assumed appreciation in the value of the program's assets.

         **HOW TO REVIEW AN
OFFERING DOCUMENT**

Your likelihood of profiting from a tax-sheltered investment depends upon the *structure* of the investment; the *economic soundness* of the projects to be undertaken; and the *caliber of management*. Your initial source of information concerning these prerequisites for profitability will be the *offering document* that State and Federal securities laws require be delivered to you even in "private placements." In some smaller tax shelter syndications, costs of preparing a proper offering document, or the ignorance of the syndicator concerning his obligations under Federal and State securities laws, results in no such offering document being prepared for your benefit. Admittedly, the plight of the small syndicator in attempting to comply with these securities law requirements is a serious one, and many small real estate syndicators and members of the oil and gas industry raise their capital through arrangements that offer you little more in the way of information than their expectations concerning the project and a brief contract. However, your plight as an investor is equally serious: how do you or your advisor analyze the likelihood of profit from a given investment unless you are provided adequate background information. Thus, unless the investment sponsor is willing to provide you with sufficient information to make an informed investment decision, you should not invest unless you have particular reason to have personal confidence in the sponsor's ability and integrity.

This offering document that you will use as the point of departure for your investment analysis may tell you more about your proposed investment than you care to know. If prepared in compliance with securities law guidelines, you will be given considerable generic information concerning the risks of tax-sheltered investments in general. While these are facts of which you must be aware, the "scare" language, which will be applicable to the best along with the worst tax-sheltered investments, and the general "formal" approach, may make it seem tedious for you also to extract the particular nuggets which can serve as guidelines in determining whether you wish to proceed further in considering this investment. However, while extracting this information may seem a chore, it can save you much greater distress if it helps you avoid a potentially disastrous investment.

What can the offering document reveal to you? Zero in on the following areas:

☐ *The sponsor's compensation.* Is it performance oriented, so that there is sufficient incentive for the sponsor to perform well on your behalf? Does the syndicator take fees at every turn? This may be an indication that he is attempting to direct attention away from the amount

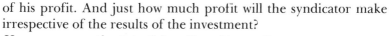

of his profit. And just how much profit will the syndicator make irrespective of the results of the investment?

☐ How severe are the *potential conflicts of interest?*

☐ Does *management* seem to have an *experience* in the type of projects they are now undertaking? Are they suddenly taking on much larger activities then they have attempted in the past? Is management's experience primarily in financial areas, or do they possess expertise in the technical side of the industry in which they will be operating? Are they adequately financed? Do they possess a sufficient, and well qualified, staff?

☐ How well has *management* performed in the past for its investors? This *"track record"* analysis is the single most important factor in evaluating a proposed tax-sheltered investment.

It is not as easy a task as might be expected to analyze the information contained in an offering document to determine whether or not there is validity to the program being offered you. As mentioned, disclosure concerning the reputable tax-sheltered investment often conspicuously parallels the disclosure on an offering which has little if any chance for profit. All programs are structured so that the sponsor will make *some profit* even if you lose money. Almost all contain conflicts of interest. And the sponsor may have impressive credentials but far less impressive actual ability or integrity.

This does not mean, however, that studying the offering document is a waste of time. It will highlight the problem areas in the particular type of offering and alert you to the need to be prepared for potential recapture, taxes on phantom income, or additional cash requirements, thus permitting you to prepare in advance for these eventualities. Furthermore, a review of the information concerning compensation and conflicts, management credentials, and past performance, should enable you to eliminate a number of potential investments from further consideration.

[¶2903.1]   Guidelines on Compensation and Conflicts of Interest

Insofar as compensation and conflicts of interest are concerned, certain guidelines can assist your review. The various guidelines adopted for publicly registered programs by the North American Securities Administrators Association, the Midwest Securities Commissioners Association and the National Association of Securities Dealers, all contained in Appendix 3100-1, will assist you in analyzing whether a proposed private investment is unnecessarily risky. Compliance with these guidelines does not insure a potentially profitable investment. Here, your track record review and the economic evaluation performed on your behalf by your broker-dealer or investment advisor will be your key guides.

Some of these guidelines may be unduly restrictive. A number of sponsors of high quality oil and gas offerings have now departed the "public program" ranks, due in part to their reluctance to comply with State blue sky guidelines. A number of former public program sponsors have also been driven out of the market place by the blue sky guidelines for the very reasons that lead to their adoption, they highlight potential problem areas.

Your review of the structure of your tax-sheltered investment, and of the basic credentials of management, should help you eliminate a large number of potential investments from further consideration. However, in both the public and private area, a number of investments will remain which, on their face, offer little to distinguish them from a structure review alone. (Some investments may even offer a better structure, but less profit potential, than those put together by a "premium" management who can afford to ask a higher price for their product.) It is at this point that *reviewing the sponsor's track record* will help you determine not only how past investors have fared in general—a key to management's ability and credentials—but whether or not the potential problems created by the sharing arrangement and conflicts of interest in even the best-structured tax-sheltered investment have in practice worked to the economic disadvantage of prior investors.

[¶2903.2]   Techniques for Analyzing A
Sponsor's Track Record

Analyzing a sponsor's track record, particularly based upon the data which can be included in the offering document to be provided a prospective investor without running afoul of securities law requirements, is not an easy task. Often, an analysis of the profitability of prior ventures requires an estimation of the present worth of the venture's properties. However, appraisals of such net worth, even when secured from "independent" sources, create serious "fraud" potential when such appraisals are secured at the sponsor's request. (A possible exception is a reserve evaluation of the present worth of oil and gas reserves prepared by an independent petroleum engineering firm, since such information could be included in an SEC-registered prospectus.) Thus, your track record analysis of the results of prior real estate, agricultural syndication, or cattle breeding projects often must be based upon data secured by an independent evaluation by consultants hired *on your behalf*, rather upon data provided in a sponsor-prepared offering document. It is virtually impossible to tell the results of prior real estate, cattle breeding, and agricultural syndications from the data permitted to be included in an offering document, although the included information will permit you to determine the level of initial tax deductions generated for prior programs, and whether or not any cash flow is presently being generated by such investments. However in the oil and gas area, a comparison of dollars invested versus dollars distributed, with the most current figures being used to project future revenues, will furnish useful information concerning the likelihood of "payout" of prior investments. For further discussion, see ¶1301. Even in oil and gas, the prospectus-based analysis of prior performance can be misleading. Results for programs less than two years old will be of little value, since in most instances development drilling is not complete and a number of wells may not as yet be "on stream." Also, since the production from oil and gas is "flush" in its early period and thereafter declines, a "straight line" rather than "declining curve" projection of current incomes will overstate return. And there is no assurance as to the length of time existing wells will continue to produce. However, the analysis mentioned should permit a targeting of prior programs which will clearly *not* pay out. Similarly, since results of the feeding of a given lot of cattle can be determined within a period of months after the investment, track record analysis in the cattle feeding area is substantially easier than cattle breeding.

Track record analysis based upon offering circular data is not an infallible means of judging program performance. If the size of the offering, the type of project, or the area of operations have changed, or if key personnel have left the company, prior performance may not be representative of present potential. Likewise, the existing projects to be undertaken may be of higher or lower quality than those undertaken in the past. Furthermore, track record analysis should not be used to "rate" programs, but merely to eliminate (or at least emphasize the need for further investigation) of those syndicators who have, in the past, sponsored ventures which have consistently proven unprofitable.

[¶2903.3]   Compare Past Performance With Sponsor's Representations

Comparing past performance with representations as to anticipated results can also prove quite useful in evaluating a sponsor's "bona fides." If a sponsor represents that a given level of tax deductions will be generated by his current project, with an early and specified cash flow, compare his earlier ventures to see if they have achieved similar results. Such prior projects may have differed in their objectives from the present one. However, the information should prove of considerable assistance to you in proceeding further. Likewise, a comparison of projections provided investors in connection with past ventures with the actual result of those programs should help you in evaluating the reliability of the syndicator's current projections.

By now, you should realize that analyzing a proposed tax-sheltered investment is indeed a complicated process. Reading the track record, analyzing the sharing arrangement and conflicts of interest, and projecting tax benefits going in and coming out, clearly call for expert counseling from your lawyer, accountant, or financial advisor. Even if you are a highly competent financial counselor, you have probably realized that it will be necessary for you to go beyond the prospectus to determine the true profit potential for the industry in question and for the projects to be undertaken by this program; the actual profitability of prior ventures; and the true capabilities of management. And you may have determined that making certain of these decisions is beyond your personal capacities. If so, you are ahead of most investors and financial advisors, who often make the potentially fatal mistake of assuming that a knowledge of basic tax consequences and various general rules concerning compensation arrangements, conflicts of interest, and other "structuring" considerations, is enough to analyze the potential profitability of a tax-sheltered investment.

[¶2903.4]   A Checklist You Should Use Before Investing

There are many essential questions concerning the potential profitability of a particular tax-sheltered program that are not answered by the offering document and the other information which is generally available to you (or which could be intelligently analyzed by you) as a potential tax shelter investor. Before actually commiting to a tax shelter program, you must have secured satisfactory answers to the following questions:

- ☐ I understand the basic tax concepts, but how "sure" is it that these tax benefits will stand up on audit? And how likely are they to be taken away by subsequent changes in the tax law?
- ☐ What are the pros and cons of the program structure as compared with other offerings within this industry?
- ☐ What are the actual capabilities of the management of this program?
- ☐ How profitable have the prior ventures sponsored by this syndicator actually proved to his prior investors?
- ☐ What is the true profit potential of the present projects, both in general and under the sharing arrangement and conflicts of interest present in this particular investment?

It is impossible for you to make an intelligent investment decision unless you can secure reliable answers to these questions. To do so, you will need expert help.

**EXPERT COUNSEL —
AVAILABLE AND WORTH IT**

As indicated in ¶2902, your final screening of the tax shelter programs available to you will require expert assistance. Only your own personal tax and financial advisor can counsel you on your personal economic and tax needs, and the tax and economic ramifications of the proposed investment on your personal situation. This same advisor will frequently be able to give you highly competent advice on the accuracy of the representations concerning the tax consequences of the proposed investment, and the degree to which the anticipated benefits are subject to disallowance on audit or a loss through changes in the tax laws.

If your advisor specializes in the tax shelter area, he often can counsel you on the program structure—on whether it possesses the various "plus" features which you should look for in this type of tax-sheltered investment and whether customary safe-guards and restrictions have been imposed on syndicator "profiteering."

The final step in analyzing the tax shelter offerings which have survived the initial screening and are now competing for your tax shelter dollars requires an informed investigation of the *true capabilities of management*, the *profitability of prior investment,* and the *potential of the present projects.* Even if you were a highly skilled tax shelter consultant, at this stage you would need to retain industry technicians to assist you in this evaluation. There is no one like another geologist to determine if an oil sponsor's geological staff in fact possesses true expertise or merely knows how to talk the "oil game." The geologist or engineer retained on your behalf can talk to management, sizing up their potential; can review prior "discoveries" to estimate how many dollars have in fact been discovered to the investors' account and over how long a period these moneys will be received; and can review the profit potential of the wells to be drilled in a forthcoming program or the prospects available to a "blind pool" syndication from the sponsor's "inventory." An independent accountant can verify the thoroughness with which prior records have been kept, the accuracy of the tax treatment and reporting, and whether sufficient steps have been taken properly to account for and protect investor funds. Similar industry professionals in cattle, real estate and other tax-sheltered investment areas can be used to judge the profit potential of other types of tax-sheltered investment.

A "typical" thorough evaluation of a tax shelter offering involves a "team manager"—usually a financial expert—who will retain necessary technicians, accountants, and attorneys to evaluate the adequacy of program structure, the tax and legal ramifications of the program, and its profit potential, relying both on meetings with management; a review both the programs structure, the prior programs of the sponsor, and the existing inventory of properties; and a thorough checking out of the syndicator through the "jungle telegraph." The reports of each of the retained consultants will be forwarded to the team manager, who will analyze them and present his conclusions to you or your personal financial advisor. From this, a truly informed decision can be made concerning whether or not you should consider investing in this particular tax shelter offering.

But isn't this process expensive? If you are a very wealthy investor, sheltering hundreds of thousands of dollars a year, the costs of such a review will represent only a fraction of the dollars you are putting at risk. Obviously, if your tax shelter needs are more modest—from $5,000 to $25,000 a year, or in a single program—the costs of such a thorough analysis would be impractical *IF* it were performed solely for your account and solely at your own expense. However, no matter how small your tax shelter needs, such an investment analysis is just as necessary for you as it is for the more wealthy investor. And such advice is available to you, at a price which you can afford, by utilizing sources where the investment advisory needs of many investors just like you permit a *"pooled review"* to make such a proper analysis economically feasible.

[¶2904.1]   Sources of Pooled Reviews

There are many *sources of* such *pooled reviews* available to you. *Brokerage houses,* large and small, which offer tax-sheltered investments normally have a tax shelter investment department which will make such analyses as a part of their "due diligence" investigation. *Investment advisors* advising numerous clients with tax shelter needs frequently retain industry consultants to provide such information for them. And many *banks* provide similar services for that portion of their clientele in need of tax-sheltered investment advice.

Unfortunately, not all banks, investment advisors, and brokerage houses perform the type of in-depth, objective, and technically oriented analysis which is necessary to provide you with informed investment advice. The size of the firm, or the fact that it possesses a "tax shelter" department, offers no assurance that it is providing proper backup review before it advises you to invest. However, while it is difficult for you to analyze the bona fides of a particular sponsor or syndicator, it is not hard for you to quiz your potential advisor to determine whether or not he has performed the proper in-depth analysis on which to base his advice. If your questions show that he is simply relying upon his own review of the offering document and his personal "feel" concerning management, whether or not based upon personal meetings, or if his advice is based primarily upon tax and "structure" analysis, without the benefit of a review by experienced industry technicians of the economic potential of the program and the other factors which we have discussed, be very careful in relying on his advice. Similarly, as an investment advisor, you will find that retaining such industry reviewing sources is well worth it in the increasingly reliable and valuable advice you are able to provide your clients.

You should also insure that this "advisor" will be *monitoring the investment* to determine whether or not the syndicator is living up to his promises concerning what will, and will not, be done in connection with your investment. In addition, if things start going badly for your investment—even if this is not the syndicator's fault—early steps may lead to correction of the problems and the saving of the project before it is too late. Without monitoring on your behalf, the syndicator may "panic," and fail to take necessary steps, such as securing additional capital contributions, where this is required, or continuing to maintain distributions to investors when such moneys should instead be held as working capital reserve.

With proper monitoring, failures to comply with contractual obligations or good business practices can "politely" be brought to the syndicator's attention and the problems corrected. If necessary, your advisor can alert you and your fellow investors to the need to step in to remove the general partner or property manager—rights frequently granted to investors under the syndicate agreement (see Chapter 30)—before the venture has reached the point of no return.

Expert advice is available to you as a tax-sheltered investor and is well worth the price.

30.

How to Get Out of a "Bad" Tax-Sheltered Investment

[¶3001]   **HOW TO GET OUT OF A
                        TAX-SHELTERED INVESTMENT**

Up to this point, we have considered ways for you to *get into* a tax-sheltered investment. However, tax shelters *are* speculative. And the risks of investing in a tax shelter that was poorly thought out (or even fraudulent), or poorly managed, create a real possibility that your tax shelter will find itself in trouble. Even when the venture has been highly profitable, the time will come when, due to cash needs or "crossover" problems, it is to your advantage to dispose of your tax-sheltered investment. Thus, investors have been known to wail, "Don't tell me how to *get into* a new tax shelter; tell me how to *get out of* the ones that I am in!"

Unfortunately, it is much easier to invest in a tax shelter than to get out of one. Both State securities laws, and economic and tax realities, highly restrict both the legal right to transfer your partnership interest and the availability of any market in the event that a transfer is theoretically possible. Furthermore, due to the tax consequences of disposing your interest, either directly or through an involuntary sale upon the foreclosure of outstanding mortgage indebtedness, "getting out" may be the worst possible solution for you.

This chapter will explore what you should do when you find that either you, or your project, are "in trouble." As we shall see, in some instances a proper solution is to dispose of the property or your partnership interest, taking all available steps to limit undesirable tax consequences. In other instances, it may be to your advantage to salvage the venture, even if this calls for additional capital contributions by you.

You have just discovered that your project is "in trouble." That nonrecourse financing which seemed so desirable when the project was

Providing additional capital will normally require an amendment to your syndicate agreement. Here, the typical restrictions on assessments imposed by State and NASD registration guidelines may actually work to your disadvantage. While amending the syndicate agreement to provide for additional contributions, which might even run afoul of registration guidelines, raises unresolved securities law questions, practicality normally dictates that these risks be taken rather than risking unnecessary loss of the project.

In the optimum situation, all investors will agree to make the additional contributions. However, in the syndicate in trouble, the situation is seldom "optimum." Hopefully, an agreement can be reached as to a preferred treatment for those investors who are willing to make contributions. If not, the salvage attempts may founder. Here, it may be to the advantage of the existing investors to buy out the recalcitrant parties.

[¶3003.1]   How to Seek Outside Sources of Capital

If too few investors are willing to make additional contributions, outside capital sources must be sought. Usually, an amendment to the syndicate agreement will be required to give such new investors preferential treatment on both tax losses and return of capital to give them sufficient incentive to pour dollars into a project already in trouble. Such "special allocations" would seem to possess sufficient "economic substance" that they would not run afoul of the restrictions on special allocations imposed by the Tax Reform Act of 1976. However, here again, it may prove difficult to secure the cooperation of the existing investors. (The most effective method of securing their cooperation is to remind them that the alternative is the total loss of the project, with its adverse tax consequences.)

At this stage, working with the lender becomes a must. The lender must be convinced that every effort is being made to save the project, and that these efforts will in all probability succeed. If so, the lender frequently will be willing to ease the strict terms of the mortgage. However, it is critical that these negotiations be begun as quickly as possible and that every effort be made to convince the lender that the project can and will be turned around.

The lender, as a condition of his cooperation, may suggest or require that debt be converted from nonrecourse to recourse. You should think a long time before you agree to any such change, since many attempts to "turn around" a faltering project do not meet with success. If you do agree to taking on a recourse liability, the dollar amount of this recourse should be strictly limited. If at all possible, each investor should be liable only for his pro-rata portion of any such agreed recourse amount. You should only accept recourse liability to the extent you are willing and able to pay off these amounts in the event the project cannot be saved. (See ¶2703.)

[¶3003.2]   Selling Your Project

It may become obvious that, due to an inability to secure agreement among the investors to the necessary syndicate agreement modifications, or because of the financial requirements involved, the existing syndicate will not be able to save the project. Consideration should then be given to disposing of the project to a buyer who is willing to assume the obligations. A "deed in lieu of foreclosure" normally will trigger the same tax consequences as if the property had been foreclosed. (See Rev. Rul. 76-111.) If, however, despite the problems, there is still a marketable equity in the property, the possibilities of a "like for like" tax free exchange of the project for another, less troubled, real estate property should be considered. While you undoubtedly will be required to take a substantial "hair cut" on the value of your equity, and finding such a property and negotiating the exchange will not be easy, avoiding the immediate adverse tax consequences are far preferable to a sale of your project.

[¶3003.3]   What to Do When Foreclosure Is Unavoidable

In some instances, you will find that foreclosure cannot be avoided. In that event, the adverse tax consequences we have previously discussed—tax on the difference between your "adjusted basis" in the property and the full amount of the mortgage, and recapture—will result, with a substantial portion of the "gain" being taxed as ordinary income. (The excess will, however, be taxed as long-term capital gain. See Rev. Rul. 76-311.) However, you can at least make an effort to direct when this gain will be received, so as to mitigate, to the greatest degree possible, the adverse tax consequences.

In the past, the syndicate often engaged in every possible delaying tactic to put off the actual entry of the degree of foreclosure and the sale of the property. However, as a result of the Tax Reform Act of 1976, your adverse tax consequences will now date from the time at which the foreclosure petition is filed, assuming the property is eventually foreclosed and sold.

Even if you are prepared to "let the property go," it may be to your best interest to prolong the loss of the property, with its adverse tax consequences, to permit you to do some tax planning to cushion the adverse tax impact. Other tax-sheltered investments can be found—hopefully of better economic merit—to offset the taxable gain. Or careful tax planning may permit you to "bunch" losses and deductions in such a manner that "income averaging" (see ¶701) will be of assistance. To permit such advantageous planning, you will have to work with the lender, and at least consider the possibility of additional advances.

[¶3003.4]   Do Your Have the Right to Demand
             Your Money Back?

Another remedy you may wish to consider with the project "in trouble" is to determine whether you have a "right of rescission"—the right to demand that the syndicator return your entire investment, plus interest, less amounts previously distributed to you—under Federal and State securities laws.

Your right to rescind for an improper failure on the part of the syndicator to "register" the security, to secure your investment through the services of a registered broker-dealer, or to comply with the "full disclosure" ("anti-fraud") provisions of Federal and State securities laws, are discussed in Chapter 31. An appropriate assertion of your rights under these securities laws will at least return to you the amount of your original investment, assuming you are successful in asserting these rights. This may be far more than any cash that would be available to you if the syndicate property could be sold. However, the tax consequences of this rescission will be the same as if you had sold your interest. This creates a particular pitfall in "exotic" investments, when asserting your rights, even when you have been defrauded, will trigger recapture of most of the tax benefits.

[¶3004]   **COURSES OF ACTION YOU MAY CHOOSE WHEN YOUR PERSONAL CIRCUMSTANCES CHANGE**

Up to this point, we have assumed that you are dealing with a syndicate in trouble. However, in many instances, it is you, rather than the syndicate, who are "in trouble." Your financial circumstances may have changed, and it may be necessary for you to liquidate your tax-sheltered investment. Or your investment may now be generating a positive cash flow, or have reached a "crossover point," which is compounding your tax problems. At this stage, you may wish to consider a sale or gift of your partnership interest.

The problems of finding a purchaser for your syndicate interest have already been discussed. While efforts have been made to create trading markets in public limited partnership interests, these "secondary markets" have seldom worked well in practice. Accordingly, you will normally find that your partnership interest is a true "frozen asset."

The tax consequences on the sale of your interest will normally eat up far more of those proceeds than you may have anticipated. The taxable gain should be taxable, except for "recapture" portion, at *long-term capital gains rates*. However, this "gain" will be based on your substantially reduced "adjusted basis" in the property. Also, you will find that your deductions, which frequently only served to offset "personal service" income (which would have been taxed at a maximum 50% rate) will now be treated, where the "ordinary gain" portion of the proceeds is concerned, as *"unearned income"* taxable without the benefits of any "maxi-tax" protection. Furthermore, the long-term capital gains portion of the proceeds will create an *item of tax preference* which will lead to a dollar for dollar loss of "personal service" income protection on your current earned income and may result in a minimum tax liability. For this reason, you need to carefully discuss the tax consequences of any sale with your personal tax advisor to determine whether the tax detriments of a sale outweigh your current "crossover" and other current tax problems.

[¶3004.1]   Is a Gift Transaction The Answer?

If a sale is not called for, you may wish to consider a gift of your tax-sheltered investment. While the gift may subject you to gift tax liability on the current fair market value of your interest and will result in taxable gain if the mortgage balance exceeds your adjusted basis (see *James W. Johnson, Jr.,* 495 F.2d 1079 (1974)), the gift otherwise is a nontaxable transaction both to you and the donee of the partnership interest. However, the donee will receive a "carry over basis" in the property. In other words, when the donee sells the property, he will be taxed on the gains in the same manner that you would have been if you had held the property. Even as to substantially appreciated property, the tax consequences on sale may be so great that you will have in fact created an economic detriment for the donee by your gift rather than an economic benefit. Thus, while it may seem to your advantage to transfer property which is generating not only positive cash flow but taxable income or is in a "crossover" situation, to your children, who presumptively are in lower tax brackets, careful consideration of all the tax ramifications is clearly called for before such a transfer is made. If the transfer is made of a property which is in imminent danger of foreclosure, any predetermined plan to lessen the tax impact by such a transfer to a lower-bracket family member may be subject to being set aside by the IRS. Similarly, special rules apply to a transfer to a trust for children where the property is sold within two years of the transfer.

[¶3004.2]   Former Solutions May Not Offer
Tax Relief Under New Rules

In the past, one solution to the problems just mentioned was a gift to charity. However, under current tax rules, the gift may create little tax relief for you, particularly where debt exceeds basis, or substantial recapture is threatened.

Prior to the Tax Reform Act of 1976, the "final solution" to the problems of the tax due on the sale of appreciated property with a low adjusted basis was to hold the property until your death. At that time, your beneficiaries would receive a "stepped-up" basis equal to the fair market value of the property. However, as a result of the Tax Reform Act, your beneficiaries will be taxed upon their sale of the property at its "carry over basis". Thus, this final means of avoiding eventual recapture of excess tax benefits has been eliminated; and, as in the case of the gift, you may actually have passed on an economic detriment to your heirs rather than an economic benefit. As to properties acquired through tax-sheltered investment prior to December 31, 1976, the Tax Reform Act does provide for a partial step up in basis based upon the length of time which the property was held before and after December 31, 1976.

"Getting out" of a tax shelter project which is in trouble, or which is now creating tax problems rather than tax benefits for you, presents no easy solutions. The best solution is a careful screening prior to investment, and insisting upon prior "monitoring" arrangements and provisions in the syndicate agreement which will help keep the property out of trouble or provide prearranged methods of dealing with problems as they arise. However, when problems do strike, careful tax planning, even after the fact, can help you cushion the adverse tax consequences and hopefully save all or a part of your investment.

31.

Rights Under Federal and State Securities Laws

[¶3101]   **BE AWARE OF YOUR LEGAL RIGHTS AND OBLIGATIONS**

No matter what part you play in the "cast of characters" in a tax-sheltered investment, the implications of Federal and State securities laws as applied to tax-sheltered investments will be highly important to you. If you are the *sponsor* of a tax-sheltered investment, a failure to comply with these laws can subject you to various *civil and criminal penalties*. Even more importantly, from a practical standpoint, they will give your investor a right to recover his entire investment in your program, cash on cash, less the moneys that you have distributed to him: *tax benefits are not taken into account*. Furthermore, this "right of rescission" will apply irrespective of any actual wrongdoing on your part, and even though the venture as structured by you made good economic sense and was properly managed.

If you are a *broker-dealer* or *investment advisor,* the securities laws impose special obligations on your conduct, and often give the investor a direct right of action for recovery of his moneys from you, in addition to (and, in some instances, instead of from) the sponsor. And if you are an *investor*, securities laws give you special rights against the sponsor, the investment advisor whom you consulted concerning the investment, and the broker-dealer who sold it to you.

Federal and State securities laws impose these obligations irrespective of the nature of the "security" being offered. However, some special obligations are imposed in connection with the offering of tax-sheltered investments.

[¶3101.1]   Why Your Investment Is
                  Considered a Security

You may wonder why your tax-sheltered investment is considered a *"security"* for the purposes of these laws. After all, you are buying an interest in an oil well, an apartment house, or a cattle herd or farm, not a stock or a bond. However, as defined in both Federal and State securities acts, the term "security" includes an *"investment contract."* And any time money is accepted by a "professional" in an industry from nonindustry investors who will rely on the skill and facilities of some experienced third party in the industry—not necessarily the promoter of the investment—to employ their money with the hope of making a profit, an "investment contract" arises.

In some instances, a "one-on-one" transaction, such as an "agency" arrangement by a cattleman with a single investor, or the sale of an entire farm to one purchaser, may not involve the "common endeavor" element which is necessary for the "investment contract" characterization. Similar arguments can be made concerning book or master record/master artwork purchases. However, where there have been a number of such individual investments, the necessary "commonality" may still be present. See Bloomenthal, *Securities and Federal Corporate Law,* §2.19[10] (Clark Boardman Co., Ltd.: 1975).

So what does it mean that your tax-sheltered investment involves a "security?" Under Federal law, and the law of most states, the offering must either be *registered* with the Securities and Exchange Commission and State securities agencies, or the sponsor must bring his offering within certain specified *exemptions* from securities registration.

The most frequently asserted exemptions from Federal securities registration are the *"private offering"* and *"intrastate offering"* exemptions. The private offerings exemption, arising under §4(2) of the Securities Act, requires that the investors be "able to fend for themselves", i.e., have sufficient investment acumen that they are able to intelligently analyze the risks and *merits* of the offering, and are provided or given access to the same kind of information a registration statement would make available. Such offerings in the tax shelter area are frequently made pursuant to the conditions of the SEC's Rule 146, which imposes complicated conditions for claiming the private offering exemption. (It is definitely a mistake for the sponsor to assume that offerings to "twenty-five sophisticated investors"—the common "private placement" folklore—comply with the private offering exemption.) Both Rule 146 and the cases discussing the private offering exemption also impose additional requirements, including a prohibition of any use of "public" methods of soliciting prospective investors. The intrastate offering exemption can be claimed when the investors and the project are all located within the same State, and where the sponsor or the partnership are likewise organized under that State's laws. Here, again, the SEC provides guidelines for claiming the exemption under its Rule 147. It is critical to know that not only all investors, but all "offerees" must be located within the same state, and that the projects must likewise be located within that state. An offer to a single nonresident of the state will vitiate the availability of the exemption even though all persons who invest are residents of the state.

State laws vary substantially in the exemptions from securities registration available under their securities acts. The most common exemption is the "limited offering" exemption, although sales to institutional investors, and, in some states, to corporations and to certain professionals may likewise be exempted from securities registration.

It is just as important to comply with the exemptions from *State securities registration* as to secure the Federal exemption: complying with the Federal "private offering" exemption does not eliminate the necessity for complying with State law or coming with the State's exemption; and a failure to secure State exemption will create the same right of rescission for the investors.

[¶3101.2]   You Are Entitled to Full Disclosure and Other Protections

Even when an offering is properly exempt from securities registration, the sponsor is required to make *"full disclosure"* to his investors of all pertinent facts which might affect their investment decision. While this requirement is normally referred to as "anti-fraud," the term "full disclosure" is much more descriptive of the actual obligation. And this requirement applies to *all* offerings of securities, including offerings which are appropriately exempt from securities registration requirements: there is no exemption from the anti-fraud requirements of Federal and State securities laws.

Both Federal and State securities laws impose various controls on the manner in which the sponsor of an investment can attempt to interest you in his proposal. Highly important among these "distribution" requirements is the necessity that all persons who attempt to interest you in investing be *registered as "broker-dealers."* While it is not entirely clear, it would appear that a failure to register as a "broker-dealer"—and many syndicators who do not sell their interests through established brokerage houses do not so register—could give you a right of rescission even though the offering was properly exempt from securities registration and there was no violation of the "anti-fraud" requirements. The exemptions from Federal and State *securities registration* do not provide an exemption from *broker-dealer registration* requirements. As to those tax-sheltered syndicators required to register as broker-dealers, see SEC Exchange Act Rel. No. 34-13, 195, "Persons Deemed not to be Brokers" (January 21, 1977).

In order to claim certain protections under the Securities Act, a broker-dealer, whether or not registered, is required to conduct a *"due diligence" investigation* to determine whether or not the sponsor's SEC registration statement contains any misstatements or omissions of material facts. A similar obligation, affirmative in nature, is imposed on a broker-dealer in private offerings under the NASD *"Know Your Customer" rules.* And, while again not totally settled, "due diligence" and "know your customer" obligations would appear to require that the broker-dealer thoroughly investigate the economic substance of the project to be undertaken by the venture and the results of prior syndications.

[¶3102]   **HOW TO DETERMINE "FAIR,
                          JUST AND EQUITABLE"**

SEC registration requirements and the conditions necessary to claim the private offering exemption primarily turn around the requirement of "full disclosure." The private offering exemption also requires a high degree of investor knowledgeability and the absence of any "public" solicitation methods. However, State registration requirements, and the rules of the National Association of Securities Dealers applied to "public" offerings, impose an additional test that the terms of the offering must be "fair, just, and equitable." State and NASD registration and filing requirements apply primarily to offerings to the "public." However, an offering which is a nonpublic offering for Federal securities law purposes may not be exempt from the State or NASD requirements.

This fairness review does not involve an examination by the State or NASD authorities of the underlying economic merit of the projects to be undertaken; this would be far beyond the abilities of the staff. ("Due diligence" and "know your customer" obligations imposed on broker-dealers would seem to impose such a requirement.) Instead, review by the States and the NASD involves a testing of the *structure* of the investment in such areas as sponsor experience and net worth; investor suitability; sharing arrangement and compensation to the sponsor and its affiliates; conflicts of interest and other possibly abusive practices; rights of participants, including voting rights and the right to receive specified reports; permissible and impermissible marketing methods; and marketing compensation.

Determining when the structure of a tax shelter offering is "fair, just and equitable" is obviously a complicated task. After several years of case-by-case attempted resolution, State and NASD regulatory authorities have developed detailed guidelines to be applied to tax-sheltered offerings, with specific rules for real estate, oil and gas, and cattle feeding offerings. These rules are contained in appendix 3100-1.

The State and NASD guidelines are not directly applicable to private offerings. However, even in the "private"area, which constitutes most of the investment opportunities in tax shelter fields other than "public" oil, the guidelines cannot be ignored. If you are an investor, they present a highly important outline of various practices that, in the past, have proved abusive and have lead to a loss of investor funds. If you are a sponsor, a failure to disclose the risks created by your failure to comply with the substance of such guidelines would appear to violate Federal and State "full disclosure" requirements. And certain of the requirements are so basic that to ignore them would violate the fiduciary responsibility owed by the sponsor to his investors. (Violation of the sponsor's fiduciary obligation would not give the automatic right of rescission which arises for a violation of securities laws, but would give the investor a right to sue for damages.)

The State and NASD guidelines are also important to the broker-dealer and the investment advisor, even in private offerings. A broker-dealer would clearly be required under his NASD and similar obligations to justify selling a program which significantly varied from these standards. And, an investment advisor would owe similar responsibilities to his clients under his contractual and implied obligations.

This is not to say that strict compliance with the State and NASD guidelines is required in private offerings. The guidelines are aimed at correcting *potential* abuses; and, in many instances, work to the detriment of an investor who is dealing with a legitimate sponsor who could safely be entrusted with greater flexibility. However, the general tendency of ignoring the State and NASD restrictions in private offerings creates potential headaches for all the parties in a tax-sheltered investment.

Federal law, and the laws of nearly half of the States, require registration of investment advisors. Unfortunately for the investor, however, these laws are relatively limited in their requirements, and for the most part do not require the taking of an examination or other test concerning an investment advisor's qualifications to advise his clients. However, it is clear that under common law principles, the investment advisor would be under a duty to use the same diligence and care in advising his clients as should be utilized by any skilled professional holding himself out as capable of performing such services. In the tax shelter area, this would appear not only to require that the investment advisor fully understand the taxation principles applicable to such investments, but that he also be aware of nontax investment considerations, unless he advised his client of the necessity for such consideration and his inability to provide such advice.

[¶3102.1]   Interpreting Rule 146 of The
                Securities Act

A particular problem created for investment advisor and sponsor alike in the tax-shelter area are the provisions of Rule 146 under the

Securities Act—the rule providing objective guidelines concerning the availability of the private offering exemption—dealing with the "offeree representative." Rule 146, which has primarily been utilized in connection with offerings of tax-sheltered investments, requires that, before accepting an investment or permitting a prospective investor to attend a group meeting, the sponsor must reasonably believe that the investor possesses "such knowledge and experience in financial and business matters that he is capable of evaluating the merits and risks of a prospective investment." If not, he must be represented by one or more similarly qualified "offeree representatives"—in other words, financial/investment advisors.

Considerable controversy exists over whether or not general business judgment, or experience in tax-sheltered investments, is sufficient to supply the investment acumen required under Rule 146. However, since the Rule requires that the investor possess the ability to both evaluate the risks *and merits* of the investment, in most instances it would seem necessary for the investor to be represented by an investment advisor. Compare *Lively vs. Hirschfeld*, 440 F. 2d 631 (10th Cir. 1971), with *Garfield vs. Strain*, 320 F. 2d 116 (10th Cir. 1963). See also SEC Exchange Act Release No. 12, 195 (March 11, 1976)

The offeree representative under a Rule 146 offering is required to be relatively independent of the sponsor—cannot be an officer, director, employee, affiliate, or a 10 percent equity owner of the "issuer"—and all relationships between the advisor and the sponsor or any of their affiliates must be disclosed in writing to the offeree by both the sponsor and the offeree representative. Rule 146(a)(1) and (e)(3). Under a recently adopted amendment to Rule 146, the "notification" now required to be filed with the Commission to claim the benefits of the rule must also list the names and addresses of all offeree representatives. See SEC Securities Act Rel. No. 33-5912 (March 3, 1978). The combined investment talents of the investor and his offeree representative or offeree representatives must also meet the "investment acumen" requirements of Rule 146.

The affluent investor considering a substantial investment in a tax-shelter offering can afford the type of investment advice required by Rule 146 (and also required by good business judgment—see Chapter 29). However, if your tax-sheltered investments in a particular program are to be more modest, the only way of securing such investment advice is through a "pooled" review by the investment advisor on behalf of a number of clients. While such advice has frequently been provided, and the "offeree representative" requirement met, by professional investment advisors representing a number of clients with tax shelter needs, many tax-sheltered investors who are appropriate targets for private offerings do not have such advisors available to them.

[¶3102.2]   How A Broker-Dealer-or Financial Advisor
Can Benefit You

Many schemes have been utilized by sponsors to attempt to satisfy the "offeree representative" requirements of Rule 146. Many of these are patently contrary to the spirit of the offeree representative requirement. However, one technique which has in the past frequently worked to the advantage of the investors has been to combine the role of broker-dealer and investment advisor.

Obviously, if the broker-dealer is more interested in his selling role than he is in his analytical one, the purposes of Rule 146 in requiring an independent advisor will be frustrated. However, in many instances, combining the broker-dealer and offeree representative roles has proved beneficial to investors. Now, however, a proposed amendment to Rule 146 would prohibit the offeree representative from receiving compensation directly or indirectly from the issuer, which would prohibit most broker-dealers from also serving as offeree representatives. While this proposed amendment has not as yet been, and may not be, adopted by the SEC, its mere presence casts a cloud on the use of the combined broker-dealer/offeree representative.

The obligations imposed on the investment advisor under common law principles, previously mentioned, clearly apply to the "offeree representative." These include both the duty to use adequate professional skill in reviewing the proposed investment and to act only in the best interest of his client—a fiduciary responsibility. In addition, the fact that the offeree representative is acting pursuant to a rule adopted under the Securities Act may impose an even increased duty of the highest possible fair dealing upon him. In this connection, Rule 146 specifically provides that the disclosure of conflicts by the offeree representative does not relieve him of his obligation to act in the best interest of the offeree. (See Rule 146(a)(1), note 3.)

The foregoing brief description of certain aspects of the securities laws as they apply to tax-shelter offerings represents only a brief summary of the various rights and obligations created under Federal and State securities laws. However, if you are an investor, you need fully to understand how these provisions of the securities laws translate into rights for you when a tax-sheltered investment goes "sour."

[¶3102.3]   Asserting Your Rights as an Investor

Most investors fail to utilize the rights provided them under the Securities Act. While an indiscriminate assertion of technical securities law violations against a sponsor who has functioned competently in your behalf, and has only inadvertently violated some securities law provision, may not be in your best interests from a *business* standpoint—you may wish to invest with that sponsor in the future—you should be aware of what you, as an investor, are entitled to expect from your syndicator.

Translating the securities law requirements we have just discussed into positive rights, you are entitled to the following:

☐ Prior to investing, *you are entitled to be advised by the syndicator of all factors,* negative as well as positive, *which might affect your investment decision.* In other words, "caveat emptor" does not apply in securities transactions. This "full disclosure" requirement is not limited to a prohibition against actively and intentionally misleading you; you are entitled to full disclosure of every possible negative aspect of the investment.

☐ *You are entitled to expect that your program interest has been sold to you by a registered salesman who has met various qualifying standards,* including passing a qualifying examination conducted by an appropriate securities regulatory agency, to insure that the salesman understands the nature of securities investments and has taken the steps to insure that this is an appropriate investment for you.

☐ *You are entitled to prompt and thorough reporting from your syndicator,* advising you realistically as to the progress of your venture and furnishing you detailed financial information concerning the venture, including what amounts he and his affiliates have taken out of the syndicate, directly or indirectly, and what they did to earn these payments.

☐ *You are entitled to expect that the syndicator will live up to his fiduciary responsibility* of treating you fairly, or, to use the legal terminology, of "utmost fair dealing."

These requirements are in addition to your contractual rights under your partnership agreement—see Chapter 30—which will include prohibitions against various conflicts of interest, restrictions on self-dealing between the syndicate and the syndicator or his affiliates, (including various restrictions on what the syndicator or its affiliates can or cannot do), limitations on the compensation which can be received by the syndicator or by any selling broker-dealers, various steps which should have been taken by the syndicator to determine whether or not this was an appropriate investment for you, and various rights which you may exercise, including the right to cancel contracts with the syndicator or its affiliates, to remove the syndicator as manager of the program, to participate in certain major decisions such as the sale of all or substantially all of the ventures assets and to hold meetings and to call for votes of the other limited partners.

Many of these contractual rights, while not giving a right to sue for rescission, are granted to you as a result of the securities laws.

[¶3103]   **WHAT YOU CAN DO IF A**
                           SYNDICATOR FAILS YOU

What is your recourse if the syndicator fails to live up to his responsibilities under the securities law? Consider the following:

☐ *If the interests were not registered with both Federal and State securities agencies*—and, except in the case of "public" oil and gas offerings and a few real estate offerings, the offering usually will not have been registered—*you have an absolute right to return of your money, with interest, unless the offering was exempt from registration.* While most syndicators who offer unregistered securities claim a "private placement" exemption, the vast majority of these offerings do not, in fact, meet the conditions required for exempt status. However, *you must act promptly to claim this right,* normally within one year from investment for improper failure to register under Federal law and two years for improper failure to register with the appropriate State.

☐ Whether the offering is registered or unregistered, *if you were not furnished complete information, or if any of the supporting presentations* outside any offering document furnished you *were in anyway misleading,* you similarly have an *absolute right to get your money back with interest.* A similar right may exist if *reporting proved misleading or incomplete.*

☐ *An action for damages* can be brought *if the syndicator has violated any of his obligations under the syndicate agreement, the representations contained in his offering document, or his fiduciary obligations.*

You may feel, "So what good does this do me? I could never afford the expense of such a legal action". However, normally the action may be brought as a "class action" on behalf of you and your fellow investors, or as a "derivative action" on behalf of the partnership. So remember, if you feel you have been dealt with unfairly by your syndicator, you have a powerful weapon available to you in the form of your rights under Federal and State securities laws.

Additional Readings: Part Four

Chapters 27-29; Investment Analysis

GRACER, *What Every Investor Should Know About Oil and Gas Investments* (Investment Dealers' Digest: 1973)

MOSBURG, "Due Diligence Investigation of Tax-Shelter Offerings," *Investment Dealers' Digest* (Apr. 3, 1973)

MOSBURG, "Evaluating Drilling Program Performance," *Financial Planner* (Dec. 1972/Jan. 1973)

MOSBURG, "How to Evaluate Tax Shelters," *Financial Observer* (Oct. 1972/Nov. 1973)*

MOSBURG, *The Tax Shelter Coloring Book* (The Institute for Energy Development, Inc.: 1977)

OPPENHEIMER, *Cowboy Arithmetic* (Interstate Printers & Publishers, Inc.: 3rd ed. 1976)

ROULAC, *Modern Real Estate Investment* (Property Press: 1976)

SHOCKEN, "Cash In vs. Cash Out—The Real Question in Evaluating Oil and Gas Drilling Programs," *Investment Dealers' Digest* (Sept. 3, 1974)*

STEWART, "Evaluating Investment Merits of Oil and Gas Drilling Programs," *The Commercial and Financial Chronicle* (Sept. 24, 1970)

Chapter 30: Getting Out of a Tax-Shelter

LEVINE, *Real Estate Tax Shelter Desk Book*, Chapters 10-11, 19

ROULAC, "Resolution of Limited Partnership Disputes: Practical and Procedural Problems," *Real Property, Probate and Trust Journal* (Summer, 1975)**

SCHILLINGBURG, "Winding Up Real Estate Tax Shelters: Problems and Solutions," *Journal of Real Estate Taxation* (Summer, 1975)

---

* Reproduced in Mosburg (ed.), *Structuring Tax-Sheltered Investments under the Tax Reform Act of 1976* (The Institute for Energy Development, Inc.: 1977)
** Reproduced in *New Challenges for Real Estate: Integrating the Disciplines* (Property Press: 1977)

Chapter 31: Securities Law Considerations

BLOOMENTHAL, *Securities and Federal Corporate Law* (Clark Boardman Co., Ltd.: 1975)

HAFT and FASS, *Tax Sheltered Investment,* Chapters 2-4 (Clark Boardman Co., Ltd.: 2d ed. 1974)

JACOBS, *The Impact of Rule 10b-5* (Clark Boardman Co., Ltd.: 1977)

MOSBURG, "Due Diligence Investigation of Tax-Shelter Offerings," *Investment Dealers' Digest* (Apr. 3, 1973)

MOSBURG (ed.), *Financing Oil & Gas Ventures* (The Institute for Energy Development, Inc.: 1977)

MOSBURG, (ed.), *Real Estate Syndicate Offerings Handbook* (Property Press: 3rd ed. 1976)

MOSBURG, *Real Estate Syndicate Offerings: Law & Practice* (RESD, Inc.: 1974)

MOSBURG, "Securities Regulation of Tax-Sheltered Investments," from *Structuring Tax-Sheltered Investments under the Tax Reform Act of 1976* (The Institute for Energy Development, Inc.: 1977)

32.

Final Tips on Selecting
The Right Investment

[¶3201] **GUIDES TO AN INTELLIGENT
TAX SHELTER STRATEGY**

Most investment "scandals" do not involve embezzlement or fraud in the legal sense. Instead, they involve a venture put together by skillful promoters who may know little of the real estate, oil and gas, or cattle business (not to mention motion pictures or coal), but who thoroughly understand investor psychology. These promoters are expert at structuring a proposal with little investment merit, but which takes advantage of an idea which appears new and glamorous and which will appeal to the virtual paranoia with which most of us view the nearly confiscatory Federal income taxation that faces the affluent American. The proposal will also be structured so that the promoters will receive substantial, and often enormous, profits irrespective of how you fare as an investor. It may also be surrounded by prestigious names and some well known "experts"—the more outlandish the proposal, the more prestigious the names.

The promoters of these catastrophes are for the most part rich, happy, and totally insulated from legal liability—civil or criminal—to their morally but not legally defrauded investors. And the tax shelter investment, with its appeal to our almost irrestible urge to avoid taxes, provides a perfect vehicle for this type of promoter.

[¶3201.1] A Little Research Can Help You Greatly

The classic example of how investor desire to avoid taxes can lead to disaster involves a cattle breeding program which flourished several years ago. Investor subscriptions were so leveraged that the deductions equalled 200 percent of the investor's initial cash investment. This was in part achieved by the investors paying between $2,500 to $3,500 a head for cows recently acquired by the sponsor for from $400 to $600. However, few investors bothered to ascertain that, at those prices, even the most optimistic evaluations concerning the cattle industry indicated an economic catastrophe.

The program proved a fiasco. Professional herd care and management were totally inadequate, and many of the exorbitantly overpriced cows died. Loans were foreclosed, wiping out both equity and triggering either recourse liability or taxes due on "phantom income." In many cases, deductions were disallowed on the basis that the investment lacked economic substance. All of this occurred when the slightest study of the cattle business would have showed such results were inevitable. As one commentator notes concerning this program:

> "Although you would hardly expect to make a profit by buying non-unique goods marked up from 400 to 900 percent, the ... investor was so busy calculating his tax deductions that he forgot to analyze the cattle business." Klineman, "How to Analyze a Tax Shelter," *Real Estate Syndication Digest* (October 1972).

Hopefully, this book, in addition to discussing the specifics of various tax shelters, has given you a substantially better understanding of how tax shelters work, of what they can and cannot do for you, and of the need for being selective in choosing both the right type of tax-sheltered investments which coincide with your investment objectives and a particular program among the ones offered in this category which maximizes your likelihood for profit. So we will close with some final advice to round out your tax-shelter strategy.

☐ **DO YOUR TAX PLANNING EARLY.** Year-end is normally the worst time to find high quality tax-sheltered investments. With the elimination of many types of prepayment, and the provisions of the Tax Reform Act of 1976 concerning retroactive allocations, the already shaky basis of many year-end deductions has been substantially worsened. Even if you are willing to settle for less than full deductibility, most high quality projects are not put in year-end programs. And the frantic search for year-end tax shelter often leads to investment in ventures which are significantly less promising in economic potential than those which would have been available earlier in the year.

☐ **AVOID "QUESTIONABLE" PROMOTERS.** Even in the specified property program, you are primarily investing in your sponsor's ability and integrity. While you and your advisor should do everything possible to evaluate the economic merits of the project, this is often a difficult task. And in the final analysis, it is how hard the sponsor does, or does not, work for you, and how seriously he takes his responsibilities to you, that will determine the likelihood of your profit or loss. Thus, no matter how "good" a project may be from an economic standpoint, in the hands of a less-than-responsible sponsor, it will probably turn out badly—at least from your standpoint.

☐ **BE REASONABLE IN YOUR EXPECTATIONS AND DON'T OVERREACH.** Promises of spectacular returns and excessive tax deductions are often the mark of a questionable investment. Such expectations not only make you blind to investment opportunities which, when viewed realistically, would in fact be to your benefit (and are more apt to obtain the represented results), but are a hallmark of an investment which will not only fail to obtain its unrealistic expectations, but normally will prove totally unrewarding. As a corollary, remember that excessive emphasis on tax benefits creates various dangers for you: the likelihood that the tax deductions are suspect, that they have been secured by the sacrifice of even more valuable economic benefits, and in any event will be subject to eventual recapture through taxes on phantom income.

☐ **TAX SAVINGS AREN'T ENOUGH.** You will always have some hard dollars at stake, even in the "excess write-off" programs. So ask yourself: does this project make economic sense? Then take the steps necessary to find the answer.

☐ **GET GOOD ADVICE.** "Before you invest, investigate," makes good sense in all investments, and is crucial in the tax-shelter area. As we have seen, the tax shelter con man will appear just as sincere and believable, and perhaps more so, than the legitimate syndicator. Furthermore, he would not have reached the top of his "profession" if he were an obvious swindler. So don't skimp on proper advice with your hard dollars at stake. If you can't afford to investigate, you are probably better off not investing at all, even though this means some additional tax burden.

Tax-sheltered investment can be an exciting opportunity for you if you are in an appropriate tax bracket, and follow the guides to an intelligent tax shelter strategy outlined in this book, including proper diversification and program screening, and if you understand the risk inherent in such investments. On the other hand, tax-shelter investment which considers only the tax benefits offered by such programs, without an adequate consideration of investment merit and your own personal needs, is a poor solution to your tax problems.

Chart 102-1
EFFECTIVE TAX RATES AT VARIOUS TAXABLE INCOME LEVELS

Taxable Income	Rates	
	Single	*Married*
$10,000	15.42%	11.52%
20,000	22.21	17.42
30,000	28.00	22.22
40,000	32.98	26.75
50,000	37.74	30.92
60,000	41.71	34.34
75,000	46.18	38.28
100,000	51.57	43.26
125,000	55.24	46.99
150,000	57.70	49.91
200,000	60.77	54.39

APPENDIX TWO

Chart 102-2
TAX RATE SCHEDULES*

UNMARRIED INDIVIDUALS
(OTHER THAN SURVIVING SPOUSES AND HEADS OF HOUSEHOLDS)
Taxable Years Beginning After December 31, 1976

TAXABLE INCOME	TAX
Not over $2,200	No tax.
Over $2,200 but not over $2,700	14% of the excess over $2,200.
Over $2,700 but not over $3,200	$70, plus 15% of excess over $2,700.
Over $3,200 but not over $3,700	$145, plus 16% of excess over $3,200.
Over $3,700 but not over $4,200	$225, plus 17% of excess over $3,700.
Over $4,200 but not over $6,200	$310, plus 19% of excess over $4,200.
Over $6,200 but not over $8,200	$690, plus 21% of excess over $6,200.
Over $8,200 but not over $10,200	$1,110, plus 24% of excess over $8,200.
Over $10,200 but not over $12,200	$1,590, plus 25% of excess over $10,200.
Over $12,200 but not over $14,200	$2,090, plus 27% of excess over $12,200.
Over $14,200 but not over $16,200	$2,630, plus 29% of excess over $14,200.
Over $16,200 but not over $18,200	$3,210, plus 31% of excess over $16,200.
Over $18,200 but not over $20,200	$3,830, plus 34% of excess over $18,200.
Over $20,200 but not over $22,200	$4,510, plus 36% of excess over $20,200.
Over $22,200 but not over $24,200	$5,230, plus 38% of excess over $22,200.
Over $24,200 but not over $28,200	$5,990, plus 40% of excess over $24,200.
Over $28,200 but not over $34,200	$7,590, plus 45% of excess over $28,200.
Over $34,200 but not over $40,200	$10,290, plus 50% of excess over $34,200.
Over $40,200 but not over $46,200	$13,290, plus 55% of excess over $40,200.
Over $46,200 but not over $52,200	$16,590, plus 60% of excess over $46,200.
Over $52,200 but not over $62,200	$20,190, plus 62% of excess over $52,200.
Over $62,200 but not over $72,200	$26,390, plus 64% of excess over $62,200.
Over $72,200 but not over $82,200	$32,790, plus 66% of excess over $72,200.
Over $82,200 but not over $92,200	$39,390, plus 68% of excess over $82,200.
Over $92,200 but not over $102,200	$46,190, plus 69% of excess over $92,200.
Over $102,200	$53,090, plus 70% of excess over $102,200.

*The tax rate schedules shown above apply to taxpayers with certain minimum incomes. Alternate schedules apply to taxpayers with income below these minimum levels, and to certain other types of taxpayers, such as married individuals filing separately, heads of households, and estates and trusts.

A corporation pays a 20 percent tax on its first $25,000 of taxable income, 22 percent on its next $25,000, and a combined "normal" and "surtax" of 48 percent on taxable income over $50,000.

MARRIED INDIVIDUALS FILING JOINT RETURNS
AND SURVIVING SPOUSES
Taxable Years Beginning After December 31, 1976

TAXABLE INCOME	TAX
Not over $3,200	No tax.
Over $3,200 but not over $4,200	14% of the excess over $3,200.
Over $4,200 but not over $5,200	$140, plus 15% of excess over $4,200.
Over $5,200 but not over $6,200	$290, plus 16% of excess over $5,200.
Over $6,200 but not over $7,200	$450, plus 17% of excess over $6,200.
Over $7,200 but not over $11,200	$620, plus 19% of excess over $7,200.
Over $11,200 but not over $15,200	$1,380, plus 22% of excess over $11,200.
Over $15,200 but not over $19,200	$2,260, plus 25% of excess over $15,200.
Over $19,200 but not over $23,200	$3,260, plus 28% of excess over $19,200.
Over $23,200 but not over $27,200	$4,380, plus 32% of excess over $23,200.
Over $27,200 but not over $31,200	$5,660, plus 36% of excess over $27,200.
Over $31,200 but not over $35,200	$7,100, plus 39% of excess over $31,200.
Over $35,200 but not over $39,200	$8,660, plus 42% of excess over $35,200.
Over $39,200 but not over $43,200	$10,340, plus 45% of excess over $39,200.
Over $43,200 but not over $47,200	$12,140, plus 48% of excess over $43,200.
Over $47,200 but not over $55,200	$14,060, plus 50% of excess over $47,200.
Over $55,200 but not over $67,200	$18,060, plus 53% of excess over $55,200.
Over $67,200 but not over $79,200	$24,420, plus 55% of excess over $67,200.
Over $79,200 but not over $91,200	$31,020, plus 58% of excess over $79,200.
Over $91,200 but not over $103,200	$37,980, plus 60% of excess over $91,200.
Over $103,200 but not over $123,200	$45,180, plus 62% of excess over $103,200.
Over $123,200 but not over $143,200	$57,580, plus 64% of excess over $123,200.

APPENDIX THREE

Chart 303-1
EFFECTS OF TAX OVERREACHING
ON ECONOMIC RETURN©

A record can reasonably be estimated to sell 20,000 copies at $5 a copy. Costs of distributing the record should run 25 percent of sales revenues.

As investor in the 50 percent bracket, you are interested in a $10,000 equity investment with "excess write-off" potential. You are told that by increasing your purchase price through a non-recourse note, you can increase your deductions.

Look at the effects of unreasonably inflating the selling price to increase deductibility.

	Purchase Price	
	$40,000: (a) $10,000 Cash (b) $30,000 Non-Re-course Note	$100,000: (a) $10,000 Cash (b) $90,000 Non-Non-Recourse Note
1. First-year Tax Savings		
(a) 50% of depreciation deduction (200% double declining balance over 3 years)	$13,300	$33,000
(b) Investment Tax Credit	1,330	3,300
(c) TOTAL INITIAL TAX SAVINGS	$14,630	$36,300
(d) DEDUCTIBILITY IN 50% BRACKET	292%	726%
2. Economic Effect Over 3 Years		
(a) Total Record Sales	$100,000	$100,000
(b) Costs of Distribution	(25,000)	(25,000)
(c) Proceeds to Owner	$ 75,000	$ 75,000
(d) Payment on Non-Recourse Loan (75% of gross sales)	(30,000)	(75,000)
(e) Cash Remaining from Sales	$ 45,000	—0—
(f) Net Taxes Payable on Sale and/or Foreclosure	(30,850)	(28,500)
(g) Net After-Tax Profit (Loss) from Sales	$ 14.150	($28,500)
(h) Initial Tax Savings	14,630	36,300
(i) Total Net Benefits	$ 28,780	$ 7,800
(j) Cash Investment	(10,000)	(10,000)
(k) NET PROFIT (LOSS)	$ 18,780	($ 2,200)

Chart 502-1©
EFFECTS OF TRA 1976 ON
TAX-SHELTERED INVESTMENT

General Provisions
- ☐ Maximum Tax
  - ☐ Exemptions eliminated
  - ☐ New tax preference items added
- ☐ Minimum Tax
  - ☐ Rate increased to 15%
  - ☐ Exemptions reduced
  - ☐ New tax preference items added
- ☐ Prepaid Interest eliminated
- ☐ Investment Interest restrictions increased
- ☐ Capital Gains
  - ☐ Stepped-up basis on death eliminated
  - ☐ Holding period lengthened
- ☐ Partnerships
  - ☐ Syndication Fees non-deductible
  - ☐ Special Allocations must have substantial economic effect
  - ☐ Retroactive Allocations eliminated
  - ☐ Partnership Borrowings limited to amount "at risk"
- ☐ Borrowing Restrictions
  - ☐ 4-activity "at risk" restrictions
  - ☐ "Partnership borrowing" restrictions
    (see above)
  - ☐ Investment Interest restrictions
    (see above)

Real Estate
- ☐ Construction Period Interest and Taxes
  capitalized and amortized
- ☐ Recapture of Excess Depreciation extended
  to new construction (except government-
  assisted housing)
- ☐ Particularly affected by changed rules
  concerning prepaid interest, investment interest, basis on death, syndication fees, and special and retroactive
  allocations
- ☐ Not affected by "at risk" or "partnership borrowing" restrictions

Oil and Gas
- ☐ Productive Well IDC
  - ☐ Item of Tax Preference
  - ☐ Subject to recapture
- ☐ A named "at risk" activity
- ☐ Particularly affected by minimum and maximum tax changes

Cattle and Agriculture
- ☐ Farming Syndicates
  - ☐ Prepayments for feed and farm supplies eliminated
  - ☐ Preproductive expenses capitalized for groves, orchards, and vineyards
  - ☐ Poultry expense capitalized
- ☐ A named "at risk" activity—special "stop loss", etc., restrictions
- ☐ Timber not subject to "farming syndicate" or "at risk" restrictions

"Exotic" Investments
- ☐ Production Service Company must capitalize and amortize costs
- ☐ Excess depreciation on all equipment leases an item of tax preference
- ☐ Leasing and films a named "at risk" activity
- ☐ Subject to partnership borrowing and investment interest restrictions

(d) **Limitation on Allowance of Losses.**—A partner's distributive share of partnership loss (including capital loss) shall be allowed only to the extent of the adjusted basis of such partner's interest in the partnership at the end of the partnership year in which such loss occurred. Any excess of such loss over such basis shall be allowed as a deduction at the end of the partnership year in which such excess is repaid to the partnership. For purposes of this subsection, the adjusted basis of any partner's interest in the partnership shall not include any portion of any partnership liability with respect to which the partner has no personal liability. The preceding sentence shall not apply with respect to any activity to the extent that section 465 (relating to limiting deductions to amounts at risk in case of certain activities) applies, nor shall it apply to any partnership the principal activity of which is investing in real property (other than mineral property).

25,402 *(I.R.C.)* Internal Revenue Code of 1954

Addition.—Sec. 464 was added by Sec. 207(a)(1) of Public Law 94-455, Oct. 4, 1976, (qualified effective date rule in Sec. 207(a)(3) of P.L. 94-455).

SEC. 465. DEDUCTIONS LIMITED TO AMOUNT AT RISK IN CASE OF CERTAIN ACTIVITIES.

(a) **General Rule.**—In the case of a taxpayer (other than a corporation which is neither an electing small business corporation (as defined in Section 1371(b)) nor a personal holding company (as defined in section 542)) engaged in an activity to which this section applies, any loss from such activity for the taxable year shall be allowed only to the extent of the aggregate amount with respect to which the taxpayer is at risk (within the meaning of subsection (b)) for such activity at the close of the taxable year. Any loss from such activity not allowed under this section for the taxable year shall be treated as a deduction allocable to such activity in the first succeeding taxable year.

(b) **Amounts Considered at Risk.**—

(1) **In general.**—For purposes of this section, a taxpayer shall be considered at risk for an activity with respect to amounts including—

(A) the amount of money and the adjusted basis of other property contributed by the taxpayer to the activity, and

(B) amounts borrowed with respect to such activity (as determined under paragraph (2)).

(2) **Borrowed amounts.**—For purposes of this section, a taxpayer shall be considered at risk with respect to amounts borrowed for use in an activity to the extent that he—

(A) is personally liable for the repayment of such amounts, or

(B) has pledged property, other than property used in such activity, as security for such borrowed amount (to the extent of the net fair market value of the taxpayer's interest in such property).

No property shall be taken into account as security if such property is directly or indirectly financed by indebtedness which is secured by property described in paragraph (1).

(3) Certain borrowed amounts excluded.—For purposes of paragraph (1)(B), amounts borrowed shall not be considered to be at risk with respect to an activity if such amounts are borrowed from any person who—

(A) has an interest (other than an interest as a creditor) in such activity, or

(B) has a relationship to the taxpayer specified within any one of the paragraphs of section 267(b).

(4) Exception.—Notwithstanding any other provision of this section, a taxpayer shall not be considered at risk with respect to amounts protected against loss through nonrecourse financing, guarantees, stop loss agreements, or other similar arrangements.

(5) Amounts at risk in subsequent years.—If in any taxable year the taxpayer has a loss from an activity to which this section applies, the amount with respect to which a taxpayer is considered to be at risk (within the meaning of subsection (b)) in subsequent taxable years with respect to that activity shall be reduced by that portion of the loss which (after the application of subsection (a)) is allowable as a deduction.

(c) Activities to Which Section Applies.—

(1) Types of activities.—This section applies to any taxpayer engaged in the activity of—

(A) holding, producing, or distributing motion picture films or video tapes,

(B) farming (as defined in section 464(e)),

(C) leasing any section 1245 property (as defined in section 1245(a)(3)), or

(D) exploring for, or exploiting, oil and gas resources as a trade or business or for the production of income.

(2) Separate activities.—For purposes of this section, a taxpayer's activity with respect to each—

(A) film or video tape.

(B) section 1245 property which is leased or held for leasing.

(C) farm, or

(D) oil and gas property (as defined under section 614),

shall be treated as a separate activity. A partner's interest in a partnership or a shareholder's interest in an electing small business corporation shall be treated as a single activity to the extent that the partnership or an electing small business corporation is engaged in activities described in any subparagraph of this paragraph.

(d) Definition of Loss.—For purposes of this section, the term "loss" means the excess of the deductions allowable under this chapter for the taxable year (determined without regard to this section) and allocable to an activity to which this section applies over the income received or accrued by the taxpayer during the taxable year from such activity.

Chart 802-1
Real Estate Investment
Example©

Assume that an investor has $25,000 and desires to invest in the Construction of a New Apartment project through leverage and the partnership vehicle. The costs of the project are as follows:

Actual Construction cost	$ 395,000.00
Construction period interest and taxes	22,775.00
Prepaid interest	17,775.00
Syndication fees	5,000.00
Organizational Cost	4,450.00
Total first year cost	$ 445,000.00

Tax-benefit in year of investment to the investor	Pre-TRA of 1976	Post-TRA of 1976
1. Taxable (loss):		
• Construction period interest and taxes	(22,775.00)	(5,693.75) (1)
• Prepaid interest	(17,775.00)	— (2)
• Syndication fees	(5,000.00)	— (3)
• Organizational costs	(4,450.00)	(890.00)
	(50,000.00)	(6,583.75)
2. Divided by initial investment	÷ 25,000.00	÷ 25,000.00
3. Percentage write-off	200%	26%

(1) Assuming the investment is made in 1978 the regulations allow construction period interest and taxes to be amortized at a rate of 25% in the year the expense is paid or incurred.
(2) Prepaid interest is not-deductible until accrued
(3) Syndication fees are not deductible
(4) Organization charts must be amortized over 60 months.

With the change in the Tax law in 1976 the real estate investment was not as attractive as before the Act. However, a simple restructuring of the shelter helped offset some of the blow delivered by TRA 1976. For instance, in the previous example the construction period interest, syndication fees and organizational costs are fairly well locked in as to their tax treatment. However, let's assume that the investor agrees to pay the prepaid interest as part of his $25,000 investment but that he does not have to pay the $17,775 until the following year when it is due. The tax-benefit in the first would be as follows:

1. Taxable (loss):	
• Construction—period interest and taxes	$(5,693.75)
• Prepaid interest	—
• Syndication fees	—
• Organizational costs	(890.00)
	(6,583.75)
2. Divided by initial first year investment ($25,000 - 17,775)	÷ 7,225.00
3. Percentage write-off	91%

XYZ Limited - Oklahoma City
Preforma Application of Funds
Proforma Acquisition and Operations
(Unaudited)

Initial Applications of Funds		
Gross amount of capital raised by the program		$ 500,000
Syndication fees		25,000
Organizational costs		25,000
Net proceeds for acquisitions and operations		$ 450,000
Acquisition and Operations		
Prepaid financial items:		
Loan Organization fee	27,000	
Mortgage broker fee	27,000	
		54,000
Initial principal payments		348,800
Net proceeds applied to acquisition		402,800
Working capital and reserves		47,200
		$ 450,000

The accompanying assumptions are an integral part of this statement.

XYZ Limited - Oklahoma City
Preforma Allocation of Purchase Price
(Unaudited)

Land	$ 189,800
Real Property Improvements	1,509,000
	$ 1,698,800

The accompanying assumptions are an integral part of this statement.

XYZ Limited - Oklahoma City
Proforma Statement by Operations
(Unaudited)

	December 1, 1978 to December 31, 1978	1979	1980	1981	1982	1983	1984
				Year ended December 31			
Schedule of gross revenues	$ —	237,000	237,000	261,300	261,300	288,100	288,100
Less: vacancy factor 5%	—	11,900	11,900	13,100	13,100	14,400	14,400
Elective gross revenue—	—	225,100	225,100	248,200	248,200	273,700	273,700
Property Administration and Management	—	6,800	6,800	7,500	7,500	8,200	8,200
Operating expenses	—	36,900	36,900	36,900	36,900	36,900	36,900
Cash flow from operations	—	181,400	181,400	203,800	203,800	228,600	228,600
General partures participation	—	3,750	3,750	6,290	6,290	8,770	8,770
Cash flow before - debt service and initial cost	—	177,650	177,650	197,510	197,510	219,830	219,830
Debt service	—	139,200	139,200	139,200	139,200	139,200	139,200
Initial costs	104,000	—	—	—	—	—	—
Cash flow before income takes	$(104,000)	38,450	38,450	58,310	58,310	80,630	80,630
Taxable income (loss)							
Cash flow before debt service and initial cost	—	177,650	177,650	197,510	197,510	219,830	219,830
Interest	(11,600)	(131,300)	(130,500)	(129,600)	(128,600)	(127,500)	(117,500)
Depreciation	(5,000)	(60,400)	(60,400)	(60,400)	(60,400)	(60,400)	(60,400)
Acquisition of organizational arts	(5,000)	(5,000)	(5,000)	(5,000)	(5,000)	—	—
Acquisition of prepaid financial items	(6,750)	(6,750)	(6,750)	(6,750)	—	—	—
Insaleable Income (Loss)	$(28,350)	(25,800)	(25,000)	(4,240)	3,510	31,930	41,930
Analysis of cash flow:							
Tax savings (costs) at the 30% tax bracket	8,505	7,740	7,500	1,272	(1,053)	(9,579)	(12,579)
Cash flow before income taxes	(104,000)	38,450	38,450	58,310	58,310	80,630	80,630
Net cash flow at the 30% tax bracket	$ (95,495)	46,190	45,950	59,582	57,257	71,051	68,051
Tax savings (costs) at the 50% tax bracket	14,175	12,900	12,500	2,120	(1,755)	(15,965)	(20,965)
Cash flow before income taxes	(104,000)	38,450	38,450	58,310	58,310	80,630	80,630
Cash flow before income taxes	$(89,825)	51,350	50,950	60,430	56,555	64,665	59,665

The accompanying assumptions are an integral part of this statement.

XYZ Limited - Oklahoma City
Proforma Projected Sale Consequences
(Unaudited)

	Tax Bracket 30%	Tax Bracket 50%
Taxable gain:		
Sale price	$ 2,406,400	2,406,400
Cost of sale	96,000	96,000
Net selling price	2,310,400	2,310,400
Less basis in property @ time of sale	1,331,400	1,331,400
Gain taxable at capital gains rates	$ 979,000	979,000
Rate of Return		
Net selling price	2,310,400	2,310,400
Less existing debt at time of sale	1,279,800	1,279,800
Net sales proceeds	1,030,600	1,030,600
Less sponsor's participation in net sales proceeds	80,600	80,600
Net sales proceeds distributable to investors	950,000	950,000
Income tax liability (exclusive of any minimum tax that otherwise might be due)	(142,500)	(237,500)
Add cash distributions to the investors over the six year period, net of tax	356,586	357,790
Net after tax proceeds to inves-tors	1,070,290	$ 1,164,086
Discounted rate of return after taxes	9.4%	7.6%

The accompanying assumptions are an integral part of this statement.

XYZ Limited - Oklahoma City
Proforma Assumptions
(Unaudited)

ASSUMPTION—A: Financing

A first trust deed will be obtained in the amount of $1,350,000.

    (A) Lender of record will be Union Federal Savings and Loan.

    (B) Annual interest rate at 9¾%.

    (C) Loan will mature in 30 years.

    (D) Annual loan constant at .1031.

    (E) Loan contains no subordination, lock-ins, or acceleration provisions.

    (F) Loan can be assigned.

    (G) Prepayment penalty—6 months interest on portion of principal prepaid.

ASSUMPTION—B: Estimated annual gross rentals
    Schedules gross rentals
        34,235 sq. ft. @ $.577 .... $237,100
        Vacancy factor approximately 5% .... $ 11,900
    All projections comply with the assumptions of the project appraisal dated
September 1, 1978.
    A lease will be for a minimum of sixty (60) months. Provisions of the lease
provide that at the end of twenty-four (24) months and forty-eight (48) months the
rent would be increased by the percentage increase upward of the consumer price
index (Oklahoma City zone) over the initial base year. This has been estimated to
be 5% per year.

ASSUMPTION—C: Distribution to Partners
    The distributions to partners are as follows:
        (A) Limited partners receive at least 7% return on their original
            investment annually. If not paid in any one year it is cumulative
            until paid.
        (B) General partner receives fixed distributions not to exceed 10% of
            the cash flow before partners distributions. This is noncumula-
            tive and is subordinated to the amounts owed the limited part-
            ners.

ASSUMPTION—D: Depreciation

Real property improvements	Method Straight-line			Useful Life 25 years		
	1978	1979	1980	1981	1982	1983
Real property	$ 5,000	$60,400	$60,400	$60,400	$60,400	$60,400

ASSUMPTION—E: Income taxes

    Capital gains tax has been computed at the maximum rate of 25% without
regard to tax preference.

ASSUMPTION—F: Selling Price

    The selling price in 1984 was determined by capitalizing estimated cash flow
from operations at 9½%. Estimated cash flow from operations in 1984 is approximately $228,600.

ASSUMPTION—G Discounted rate of returns after taxes

The sale is assumed to have occurred at the end of the sixth year. The discounted cash flow method of calculating the rate of return was used and was computed as follows:

Discounted rate of return:	Amount Value	Discount Factor 9½%	30%	50%
Present value of net after tax proceeds to investors:				
Net sales proceeds	950,000		605,096	605,096
Income tax liability	(142,500)		(90,764)	
	(237,500)			(151,274)
Cash distributions and savings:				
30% bracket				
beginning 1st yr.	8,505		8,505	
end of 1st yr.	46,190		42,183	
2nd yr.	45,950		38,613	
3rd yr.	59,582		46,367	
4th yr.	57,257		41,491	
5th yr.	71,051		48,170	
6th yr.	68,051		43,345	
50% bracket				
beginning 1st yr.	14,175			14,175
end of 1st yr.	51,350			46,895
2nd yr.	50,950			42,815
3rd yr.	60,430			47,027
4th yr.	56,555			40,982
5th yr.	64,665			43,841
6th yr.	59,665			38,003
			783,006	727,560
			− 500,000	− 500,000
			283,006	227,560
			÷ 500,000	÷ 500,000
			56.6	45.5
			÷ 6 yrs.	÷ 6 yrs.
			9.4%	7.6%

ASSUMPTION—H

The Proforma Statement of Operations has been prepared on the assumption that the premises will be 95% leased on or about December 31, 1980 and that the leaseback will thereupon terminate and the Partnership will operate the property.

XYZ Limited - Oklahoma City
Projected Revenues in Relation To
Occupancy Levels and Expenditures

Total Expenditures

Gross Revenues

Breakeven point 77%; Revenue $186,650

Current Level of Occupancy

Area of Cash Deficit

Projected Level of Operations

Area of cash flow

Percent Occupancy

Annual Revenue (000)

250
225
200
175
150
125
100
75
50
25

0 5 10 15 20 25 30 35 40 45 50 55 60 65 70 75 80 85 90 95

XYZ Limited - Oklahoma City
Sensitivity Table
Discounted rates of Return or Other Comparable
Measure of Prefermonance for the Preformance Levels and Tax Brackets shown

Performance Level	*30%*	*50%*
1. *As projected*	9.4%	7.6%
2. *No cash flow-sale* @ mortgage balance in the projected year of sale	(7.4%)	(6.99%)
3. No cash flow-sale @ mortgage balance is the projected year of sale divided by 2	(101.4%)	(82.72%)
4. 50% of projected cash flow	4.95%	3.02%
5. 150% of projected cash flow	13.91%	12.15%

Chart 905-1
Potential Economics of Recreational
Real Estate Investment©

	With Tax Benefits	Without Tax Benefits
Purchase Price	$74,000.00	$74,000.00
Liability Assumed - 20 year 8%	66,000.00	66,000.00
Cash Investment	8,000.00	8,000.00
Taxable Income: (1st year)		
Gross Receipts	5,400.00	5,400.00
Depreciation	(4,625.00)	
Interest	(4,789.58)	(4,789.58)
Other Costs	(1,000.00)	(750.00)
Taxable Income (Loss)	(5,014.58)	(139.58)
	× 50%	× 50%
Tax Savings	$ 2,507.29	$ 69.79

APPENDIX EIGHT

Chart 1101-1

TAX EFFECTS OF OIL AND GAS
INVESTMENT ASSUMING SALE
Pre-1975 vs. Post-1976©

		Pre-1975	*Post-976*
Taxable Income Before Tax Shelter		$ 200,000.00	200,000.00
(All Income Personal Service Income)			
Oil and Gas Investment			
Tangible		50,000.00	50,000.00
Intangible		50,000.00	50,000.00
Total Investment		$ 100,000.00	100,000.00

Well is Drilled and Completed-Ten
Months Later the Well is Sold for $200,000

Taxable Income Before Tax Shelter		200,000.00	200,000.00
IDC Deduction		(50,000.00)	(50,000.00)
		150,000.00	150,000.00

Sale of Investment			
Proceeds	200,000.00		
Basis	50,000.00		
Gain	$ 150,000.00		
Portion Taxable as LTCG:			
Capital Gain	150,000.00		
LTCG Deduction	(75,000.00)		
		75,000.00	
Portion Taxable as Ordinary Income			
Recapture of IDC			
Total IDC	50,000.00		
Less IDC if Amortized	(4,170.00)		
			45,830.00
Portion Taxable as LTCG:			
(150,000 - 45,830)	104,170.00		
Less LTCG Deduction	52,085.00		
			52,085.00
Taxable Income		$ 225,000.00	247,915.00

Maximum Tax:			
Personal Service Income		200,000.00	200,000.00
Tax Preference Items		(75,000.00)	(97,915.00)
Personal Service Taxable Income		125,000.00	102,085.00
Less $55,200		(55,200.00)	(55,200.00)
Income Subject to Maximum Tax		69,800.00	46,885.00
Maximum Tax Rate		× 50%	× 50%
Maximum Tax		34,900.00	23,442.50

Tax on Taxable Income		126,240.00	142,280.50
Tax on Personal Service Taxable Income		58,732.00	44,511.00
		67,508.00	97,769.50

Tax on $55,200		18,060.00	18,060.00

Total Tax on Taxable Income		120,468.00	139,272.00

DIFFERENCE $18,804

the various State Blue Sky Authorities in order to insure
maximum uniformity with state securities laws. It is intended
that uniformity of any amendments to the rule will be maintained
by a program of coordination with Blue Sky authorities.

Following this comment period proposed Appendix F
will be reviewed by the Board, taking into consideration the
comments received and modifications to the extent deemed appropriate will be made. Thereafter, it is contemplated that
Appendix F will be adopted, pursuant to powers given to the
Board by proposed Article III, Section 35(c). It is anticipated that that proposed rule will have been approved by the
Securities and Exchange Commission prior to the time final
action is called for by the Board. The proposed Appendix F
will then be filed for approval with the Securities and Exchange
Commission under Rule 19b-4 of the Securities Exchange Act of
1934 prior to its enactment.

The proposed new Appendix F is important and merits
your immediate attention. This is the last opportunity for
the membership to comment on the substantive regulations to
be applied under proposed Article III, Section 35 prior to
their filing with the SEC under Rule 19b-4 of the Securities
Exchange Act of 1934.

All comments should be directed to Christopher
R. Franke, Secretary, National Association of Securities
Dealers, Inc., 1735 K Street, N.W., Washington, D.C. 20006.
All communications will be considered available for public
inspection. Any questions regarding this Notice may be
directed to George Warner or Harry Tutwiler of the Association staff at (202)-833-7240.

The Board of Governors believes the substantive
regulations of Appendix F are necessary and appropriate and
recommends that members carefully reflect on them and respond
promptly with any objections, modifications, or additions
that they wish to be considered.

A section by section explanation of the provisions
follows.

Very truly yours,

Frank J. Wilson
Senior Vice President
Regulatory Policy and
General Counsel

Section by Section Explanation

Article III, Section 35

Appendix F

Appendix F contains the substantive rules with resp to direct participation programs which the Board would be aut rized to adopt by the provisions of proposed Section 35 of th Rules of Fair Practice.

The various sections of proposed Appendix F contain little modification from the January 21, 1977 release (Notice to Members: 77-3), with the exception of new Sections 1, 2 an 8 and the substantial modification of Section 10(b) regarding sponsor's compensation in oil and gas direct participation pr grams. Former Sections 1 through 5 and 6 through 9 in Notice Members: 77-3 have been redesignated Sections 3 through 7 an 9 through 12, respectively.

Section 1

This section establishes the filing requirement for all direct participation programs offered to the public by members of the Association. This requirement is cross refere to the primary filing requirement contained in Article III, Section 1 of the Rules of Fair Practice - Interpretation of t Board of Governors - Review of Corporate Financing.

Section 2

This section states that where there is an irrec- oncilable conflict with the requirements of state or federal regulatory authorities, the regulations of those authorities shall prevail. In order to allow a maximum of creativity and innovative freedom to those members engaged in this evolving industry, a variance provision has also been added to this section. This provision would allow the interpretation and waiver of provisions of the rule in the case of new or unusua circumstances, where such does not violate the spirit or inte of the rule. Such variances might be granted by the Committe on Direct Participation Programs with the consent of the Boar of Governors. Such a procedure is essential if the dual obje tives of effective regulation in a context of maximum operati freedom are to be achieved.

Section 3 -- Definitions

Section 1 of proposed Appendix F contains a series

of definitions of words used throughout the Appendix. These
terms were discussed in previous notices and are self-explanatory.

Section 4

This section would disallow a member or a person
associated with a member from underwriting or participating
in the distribution of a public offering of a direct participation program in which a member or an affiliate of a
member is a sponsor if the program permits or does not
prohibit certain conduct, or if it contains certain terms
or conditions, or if certain other terms or conditions are
not included within its provisions. Section 4 would thus
prevent members from distributing units of direct participation programs unless a variety of terms and conditions
are first satisfied by the program and/or the member-
sponsor or its affiliate.

Subsection (a) would require that a member-sponsor
or its affiliate have three years experience in the industry
represented by the program, or in services to be performed
for the program. It would not require the expertise called
for to be "in-house" if it were readily available to the sponsor
within its corporate complex, under contract or otherwise.
This recognizes a practical situation in which some companies find themselves, i.e., a sponsor-member subsidiary
may not have the industry expertise "in-house" but such
is available to it within the company's corporate complex
and is, in fact, drawn upon in managing the program in
question. This procedure is followed by a number of companies. It also recognizes the situation where the
sponsor of a program will contract for such expertise.
An example of this would be a cattle operation where an
experienced ranch manager would provide the day-to-day
management function under contract with the sponsor.
The provision is considered important since the Board
does not believe it to be in the public interest if a
person unskilled in the industry represented by a direct
participation program is the sponsor of the program unless
the expertise is readily available to it.

Subsection (b) would require that the member-
sponsor of a program or its affiliate have a fair market
net worth at least equal to the greater of $50,000 or
the lesser of $1,000,000 or 5% of the total capital con-
tributions made by the holders of the program participations issued by all programs of which such persons are a
sponsor organized within the twelve-month period immediately preceding the offering date of the program plus
5% of the gross amount of the current offering. Certain
exceptions from the term "sponsor" are also contained in

this section, i.e., members of the immediate family of,
or persons associated with, the sponsor except to the
extent that such persons are guarantors of obligations
entered into by the sponsor in its capacity as sponsor
of the program in question. In addition to having expertise in the industry represented by the program, the
Board also believes a sponsor should have the financial
capability to carry out its duties as a sponsor and that
the requirement of this paragraph will afford a measure
of protection to the public in that respect.

Subsection (c) would require that all funds received
be transmitted in accordance with Rule 15c2-4(b) of the Securities Exchange Act of 1934, as amended, by being placed in
an account specifically designed for that purpose until the
minimum is reached.

Subsection (d) requires that if the minimum is not
reached the entire amount deposited by participants, including
sales commissions, be returned to them.

Subsection (e) would restrict oil and gas programs (defined at Section 1(y)) to a minimum size of no
less than $500,000. It is believed that no unspecified
oil and gas program can effectively undertake exploration and development operations without funds of at least
$500,000. Even this amount is considered a bare minimum
and experience has shown that most programs are necessarily
much larger. Drilling of a specified exploratory or
development prospect or acquisition of a specified exploratory or development prospect or acquisition of a
specified producing property would be allowed below
that minimum so long as the program was registered or
exempt under applicable federal or state law. No minimum
amounts would be established at this time in connection
with other programs, including real estate programs, because
of the differences in objectives of use of proceeds. In
this connection, a real estate program could logically be,
for instance, $100,000, if the purpose of the program being
sold is to purchase a single building. Such a program
could be workable and viable because of the extensive use
of·leveraging in connection with these programs. The Board
does not believe such is the case in connection with unspecified oil and gas programs. Hence, a minimum size of
$500,000 would be applicable to them.

Pursuant to Subsection (f) however, other programs would be required to state in their prospectuses
a minimum amount which would have to be raised before the
program could be activated and that such amount must be
sufficient, after funding all organization and offering
expenses, and giving due consideration to the fixed obligations of the program, to effect the objectives of the

program without changing the nature of the investment called for by the general terms of the program. This provision is designed to prevent a situation which would find only a small amount of the proposed offering being sold with most of the proceeds being absorbed by organization and offering expenses. Where this occurs, it would be impossible for the program to implement its original purposes, hence the nature of the participants' investment would have been changed.

Subsection (g)(1) would prohibit the distribution of units by members if the program did not meet the requirements of the Internal Revenue Code enabling participants to obtain tax benefits as described in the prospectus and if such could not be demonstrated by a favorable tax ruling or a favorable opinion from independent tax counsel with respect to such requirements. Subsection (e)(2) would permit distribution of units without a favorable ruling or opinion as long as there is a right of withdrawal and a return of investment in the event the tax ruling or opinion does not indicate that participants will obtain the tax benefit described. All funds received would be required to be escrowed until such time as a ruling or opinion is received and returned in full, including sales commissions, to the participants in the program in the event an unfavorable ruling or opinion is received. Without this provision, investors could not be certain they would realize the tax benefits which may be an important reason for investing.

Subsection (h) would restrict a participant's minimum subscription commitment in an oil and gas program to $5,000, unless a higher amount is required by state or local law. Additional increments in smaller amounts over and above that minimum amount would not be prohibited. Thus, the minimum unit size would not necessarily have to be $5,000 though the minimum commitment by an individual participant would have to be $5,000 or more. This provision is consistent with the minimum commitment requirements established by many states and a majority of the oil and gas programs. The provision for minimum commitments is presently restricted to oil and gas programs.

Subsection (i) would require full payment of subscription commitments for oil and gas programs within a twelve-month period if such payment period does not otherwise violate federal credit regulations. No such twelve-month period would be imposed with respect to other programs. A maximum twelve-month payment period is accepted practice in the oil and gas program industry and is important to it because of tax considerations.

In connection with deferred payments, however, it should be noted that the Federal Reserve Board has issued an interpretation of Section 7(a) of its Regulation T, 12 C.F.R. 220.7(a), which states that a broker/dealer would be guilty or arranging credit on terms more favorable than he could himself grant to his customers if he sold units on a periodic payment basis. This interpretation effectively prohibits broker/dealers from selling programs calling for periodic payments, at least where a binding contractual obligation to make the subsequent payments exists. In addition, the SEC has interpreted that Section 11(d)(1) of the Securities Exchange Act of 1934, which was enacted by Congress to prevent the extension of credit on offerings by broker/dealers, is also applicable. It should be noted, however, that the SEC's new Rule 3(a)12-5 under the Securities Exchange Act of 1934 offers some relief for condominium securities offerings.

Subsection (j) would prohibit the use of deferred payment plans in an unspecified property program. Since there is no description of the anticipated cash needs of the program, any type of a deferred payment plan would not appear to be in the interests of the public.

Subsection (k) would prevent charging a participant interest or a comparable charge for purchasing units on an installment basis except where the program requires immediate funding of the installment proceeds through borrowing with its incidental interest expense.

Subsection (e) through (s) relate to assessments on a participant's interest in a program. Assessments have been defined in Section 1(e).

Subsection (e) would require certain minimum information to be supplied to a program participant as a part of any assessment call.

Subsection (m) would prevent sales commissions from being charged on assessments and (n) would require that the maximum amounts of additional assessments prescribed by the program be fully disclosed in the prospectus together with a statement of whether they are mandatory or optional. Only by so requiring would the participant be able to know at the outset the total potential amount of his commitment. He would thus avoid the possibility of assessments which he could not meet. The provisions of this paragraph are further enhanced by the provisions of Subsection (r) which would limit the amount of a mandatory assessment to no more than 25% of the original amount of a participant's interest.

It is customary in connection with most direct
participation programs to impose certain penalties upon
participants for failure to meet an assessment. The Association believes such is not improper because, if a participant does not fully live up to the provisions of his commitment, the other program holders and the program itself are
injured in an amount proportionate to his failure to perform.
Penalties or liquidated damages of some kind are, therefore,
not only necessary but in the opinion of the Association
entirely proper. They should, however, as provided in
Subsection (s), be disclosed in the prospectus, be fair
and reasonable and not contain a forfeiture or a significant dilution of a participant's interest in the program
for which he has already paid. The Association also
believes any penalties to be imposed should not unduly
benefit the sponsor but, rather, if there are to be
penalties, the other participants or individuals meeting
the unfulfilled commitments should receive the benefit
thereof. Subsection (s)(3), therefore provides that penalties must accrue to the benefit of the program. Subsections (s)(4) and (5) integrate specific penalty provisions
for voluntary and mandatory assessments respectively that are
followed by Blue-Sky authorities.

Subsection (t) would prohibit the forfeiture of
a participant's right to participate in a future optional
development well as a penalty for failure to meet an assessment if this intended procedure is not disclosed in the
prospectus. The Association does not believe this penalty
is inappropriate if fully disclosed because the participant
would not have invested in the future development well
since he did not meet the assessment. There is no reason,
therefore, why he should not forfeit his right to participate as long as disclosure of this intended procedure is
properly made.

Subsection (u) would require that when reinvestment of a program's distributable cash flow into a subsequent
program is provided for, such must be at the option of the
investor who shall be provided, prior to the time he exercises
his option, complete information as to the amount of money
to which he is then entitled as well as a copy of the prospectus of the subsequent program in which reinvestment is
contemplated. The decision is made by each participant and
not one left to the sole discretion of the sponsor.

Subsections (u), (w) and (v) relate to the liquidation of participants' interests in the program. Subsection
(v) would prohibit a sponsor or an affiliate of a sponsor
from selling his interest in a program without making an
offer comparable in all respects simultaneously to all
other participants and giving them a reasonable period of

time in which to sell their interests. The purpose of
this provision is to prevent a sponsor from extricating
himself from his investment in a program in preference to
the participants. Notwithstanding that a sponsor is not
required to purchase interests in a program, the fact that
he has done so undoubtedly creates a greater degree of
assurance in the minds of participants that he will perform
properly his obligations as a sponsor. A sale by him of
his units could destroy that confidence. In addition to
not being in the public interest, such action could possibly be inconsistent with his fiduciary obligation to
the participants to act at all times in their best interests.

Subsection (w)(1) would prohibit the purchase by
a program of any interests of any other program and the
repurchase by a program of its own participants' interests
in a manner or in an amount which is not in the best
interests of the program. A customer in making his
investment decision as to a given program has elected to
place his trust in the possibility of success of that
program and in the management ability of the sponsor.
If that program invests in another, his investment has
then, without any informed judgment on his part, been
transferred, in part at least, to the new program.

Subsection (w)(2), relating to repurchase by
a program of its own participants' interests, would prevent
a situation from developing whereby so many participants
chose to liquidate that an insufficient amount of funds
would remain for the program to continue viable operations. This provision would, therefore, require that
some limitation be written into each prospectus which
is reasonable in nature. The Association does not at
this time wish to prescribe the extent of such limitations other than that they be reasonable.

Subsection (x) would require that cash liquidation values be computed on the basis of an appraisal of
property made within the preceding twelve-month period
by a qualified independent appraiser pursuant to a formula
or in accordance with terms spelled out in the prospectus.
If there has been a material change in value between the
time of the appraisal and the contemplated liquidation,
a new appraisal would be required to be made prior to any
liquidation.

Subsection (y) would require that if any person
contemplates transacting business with the program in an
amount aggregating more than twenty percent (20%) of the
total dollar value of the participants' interests, such
would have to be disclosed in the prospectus. The Board
is not suggesting that such a business relationship is

detrimental to the program. However, it does feel that the knowledge of this relationship is of importance to the investing public.

Subsection (z) would require that all details with respect to all of the provisions of Subsections (a) through (x) of Section 2 be fully disclosed in the prospectus. This is in keeping with the Board's desire to not only impose a system of regulation in connection with direct participation programs but to also insure that even though the program fully complies, participants be placed on notice of all details in respect thereto so they can properly make their investment decisions.

Section 5 -- Rights of Participants

Unless there are conflicts with the laws of the state where the program is organized, this section would prevent a member, or person associated therewith, from underwriting or distributing units of a direct participation program of which a member or an affiliate of a member is sponsor which does not contain a series of provisions relating to the rights of participants. Thus, Subsection (a) would prohibit participation in the distribution where the program did not permit its participants the right by a majority vote to remove the sponsor. Subsection 6 would require that a majority of the outstanding units be allowed to amend the partnership or other agreement organizing the program entity, to dissolve the partnership or other legal entity formed to carry out the purposes of the program and/ or to approve or disapprove the sale of all or substantially all of the assets of the program. Several other rights would also be accorded to participants by Subsections (c) through (f) of this section. Generally, these provisions would prevent situations from occurring whereby significant and material provisions of a program could be changed or other action taken at the discretion of the sponsor to the possible detriment of participants. Thus they would insure ample notification (60 days) of termination of a sponsor's contract by it or the participants (Subsection (c)(1)); require the sponsor to cause a vote to be taken on any of the above listed four rights after being requested in writing to do so by at least 10% of the outstanding program interests (Subsection (c)(2)); prevent restrictions on the assignment of a participant's program interests but such would not prevent requiring approval by the sponsor prior to such a transfer (Subsection (d)); grant to all participants upon written demand the right for any proper purpose to have a list of names and addresses of, and interests held by, all participants (Subsection (e)); and require a notice by the sponsor to all participants of any material amendment to the program proposed by him and affirmative vote of not less than a majority of the outstanding number of program interests for approval if more than 10% of the participants object to the program (Subsection (f)).

The Association recognizes that as a matter of law the possibility exists in the case of limited partnerships that if the limited partners have and exercise authority to the extent that they are conducting the day-to-day operations of the partnership, limited partners could possibly be construed as general partners and lose their limited liability notwithstanding their designation as limited partners. The laws of the states vary in several respects as to the scope of activity on the part of a limited partner which could cause such a change in his status. It is not the Association's intent by the provisions of Section 5 to cause that result. The "rights of limited partners" provisions are, therefore, preceded with the lanaguage: "Unless such conflicts with any federal law or law of the state pursuant to which the program is organized." If the law would cause loss of limited partnership status under any . one of the provisions, the program would not be required to contain that provision.

Section 6 -- Conflicts of Interest

Initially, it should be noted that the Board recognizes and accepts as fact that it is not possible to eliminate all conflicts of interest in direct participation programs. It also believes that such is not necessary because all conflicts of interest are not bad if properly regulated and that some may be necessary to the success of a program and are in the best interests of the program's participants. The Board believes, therefore, that conflicts should be divided into those which are considered permissible subject to regulation and those which are considered impermissible. The impermissible conflicts should be eliminated and controls should be placed on the others. Section 4 is promulgated with these ideas in mind.

Generally speaking, one area of conflict which exists in many direct participation programs, and which is not necessarily detrimental to the program if properly regulated, is the situation of the sponsor or an affiliate of the sponsor dealing with the program. In some cases the sponsor or its affiliates will sell property, services or supplies to the program. The Association does not believe such conduct should be eliminated but it does believe that stringent controls should be imposed. Thus, the various provisions of Subsection (a) of Section 6 would place controls on these situations with regard to all programs in which a member or an affiliate of a member acts as a sponsor. In some cases, specific situations relate to specific types of programs, i.e., oil and gas or real estate, and where such is the case the pertinent provision so indicates.

Paragraphs (1) and (2) of Subsection (a) relate to situations involving the sale of property by a sponsor or an affiliate of a sponsor which has been owned, optioned or acquired by them either prior to or subsequent to the formation of the program. In the case of property obtained by a sponsor or its affiliate, except for a limited exception made for oil and gas programs, Paragraph (1) would impose the requirement that the property to be acquired by the program must be transferred at the lesser of cost or fair market value as determined by a qualified independent appraiser. A provision for an exception to these standards is included which allows the transfer of such property at a price greater than cost if all the details of the transaction, including the profit to the sponsor or its affiliates, are fully disclosed to the program participants and to subsequent program subscribers, the acquisition is at no more than fair market value, and the sponsor or its affiliate has owned the property for at least two years or there has been a material change in the value of the property.

Paragraph (2) of Subsection (a) deals with the acquisition by an oil and gas program of non-producing acreage owned by the sponsor or an affiliate of the sponsor. It provides that such acquisition shall be at cost unless the sponsor or its affiliate has reason to believe that the cost is materially different than fair market value. In that case the acquisition may be at a price determined by an independent appraiser as long as the details of the transaction are fully disclosed.

Paragraph (e) of Subsection (a) deals with the reverse situation. The purchase by a sponsor or an affiliate of the sponsor of property owned by an oil and gas program shall be at fair market value determined by an appraiser unless the sponsor or its affiliate has grounds to believe that the cost is materially higher than fair market value. In that case the purchase shall be at a price not less than cost. This paragraph contains the only exception to the prohibition in Section 6(b)(6) against a sponsor's or its affiliate's purchase of property from a program.

Paragraph (4) of Subsection (a) relates to the sale of services, supplies, equipment, furnishings or other property to the program by the sponsor or an

affiliate of the sponsor. The Board recognizes that
conflicts of interest exist in such situations and
that the possibility of overreaching is present. At
the same time, however, it believes that in many cases
such sales by a sponsor and its affiliates are beneficial
to the program and its participants. Because the possibility of overreaching does exist, proper guidelines
must be established to reduce that possibility. Paragraph (4) would, therefore, require, in order for a member
to participate in the distribution of units of a program
which permits such activity, that the fees and prices
charged be no higher than those customarly charged for
-similar services in the same or a comparable geographical
location by persons who are dealing at arms'-length
and have no affiliation with the recipient. A further
provision states that if there exists no basis for
comparing fees or if the sponsor or its affiliates are
not engaged in an ongoing business of providing such
services, the services shall be provided at no more
than cost.

In addition to the requirements stated above
concerning self-dealing by a sponsor or an affiliate
of the sponsor with a program, additional protections
to the investor are required by Section 11 dealing with
periodic reporting to participants. Subsection (d)
thereof would require that the total amount of expenditures made by a program in connection with the sale to
it of services, supplies, equipment, furnishings or
other property by the sponsor or its affiliates be fully
disclosed in the annual audited financial statements
required by Subsection (b) of Section 11. The same
requirement is made as to any person with whom the
program transacts business in a material amount. Also,
where a sponsor or its affiliates have sold services,
supplies, equipment, furnishings or other property to
previous programs sponsored by them, the full details
with respect to this activity must be made available in
the prospectus of the current program (Section 11(d)).
The potential participant is, therefore, able to take
these activities into consideration prior to making his
investment decision.

Paragraph (5) of Subsection (a) prevents the
retention by the sponsor or an affiliate of the sponsor
of an oil and gas program of any rights of any kind in
property which he has transferred to the program unless
the sponsor or its affiliate is required by the terms of
the program to participate in the development of the
property on a cost basis proportionate to his retained
interest in the property. Those rights created by virtue of its status as sponsor of the program are excepted

from this prohibition so long as those rights are fully disclosed in the prospectus. This latter provision relates to sponsors' compensation which is covered in Section 10. The purpose of this paragraph is to prevent a sponsor or its affiliate from benefiting at the expense of the program carrying on the development by retaining rights in a property. By requiring the sponsor and its affiliates to participate with the program in the development of the property on a cost basis proportionate to their retained interest, the possibility of it benefiting at the expense of the program is decreased.

Paragraph (6) of Subsection (a) relates solely to real estate programs and requires that in cases where the sponsor or an affiliate of the sponsor is to provide development or construction services for the program, the program shall require that such be done on a firm contract basis at a price not to exceed the appraised value of the property when completed, including the total cost of the real property as determined by a qualified independent real estate appraiser at the time of the commitment for such service. It provides further that if any developing or contracting is to be supplied by the sponsor or its affiliates after the formation of the program it must be done in accordance with the provisions set forth in Subsection (a)(4) relating to the rendition by a sponsor or its affiliates of services, supplies or equipment to the program.

Section 6(b) -- Impermissible Conflicts of Interest

As noted above, the Board believes several situations exist which constitute impermissible conflicts of interest and should not be allowed in connection with any direct participation programs of which a member or an affiliate of a member is a sponsor. One of these, relating to retention of rights in adjacent or surrounding acreage, has been discussed above.

Subsection (b)(1) related to real estate programs and would prohibit the sponsor or an affiliate of the sponsor from being a principal or prime tenant on property owned by the program. This provision would tend to minimize the potential detriment to participants in a situation where a sponsor and/or its affiliates would be dealing with the program on a non-arms'-length basis. There is no real reason why a sponsor or its affiliates should not be permitted to be a tenant of program property but they would have great leverage to cause it to operate less than optimally to their benefit if they were the only or principal tenant. Subsection (b)(1) excludes from its proscriptions a fully guaranteed lease back

arrangement (defined in Section 1(q)) where the terms
of such are fair and reasonable and no more favorable
to the sponsor or its affiliates than those offered to
other persons. A "principal or prime tenant" has been
defined in Section 1(ii).

Subsection (b)(2) would prevent the rendition
by the sponsor or an affiliate of the sponsor of professional services to the program, such as legal services or
auditing services, or the payment of fees in that connection. The purpose of this provision is to insure that a
program has the benefit of independent legal opinions,
auditing, and other professional services. This would
not prevent the payment to the sponsor or its affiliates
for services which are offered in connection with the day-
to-day management of the program, such as day-to-day legal,
accounting and recordkeeping services, leasing agreements,
settlement arrangements and property management, among
others.

Subsection (b)(3) would prevent the sale or
exchange of any property between programs with the same
sponsor. An exception would be made, however, to allow
such sales and exchanges in the case of oil and gas programs where the sales and exchanges are of non-producing
exploratory acreage, are at cost or, if there is reason
to believe there has been a material change in value, at
fair market value as determined by a qualified independent
appraiser, and are between programs whose compensation
arrangements with the common sponsor are substantially
comparable. This paragraph would also allow transactions
among oil programs by which property is transferred from
one to another in exchange for the transferee's obligations
to conduct drilling activities on the property transferred
or to joint ventures among such oil programs, provided
that the compensation arrangement of the manager and each
affiliated person in each such oil program is the same,
is reasonably calculated to be the same, and is in the
best interest of the program. This paragraph would prevent
one program from benefiting at the expense of another program. Unless such a prohibition were imposed, the possibility would exist for the transfer of property on a
preferential basis depending upon, for instance, the
interests of the sponsor in the respective programs or
other considerations. The overall intent of the paragraph
is to prevent improper self-dealing.

The provision contained in Subsection (b)(4) of
Section 6, relating to impermissible conflicts of interest,
prohibits the retention by the sponsor or an affiliate of
the sponsor of any interests in adjacent acreage (as defined

in Section 1(b)) to property transferred to an oil and gas program or, in the case of all other programs, in property in the general area of the property so transferred. The purpose of this prohibition is to prevent a sponsor or its affiliates from capitalizing on a program's expenditures on the property in question. This possibility is more acute in the case of oil and gas programs. In such cases, a sponsor or its affiliates, retaining surrounding properties to that transferred to the program, could cause the program to expend its funds for drilling operations on the transferred property. If oil or gas were discovered, a reasonable possibility would exist that the discovery would extend to their own surrounding property. This conflict is especially acute since the sponsor would have available the geological reports and could specify where the program's drilling operations should take place. They could then tap into the reservoir with a high probability of profit. The cost of exploration in such a case would have been borne by the program for the benefit of the sponsor and its affiliates. Such is considered to be an impermissible conflict of interest and inconsistent with the sponsor's fiduciary duty to the participants.

An exemption would be granted in the case of real estate programs to the prohibition of retaining an interest in surrounding property as long as such is fully disclosed in the prospectus including a disclosure of any potential benefits to the sponsor or an affiliate of the sponsor or any conflicts of interest which could result from any type of service or supplies rendered by them to the surrounding properties. This exclusionary provision recognizes an accepted, and not improper, course of doing business in the real estate industry. When a real estate program expends funds in connection with the development of a property it assuredly adds value to it, i.e., it constructs a building, as distinguished from expenditures by an oil and gas program which do not necessarily add value to the property. Indeed, expenditures could lead to the discovery that the oil property is a worthless prospect. The provisions also recognize the fact that oil and gas is a depletable asset and to the extent a sponsor draws oil or gas from a reservoir discovered by the program, it assists in the depletion of the asset to the detriment of the program and its participants. This does not occur in the case of real estate programs since there is no depletable asset from which the sponsor can draw to the detriment of the participants. Further, notwithstanding the fact that the sponsor's surrounding property would increase in value because of expenditures by the program, more often than not, the sponsor or his transferee would himself, sooner or later, develop that property thus

adding to the overall value of the property in the neighborhood including property owned by the program.

Subsection (b)(5) would prevent the sale to the
program by a sponsor or an affiliate of the sponsor of an
unspecified property program of any services including
development and construction contracting on any property
owned by it unless the property is specifically designated
and detailed information concerning the services to be
rendered is disclosed in the prospectus. An unspecified
property program has been defined in Section 1(bbb).

Subsection (b)(6) of Section 6 would prevent
the sale to the sponsor or an affiliate of the sponsor by
the program of any property except as provided in Subsection
(a)(3).

Subsection (b)(7) would prevent the direct or
indirect payment of a commission or fee to a sponsor or
an affiliate of the sponsor in connection with the reinvestment of the proceeds of the resale, exchange, or
refinancing of program property except when the aggregate
of initial acquisition fees and the reinvestment fee are
within the limits of Section 10(a)(1).

Subsection (b)(8) would prevent a sponsor or an
affiliate of the sponsor from having an exclusive right to
sell or exclusive employment to sell property for the program

Subsection (b)(9) would prohibit the program from
making loans to the sponsor or an affiliate of the sponsor.

Subsection (c) of Section 6 is a general provision
relating to all other conflicts of interest not specifically
provided for in Section 6 and states that all such conflicts
shall be considered impermissible and members shall not be
permitted to distribute units of programs containing them
where a member or an affiliate of a member is a sponsor
unless justified taking into consideration standards of
fairness and reasonableness to participants. Thus, if a
program of which a member or an affiliate of a member is
a sponsor contains any conflict not specifically covered
by this Appendix F, it would be considered impermissible and
prior to distribution by a member it would be mandatory that
justification for the fairness and reasonableness of the
conflict be affirmatively demonstrated to the Association.
Such justification would include not only the basis for
functioning in the given manner but would also include a
demonstration of the measures which are proposed to be
taken for the purpose of protecting the interests of participants in view of the conflict. It seems, in evaluating

conflicts of interest the predominate consideration in the specific provisions discussed above is that all conflicts are not improper as long as proper controls are imposed for the protection of participants.

Section 7 -- Suitability

The suitability of a direct participation program for a particular customer is an extremely important matter to be considered by members. Usually, because of the tax consequences inherent in such programs, they are a suitable investment only for persons of substantial financial resources who are in an income tax bracket appropriate to enable them to obtain the tax benefit described in the prospectus. Higher than normal suitability standards would be imposed by the Association under Subsection (b) of this section in connection with investment in oil and gas programs which are not formed to acquire producing properties.

However, while the Association believes that suitability standards for investment in certain direct participation programs should be higher than those for investment in general securities, it does not believe they should be so rigid that exceptions could not be made in appropriate circumstances or that discretion to make a suitability determination should be taken completely from the member. Thus a provision is included in Subsection (c) to permit deviations from the provisions of Subsections (a) or (b) if such can be justified. However, certain additional record-keeping must be maintained with respect to this prerogative.

Subsection (a) of Section 7 would prohibit a member from participating in the distribution of a direct participation program unless standards of suitability have been established by the program for its participants which are fully disclosed in the prospectus and are not inconsistent with the provisions of Subsection (b) of this section.

Subsection (b)(1) of Section 7 would require that a member, in recommending the purchase of a direct participation program, whether it be an initial distribution or a subsequent sale, inform his customer of all pertinent facts relating to the liquidity and marketability of the program, the tax aspects of the program during the term of the investment and the tax consequences upon dissolution of the program. This would add a measure of protection for participants who may not be aware of these factors or who may not have the sophistication to determine investment consequences on their own. Mere notification to customers of these factors, however, would not relieve a member from the responsibility of being assured that the other requirements of Subsection (b) are satisfied and that the investment is suitable to that particular customer.

In addition to informing the customer of the
stated pertinent facts, a member, pursuant to Subsection
(b)(2), would have to be assured on the basis of information
obtained, that the customer, after giving effect to all of
his direct participation investments, is reasonably antici-
pates to be in a federal tax bracket (defined at Section
l(aaa)) appropriate to enable him to obtain the tax benefit
described in the prospectus. Pursuant to Subsection (b)(3)
the investor must have a fair market net worth sufficient
to sustain the risk inherent in the program including loss
of investment and loss of liquidity. The investor's commitment to all direct participation programs must bear a reasonable relationship to his net worth. Subsection (b)(4) would
require a member, in addition to the above, to have reasonabl
grounds for believing that the purchase of the program is
suitable for each customer on the basis of information furnished by that customer concerning his investment objectives,
financial situation and needs, and any other information know
by the member. Subsection (b)(5) would require that the memb
maintain in its files the basis for the determination of
suitability with regard to each customer.

Thus, under the proposals a member would have a
strict obligation to not only inform each of his customers
of the tax consequences of the investment as well as the
liquidity and marketability of the program, but also to be
assured on the basis of information received from the custome
that his tax bracket and net worth indicate the investment t
be suitable. The member thereafter would be required to
maintain in its files a statement containing the basis for
and the reasons upon which the determination was made.

As stated, exception procedures are contained in
Subsection (c). The procedures would impose the burden of
justifying a determination of suitability which departs from
the provisions of Subsections (a) and (b) upon the member who
makes that determination and would require that the member
document in writing the basis for his departure from the
provisions and retain such documentation in its files. Thus
whether a determination of suitability is made pursuant to
the provisions of Subsections (a) and (b) or pursuant to a
departure therefrom, a record of suitability bases would be
required to be kept in the member's files in connection with
all participants.

Subsection (d) would require a member soliciting
or recommending the resale, transfer or other disposition of
an outstanding direct participation program interest to info
the seller of any evaluations which were made by the program
sponsor and of the tax consequences of the transaction.

Subsection (e) would prohibit the sale of a direct
participation program interest without first receiving specific authority from the customer to execute that transaction.

Section 8

Although this section is entirely new to Appendix F, it consists of modified portions of Notice to Members 75-33, dated April 25, 1975, and previously considered by the membership, concerning a Proposed Statement of Policy of the Board of Governors Concerning Due Diligence Requirements For Public Offerings of Securities. The main provisions of that proposal have been withdrawn by the Association. However, in view of the overwhelmingly favorable comments received regarding the need for investigative measures in the offering of direct participation programs, the provisions which apply to offerings of these programs have been partially preserved and restated here. In the case of direct participation programs, the Association believes, in view of the nature of the offerings, that investigation of the issuer's activity should be intensive. The lack of traditional underwriting methods used in the distribution of these securities and the need for highly technical knowledge in the specific area of program enterprise require these additional measures. This section as reconstructed makes NASD member firms responsible for conducting a reasonable evaluation of the accuracy and adequacy of disclosure in any direct participation program offering in which they participate.

Section 9 -- Organization and Offering Expenses

This section is designed to assist in insuring that expenses incurred in connection with organizing and offering a program are fair and reasonable. Thus Subsection (a)(2) would place a limitation on organization and offering expenses to be paid directly by any member-sponsored program of fifteen percent (15%) of the dollar amount of the cash receipts of the offering. It should be noted that "Organization and Offering Expenses" has been defined in Section 1(bb) to include all sales commissions paid to broker/dealers in connection with the distribution and all other expenses incurred in connection with preparing a direct participation program for registration. Further, the fifteen percent (15%) relates to the total dollar amount of the cash receipts of the offering as distinguished from the total stated amount of the proposed offering. Thus, if an offering were for $1,000,000, the maximum permissible organization and offering expenses would not necessarily be $150,000 if all the units of the program were not sold. If, for instance, units representing only $500,000 were sold, total organization and offering expenses paid by the program could not exceed $75,000. Should a substantial portion of a proposed offering not be sold and if limitations such as these were not imposed, it would be possible for organization and offering expenses to absorb a significant portion of the invested funds. Such would obviously be detrimental to investors.

Subsection (a)(3) would restrict sales commissions paid to members to a standard of fairness and reasonableness taking into consideration the size of the program being offered. In this connection, it should be noted that the Association has reviewed many offerings of all types of programs and has ascertained that certain norms have developed in the various industries offering direct participation programs. It should be expected that these norms would be considered by the Association in its determination of whether the sales commissions and other offering expenses in a given direct participation program are fair and reasonable. Presently, a maximum underwriting compensation of 10.0% of the gross dollar amount of units sold is being applied in all direct participation programs. In an integrated program, i.e., one where the sponsor or its affiliate also acts as the distributor, a lower compensation would be expected except where specifically justified. Included in the maximum suggested figure of compensation would be all items of compensation to distributors such as expenses of underwriter's counsel, advertising, wholesaling, retailing, investor relations fees, due diligence expense reimbursements, and all other items of value.

Subsection (a)(4) would prohibit the direct or indirect payment or awarding of commissions or other compensation to any person engaged by a potential investor for investment advice as an inducement to such person to advise the purchaser of interests in a particular program, unless such person is a registered broker/dealer or other person properly licensed for selling program interests. Subsection (a)(4) is reflective of other rules of the Association and is designed to prevent the granting of sales commissions to accountants, legal counsel or investment advisors who may be giving advice to the investor but who are not properly registered under the appropriate securities laws.

Subsection (a)(5) would prohibit members or persons associated with members from receiving compensation in forms other than cash if of an indeterminate nature for services of any kind rendered in connection with the distribution of units of a direct participation program. Items such as, but not necessarily limited to, a percentage of the program management fee, a profit sharing arrangement, brokerage commissions, overriding royalty interests, a net profits interest, a percentage of revenues, a reversionary interest, a working interest, or other similar incentive items are included in the prohibition.

Subsection (b) of Section 9 prescribes the various types of compensation to underwriters or dealers, deemed to be in connection with the offering, which will be taken into consideration in calculating the amount of sales commissions to determine compliance with the provisions of Subsection (a)(3).

Subsection (c) of Section 9 prohibits a member or person associated with a member from receiving in connection with an offering any warrants, options, stock or partnership interests in a sponsor or an affiliate of a sponsor. What is in connection with an offering shall be determined on the basis of factors such as, but not necessarily limited to, the timing of the transaction, the consideration rendered, the investment risk and the role of the member or person associated with the member in the organization, management and direction of the enterprise in which the sponsor is involved. The guidelines set forth in the Interpretation of the Board of Governors With Respect to Review of Corporate Financing shall govern so far as applicable for purposes of determining the factors utilized in computing compensation derived from securities received prior to the filing of an offering with the Association.

Subsection (d) of Section 9 is directed at an area of compensation to members in which the Association has noticed much abuse. It has been found that sales incentive compensation has been awarded to members and their sales-persons in the form of free vacation trips and merchandise but that these incentive compensation arrangements have not been disclosed to the Association as part of the compensation package. Not only will the use of such items when undisclosed violate the compensation arrangements under Subsections (a)(4) and (5) and Subsection (b) of this section but such nondis-closure may violate the disclosure laws under the federal and state securities laws. This paragraph prohibits the allowance of any sales incentive items by a sponsor or an affiliate of a sponsor or a program to a member or person associated with a member such as, but not necessarily limited to, travel bonuses, prizes and awards in an amount in excess of $25. The payment of any incentive compensation must be disclosed and the dollar amount of the incentive items shall be taken into consideration in computing the amount of sales commissions to determine compliance with the provisions of Subsection (a)(3).

Section 10 -- Sponsor's Compensation

This section addresses itself to various sponsor's compensation arrangements which are believed to be improper in any direct participation program and also to specific arrangements in the oil and gas and real estate areas.

Subsection (a) of Section 10 is composed of several paragraphs dealing with specific situations which apply to

all direct participation programs. Its provisions are
applicable only to public programs of which a member or an
affiliate of a member is the sponsor. Subsection (a)(1)
provides generally that compensation to a sponsor or an
affiliate of a sponsor must be fair and reasonable taking
into consideration all relevant factors. The following
paragraphs would require complete disclosure in the prospectus of all compensation to the sponsor and affiliates,
whether direct or indirect, and a summary of compensation
arrangements to appear in one section so entitled with a
clear reference to other parts of the prospectus where
more detail can be found (Subsection (a)(2)); prohibit
payment of compensation directly or indirectly to a sponsor
in connection with the dissolution of a program unless such
payment is consistent with the sharing arrangement and is
fully disclosed in the prospectus (Subsection (a)(3));
require that any interest and fees earned on funds held for
the sole account of the program be payable only to it and
not to the sponsor or any other person (Subsection (a)(4));
and prohibit rebates, give-ups, or reciprocal business arrangements in the conduct of the sponsor's duties (Subsection (a)
(5)).

Subsection (b) of Section 10 establishes more
specifically certain acceptable standards of compensation
with regard to oil and gas programs. Subsection (c) does
likewise with regard to real estate programs. Subsections
(b) through (e) are applicable only to programs of which a
member or an affiliate of a member is a sponsor.

Subsection (b) sets forth permissible levels of
sponsor's compensation in oil and gas drilling programs and
production programs. These provisions are essentially uniform
with those which were adopted by the North American Securities
Administrators Association on September 22, 1976. While these
provisions represent a substantial departure from previous
proposals filed under this rule, they clearly adhere much more
closely to the current organization and structure of arrangements in public oil and gas programs.

Subsections (b)(1) through (b)(6) indicate permissible
spreads between cost and revenue participation and related
arrangements for programs in which the general partner contributes to operating capital. Subsection (b)(7) indicates the
permissible participation of program sponsors in revenues on
a subordinated basis where they contribute nothing to the
program's operating capital. Subsections (b)(8) through
(b)(10) indicate permissible levels of participation in the
revenues of production programs depending on the role of the
sponsor in management of operations. Subsection (b)(11)
indicates the manner in which and extent to which expenses may
be allocated to and paid by an oil and gas program.

Subsection (c) of Section 10 relates to sponsor's compensation in real estate programs and, as stated, these provisions are in addition to those specified in Subsection a. as being applicable to all programs. These provisions adhere closely to the Statement of Policy adopted by the Midwest Securities Commissioners Association of February 28, 1973 and subsequently amended February 26, 1974 and July 22, 1975. Subsection (c)(1) would prohibit the payment of an "acquisition fee" any greater than the lesser of a. the customary real estate commission charged by others rendering similar services in the same area, or b. 18 percent of the gross proceeds of the offering provided the total purchase price, including all commissions paid by both the seller and the program, do not exceed fair market value. Subsection (c)(2) would provide that payment of a real estate brokerage commission or similar fee to the sponsor or an affiliate of the sponsor on the resale of property by the program may not exceed 50% of the standard real estate commission and require that such must be subordinated to a return of 100% of the participant's capital contribution plus a 6% per annum cumulative return thereon; Subsection (c)(3) would prohibit the payment of more than one standard real estate or other commission or fee of a similar nature for the sale of any program property in any transaction in which the sponsor or an affiliate of the sponsor is a participating broker.

Subsection (c)(4) would prohibit the payment of any real estate acquisition fees, brokerage fees or other commissions except for services actually rendered by a sponsor or an affiliate of the sponsor that is licensed as a real estate broker or agent and that is engaged in the ongoing business of offering similar services to others. Subsection (c)(5) would prohibit leasing fees or similar types of compensation from being paid to a sponsor or an affiliate of a sponsor on property leased to them. Subsection (c)(6) would require that no more than one mortgage placement fee be paid on any property owned by a program with the proviso that fees received for securing both a construction loan and a permanent mortgage on a property shall be deemed to be one fee. Subsection (c)(7) would require that, where the sponsor or an affiliate of the sponsor is to manage the property of a program, the property management fees to be paid be for services actually rendered and be at a rate based on a percentage of the cash received during the period of operation of the program and no higher than those fees which would customarily be charged for similar services in the same geographical area on similar property by property management as an ongoing business activity.

Subsection (c)(8) would impose limitations on the fees to be paid to a sponsor or an affiliate of a sponsor

for the administration of a program. These provisions are
limited to those programs which invest in raw land and in
government subsidized housing.

Subsection (c)(9) would allow the sponsor or an
affiliate of the sponsor two alternatives of receiving
promotional compensation in the form of a sharing arrangement. The first would be on the basis of a 25 percent
sharing arrangement fully subordinated after payment to
investors of an amount at least equal to 100 percent of
their capital contributions. The second would allow the
sponsor or its affiliate to receive an interest equal to
10 percent of the cash available for distribution, unsub-
ordinated, and a 15 percent sharing arrangement subordinated until after a return to investors of an amount at
least equal to 100 percent of their capital contributions
plus an amount equal to 6 percent of the capital contributions per annum on a cumulative basis.

Subsection (d) of Section 10 would provide for
flexibility in programs of which a member or an affiliate of
a member is a sponsor for levels and methods of compensation other than those listed but would require that justification for alternative arrangements be demonstrated by
the persons proposing them. This provision would require,
however, that such levels or methods be comparable or
equitably equivalent to those listed, that they should
be fair and reasonable taking into consideration all relevant factors and that they should not include levels or
methods of compensation prohibited by those paragraphs.
The purpose of the exception provision is to provide a
flexibility to businessmen. It is recognized that new
methods of compensation may develop in the future and that
alternative arrangements must be consistent in total effect
with the methods and levels of compensation which have been
specified in Section 10.

Subsection (e) would specify that income received
by a sponsor or an affiliate of a sponsor as a result of an
interest held as a participant in a program will not be
included in computing sponsor's compensation for purposes
of Section 10.

Section 11 -- Periodic Reports

Section 11 would prohibit a member from distributing
units of a direct participation program of which a member or
an affiliate of a member is a sponsor unless certain periodic
reports are required by the terms of the program to be sent
to participants. These reports generally are divided into
quarterly and annual reports.

Subsection (a) of Section 11 contains provisions requiring quarterly operations reports to be sent by oil and gas programs on the one hand and all other programs on the other hand. This provision is necessitated because of differences in the nature of the operations of oil and gas programs for those of other types of programs. Thus, in the case of an oil and gas program, a quarterly report covering the period prior to the commencement of drilling operations would not be meaningful. It is required, therefore, that the report be sent quarterly to all participants during the drilling phase of operations disclosing in reasonable detail the progress of drilling operations, the amount of production, if any, receipt and disbursement of revenue and any other relevant information. In the case of all other programs the quarterly reports are required for each quarterly period after the activation of the program and similar information must be disclosed. The purpose of these reports is to enable an investor to follow the progress of operations as well as the success or failure of his program's undertakings.

Subsection (b) would require that participants receive audited financial statements and tax information within 75 days after the close of each fiscal year in order to allow the participant sufficient time in which to file his tax return.

Subsection (c) relates only to an oil and gas program and would require the sponsor to send to each participant within 90 days after the end of the second year of the program, and at least annually thereafter, a report of projected cash flow by years from proven reserves as determined by an appraisal made by a qualified independent petroleum engineer. It is unlikely that such a report would be meaningful prior to the end of the second year of operations, hence the reason for that period.

Subsection (d) would require that the details of arrangements between a sponsor or an affiliate of a sponsor and any person with which the sponsor transacts a large amount of business be set forth in periodic reports. Subsection (d) would also require that the gross receipts received by the persons delineated in this Subsection from prior programs be also disclosed in the prospectus of the current program. This enables the potential participant in the current program to evaluate previous expenditures to such persons prior to making his investment decision.

Section 12 -- Sales Literature

The increase in interest in direct participation programs has resulted in a corresponding increase in the flow of brochures, pamphlets and other forms of sales literature used as supplements to prospectuses. The Association has developed what it considers to be basic requirements for sales literature which are related to the specific features and unique characteristics of direct participation programs.

Subsection (a) under "General Requirements" deletes the previous filing requirement in conformance with the provisions of proposed Section 37 of Article III of the Rules of Fair Practice forwarded to the membership for comment under Notice to Members 77-34 and shortly to be submitted to it for vote.

Subsection (b) under "General Requirement" sets forth the general requirements of accuracy and clarity of sales literature on which the provisions of this section are based.

Subsection (c) under "General Requirements" specifies that the standards of this section are applicable to both oral and written statements which would not conform to the standards outlined.

Subsections (d)(1) through (8) under "Required Content" set forth certain factors which must be explained in the sales literature, including the general nature of the program, suitability factors, sales and management charges, assessments, liquidity limitations, the tax aspects of the program and the sponsor's expertise in order that the sales literature not be considered materially misleading. These paragraphs also contain a statement regarding the necessity of a prospectus accompanying or preceding sales literature. If a sales kit or other integrated grouping of sales material is used collectively, the data required by these paragraphs would be permitted to be contained in only one or more pieces except that the requirement covering delivery of a prospectus would be required to be in each piece of the integrated grouping of materials. The grouping in the aggregate, however, must contain all of the required data.

Subsections (e)(1) through (11) under "Prohibited Content" set forth specific prohibitions with respect to the content of sales literature and prescribe that sales literature containing such data shall be considered materially misleading.

Paragraph (1) thereof generally prohibits projections or forecasts of future returns from an investment in a program. Specific exceptions are provided for oil and gas and reasl estate programs when illustrations or tables are limited in format and content to the standards set forth

Paragraph (2) prohibits forecasts and projections of capital appreciation and assurances of safety or protection against loss.

Paragraph (3) prohibits any discussion of appreciation or profit potential unless balanced with a clear statement of the potential risks of investment in a direct participation program.

Paragraph (4) prohibits undocumented claims of management expertise and is self-explanatory.

Paragraphs (5) and (6) prohibit misleading references to approval or endorsement of regulatory organizations including the Association.

Paragraph (7) would prohibit any statistical statement, table, graph, chart or illustration unless the source of data is disclosed.

Paragraph (8) would prohibit any statement of potential tax benefits unless accompanied by disclosure of the basis for such statement, such as the opinion of independent tax counsel or an Internal Revenue Service ruling.

Paragraph (9) would prohibit any type of stated or implied comparison of the structure or performance of an investment in a direct participation program with that of an investment in another non-affiliated program or of any other investment or industry.

Paragraph (10) would prohibit references to or statement of the financial condition of any affiliate of a management or sponsoring organization which does not have a direct financial responsibility for the program.

Paragraph (11) would prohibit any projection of the results of an exchange of program interests for other securities as well as illustrations of actual exchanges which have no direct relationship to the program being offered. The last sentence of the paragraph clarifies that its purpose is not to prohibit the presentation of factual data regarding completed exchanges of prior programs in accordance with the provisions of the paragraphs concerning oil and gas and real estate programs, respectively.

Subsection (f) under "Oil and Gas Programs" is limited in scope to illustrations and performance data on oil and gas programs and would be applicable to oil and gas program sales literature in addition to the paragraphs discussed above. Subsection (f)(1) is concerned with the format and content of hypothetical illustrations while Subsection (f)(2) is related to historical presentations of the results of previously offered programs.

The basic intent of Paragraph (1)a. is to standardize the format and terminology used in illustrating the major tax advantages of an oil and gas program.

Subparagraph a.1. would require the illustrations of the effects of intangible drilling costs deductions be based on an assumed investment of $10,000 regardless of the minimum investment requirements of the program. In addition to the $10,000 illustration, however, illustrations based upon the total value of the program or the minimum subscription commitment would be permitted. Subparagraphs a.2. through 2.8. set forth the specific content, terminology and sequence which would be required in such an illustration. Subparagraph a.7. sets forth certain minimum disclosures and explanatory statement which would also be required to be included in such an illustration. Schedule I, entitled "Hypothetical Illustration of Tax Treatment of a $10,000 Investment in an Oil and Gas Program," is attached to Appendix F to assist members in preparing illustrations which conform to the requirements.

Paragraph (1)b. would set forth the requirements of content, terminology and sequence for all illustrations of the effects of the depletion allowances and/or depreciation on the taxability of income as well as the minimum disclosures and explanatory statements which would also be required to be included in such an illustration. It also requires that such illustrations be uniformly based on $1.00 of gross income since it is considered unnecessary to use higher figures to illustrate depletion and the use of higher figures may carry implications of future income results. Schedule II, entitled "Hypothetical Illustration of the Tax Treatment of Cash Flow in an Oil and Gas Program on a per $1.00 Basis," is attached to Appendix F to assist members in preparing illustrations conforming to the provisions.

Paragraph (1)c. would require that illustrations of both the intangible drilling costs deduction and the depletion allowance be used if either illustration is used. While there is no requirement that illustrations be used, this provision would prohibit the selective use of an illustration reflecting only one of these major tax features.

Subsection (f)(2) has as its primary goal the development of standardized illustrations of the results of

previously offered programs. While there would be no requirement that such illustrations be used, this section sets
forth what would be the minimum required content of any
illustration which is used.

Paragraph (2)a.1. would require that all programs
offered within the previous ten years be reflected. This
provision would thus prohibit the illustration or analysis
of selected programs which may show the most favorable
results. This paragraph would also permit the use of programs offered more than ten years prior to the date of the
analysis as long as the results of all earlier programs are
included.

Paragraph (2)a.2. would require that results be
reflected both in terms of cash liquidation value and distributable cash flow if the program has a liquidation provision. Neither would be required but if one is used both
must be.

Paragraph (2)a.3. would require that figures used
in such illustrations be updated annually based on appraisals
of reserves made by a qualified independent petroleum
engineer.

Paragraph (2)a.4. would require that distributable
cash flow estimates be based only on proven, producing
properties and cash liquidation values, as of the date of
the illustration, calculated in accordance with a formula
or in accordance with terms contained in the prospectus.

Paragraph (2)a.5. would require that all illustrations be based on an assumed investment of $10,000, including
actual assessments which must be prorated in such a manner
as to reflect that $10,000 is the total investment. This
provision would in certain circumstances also permit higher
or lower investment illustrations but only as a supplement
to the $10,000 illustration. A statement would also have
to be made on the $10,000 illustration in connection with
a program with a minimum investment requirement in excess of
this amount that that figure has been used for clarity of
illustration only and that an investment below the program's
minimum is not possible.

Paragraph (2)a.6. would require that the illustration be updated annually based on the independent appraisals
discussed above. It would permit more frequent updating,
using figures based on reserve estimates of "in-house"
engineers, so long as their update is based on the annual
appraisal by a qualified independent petroleum engineer.

Paragraph (2)a.7. requires a caveat legend regarding the nature of the analysis.

The remaining provisions of Subsection (f)(2) specify the content, terminology and sequence of the items which would be required in the illustration. Schedule III, entitled "Analysis of XYZ Exploration Co., Inc. Programs' Return to Participants in 50% Federal Tax Bracket as of _____," is attached to Appendix F to assist members in preparing illustrations conforming to the provisions of Subsection (f)(2).

Subsections (g) and (h) under "Real Estate Programs" are limited in scope to illustrations and performance data on real estate programs and are supplemental to Subsections (a) through (e) of this Section 12. Subsection (g) is concerned with hypothetical illustrations of potential benefits while Subsection (h) is related to historical presentations of the results of previously offered programs.

Subsection (g)(2) prohibits the use of projections in the prospectus or sales literature of unspecified property programs.

Subsections (g)(3) and (g)(4) allow use of projections meeting certain minimum information requirements for specified property programs and unimproved land programs, respectively. The tables and charts in these subsections are largely self-explanatory.

Finally, Subsection (h) would require that any track record analysis contain the results of all programs offered in the last five years, be factually accurate and comply with federal or state regulations under which the program has been qualified.

These subsections follow almost verbatim the rules for Track Records and Projections adopted by the Commissioner of Corporations of the State of California (Rule 250.140.117.3(k) and Rule 260.140.117.4).

It is intended that all sales literature in connection with real estate programs will conform to the general provisions of Subsection (g)(1) as well as the specific provisions of Subsections (G)(2) through (g)(4), Subsection (h), and the requirements of the Securities and Exchange Commission and/or the regulations of the state or states under which the program is qualified.

PROPOSED APPENDIX F TO
ARTICLE III, SECTION 35
OF THE RULES OF FAIR PRACTICE

Section 1 - Filing Requirements

All members and persons associated therewith making a distribution of securities to the public which is subject to the provisions of this Rule are required to file with the Association for review the appropriate documents and filing fee referred to under the subsection "Filing Requirements" as contained in the "Interpretation of the Board of Governors With Respect to Review of Corporate Financing" of Article III, Section 1 of the Rules of Fair Practice.

Section 2 - Conflicts with Requirements of Appendix F

The requirements of this Appendix shall apply except where there is an irreconcilable conflict between Sections 4, 6, 10 or 11 and the regulations or guidelines established by state securities administrators' associations to the extent adopted by the state or states with jurisdiction. An irreconcilable conflict shall be limited to instances where compliance with both these sections and state regulations is impossible.

All public offerings of direct participation programs must conform to the standards set forth in this Appendix. However, arrangements which do not conform explicitly thereto, but which are not inconsistent with the spirit thereof, may to the extent appropriate be permitted if they can be justified to the Association taking into consideration standards of fairness and reasonableness to participants.

Section 3 - Definitions

The following words shall have the stated meanings whenever used in this Appendix:

(a) ACQUISITION FEE - the total of all fees and commissions paid by any party in connection with the selection or purchase of property by a program. Included in the computation of such fees or commissions shall be any real estate commission, acquisition fee, development fee, selection fee, construction fee, guaranteed payment, nonrecurring management fee, or any fee of a similar nature. Excluded from the computation of such fees and commissions shall be such items as legal expenses, independent appraisals, settlement costs, title insurance and a development fee paid to a person not affiliated with a sponsor, in connection with the actual development of a project after acquisition of the land by the program.

(b) ADJACENT ACREAGE - producing or nonproducing leases located within four spacing units of any well site or located within the boundaries of the same prospect, whichever is larger.

(c) AFFILIATE - when used with respect to a member or sponsor, shall mean any person which controls, is controlled by, or is under common control with, such member or sponsor, and includes:

   (1) any partner, officer or director (or person performing similar functions) of (a) such member or sponsor or (b) a person which beneficially owns 50% or more of the equity interest in, or has the power to vote 50% or more of the voting interest in, such member or sponsor.

   (2) any person which beneficially owns or has the right to acquire 10% or more of the equity interest in or has the power to vote 10% or more of the voting interest in (a) such member or sponsor or (b) a person which beneficially owns 50% or more of the equity interest in, or has the power to vote 50% or more of the voting interest in, such member or sponsor.

   (3) any person with respect to which such member or sponsor, the persons specified in paragraphs (1) or (2), and the immediate families of partners, officers or directors (or persons performing similar functions) specified in paragraph (1) or other persons specified in paragraph (2), in the aggregate beneficially own or have the right to acquire, 10% or more of the equity interest or have the power to vote 10% or more of the voting interest.

   (4) any person an officer of which is also a person specified in paragraphs (1) or (2) and any person a majority of the board of directors of which is comprised of persons specified in paragraphs (1) or (2); or

   (5) any person controlled by a person or persons specified in paragraphs (1), (2), (3) or (4).

(d) APPRAISAL - a written opinion of the value of property

prepared by a qualified independent appraiser of the type of property which is the subject of the appraisal.

(e)   ASSESSMENTS - additional amounts of capital which a participant may be called upon to furnish beyond his subscription amount. Assessments may be mandatory or optional.

(f)   AUDITED FINANCIAL STATEMENTS - financial statements of a program including the balance sheet, the profit and loss statement, and cash flow and source and application of revenues statement which have been audited by an independent certified public accountant.

(g)   CAPITAL CONTRIBUTION - the gross amount of investment in a program by a participant, or all participants, not to include any units purchased by the sponsors.

(h)   CAPITAL EXPENDITURES - costs of lease acquisitions and drilling and completing wells which are generally accepted as capital expenditures pursuant to the provisions of the Internal Revenue Code.

(i)   CASH LIQUIDATION VALUE - the amount, based upon an evaluation made by a qualified independent appraiser and computed in accordance with a formula or in accordance with terms contained in the prospectus, which will be paid for an interest in a program upon exercise by the participant of his right to receive such value.

(j)   CASH AVAILABLE FOR DISTRIBUTION - cash flow less that amount set aside for restoration or creation of reserves.

(k)   CASH FLOW - program cash funds provided from operations, including lease payments on net leases from builders and sellers, without deduction for depreciation, but after deducting cash funds used to pay all other expenses, debt payments, capital improvements and replacements.

(l)   DEVELOPMENT FEE - a fee for the packaging of a program's property, including negotiating and approving plans, and undertaking to assist in obtaining zoning and necessary variances and financing for the specific property, either initially or at a later date.

(m)   DIRECT PARTICIPATION PROGRAM (PROGRAM) - a program which provides for flow-through tax consequences regardless of the structure of the legal entity or vehicle for distribution including, but not limited

334

to, oil and gas programs, real estate programs, agricultural programs, cattle programs, condominium securities, Subchapter S corporate offerings and all other
programs of a similar nature, regardless of the industry
represented by the program, or any combination thereof.
A program may be composed of one or more legal entities
or programs but when used throughout this Appendix
the term shall mean each of the separate entities or
programs making up the overall program and/or the
overall program itself. Excluded from this definition
are real estate investment trusts, tax qualified pension and profit sharing plans pursuant to Sections 401
and 403(a) of the Internal Revenue Code and individual
retirement plans under Section 408 of the Internal
Revenue Code, tax sheltered annuities pursuant to the
provisions of Section 403(b) of the Internal Revenue
Code, and any company, including separate accounts,
registered pursuant to the Investment Company Act of
1940.

(n) EQUITY INTEREST - when used with respect to a corporation,
means common stock and any security convertible into,
exchangeable or exercisable for common stock, and, when
used with respect to a partnership, means an interest
in the capital or profits or losses of the partnership.

(o) FAIR MARKET NET WORTH - the difference between total
fair market value of assets and total liabilities
including, in the case of an oil and gas program
sponsor, the present value of proven reserves of oil,
gas and other minerals as determined by an appraisal
by a qualified independent appraiser.

(p) GENERAL AND ADMINISTRATIVE EXPENSE - all costs and
expenses incurred by the sponsor in connection with
administering a program, including salaries paid by
the sponsor, which costs and expenses are not directly
allocable to the operations of the program.

(q) GUARANTEED LEASE - an arrangement whereby the leasee of
a property makes an agreement or has the right to lease
the property from the buyer pursuant to terms and conditions which are non-renegotiable for a reasonable
length of time.

(r) IMMEDIATE FAMILY - parent, mother-in-law or father-in-law,
husband or wife, children, or any relative to whose support
the sponsor, the member, or person associated with the
member contributes directly or indirectly.

(s) MANAGEMENT FEE - a fee paid to a sponsor of a program
for management and administration of the program.

(t)   MINIMUM SUBSCRIPTION AMOUNT - the minimum amount to which a person must initially subscribe in order to be a participant in a program.

(u)   NET PROCEEDS - the total gross proceeds received from an offering less organization and offering expenses incident thereto.

(v)   NET PROFITS INTEREST - that interest measured by net profits from a property or program, without any liability for losses, which becomes payable after receipt by the participants in a program of net profits equal to certain specified expenditures as detailed in the prospectus for the program.

(w)   NET OPERATING PROFITS INTEREST - a special class of net profits interest which means an interest in net profits from the commencement of production without regard for expenditures for leasehold, exploration or development.

(x)   NON-CAPITAL EXPENDITURES - any expenditures incurred by an oil and gas program in drilling and completing wells which are generally accepted as current expense items pursuant to the appropriate provisions of the Internal Revenue Code.

(y)   OIL AND GAS PROGRAM - a direct participation program which has for its primary purpose oil and gas exploration, development, or purchase of production.

(z)   OPERATING EXPENSES - production and/or leasehold expenses of an oil and gas program incurred in the operation of a producing lease, including district expenses, direct out-of-pocket expenses for labor, materials and supplies, and that share of taxes and transportation changes not borne by overriding royalty interests.

(aa)   OPERATOR - a person designated to supervise and manage the exploration, drilling, production and leasehold operations of an oil and gas program or a portion thereof.

(bb)   ORGANIZATION AND OFFERING EXPENSES - those expenses which are incurred in preparing a direct participation program for registration and subsequently offering and distributing it to the public, including sales commissions paid to broker-dealers in connection with the distribution of the program.

(cc)   ORIGINAL COST - the sum of the price paid by the seller for property plus all costs and expenses, if any, reasonably and properly allocable to the property in accordance with generally accepted accounting principles, except, in the case of oil and gas programs, the costs of drilling wells which are not commercial producers.

(dd) OVERRIDING ROYALTY INTEREST - an interest in oil and gas produced or in the proceeds from the sale of oil and gas, free of operating expenses but subject in some cases to production and ad valorem taxes and transportation charges.

(ee) PARTICIPANT - the purchaser of an interest in a direct participation program.

(ff) PAYOUT - that point at which the gross revenues from production attributable to a program equal the sum of all costs. As used herein, costs shall include expenditures for leasehold, exploration, development, operation and overhead but do not include depletion, depreciation or income taxes.

(gg) PERSON - any natural person, partnership, corporation, association or other legal entity.

(hh) PERSON ASSOCIATED WITH A SPONSOR - any person or member of the immediate family of any person who is employed in any capacity by a sponsor, who is contractually obligated to the sponsor or to whom the sponsor is contractually obligated, or who is, directly or indirectly, controlling or controlled by such sponsor; provided, however, that independent contractors such as attorneys and accountants shall not be deemed to be persons associated with a sponsor.

(ii) PRINCIPAL OR PRIME TENANT - a person, or group of related persons, who is the largest single occupant of a piece of real property and who occupies more than 25 percent of the aggregate square footage thereof.

(jj) PROPERTY MANAGEMENT FEE - the fee paid to a sponsor or others for day-to-day professional property management services in connection with a real estate program's real property project.

(kk) PROSPECT - an area geographically defined by the sponsor of an oil and gas program in which the program owns or intends to own an interest in one or more oil and gas lease and which is reasonably anticipated by the sponsor to have possibilities for the production of oil and gas.

(ll) PROSPECTUS - shall have the meaning given to that term by Section 2(10) of the Securities Act of 1933, including a preliminary prospectus; provided, however, that such term as used herein shall also include an offering circular as described in Rule 256 of the General Rules and Regulations under the Securities Act of 1933 or, in the case of an intrastate offering, any document by whatever name known, utilized for the purpose of announcing the offering and selling securities to the public.

(mm)   QUALIFIED INDEPENDENT APPRAISER - a person, including a qualified independent petroleum engineer and a qualified independent real estate appraiser, who holds himself out as an appraiser of a particular type of property and who:

(1)   is licensed or registered to practice his profession with the appropriate professional and/or regulatory body, if any, within the state of his business activity, if such is required, and can demonstrate himself to be qualified to appraise the type of property in respect to which he holds himself out; and,

(2)   is totally independent in that:

a.   he is informed of the purpose for which the appraisal is to be used and that it is to be relied upon for the public program;

b.   he has relied upon sufficient competent evidence of value and has based the appraisal upon his own experience and judgment;

c.   he has no present interest or contemplated future interest, either legal or beneficial, in the property appraised;

d.   he has no interest in any proposed transaction involving the property or in the parties to such transaction;

e.   his employment and compensation are not contingent upon any value found by him or upon anything other than the delivery of his report for a predetermined fee; and,

f.   he is not an affiliate of a sponsor.

(nn)   QUALIFIED INDEPENDENT PETROLEUM ENGINEER - a person who holds himself out as an evaluator of producing petroleum properties and who:

    (1) is licensed to practice petroleum engineering in the state of his professional activity, if such is required, and can demonstrate himself to be qualified to appraise oil and gas properties and petroleum reserves; and

    (2) is totally independent in that:

        a. he is informed of the purpose for which the appraisal is to be used and that it is to be relied upon for the public program;

        b. he has relied upon sufficient competent evidence of value and has based the appraisal upon his own experience and judgment;

        c. he has no present interest or contemplated future interest, either legal or beneficial, in the property appraised;

        d. he has no interest in any proposed transaction involving the property or in the parties to such transaction;

        e. his employment and compensation are not contingent upon any value found by him or upon anything other than the delivery of his report for a predetermined fee; and,

        f. he is not an affiliate of a sponsor.

(oo) QUALIFIED INDEPENDENT REAL ESTATE APPRAISER - a person who holds himself out as an appraiser of real property and who:

    (1) is registered with a recognized national real estate appraisal organization within the state of his professional activity, if such is required, and can demonstrate himself to be qualified to appraise the type of real property at issue; and

    (2) is totally independent in that:

        a. he is informed of the purpose for which the appraisal is to be used and that it is to be relied upon for the public program;

        b. he has relied upon sufficient competent evidence of value and has based the appraisal upon his own experience and judgment;

       c.   he has no present interest or contemplated
              future interest, either legal or beneficial,
              in the property appraised;

       d.   he has no interest in the proposed transaction
              for acquisition of the property by the program
              or in the parties to such transaction;

       e.   his employment and compensation are not con-
              tingent upon any value found by him or upon
              anything other than the delivery of his
              report for a predetermined fee; and,

       f.   he is not an affiliate of a sponsor.

(pp) REAL ESTATE PROGRAM - a direct participation program
which has for its purpose the expenditure of a deter-
minable sum of money for the investment in and/or the
operation of or gain from an investment in real property.

(qq) REGISTRATION STATEMENT - shall have the meaning given
to that term by Section 2(8) of the Securities Act of
1933; provided, however, that such term as used herein
shall also include a notification on Form 1-A filed
with the Securities and Exchange Commission pursuant
to the provisions of Rule 255 of the General Rules and
Regulations under the Securities Act of 1933 and, in
the case of an intrastate offering, any document, by
whatever name known, initiating the registration or
similar process by whatever name known for an issue
of securities which is required to be filed by the laws
or regulations of any state.

(rr) REVERSIONARY INTEREST - an interest in a program the
benefits of which accrue in the future upon the
occurrence of some event.

(ss) SALES LITERATURE - any communication (including radio,
television and slide presentations, photographs,
recordings and illustrations) used to supplement a
prospectus; provided, however, such shall not mean:

    (1) letters of transmittal which do no more than
         refer to the enclosed prospectus and sales
         literature; and,

    (2) periodic reports required by Section 11 hereof
         supplied by issuers to members and current
         participants in the program, provided that said
         reports are used in no way as sales literature
         and do not contain an expressed or implied
         offer to sell a security.

(tt) SALES MEMORANDA - any communication used as a supplement to the prospectus or selling agreement and intended solely for use by broker-dealers distributing the program.

(uu) SHARING ARRANGEMENT - an interest in a program granted to the sponsor for his services at a lower cost than that charged participants.

(vv) SPACING UNIT - that area or distance between wells specified in an order of a regulatory body, or in the absence of such an order, the customary spacing pattern followed in the area which establishes the number and location of wells over an oil and gas reservoir as a conservation measure.

(ww) SPONSOR - a person who directly or indirectly provides promotional or management services for a direct participation program whether as general partner, pursuant to contract or otherwise.

(xx) SUBORDINATED INTEREST - one which is junior to the rights of participants until such time as they have received cumulative distributed cash or net revenues in an amount at least equal to their capital contribution.

(yy) SUBSCRIPTION AMOUNT - the total dollar amount for which a participant in a direct participation program has subscribed for his participation in the program.

(zz) TAXABLE INCOME - shall have the meaning given that term in Section 63 of the Internal Revenue Code of 1951, as amended, without taking into consideration investment in the program.

(aaa) TAX BRACKET - the maximum rate at which a portion of a person's taxable income would be taxed.

(bbb) UNSPECIFIED PROPERTY PROGRAM - a program which, at the time the registration statement becomes effective, does not have 75 percent or more of the net proceeds of the total dollar amount of the offering allocable to specific purposes or, in the case of a real estate program, allocable to the purchase or construction of specific properties. Cash reserves shall be included in the unspecified 25 percent.

(ccc) WORKING INTEREST - an operating interest entitling the holder to a share of production under an oil and gas lease which carries with it the obligation to bear a corresponding share of all costs associated with the production of income.

Section 4 - General Requirements and Requirements Concerning Subscriptions, Assessments, Reinvestment of Revenue and Liquidations

A member or person associated with a member shall not underwrite or participate in the distribution to the public of a direct participation program of which a member or an affiliate of a member is the sponsor unless:

General

(a)   such sponsor and affiliates of the sponsor have expertise appropriate to the program and in services to be rendered of not less than three (3) years or such expertise is directly or readily available to it within its corporate complex, under contract or otherwise and there is full and complete disclosure of the details of that expertise in the prospectus;

(b)   the sponsor or sponsors of the program have a combined fair market net worth at least equal to the greater of (1) $50,000, or (2) the lesser of $1,000,000 or 5 percent of the total capital contributions made by the holders of program participations issued by all programs of which such persons are a sponsor organized during the twelve (12) month period immediately preceding the offering date of the program plus 5 percent of the gross amount of the current offering; provided, however, that for purposes of this subsection the term "sponsor" shall not include members of the immediate family of or persons associated with a sponsor except to the extent that such persons are guarantors of obligations entered into by the sponsor in its capacity as sponsor of the program in question;

(c)   until the minimum subscription is raised all monies received are transmitted in accordance with the provisions of Rule 15c2-4(b) of the Securities Exchange Act of 1934, as amended;

(d)   the minimum amount or conditions are not met, the total capital contributions of all participants, including sales commissions, shall be returned to them promptly following termination of the offering period which period shall not be unreasonably extended;

(e)   in the case of an oil and gas program, the program requires, as a prerequisite to the activation thereof, minimum public sales in the amount of no less than $500,000 per program (except specified oil and gas operations registered pursuant to or validly exempt from registration under the Securities Act of 1933, including Regulation B exemptions, or under applicable state laws);

(f)   the program, other than an oil and gas program, contains a provision preventing the activation of the program if a stated minimum amount of money is not raised which shall be sufficient, after funding all of the organization and offering expenses and giving due consideration to the fixed obligations of the program, to effect the objectives thereof without changing the nature of the investment called for by the general terms of the program;

(g)   (1)   the program meets the requirements of the Internal Revenue Code which enable participants to obtain tax benefits as described in the prospectus and such can be demonstrated by a tax ruling or an opinion with respect to such requirements by independent tax counsel; or,

        (2)   in the case where such a tax ruling or opinion has not been received:

                a.   the program provides for a right of withdrawal and the return of the capital contribution including commissions to all participants from the program in the event a tax ruling or opinion is subsequently received which states in substance that the program will not enable participants to obtain the tax benefits as described in the prospectus; and,

                b.   the program requires that all funds received will be placed in an escrow account and not used until a tax ruling or opinion has been received which states in substance that the program will enable participants to obtain the tax benefits described in the prospectus.

Subscriptions

(h)   in the case of an oil and gas program:

        (1)   the drilling program's terms require that the minimum subscription in a unit of investment, whether as a result of a direct purchase or an

assignment, except by gift or operation of law, shall not be less than $5,000, or such higher amount as required by state or local law.

(2)   the income or production purchase program's terms require that the minimum subscription be limited so that assignees or assignors may not hold less than the program's prescribed minimum except by gifts or operation of law.

(i)   the program's terms require that all subscriptions be fully paid for within a twelve (12) month period following the date of the commencement of the program or as otherwise required to conform with applicable federal credit regulations; however, a period of deferred payment in excess of the twelve months may be granted in certain types of offerings, i.e., farming, real estate development, among others, where the nature of the investment and development of the product demand a longer period provided, however, the period of payment shall coincide with the anticipated cash needs of the program;

(j)   in the case of an unspecified property program, it prohibits deferred payment plans;

(k)   the program prohibits interest or other similar charges assessed against a participant purchasing units on an installment basis where those installment or benchmark payments are scheduled so as to meet future capital requirements; in cases where installment payments are utilized as a convenience to contributors but the underlying capital is immediately required for program operations, interest payments on the installment proceeds may be considered appropriate;

Assessments

(l)   in any assessment, the sponsor includes with the call for the assessment a statement of the purpose and intended use of the proceeds from such assessment, a statement of the penalty to be imposed for failure of the participant to meet the assessment, and to the extent practicable, a summary of pertinent data on the properties to which the assessment relates;

(m)   the program prohibits payment of sales commissions for assessments on units;

(n)   the possibility of assessments is fully disclosed in the prospectus with a statement as to the maximum amount which the units may be assessed and whether the assessments are mandatory;

(o) in a real estate program, it prohibits the levying of assessments other than to the extent necessary to meet any deficiencies in partnership obligations, including default;

(p) in the case of unspecified property programs, it prohibits the levying of assessments;

(q) all voluntary assessments do not exceed 100% of the participant's initial capital contribution;

(r) mandatory assessments of the program are not in excess of 25 percent of the participant's initial capital contribution in the offering of the securities and provided further, the total of all assessments are not to be in excess of 100% of the participant's initial capital contribution;

(s) when penalties are to be imposed upon participants for failure to meet assessments, the penalty:

    (1) is fair and reasonable;

    (2) is disclosed in the prospectus;

    (3) accrues to the benefit of the program rather than the sponsor;

    (4) for voluntary assessments is,

        a. a proportionate reduction of the participant's percentage interest in revenues derived from future development based on the ratio of his unpaid assessment to all capital contributions and assessments used for such future development, or

        b. a subordination of the defaulting participant's right to receive revenues from future development until those nondefaulting participants who have paid the defaulting participant's assessment have received an amount of revenues from revenues of the program from future development equal to 300% of the proportionate amount of the defaulted assessment which they paid.

(5) for mandatory assessments is,

    a.   a proportionate reduction of the participant's percentage interest in program revenues based on the ratio of his unpaid assessment to all capital contributions and assessments, or

    b.   a subordination of the defaulting participant's right to receive revenues from the program until those non-defaulting participants who have paid the defaulting participant's assessment have received an amount of revenues from all revenues of the program equal to 300% of the proportionate amount of the defaulted assessment which they paid, or

    In the case of a mandatory assessment, the sponsor may enforce such personal liability through a lien on the participant's program interest, which permits the sponsor to withhold and apply all revenues attributable to the participant to the payment of any delinquent assessment.

    For purposes of this subsection, voluntary assessments which a participant has committed to pay will be considered mandatory assessments.

(t) if a failure on the part of a participant to meet an assessment in the case of an oil and gas program is to result in a forfeiture by him of a right to participate in future optional development wells, this fact is disclosed in the prospectus;

Reinvestment of Distributable Cash Flow

(u) when the reinvestment of a program's distributable cash flow into a subsequent program is provided for, such reinvestment is optional to the investor who shall be given the opportunity to elect whether he desires to have his interest therein so invested, and who shall, pursuant to the terms of the program being offered, prior to his election, be provided with complete information on the amount of money to which he is entitled and a copy of a prospectus relating to the subsequent program in which reinvestment is contemplated;

Liquidation of Program Interests

(v) the program prohibits the sponsor or an affiliate of the sponsor from transferring or selling his program interest therein except as may be required for mortgage purposes without requiring that an offer comparable in all respects simultaneously be made to all participants and a reasonable period of time be given to them to transfer or sell their interests;

(w) the program prohibits:

(1) the purchase by it of the program interests of any other program with the same sponsor; however, nothing herein shall preclude entering into partnerships or ventures to acquire and operate a particular property; or

(2) the repurchase by the program of its participants' interests in a manner or in an amount which is not in the best interests of the program; provided, however, this shall not be construed so as to prevent the sponsor of a program from purchasing and reselling such interests on a non-exclusive basis;

(x) when the liquidation of participants' interests in a program are provided for other than as a result of the resale of properties in a program, cash liquidation values are required to be computed on the basis of an appraisal of the program's properties made within the preceding twelve (12) months by a qualified independent appraiser pursuant to a formula or in accordance with terms clearly spelled out in the prospectus; provided, however, if there has been a material change in value subsequent to the last appraisal a new appraisal must be made prior to any liquidation;

Business Transacted

(y) when the program contemplates transacting business with any person in an amount aggregating at least 20 percent of the total dollar value of the participants' interests therein, that fact is disclosed in the prospectus; and,

(z) the details with respect to subsections (a) through (v) hereof are fully disclosed in the prospectus.

Section 5 - Rights of Participants

Unless such conflicts with federal law or rules and regulations or interpretative positions of the Internal Revenue Service or the law of the state within which the program has been organized, a member or person associated with a member shall not underwrite or participate in the distribution to the public of a direct participation program of which a member or an affiliate of a member is a sponsor which:

(a) does not permit its participants the right by a majority of the then outstanding units to remove the sponsor as general partner or manager;

(b) does not require the approval of its participants by a vote of at least a majority of the outstanding units:

    (1) to amend the partnership or other agreement organizing the program entity;

    (2) to dissolve the partnership or other entity formed to carry out the purposes of the program; and/or,

    (3) to approve or disapprove the sale of all or substantially all of the assets of the program in a single sale, or in multiple sales in the same twelve (12) month period, except in the orderly liquidation and winding up of the business of the program upon its termination and dissolution;

(c) does not:

    (1) provide for the termination of all contracts between the program and the sponsor or affiliate of the sponsor, and the sponsor and the underwriter of the program without penalty on 60 days notice in writing; and/or,

    (2) require the sponsor upon the written request of 10 percent of the outstanding program units to cause a vote to be taken on any of the matters referred to in subsections (a) and (b) hereof;

(d) imposes any restrictions on the assignment of a participant's program interests; provided, however, such shall not be construed to prohibit a requirement for approval by a sponsor of the transfer of a participant's interests nor shall such prohibit a restriction on transfer imposed by any regulatory body having jurisdiction over the program.

(e) does not grant the right to every participant in the program to obtain a complete list of names and addresses of, and interests held by, all participants in the program, upon written request to the sponsor and payment of the cost of reproduction thereof, for exercise of rights under the program; and,

(f)   does not prevent the amendment of the partnership or
other agreement establishing the program entity in any
material respect affecting the rights or interests of
the participants unless notice is previously given to
all participants and, if 10 percent or more of the
then outstanding unit interests object, by the affirmative vote of not less than a majority of the outstanding
number of program interests.

Section 6 - Conflicts or Potential Conflicts of Interest

Permissible Conflicts of Interest

(a)   A member or person associated with a member shall not
underwrite or participate in the distribution to the
public of units of a direct participation program of
which a member or an affiliate of a member is a sponsor
which does not fully disclose all potential conflicts
of interest in the prospectus and does not by its
terms, in addition, conform to the following standards
concerning conflicts of interest. Thus, if the program
permits:

   (1)   the acquisition by the program of property owned
by the sponsor or an affiliate of a sponsor,
except as otherwise provided herein, such acquisition by the program shall be at the lesser of
original cost to the sponsor or its affiliate or
fair market value as determined by an appraisal
made by a qualified independent appraiser; provided, however, such an acquisition may be at a
price greater than cost if all details in respect
thereto, including the profit to the sponsor or
its affiliate, are fully disclosed to program
participants and to subsequent program subscribers,
the acquisition is at no more than fair market
value as determined by an appraisal made by a
qualified independent appraiser and:

      a.   the property has been owned for at least a
period of two years prior to the acquisition
by the program; or,

      b.   a material change in the value of the property
has occurred since the acquisition thereof by
the sponsor or its affiliate in which case the
change and the basis for the change are disclosed;

   (2)   the acquisition by an oil and gas program of non-
producing acreage owned by the sponsor or an affiliat
of the sponsor, such acquisition shall be at cost
unless there is reason to believe that the cost is
either materially in excess of, or materially lower

than, fair market value. Where property is acquired at a price other than cost the price shall be based on the opinion of a qualified independent appraiser and all details shall be disclosed with respect to the acquisition, including the profit to the sponsor or its affiliates, to program participants and to subsequent program subscribers;

(3)   the purchase of property owned by an oil and gas program by the sponsor or affiliates of the sponsor, such purchase shall be made at fair market value as determined by a qualified independent appraiser unless the sponsor has reasonable grounds to believe the cost is materially higher than fair market value, in which case the purchase shall be made for a price not less than cost;

(4)   the sale of services, other than those provided for hereafter in Section 10, or the sale or lease of supplies, equipment, furnishings or other property of any kind except as otherwise provided herein to the program by its sponsor or an affiliate of the sponsor, the program must require that the fees and prices to be charged for such services, supplies, equipment, furnishings or other property shall not exceed those customarily charged for such in the same or in a comparable geographical location by persons dealing at arms'-length and having no affiliation with the recipient; provided, however, that if there exists no basis for comparing such fees and prices or if the sponsor or its affiliate is not independently and as an ongoing business activity actively engaged in the business of rendering such services or selling such supplies, equipment, furnishings or other property, they shall not exceed cost;

(5)   the sponsor or an affiliate of the sponsor of an oil and gas program to sell or transfer property to the program, the program must also provide that the sponsor shall not retain therein any interest or rights of any kind whatsoever except those rights created by virtue of the sponsor's status as sponsor of the program and that those rights are fully disclosed in the prospectus, unless the sponsor or its affiliate is required by the program to participate with the program in the development of the property on a cost basis proportionate to its retained interest in the property; or,

(6)   the sponsor or an affiliate of the sponsor of a real estate program to provide development or

construction of a property for the program in accordance with the terms of the program, the program shall require that:

a.   the specified terms of the development and construction of identifiable properties are ascertainable and are fully disclosed in the prospectus;

b.   such be done only on a firm contract basis at a price not to exceed the appraised value of the property when completed, including the total cost of the property as determined by a qualified independent real estate appraiser at the time of the commitment for such services; and,

c.   if the development or construction contracting is to be supplied by the sponsor or its affiliates after formation of the program, such shall be done in accordance with those provisions set forth under paragraph (4) of this section.

Impermissible Conflicts of Interest

(b)   The following situations are considered impermissible conflicts of interest; thus, a member or person associated with a member shall not underwrite or participate in the distribution of a direct participation program of which a member or an affiliate of a member is a sponsor which permits:

(1)   in the case of a real estate program, a sponsor or an affiliate of a sponsor to be the principal or prime tenant on property owned by the program. Such shall not apply to fully guaranteed leaseback arrangements where the terms of such are considered to be fair and reasonable and no more favorable to the sponsor or its affiliate than those offered other persons;

(2)   the rendering by the sponsor or an affiliate of the sponsor of professional services, such as the certifying of financial statements or legal opinions in connection with the organization and registration of the program, or the payment of fees for such services to the sponsor or its affiliates, except for services which may be offered in connection with the day-to-day management of the program such as legal, accounting and recordkeeping services, leasing agreements and settlement arrangements, among others;

his direct participation investments, is reasonably
anticipated to be in a tax bracket appropriate
to enable him to obtain the tax benefit described
in the prospectus; provided, however, that in the
case of an oil and gas program, other than a program formed to acquire producing properties, the
customer shall be reasonably anticipated to be
in at least a 50 percent tax bracket prior to
giving effect to all of his direct participation
investments;

(3)   be assured that the customer has a fair market
net worth sufficient to sustain the risk inherent
in the program, including loss of investment and
loss of liquidity of investment and that his
subscription to all direct participation programs
bears a reasonable relationship to his fair market
net worth;

(4)   have reasonable grounds for believing that the
purchase of the program is suitable for the customer
on the basis of information furnished by him concerning his investment objectives, financial
situation and needs and any other information
known by such member or person associated therewith; and,

(5)   maintain in the files of the member the basis for
and reasons upon which the determination of
suitability was reached as to that customer.

(c)   In any instance in which a determination of suitability
is made without the provisions of subsection (a) or (b)
hereof being entirely satisfied:

(1)   the burden of proving justification for the determination shall be upon the member or person
associated therewith making it; and,

(2)   the member or person associated therewith who
makes such a determination shall document in
writing the basis therefor with particular
references to its departure from the standards
specified in subsections (a) and (b) hereof and
retain such documentation in the files of the
member.

(d)   In any solicitation or recommendation of the resale,
transfer or other disposition of a direct participation
program to a customer, a member or persons associated
with a member shall advise the seller of all details
of program interest evaluations by the sponsor and
the likely tax consequences of the proposed transactions.

(e) Notwithstanding the provisions of subsections (a) through (d) hereof, a member shall in no event execute a transaction involving a unit of a direct participation program without first receiving specific authority from the customer to do so.

Section 8 - Disclosure

In participating in the distribution of securities to the public of a direct participation program, members or persons associated therewith, shall have reasonable grounds for believing that the information made available to them by the sponsor through a prospectus or other materials is adequately and accurately disclosed so as to provide a basis for evaluating the economic merits with regard to these highly technical securities.

Members shall therefore give consideration, depending on the nature of the offering, to the items of compensation; the physical properties; the tax aspects; the financial stability and experience of the sponsor; the program's conflicts and risk factors; appraisals and other pertinent reports; and any other items of material fact.

Section 9 - Organization and Offering Expenses

(a) A member or person associated with a member shall not underwrite or participate in the distribution to the public of units of a direct participation program if:

(1) organization and offering expenses are not fair and reasonable, taking into consideration all relevant factors;

(2) organization and offering expenses which are paid by the program of which a member or an affiliate of a member is a sponsor exceed 15 percent of the dollar amount of the cash receipts of the offering;

(3) sales commissions, wholesaling fees, finder's fees, consultant's fees, underwriter's counsel fees, costs of due diligence, or any other items of distributive compensation of any kind from whatever source are paid in advance of the breaking of escrow unless otherwise deemed appropriate under this section, or are not fair and reasonable in relationship to the cash receipts of the offering;

(4) commissions or other compensation are to be paid or awarded either directly or indirectly to any person engaged by a potential investor for investment advice as an inducement to such advisor to

(3) sales or exchanges of properties or any interest
therein between programs with the same sponsor,
provided, however, that such sales or exchanges
may be made in the case of oil and gas programs
where the sales or exchanges are of nonproducing
acreage, are at cost or, if there is reason to
believe there has been a material change in value,
at fair market value as determined by a qualified
independent appraiser, are in the best interests
of the program, and are between programs whose
compensation arrangements with the sponsor are
substantially comparable; provided, further, that
this paragraph shall not apply to transactions
among oil programs by which property is transferred
from one to another in exchange for the transferee's
obligation to conduct drilling activities on the
property transferred or to joint ventures among
such oil programs, provided that the compensation
arrangement of the manager and each affiliated
person in each such oil program is the same, or
such transfer is reasonably calculated to be in
the best interests of the program.

(4) the sponsor or an affiliate of the sponsor of a
program, except as otherwise provided herein, to
retain any interest or rights of any kind whatsoever in property sold or transferred to the program, or, in the case of other programs,
in the general area of such property, except
such shall not be considered impermissible in the
case of a real estate program if such is fully
disclosed in the prospectus including the disclosure of any potential benefits to the sponsor
and its affiliates of any conflicts of interest
which could result from any type of service or
supplies rendered to such properties by the sponsor
or its affiliates;

(5) the sale to the program by the sponsor or an
affiliate of the sponsor of an unspecified
property program of any services including
development and construction contracting on any
property owned by it unless any such property
is specifically designated and detailed information concerning any such service and each specified
property is disclosed in the prospectus;

(6) the sale to the sponsor or an affiliate of the
sponsor by the program of any property except as
provided in Section 6(a)(3) hereof;

(7) directly or indirectly, a commission or fee to a

sponsor or an affiliate of the sponsor in connection
with the reinvestment of the proceeds of the resale,
exchange, or refinancing of program property, except
if total acquisition fees including reinvestment fees
with regard to the property remain within the limitations of Section 10(h)(1);

(8) a sponsor or an affiliate of a sponsor to have an
exclusive right to sell or exclusive employment
to sell property for the program; or,

(9) loans to be made by the program to the sponsor
or an affiliate of the sponsor or the commingling
of program funds with the funds of the sponsor or
its affiliates.

Other Conflicts of Interest

(c) All conflicts of interest not conforming to the provisions of this Section 6 shall be considered impermissible conflicts of interest and members or persons
associated with members shall not underwrite or participate in the distribution of units in a program of which
a member or an affiliate of a member is a sponsor
which contains such unless justification therefor,
taking into consideration standards of fairness and
reasonableness to participants, can be demonstrated
to the Association and it accepts such provisions as
being consistent therewith.

Section 7 - Suitability

(a) A member or person associated with a member shall not
underwrite or participate in the distribution to the
public of units of a direct participation program unless
standards of suitability have been established by the
program for participants therein and such standards
are fully disclosed in the prospectus and are not inconsistent with the provisions of subsection (b) of
this section.

(b) In any sale, solicitation or recommendation of the
purchase of a direct participation program to a customer, a member or persons associated with a member
shall:

(1) inform the customer of all pertinent facts relating
to the liquidity and marketability of the program during the term of the investment and the tax
consequences upon dissolution of the program;

(2) be assured on the basis of information obtained
that the customer, after giving effect to all of

advise the purchaser of interests in a particular program, unless such person is a registered broker-dealer or is considered a properly licensed person for selling program interests; and,

(5)   the program provides for compensation to be paid to members or persons associated with members for sales of program units, or for services of any kind rendered in connection with or related to the distribution thereof, in a form other than cash if of an indeterminate nature, such as, but not necessarily limited to, the following: a percentage of the management fee, a profit sharing arrangement, brokerage commissions, an overriding royalty interest, a net profits interest, a percentage of revenues, a reversionary interest, a working interest, or other similar incentive items.

(b)   Miscellaneous items of compensation to underwriters or dealers, or their affiliates, such as, but not necessarily limited to, underwriter's expenses, underwriter's counsel's fees, rights of first refusal, consulting fees, brokerage commissions, investor relations fees and all other items of compensation for services of any kind or description, deemed to be in connection with or related to the distribution of the offering, paid by the program directly or indirectly shall be taken into consideration in computing the amount of sales commissions to determine compliance with the provisions of subsection (a)(3) hereof.

(c)   The acquiring of warrants, options, stock or partnership interests in a sponsor or an affiliate of a sponsor in connection with an offering shall be prohibited. The determination of what is in connection with or related to an offering as referred to in subsections (a)(5), (b), and (c) shall be made on the basis of such factors as the timing of the transaction, the consideration rendered, the investment risk, and the role of the member in the organization, management and direction of the enterprise in which the sponsor is involved. For purposes of determining the factors to be utilized in computing compensation derived from securities received prior to the filing of an offering with the Association, the guidelines set forth in the Interpretation of the Board of Governors With Respect to Review of Corporate Financing shall govern to the extent applicable.

(d)   The allowance of any sales incentive items by the sponsor, an affiliate of the sponsor or the program to any member or associated person in the form of travel bonuses, prizes or awards shall be disclosed in detail and any incentive items in excess of $25 per person per program shall be prohibited. Any sales incentive item of $25 or less shall be taken into consideration in computing the amount of sales commissions to determine compliance with the provisions of Subsections (a)(2) and (a)(3) of this section.

Section 10 - Sponsor's Compensation

General

(a)   A member or a person associated with a member shall not underwrite or participate in the distribution to the public of units of a direct participation program of which a member or an affiliate of a member is a sponsor;

    (1)   which provides for compensation to the sponsor or an affiliate of the sponsor which is unfair or unreasonable taking into consideration all relevant factors;

    (2)   which does not have in its prospectus a summary of all compensation, direct or indirect, to be paid to the sponsor or affiliates of the sponsor in one section so entitled with a clear reference to other locations in the prospectus where more detail with respect to the various items of compensation may be found;

    (3)   unless it prohibits the payment of a fee upon the dissolution of the program in any manner inconsistent with the sponsor's sharing arrangement;

    (4)   unless it requires that any interest and fees earned on funds held for the sole account of the program shall be payable only to it; and,

    (5)   unless it prohibits receipt or disbursement of rebates or give-ups, and the participation in reciprocal business arrangements by the sponsor which are deemed inconsistent with Section 6(a)(4) above.

Oil and Gas Programs

(b)   In addition to the provisions of subsection (a) hereof, a member or person associated with a member shall not underwrite or participate in the distribution to the public of units of an oil and gas program of which a member or an affiliate of a member is a sponsor:

Drilling Programs - Functional Allocation

(1) a.   if, in a functional allocation drilling program where the sponsor agrees to pay all capital expenditures of the program but in any case at least 10% of the total program's capital contributions, excluding any contribution made by the sponsor or its affiliates, his share of revenue is not determined by the following formula:

  (i) if the agreement is to pay all capital expenditures but in any case a sum of not less than 10% of the capital contribution of the program, the sponsor is entitled to receive 35% of the program revenues; and

  (ii) the sponsor's revenue sharing may be increased in additional increments of 5% for each additional 5% increase in the percentage of capital contribution agreed to be paid by him up to a maximum of 50% of revenues subject to sponsor's agreement to pay in any case all capital expenditures;

  b.   unless, as an alternative to subsection (b)(1)a., the sponsor elects to receive 15% of revenues and an additional percentage of revenues determined by computing the sponsor's capital expenditures as compared to total costs associated with obtaining production, on a prospect basis, until such time as the sponsor shall have received from such additional percentage of revenues an amount equal to his capital expenditures; after which, revenues shall be distributed as follows: 15% of revenues to the sponsor and 85% of revenues to the participants until the participants shall have received on a program basis a return of their capital contributions and then, 15% plus the additional percentage of revenues shall be paid to the sponsor and the remainder to the participants; or

    c.   unless in connection with any other possible alternatives to subsection (b)(1)a.:

        (i)   a promotional interest in excess of 25% on a program basis is prohibited; and

        (ii)   there is a minimum commitment by the sponsor to pay at least 10% of the total program's contributions.

(2)   unless any arrangement to pay capital expenditures refers to and includes all capital expenditures for the drilling and completing of wells during the life of the program, which need not include capital expenditures for facilities downstream of a wellhead. If the sponsor should enter into farm-out or other arrangements through which only he is relieved of his obligations to pay for such capital expenditures, then the sponsor's share of revenue shall be proportionately reduced, the amount to be determined on an individual basis.

(3)   unless, when electing a sharing arrangement as provided in subsections (1) and (2) above, the sponsor has a net worth of $300,000 or 10% of the total contributions to the program by the participants, whichever is greater, and is under a contractual obligation to pay his pro rata share of expenses as such expenses are paid by the program and to complete his minimum financial commitment to the program by the payment of cash by the end of the third fiscal year succeeding the fiscal year in which the program commenced operations;

(4)   unless a sponsor who does not actively participate in obtaining a significant portion of a program's wells satisfactorily demonstrates to the Association that his compensation together with the costs of procuring such services for the program from third parties does not exceed the permissible compensation to the sponsor set forth in subsections (1) and (2) above;

(5)   unless, in the case of sharing arrangements in which the sponsor pays all development costs, exploratory wells are drilled on prospects which are reasonably expected to require developmental drilling if the exploratory drilling is successful; or

(6)   in any program involving sharing arrangements where the sponsor does not pay his share or category of costs on a current basis.

Drilling Programs - Subordinated or Reversionary Working
Interest

(7)   a.   unless, as an alternative to sharing revenues
on a basis related to costs paid as provided
in subsections (b)(1) through (6) hereof, a
sponsor of a drilling program receives a
promotional interest in the form of a subordinated percentage of the working interest.
The holder of a subordinated percentage of the
working interest shall be entitled to receive
his share of revenues only after the participants have had allocated to their respective
accounts an amount determined in accordance
with either one of the following alternative
formulas:

(i)   an amount which reflects that the
participants' share of revenues from
production and other items credited
to a prospect equal the sum of the costs
of acquisition, drilling and development,
all costs of operating the leases underlying the prospect, and an appropriately
allocated portion of all other program
expenses, including organizational and
offering expenses; or

(ii) an amount which reflects that the revenues
of the program equal all the expenses of
the program.

b.   in the event the sponsor elects to utilize
the provisions of subsection (7)a.(i), his
subordinated working interest shall entitle
him to receive up to 25% of program revenues.
If he selects the second formula, he shall
be entitled to revenues equal to 33-1/3% of
program revenues. At such time as the sponsor
is entitled to receive his promotional interest,
he shall also bear program costs in the same
ratio as he participates in program revenues.

Income or Production Purchase Programs

(8)   unless in income or production purchase programs,
where a major portion of the sponsor's management
and operating responsibilities are performed by
third parties, the cost of which is paid by the
program, the sponsor takes no more than a 3%
working interest convertible to no more than a
5% working interest after the return from production to the investors of 100% of their capital
contribution, computed on a total program basis.

(9)   unless, where the sponsor maintains the operating capabilities and technical staff so as to be in a position to, and in fact does, provide the program with a major part of the management and operating responsibilities of the program, the sponsor takes no more than a 15% working interest.

(10)   unless, where the individual characteristics of specific programs warrant modification from the provisions of either paragraph (9) or (10) regarding production purchase programs, such modifications are consistent with the aforesaid compensation arrangements.

(11)   unless the sponsor's interest in a program or in properties owned by a program bears a pro rata share of all costs, expenses and obligations of the program including, but not limited to, costs of operations, debt service and any other items of expense chargeable to the operation of the program. Program expenses shall be considered to include all actual and necessary expenses incurred by the program and may be paid by the sponsor out of capital contributions or out of program revenues. A sponsor may be reimbursed out of capital contributions and program revenues for all actual and necessary direct expenses paid or incurred by it in connection with its operation of a program, and for an allocable portion of its general and administrative overhead, computed on a cost basis. All overhead costs shall be determined in accordance with generally accepted accounting principles, subject to annual independent audit. Administrative and similar charges for services must be fully supportable as to the necessity thereof and the reasonableness of the amount charged. The prospectus shall disclose in tabular form an estimate of such expenses to be charged to the program showing direct expenses and general and administrative overhead shall be broken down into the various types of services and costs, with a separate breakdown for salaries to officers, directors and other principals of the sponsor and any affiliate of the sponsor: a summary of the manner in which such expenses are allocated shall be included. In addition, the prospectus shall disclose in tabular form for each program organized in the last three

years the dollar amount of the expenses so charged and allocated, and the percentage of subscriptions raised reflected thereby.

Real Estate Programs

(c) In addition to the provisions of Subsection (a) hereof, a member or person associated with a member shall not participate in the distribution to the public of units of a real estate program of which a member or an affiliate of a member is a sponsor unless:

(1) it prohibits the payment of a real estate acquisition fee in an amount exceeding the lesser of:

a. the real estate commission customarily charges in arms'-length transactions by others rendering similar services as an ongoing business activity in the same geographical location and for comparable property; or,

b. an amount equal to 18 percent of the gross proceeds of the offering;

provided, however, that the total cost of the property, including all prepaid items and acquisition fees whether paid by the seller or the program, shall not exceed fair market value;

(2) when the program provides for payment of a real estate brokerage commission or similar fee to be paid to the sponsor or an affiliate of the sponsor on the resale of the property by the program the commission or fee to the sponsor or the affiliate is not in excess of 50 percent of the real estate commission and is subordinated to a return of 100 percent of the capital contribution of the investor plus an amount equal to 6 percent of the capital contribution per annum on a cumulative basis, less the sum of prior distributions to the investor. To the extent that the sponsor or an affiliate of the sponsor participates with an independent broker on resale, the limitations and subordination only apply to commissions paid to that sponsor and its affiliates.

(3) it prohibits the payment of more than one real estate fee or other commission for the acquisition or sale of program properties in any transaction in which the sponsor or an affiliate of the sponsor is a participating broker;

(4) it prohibits the payment of real estate acquisition fees, brokerage fees, or other commissions or fees of a similar nature to the sponsor or an affiliate of the sponsor except for services actually rendered by a sponsor or an affiliate licensed as a real estate broker or agent and engaged in the ongoing business of offering similar services to others;

(5) it prohibits leasing fees or similar types of compensation from being paid by the program to to the sponsor or an affiliate of the sponsor on properties leased to the sponsor or its affiliates;

(6) it requires that mortgage placement fees to be paid to the sponsor or an affiliate of the sponsor for the arranging and financing of a property for the program be limited to no more than one fee for the financing of the same property during the property's life in the program provided, however, that fees received separately for the services of securing both a construction loan and a permanent mortgage on a property shall be deemed one fee;

(7) it requires that property management fees to be paid to the sponsor or an affiliate of the sponsor be for services actually rendered at a rate based on a percentage of the cash receipts during the period of operation and at a price no higher than those customarily charged for similar services in the same geographical location on a similar property by a nonaffiliated person who engaged in the business of property management as an ongoing business activity;

(8) it limits program management fees to be paid to a sponsor or an affiliate of the sponsor:

   a. on a program owning unimproved land to annual compensation not exceeding 1/4 of 1% of the cost of such unimproved land for operating the program until such time as the land is sold or improvement of the land commences by the limited partnership. In no event shall this fee exceed a cumulative total of 2% of the original cost of the land regardless of the number of years held.

   b. on a program holding property in government subsidized projects to annual compensation not exceeding 1/2 of 1% of the cost of

such property for operating the program
until such time as the property is sold.

c.   program management fees other than as set
forth in a. and b. above be prohibited.

(9)   it limits the amount of any sharing arrangement,
promotional interest or similar type of compensation to be paid to the sponsor or an affiliate
of the sponsor for promotional services to no
more than the following:

a.   an amount equal to 25 percent of the undistributed amount remaining after payment
to the investors of an amount at least
equal to 100% of their original capital
contributions; or,

b.   an interest equal to:

1.   10 percent of the cash available for
distribution; and,

2.   15 percent of distributions to investors
from the proceeds of the sale or refinancing of properties remaining after
payment to investors of an amount at
least equal to 100 percent of their
original capital contributions, plus
an amount equal to 6 percent of the
capital contribution per annum on a
cumulative basis, less the sum of prior
distributions to the investor.

(d)   The burden of demonstrating justification for levels
and methods of compensation for programs in which a
member or an affiliate of a member is a sponsor other
than those listed in subsections (a) through (c) hereof
shall be upon the person proposing such. In any event,
such other levels or methods shall be comparable or
equitably equivalent to those listed in subsections
(a) through (c) and shall not be unfair or unreasonable
taking into account all relevant factors and shall not
include levels or methods of compensation prohibited
by those subsections.

(e)   Income to a sponsor or an affiliate of the sponsor from
any interest held as a participant in a program shall
not be included in computing sponsor's compensation for
purposes of this section.

Section 11 - Periodic Reports

A member or a person associated with a member shall not underwrite or participate in the distribution to the public of units in a direct participation program of which a member or an affiliate of a member is a sponsor unless:

(a)   quarterly operations reports are required by the terms of the program to be sent to all participants:

    (1)   in the case of an oil and gas program during the drilling phase of operations disclosing in reasonable detail the progress of drilling operations, the amount of production, if any, the receipt and disbursement of revenue and any other relevant information; and,

    (2)   in the case of all other programs commencing with the first full quarterly period after the activation of the program disclosing in detail the progress of the program, the receipt and disbursement of revenues and any other relevant information;

(b)   the sponsor is required by the terms of the program to send to each participant within 75 days after the close of each fiscal year audited financial statements and tax information to the extent required for the proper preparation of his income tax return;

(c)   in the case of an oil and gas program, the sponsor is required by the terms of the program to send to each participant within 90 days after the end of the second year of the program a report of the remaining proven reserve (as determined by an appraisal made by a qualified independent petroleum engineer), their present worth and a projection of the net cash distribution for the next fiscal year of the program; and,

(d)   when a sponsor or an affiliate of the sponsor is permitted by the terms of the program to sell services, supplies, equipment, furnishings or other property to the program, or if a program contemplates transacting business with any person in a material amount, the terms of the program require the audited financial statements referred to in Subsection (b) above to detail the terms of such arrangements and state the gross expenditures by the program to each such person in connection with such activity, and the gross receipts by such persons from all prior programs are disclosed in the prospectus of the current program.

Section 12 - Sales Literature

General Requirements

(a)   No member or person associated with a member shall use
       any sales literature or sales memoranda in connection
       with the offer or sale of a direct participation program
       which does not conform to the standards contained in
       this section.

(b)   No member or person associated with a member shall use
       any sales literature or sales memoranda in connection
       with the offer or sale of a direct participation pro-
       gram which is misleading, which contains an untrue
       statement of a material fact or which omits to state
       a material fact necessary in order to make a statement
       made, in light of the circumstances of its use, not
       misleading.

(c)   No member or person associated with a member shall
       make any oral statement or presentation which, if
       made in writing, would not conform to the standards
       outlined herein.

Required Content

(d)   If a sales kit or other integrated grouping of sales
       material is used collectively, such data may be con-
       tained in one or more pieces of sales literature
       except that the statement required by paragraph (7)
       shall be included in each separate piece of sales
       literature. Sales literature will be considered
       materially misleading if it fails to contain the data
       specified hereafter in paragraphs (1) through (8):

       (1)   a clear, concise statement outlining the general
              nature of the program being offered including a
              clear and accurate statement describing the pro-
              gram's proposed activities, including estimates
              of the percentages of proceeds to be applied to
              each of the proposed activities;

       (2)   a statement of the relevant factors of suitability
              for purchase of a direct participation program as
              contained in Section 7 above;

       (3)   a clear and accurate statement fully disclosing
              the amount, method, form and percentage of
              sales charge to the investor, based on a percentage
              of the gross proceeds of the offering, the manage-
              ment fee and any revenue sharing arrangement con-
              tained in the program, or in the alternative, a

clear reference to the location of such information in the prospectus;

(4)   a statement fully describing the assessments, if any, required of participants in the program; the purpose of the assessment, if such is an optional assessment, and the penalty, if any, which the participant would incur if he did not meet the call, or in the alternative, a clear reference to the location of such information in the prospectus;

(5)   a clear and accurate statement describing the liquidity and marketability of the program or the lack thereof;

(6)   a clear and accurate statement of the tax aspects during the term of the investment and the tax consequences at dissolution or liquidation of the program or upon the sale of a material percentage of the assets of the program, or upon the sale of an interest in the program, or in the alternative, a clear reference to the location of such information in the prospectus;

(7)   a statement that sales literature cannot be distributed to the public unless preceded or accompanied by a current prospectus; and,

(8)   a clear and accurate statement describing the three or more years of expertise possessed by or available to the sponsor as required by Section 4(a), hereof, or in the alternative, a clear reference to the location of such information in the prospectus.

Prohibited Content

(e)   Sales literature shall be considered materially misleading if such literature:

(1)   contains hypothetical projections of income or other benefits to be received from a program except as provided hereafter or represents or implies an assurance that the investor will receive a specific, stable, continuous, dependable, or liberal return, or rate of return, unless such is guaranteed and there is reasonable assurance that the guarantor will be able to meet the obligation of such guarantee;

(2)   represents or implies an assurance that an investor's capital will increase or will be preserved or protected against loss in value, unless

such is guaranteed by the terms of the program and there is reasonable assurance that the guarantor will be able to meet the obligation of such guarantee;

(3) discusses or portrays in any way the appreciation or profit potential of the investment without explaining the potential risks of such investment;

(4) makes extravagant claims regarding management ability, experience or competency;

(5) makes any reference to registration or regulation of the securities being offered, or of the issuer, underwriter or sponsor thereof, under federal or state securities laws which could, or in any way does, constitute or imply endorsement or approval by a regulatory body;

(6) makes any reference to the National Association of Securities Dealers, Inc. which could, or in any way does, constitute or imply endorsement or approval of the securities, the issuer, the underwriter, or the sponsor by the Association;

(7) contains any statistical statement, table, graph, chart, or illustration without disclosing the source of the information;

(8) contains any statement or claim of tax benefits resulting from an investment in the program without a clear statement as to the basis for such;

(9) contains any comparison or reference to the similarities of an investment in the program with an investment in another non-affiliated program, whether similar in nature or not, or a comparison of the performance of the program with performance of any industry or property (e.g., real estate in general or the oil and gas industry), or a comparison with an investment in other securities, including investment company shares;

(10) contains or refers to any statement of financial condition of an affiliate of a management or sponsoring organization unless such affiliate has direct financial responsibility for, or is the sponsor of, the program being offered.

(11) contains any reference to or illustration of the possible effects of an exchange of program interests for the securities of any corporation whether

based on a hypothetical projection or an assumed exchange utilizing past market performance of the security. The provisions of this paragraph shall not be construed to prohibit the presentation of factual data regarding prior exchanges if such data is presented as part of an analysis of the results of prior programs in a manner consistent with the provisions of Subsection (f)(2) hereof regarding Oil and Gas Programs and Subsection (h) regarding Real Estate Programs, even if the program currently being offered has no exchange provisions.

Oil and Gas Programs

(f)   In addition to the provisions of Subsections (a) through (e) hereof, sales literature designed to promote the sale of oil and gas programs shall be considered materially misleading unless it conforms to the provisions of this subsection.

(1)   If a hypothetical illustration of the tax benefits of an oil and gas program is used, it shall conform to the following standards:

a.   Illustration of Effects of Intangible Drilling Costs Deduction - An illustration of the effects of the non-capital expenditures deduction on an investment in an oil and gas program must:

1.   be based on an assumed investment of $10,000; provided, however, illustrations based upon the total value of the program or the minimum subscription commitment may also but shall not be required to be shown. The illustrations may give effect to future assessments but they must, in any event, be structured so that the total investment illustrated is $10,000, or such other amount as is used in the additional illustrations. Programs with minimum investments higher than $10,000 must clearly state in the illustration based on $10,000 that that figure has been used for clarity of illustration only and that an investment below the program's minimum is not possible. Programs with minimum investments lower than $10,000 may, if any illustration based upon

the lower amount is not also used,
refer to their actual minimums but an
illustration based upon $10,000 must
still be used;

2. reflect in both percentage and dollar
figures, the "estimated deductible
expenses" (non-capital expenditures
costs of abandoned acreage and general
and administrative expenses);

3. reflect the "tax savings" to the participant based on an assumed participant's
federal income tax bracket of 50 percent
which must be clearly stated in the illustration;

4. reflect the "net cost" to the investor
(total investment minus "tax savings");

5. reflect the investor's "adjusted federal
tax basis" (total investment less
estimated deductible expenses);

6. illustrate the items listed in items
1. through 5. above in the same orde
and using the same terminology, as t y
appear above;

7. contain an explanatory statement which:

   (i) states that the illustration is
   hypothetical;

   (ii) includes a description of the
   estimated deductible expenses;

   (iii) states the period over which the
   deduction would occur;

   (iv) states the source from which the
   estimated percentage deduction
   was obtained, that the percentage
   may vary and is not guaranteed;
   and,

   (v) refers to the location in the
   prospectus where more complete
   information regarding the estimated deductible expenses may be
   found;

   (Schedule I hereto is provided as a

guide to members in preparing an illustration which conforms to the above requirements.)

b. Illustration of Effects of Depletion Allowance - An illustration of the effects of the depletion allowance and/or depreciation on the taxability of income distributed to a participant from an oil and gas program must:

1. be based on one dollar ($1) of "gross income;"

2. reflect a reasonable level of "operating expenses;"

3. reflect the "net income;"

4. reflect any "depreciation" which would be passed on to participants;

5. reflect the "tax depletion allowance" in both percentage and dollar figures;

6. reflect the "taxable income" to the investor;

7. illustrate the items listed in items 1. through 6. above in the same order, and using the same terminology, as they appear above; and,

8. contain an explanatory statement which:

(i) states that the illustration is hypothetical;

(ii) includes descriptions of depreciation and depletion allowance (specifically stating that the depletion allowance deduction is limited to 50 percent of net income);

(iii) includes a brief explanation of the calculation of the depletion allowance in the example; and

(iv) refers to the location in the prospectus where more complete information regarding depreciation allowance may be found;

        (v)   depletion allowance may or may not
be available to a particular investor
depending upon the availability to
him of the independent producers
and royalty owner exemption created
by the Tax Reduction Act of 1975;

        (Schedule II hereto is provided as a
guide to members in preparing an
illustration which conforms to the
above requirements.)

c.   If an illustration of either the non-capital
expenditures deduction or the depletion
allowance is made, an illustration of both
must be made.

(2)   If an analysis of the results of previously offered
programs is used, it shall conform to the following
standards:

a.   General - All such analyses must:

    1.   include the results of all programs
offered within the previous five-year
period from registration date if the
results of any program are included.
The results of programs offered more
than five years prior to the date of
the analysis may be included if the
results of all such earlier programs
are also included:

    2.   present the results in terms of cash
liquidation value and distributable
cash flow and include an analysis of
the results on the basis of both cash
liquidation value and distributable
cash flow if an analysis on the basis
of either is included, unless the program
has no liquidation provision; provided
that the computation of such results
must take into consideration the value
of any exchange of stock for program
interests;

    3.   include only estimates of cash liquida-
tion values and distributable cash flow
which are based upon at least annual
appraisals of oil and gas reserves
made by a qualified independent petroleum engineer, whose identity is disclosed in the illustration;

4. include distributable cash flow estimates
    which must be based on proven reserves,
    whether producing or nonproducing, and
    actual cash liquidation values, as of
    the date of the illustration, calculated
    in accordance with a formula or terms
    contained in the prospectus;

5. be based on an assumed total investment
    of $10,000 which must give effect to
    and illustrate actual assessments made
    for each program, provided, however,
    illustrations based upon the total
    value of the program or the minimum sub-
    scription commitment may also but shall
    not be required to be shown. Programs
    with minimum investments higher than
    $10,000 must clearly state in the illus-
    tration based on $10,000 that that
    figure has been used for clarity of
    illustration only and that an invest-
    ment below the program's minimum is
    not possible. Programs with minimum
    investments lower than $10,000 may,
    if any illustration based upon the
    lower amount is not also used, refer
    to their actual minimums but an illus-
    tration based upon $10,000 must still
    be used;

6. be updated at least annually based on
    the appraisals referred to in item 3.
    above. More frequent revisions are
    permitted if based upon interim evalua-
    tions by a qualified petroleum engineer
    whose identity is disclosed in the
    illustration;

7. contain a prominent legend stating
    that the analysis is related solely
    to the results of previously offered
    programs and that it should not be
    construed as a representation that
    similar results will be achieved by
    any future program;

8. include the following items presented
    in the same order and utilizing the
    same terminology as appears below:

    (i)   "Initial Investment"

    (ii) "Assessments"

        (iii)   "Total Investment"

        (iv)   "Cumulative Deductible Expenses"

        (v)   "Adjusted Federal Tax Basis"

        (vi)   "Tax Savings"

        (vii)   "Net Cost"

b.   Analysis of Previously Offered Programs Based on Cash Liquidation Value - An analysis of the results of previously offered programs based on cash liquidation value must also include the following items presented in the same order and utilizing the same terminology as appears below:

    1.   "Cash Liquidation Value"

    2.   "Adjusted Federal Tax Basis"

    3.   "Taxable Gain"

    4.   "Capital Gains Tax"

    5.   "Net Proceeds After Tax"

    6.   "Net Cost" (Total Investment less Tax Savings)

    7.   "After Tax Cash Gain (Loss)"

c.   Analysis of Previously Offered Programs Based on Distributable Cash Flow - An analysis of the results of previously offered programs based on distributable cash flow must also include the following items presented in the same order and utilizing the same terminology as appears below:

    1.   "Total Net Income Paid to Participant"

    2.   "Depreciation"

    3.   "Depletion Allowance"

    4.   "Taxable Net Income Received"

    5.   "Federal Income Tax"

    6.   "Net Income After Taxes"

7. "After Tax Cash Flow"

8. "Latest Three Months' Net Income Paid to Participant"

9. "Estimated Net Future Income to be Paid to Participant Over Next Five Years (or Remaining Life of the Program, Whichever is Less)" so long as such presentation is not inconsistent with the provisions of federal and state securities law and is based on reports of qualified independent petroleum engineers

10. "Estimated Net Future Income to be Paid to Participant Over Remaining Life of the Program" so long as such presentation is not inconsistent with the provisions of federal and state securities law and is based on reports of qualified independent petroleum engineers

(Schedule III hereto is provided as a guide to members in preparing an analysis which conforms to the above requirements.)

Real Estate Programs

(g) In addition to the provisions of Subsections (a) through (e) hereof, sales literature designed to promote the sale of real estate programs which makes or includes a presentation on predicted future results (projections) of operations shall be considered materially misleading unless it conforms to the provisions of this subsection.

(1) General Requirements for Projections

a. Projections shall be realistic and shall clearly identify the assumptions made with respect to all material features of the presentation.

b. Projections shall be prepared by qualified persons or firms. Those persons or firms who participate in the preparation of the projections should be identified, together with their respective roles in such preparation.

c. No projections shall be permitted in any sales literature or in any oral or other presentation whether formal or informal which do not appear in the prospectus or offering circular. If any projections are included in the sales literature or oral or other presentations, all of the projections included in the prospectus or offering circular must be presented in total.

d. Projections shall be for a period equivalent to the anticipated holding period for the property or properties in the program.

e. Projections shall prominently display a statement to the effect that they represent a prediction of future events which may or may not occur; that they are based on assumptions which may or may not occur; and may not be relied upon to indicate the actual results which might be attained.

f. The assumptions underlying tabular and numerical presentations should be fully explained and disclosed and, where appropriate, cross-referenced to relevant sections of the prospectus.

(2) Non-Specified Property Programs. The use of projections in non-specified programs, whether contained in the offering circular, prospectus or any other advertising media, is prohibited.

(3) Material Information for Specified Property Programs. Projections for programs where any property is specified shall include as to each property specified, at least the following information:

a. Initial Application of Funds

Gross amount of capital raised by the program;	xxxx
Organizational expenses;	(xxxx)
Offering expenses;	(xxxx)
Net proceeds available for acquisitions and operations	xxxx

b. Acquisition and Operations

Prepaid financial items;	xxxx
Prepaid operating expenses;	xxxx
Other fees and expenses;	xxxx
Initial principal payments;	xxxx

                Net proceeds applied to
                    acquisitions;   xxxx
                Working capital and operating
                    reserves;   xxxx
                Net proceeds applied to
                    acquisitions and operations. xxxx

c.   Other Financial Information

       1.   Mortgages and other financing separately
              stating as to each mortgage the material
              terms thereof (e.g., interest rate,
              maturity date, annual constant, balloon
              payments, lock-in period, prepayment
              penalties, acceleration provisions,
              assignability, subordination and partici-
              pation);

       2.   Where the program develops a property,
              the predicted construction or develop-
              ment costs, including disclosures
              regarding contracts relating to such
              developments;

       3.   Allocation of the purchase price to the
              improvements, person property and
              loan including information on the
              depreciation methods, useful lives and
              salvage values as appropriate.

d.   Operations

       A proposed operating statement shall be shown
       for each year in the following format (unless
       shown to be inappropriate):

       1.   Scheduled gross revenues;   xxxx
              Vacancy and collection loss;   xxxx
              Effective gross revenues;   xxxx
              Operating expenses;   xxxx
              Cash flow from operations;   xxxx
              Partnership administration;   xxxx
              Sponsor's participation;   xxxx
              Cash flow before debt
                  service and reserves;   xxxx
              Debt service;   xxxx
              Reserves;   xxxx
              Cash flow before income
                  taxes   xxxx

2. Analysis of Cash Flow:

    Cash flow before debt service
        and reserves;   xxxx
    Interest;   xxxx
    Depreciation (attach
        schedule);   xxxx
    Taxable income (loss)   <u>xxxx</u>

    Tax savings (cost) at various
        tax brackets;   xxxx

    Cash flow before income
        taxes;   xxxx
    Total   <u>xxxx</u>

    For purposes of the foregoing, the mini-
    mum tax bracket used shall correspond to
    the minimum suitability standards based
    on combined federal and state income
    tax brackets. In addition the sponsor
    shall include projections at the com-
    bined federal and state 50 percent
    tax bracket and may show such additional
    brackets as are appropriate to the
    offering.

3. As part of the projections the sponsor
    shall include a graphic presentation
    for each specified property based on
    the proposed operating statement entitled
    "Projected Revenues in Relation to
    Occupancy Levels and Expenditures," or
    otherwise appropriately headed, which
    presentation shall include:

    Annual stabilized revenues expressed in
        appropriate dollar amounts at various
        occupancy levels in 5 percent incre-
        ments from 0 percent to 100 percent;
    The level of expenditures at all occupancy
        levels;
    The projected revenue level;
    The break-even point.

    The graphic presentation shall be in the
    following form:

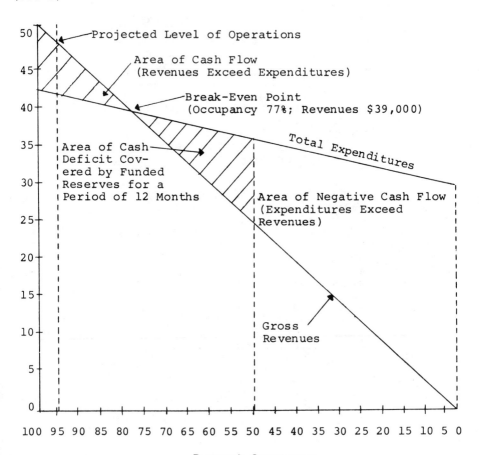

PROJECTED REVENUES IN RELATION TO
OCCUPANCY LEVELS AND EXPENDITURES

e. Refinancing

Sponsor shall be required to project the effects of any anticipated refinancing. Such refinancing must be reasonable and supported by appropriate analysis.

f. Sale

1. The projections shall include a projection of the consequences of a sale of the property. The projected resale price must be reasonable. The total consideration paid for the properties shall be deemed a reasonable resale price except in special circumstances, e.g., some leasebacks, or subsidized housing. In such special circumstances, the sponsor must justify the proposed resale price by appropriate analysis of the projected financial characteristics of the property in the assumed year of sale. The presentation of the projected sale consequences shall be in the following form:

PROJECTED SALE CONSEQUENCES

	Tax Bracket #1	Tax Bracket #2	Etc.
Sale price;	xxxx	xxxx	
Costs of sale;	xxxx	xxxx	
Net selling price;	xxxx	xxxx	
Taxable gain (loss) on sale with ordinary income and capital gain on each sale separately stated;	xxxx	xxxx	

	Tax Bracket #1	Tax Bracket #2	Etc.
Net sales proceeds;	xxxx	xxxx	
Less sponsor's participation in net sales proceeds;	xxxx	xxxx	
Net sales proceeds distributable to investors;	xxxx	xxxx	
Income tax liability;	xxxx	xxxx	

Net after tax proceeds to
investors;   xxxx   xxxx

Discounted rate of return
(internal rate of return)
or other comparable measure
of performance   xxxx   xxxx

> For purposes of the foregoing, the
> assumed tax brackets shall be the same
> as those tax brackets assumed for pro-
> jection of operations. The discounted
> rate of return or other comparable
> measure of performance shall be dis-
> closed for each assumed tax bracket.
> The discounted rate of return (internal
> rate of return) is defined as that
> interest rate which equates the present
> value of the after tax cash inflows to
> the present value of the investment.

> 2. The projections shall include a sensitivity
>   table showing discounted rate of return or
>   other comparable measure of performance
>   under various operating and sale assump-
>   tions for the various combined federal
>   and state income tax brackets which have
>   previously been used in the projections.
>   The table shall be in the following form:

SENSITIVITY TABLE

Discounted Rates of Return or Other Comparable Measure of
Performance for the Performance Levels and Tax Brackets Shown

	Tax Brackets			
Performance Level	_____ %	_____ %	_____ %	_____ %

1. As Projected

2. Disposition without equity

    a. No cash flow - sale at
       mortgage balance in the
       projected year of sale

    b. No cash flow - sale at
       mortgage balance half
       way through the originally
       projected holding period

3. 50 percent of projected cash flow with the sale price determined by a capitalization rate[1] based on that level of operating income - sale in projected year of sale

4. 150 percent of projected cash flow - sales price determined by a capitalization rate[1] based on that level of operating income - sale in projected year of sale

----------------(End of Sensitivity Table)------------------

      3. Where the net sales proceeds resulting from any of the sales assumed on the foregoing chart are less than the tax liability resulting from such sales, that fact shall be so stated as to each such sale as a specific dollar figure per thousand dollar investment.

(4) Material Information for Unimproved Land. Projections for unimproved land programs shall include all of the following information:

    a. Initial Application of Funds

Gross amount of capital raised by program;	xxxx
Organizational expenses;	(xxxx)
Offering expenses;	(xxxx)
Net proceeds available for acquisitions and operations.	xxxx

    b. Acquisition Expenditures

Prepaid financial items;	xxxx
Prepaid operating expenses;	xxxx
Other fees and expenses;	xxxx
Initial principal payments;	xxxx
Net proceeds applied to acquisitions;	xxxx

---

1 The capitalization rate to be used is the rate computed by reference to the original total consideration (rather than contract price) for the property unless a lower capitalization rate can be justified.

Working capital and operating
reserves;   <u>xxxx</u>
Net proceeds applied to
acquisitions and working
capital and reserves.   <u>xxxx</u>

c.   Other Financial Information

Mortgages and other financing separately stating
as to each mortgage, the material terms thereof
(e.g., interest rate, maturity date, annual
constant, balloon payments, lock-in period,
prepayment penalties, acceleration provisions,
assignability, subordination and participation).

d.   Holding Costs

    1.   Operations:

Gross revenues;	xxxx
Taxes;	xxxx
Insurance;	xxxx
Maintenance and repairs;	xxxx
Debt service;	<u>xxxx</u>
Cash requirements (cash investment)	<u>xxxx</u>

    2.   Analysis of Cash Flow:

Cash investment;	xxxx
Add: equity build up;	xxxx
Less: depreciation (attach schedule);	<u>xxxx</u>
Taxable income (loss)	<u>xxxx</u>

Tax Savings (detriment):

Tax Savings (liability) for various tax brackets;	xxxx
Cash investment before taxes;	<u>xxxx</u>
Net cash investment	<u>xxxx</u>

    3.   Sale

The projections shall include a projection of the consequences of a sale of the
property. The minimum sales price shall
be the total consideration paid for the
property, plus the necessary increase to
cover all holding costs and thereby

achieve a sale of the property at a break-
even price. All projections of sales shall
be based on a minimum holding rate of at
least 5 years. The projections shall
include information as to the timing of
the sale as well as the sale price.

4. Rate of Return

The projections shall include a schedule
of anticipated discounted rate of return
or other comparable measure of performance
over the life of the program.

(h) If an analysis of the results of previously offered programs is used, it shall include the results of all programs
within the past five (5) years from the registration date,
be disclosed in both the prospectus or offering circular
and the sales literature, be summarized in tabular form,
be consistent with the requirements established by the
Securities and Exchange Commission and/or the regulations
of the state(s) under which the program has been qualified,
and shall in addition conform with the provisions of subsection (b) of Section 12.

SCHEDULE I

Hypothetical Illustration of Tax Treatment of a
$10,000 Investment in an Oil and Gas Program

Initial Investment	$ 7,000	
Assessments	3,000	
Total Investment	$10,000	
Estimated Deductible Expenses (70%)		($7,000)
Tax Savings (based on participant's federal income tax bracket of 50%)	($ 3,500)	
Net Cost	$ 6,500	
Adjusted Federal Tax Basis		$3,000

This illustration is hypothetical and should not be construed as a guarantee of the amount or percentage of expenses which will be deductible. The estimated deductible expenses illustrated represent costs associated with drilling which are deductible under federal income tax law, such as non-capital expenditures, acquisition expenses of abandoned acreage and overhead expenses. The above illustration reflects an investor's net cost in "after-tax" dollars, assuming a 70 percent expense write-off in the first year of the program; however, actual deductible expenses may be more or less than 70 percent depending on drilling results. It is estimated by tax counsel that deductible expenses in the year 19__ will approximate 70 percent to 80 percent of the initial investment. The illustration does not give effect to possible taxable income to the participant which would reduce the tax benefits illustrated. Please refer to page __ of the prospectus for further information.

NOTE: Schedules I, II, and III are presently being modified to reflect the necessary tax changes as a result of the Tax Reform Act of 1976.

SCHEDULE II

Hypothetical Illustration of Tax Treatment of Cash Flow
in an Oil and Gas Program on a Per $1.00 Basis

Gross Income		$1.00
Operating Expenses		(.25)
Net Income		.75
Depreciation	.10	
Tax Depletion Allowance (22% of gross income)	.22	(.32)
Taxable Income		$ .43

In this example, of $.75 net income, $.32 is tax free due to the depletion allowance and depreciation, leaving $.43 taxable income, which, combined with the $.32 tax free amount, results in a total net to the participant of $.535 per $1.00 gross income to the program.

This illustration is hypothetical and should not be construed as a guarantee that there will be income from the program or that there will be any specific level of income or expenses. The illustration is designed to show the advantages of the tax shelter provided by the depletion allowance and depreciation on the income earned by the program, if any. Since oil and gas are "depletable assets," i.e., eventually the supply will be completely exhausted by production, the federal income tax law permits, as an allowance for depletion, 22 percent of gross income (but not more than 50 percent of net income) to be earned tax free. This allowance commences when commercial production of a well begins and continues for the life of the well. Please refer to page __ of the prospectus for further information.

NOTE: Schedules I, II, and III are presently being modified to reflect the necessary tax changes as a result of the Tax Reform Act of 1976.

SCHEDULE III

Analysis of XYZ Exploration Co., Inc., Programs Return
to Participants in 50 Percent Federal Tax Bracket as of _____

This is an analysis of the results of previously offered programs and should not be construed as a representation that these or similar results will be achieved by any future program.

Analysis of a $10,000 Investment in Each Program Assuming a 50% Federal Income Tax Bracket:

	1969 Program	1970 Program	1971 Program	1972 Program	1973 Program	1974 Program	1975 Program	1976 Program	Total All Programs
Initial Investment	$ 7,000								
Assessments	3,000								
TOTAL INVESTMENT	$10,000								
Cumulative Deductible Expenses (a)	(7,000)								
Adjusted Federal Tax Basis	3,000								
Tax Savings	3,500								
NET COST (total investment less tax savings)	$ 6,500								
Cash Liquidating Value									
Cash Liquidation Value (b)	$ 7,000*								
Adjusted Federal Tax Basis	(3,000)*								
Taxable Gain	$ 4,000								
Capital Gains Tax (based on an assumed liquidation by a taxpayer paying a capital gains rate of 25%)	(1,000)*								
NET PROCEEDS AFTER TAX	$ 6,000*								
NET COST	$ 6,500*								
AFTER TAX CASH GAIN (LOSS)	$(500)*								
Cash Flow									
TOTAL NET INCOME PAID TO PARTICIPANT	$ 8,000								
Depreciation	(2,240)								
Depletion Allowance**	(2,347)								
TAXABLE NET INCOME RECEIVED	$ 3,413								
Federal Income Tax (50% federal income tax bracket)	1,706								
NET INCOME AFTER TAXES (exclusive of tax-free income)	$ 1,707								
AFTER TAX CASH FLOW (depreciation and depletion allowance plus net income after taxes)	$ 6,000								
Latest Three Months' Net Income Paid to Participant	$ 500*								
Estimated Net Future Income to be Paid to Participant Over Next 10 Years (or remaining life of program, whichever is less)(b)	$10,000*								
Estimated Net Future Income to be Paid to Participant over Remaining Life of Program (b)	$15,000*								

(a) Total of actual deductible expenses incurred since inception of program. (Actual deductible expenses for the first year of each program may also be reflected as a part of this footnote.

(b) Based on appraisals of oil and gas reserves made by a qualified independent petroleum engineer.

* Where program interests have been exchanged for stock, these lines would be blank, footnoted to an explanation of the terms of the exchange; where some program interests have been exchanged and others remain outstanding, two columns would be required showing the alternative results. Any data on an exchange of stock must conform to the requirements of Section 9(f)(2)a.2.

** Assuming gross income of $10,667 and operating expenses of 25 percent, depletion allowance would be as shown.

NOTE: Schedules I, II and III are presently being modified to reflect the necessary tax changes as a result

MIDWEST SECURITIES COMMISSIONERS ASSOCIATION

GUIDELINES FOR REGISTRATION OF

PUBLICLY OFFERED CATTLE-FEEDING PROGRAMS

(Adopted at San Francisco, California   February 28, 1973)

PREFACE

Nothing contained in these Guidelines shall prevent a securities administrator from considering variations therefrom to be fully justified when viewed in the light of the facts of the entire offering.

PURPOSE

These Guidelines have been constructed with a threefold purpose:

To provide for uniform treatment of certain problem areas encountered in the analysis and registration of securities consisting of interests in cattle feeding ventures; by defining terms, establishing maximums and minimums, restrictions, prohibitions and requirements to set out in orderly form a policy which may be adopted by Administrators of States to formulate standards for the evaluation of cattle feeding ventures.

To assure industry that programs with plans of business falling within the bounds of these Guidelines are fair and reasonable, and that other plans of business not contemplated herein may be equally fair and reasonable.

To assure public investors that sponsors are adequately capitalized to perform their commitments and that success of the ventures will be fairly shared between investors and sponsors.

DEFINITIONS OF TERMS AS USED IN THE GUIDELINES

The following terms mean:

Affiliate: An affiliate of another person (any entity) means (a) any person directly or indirectly owning, controlling or holding power to vote ten percent or more of the outstanding voting securities of such other person; (b) any person ten percent or more of whose outstanding voting securities are directly or indirectly owned, controlled, or held with power to vote, by such other person; (c) any person directly or indirectly controlling, controlled by, or under common control with such other person; (d) any officer, director, partner, co-partner, or employee of such other person.

Pay-out: That point at which public investors have received a 100 percent return of their investment, before taxes, and without considering any tax deductions.

Sponsor: Any corporation, partnership or individual which originates, promotes and/or manages a cattle-feeding venture; for example, a general partner in a limited partnership set up for that purpose. An Attorney or accountant who only renders professional advice and services to a cattle-feeding venture shall not be deemed a sponsor only as a result of such advice and services.

Net Assets: Total assets less total liabilities.

Affiliate Dealings: Dealings in which feed is purchased, directly or indirectly, from the sponsor or an affiliate, or cattle are fed in feed lots owned by the sponsor or an affiliate; provided, however, the sale of proprietary feed supplements by an affiliate to independent feed lots shall not be deemed "affiliate dealings" if such sales are at prices not greater than those in completely unrelated sales.

Custom Feeding: Includes the feeding of all cattle, other than those fed for publicly offered ventures and those fed for the account of the sponsor and/or any affilitate of the sponsor.

Administrator: The State Securities Administrator or Commissioner or other person designated under State law to approve or disapprove the application to register securities for sale in his jurisdiction.

Hedging: The sale of futures against a purchase of spots (cattle or other commodities) or the purchase of futures against commitments for spot purchases. Hedging is a medium through which offsetting commitments are employed to eliminate or minimize the impact of an adverse price movement on inventories or other previous commitments.

Speculation: Frequent movement in and out of the commodity futures market, holding either long or short positions, or both, without corresponding sales or purchases of commodities on the cash market.

Basic Feed Cost: Costs of the ration ingredients, plus the milling charge. This excludes the mark-up charge for yardage and management.

GUIDELINES

FOR THE REGISTRATION OF

CATTLE FEEDING PROGRAMS

I. The Plan of Business.

The form of the business entity (herein sometimes referred to
as the "venture") must be a limited partnership, or such other
form of entity as to ensure that liability of public investors
will be limited to the amounts of their respective investments,
must provide adequate capitalization and investment in the venture by the sponsors and must reasonably assure the flow-through
of tax deferral benefits to public investors.

A. Experience of Management

At least one principal of the sponsor must have adequate
experience in the cattle feeding business, including buying, selling, feeding and maintenance of beef cattle.
Such experience must be of at least five years duration,
with three of such years in feed lot operations exceeding
1,000 head capacity, and recently preceding the commencement of the publicly financed venture.

B. Capitalization of Sponsor and Investment by Sponsor

1. The prospectus must contain audited financial
statements of all sponsors which are corporations or partnerships indicating an ability
to perform any commitment which is made in regard to the venture.

2. The corporation or partnership, acting as a sponsor, must have a net worth sufficient to meet the
requirements of the Ruling Branch of the Internal
Revenue Service and have a favorable tax ruling,
or an opinion of qualified tax counsel (acceptable
to the administrator), assuring flow-through of
tax benefits to the public investor.

3. The sponsor must purchase for cash a minimum of
$100,000 in participation interests (which will
be treated equally with investments by public
investors) in any entity which offers its cattle
feeding interests to the public. If the aggregate offering of the entity (less underwriting
discounts and commissions) is less than $1,000,000,
the sponsor may, in lieu of this requirement, purchase 10% of the offering, less underwriting discounts and commissions. In either case, the sponsor's required investment in participation interests
may be reduced by 10% for each $35,000 in tangible
net equity possessed by the sponsor. In lieu of
the sponsor making the above-described investment
(if any is required), such investment may be made
by any person or company owning 50% or more of
the voting control of the sponsor.

cable to initial public offerings by such entities. The
public investors must be advised, in the prospectus, that
any future exchange offers may not be available to them
if the exchange offer fails to meet the registration requirements of the particular jurisdiction in which the
investor resides. The sponsor must undertake to continue
management, on the same terms, of the interest of investors who do not exchange their interests for interests
in the new entity, until orderly liquidation of all cattle in the venture is completed.

F. Exculpatory Clause

The sponsor of a venture shall be deemed to be in a
fiduciary relationship to the public investors, and
the prospectus shall so state. Sponsors and affiliates shall not be exonerated from liability to investors for any losses caused by gross negligence or
willful or wanton misconduct.

G. Insurance and Death Loss

1. Casualty insurance or full mortality insurance may
be maintained on all cattle belonging to the venture,
in the discretion of the sponsor, and if in the best
judgment of the sponsor the costs of such insurance
are economically feasible.

2. The sponsor, at no additional cost to the venture,
must guarantee against death loss above 4% occurring during the term of the venture or upon earlier
termination of the management agreement. Such guarantee must include a specified indemnity which will
be made at the earlier of termination of the venture
or termination of the management agreement. Proof
of loss must be produced in order for the sponsor
to receive credit toward the 4% (in some manner
subject to audit). The sponsor must provide for
indemnification for any death loss whatever brought
about due to negligence or misconduct on the part
of the sponsor and/or its employees.

H. Leverage

A venture may not engage in leveraging in excess of four
to one and a limitation of the leveraging to be used must
be set out in the prospectus, along with a clear explanation of the risk involved in leveraging.

I. Hedging and Speculation

If the plan of business of the venture includes the purchase or sale of commodities futures contracts, such purchases and sales must be limited in extent and frequency
to those instances deemed reasonably necessary to protect
the venture against price fluctuations in the cattle or
grain market. The purchase or sale of commodities futures contracts may be for the purpose of hedging only
and such transactions may not be for purposes of speculation. The public investors must be notified, in writing, at the earliest practicable time (at least monthly)
of the terms of any commodity futures contract transactions for the venture.

J. Facilities

Feed lots in which the venture's cattle are to be fed
must have a capacity of 5,000 head or more. The sponsor must have reasonable assurance that it will have
access to feed lots with combined total capacity of
20,000 head or more for feeding of the venture's cattle
prior to the public offering. All such feed lots must
have available the services of a veterinarian and nutri-
tionist and must keep detailed records of all cattle
processed, including the venture's cattle, and all services and goods provided for all cattle in the feed lot,
and must agree to make all such records available to the
venture's auditors and to the sponsor. In geographic
areas where feed lots of 5,000-head capacity or more are
unusual, the numbers mentioned above in this paragraph
may be reduced by as much as one half in the administrator's discretion.

K. Branding & Accountability of Property

Cattle belonging to the venture must be clearly dis-
tinguishable (branded with the venture's brand) at the
earliest practicable time, and not more than 24 hours
after placement in the feed lot under normal circumstances.

All cattle, feed and funds belonging to the venture must
be strictly accounted for, and identified to the extent
practicable, throughout the life of the venture. The
cost of feed and services to the venture shall not be
in any way artificially increased (other than customary
mark-ups mentioned elsewhere herein. See Section I.C.3.),
which duty the sponsor shall indicate in the prospectus.

The weighing of all feed and cattle to be sold to the
venture and all cattle to be sold by the venture shall
be done on sealed certified scales, certified by the
governmental authority (if any) having jurisdiction
thereof in the particular locality. The weighing of
feed ration upon delivery to the venture's cattle shall
be done on certified scales when practicable, and otherwise on truck scales which are daily compared for accuracy with certified scales.

L. Conflicts of Interest

1. The prospectus must fully describe all conflicts of
    interest between the public investors and the spon-
    sor and its affiliates.

2. No fees, commissions, or other remuneration of any
    kind may be received by the sponsor or its affili-
    ates, directly or indirectly, in connection with
    the venture which are not set out and fully dis-
    closed in the prospectus.

3. No fee may be charged the venture upon the sale of
    venture cattle.

4. The venture's cattle may not be sold to the sponsor
    or its affiliates, directly or indirectly, except

that finished cattle may be sold to an affiliated
packer on a dressed carcass basis with payment on
the basis of U.S.D.A. quality and yield grades,
provided the packer reports to the public investors
prices paid for other cattle on the same date and
reports the nearest U.S.D.A. Market News Quotations
of comparable grade and yield. The venture's cattle may not be purchased from the sponsor or its
affiliates, directly or indirectly. When an affiliate acts as a commission buyer, he may be paid
commissions on the purchase of cattle for the venture at rates not exceeding those customary in the
industry, and may take title to the cattle on behalf of the registered ventures during any necessary interim while pen-size lots are being formed.

II. Plan of Distribution

A. Minimum Unit

The minimum investment by a public investor shall be
$5,000 and the initial investment by a public investor
shall be no less than $5,000, all of which must have
been paid at the date the venture commences. Assignability of a public investor's interest must be limited so that no assignee (transferee) or assignor
(transferor) may hold less than a $5,000 interest,
except by gift, inheritance, or Court decree.

B. Public investors' interests in a cattle feeding venture
may not be assessed (the public investors may not be
compelled in any way to make additional capital contributions to the venture).

C. Advertising Materials

Sales of the venture interests must be made by and through
a prospectus. Supplementary material must be submitted to
the administrator in advance of use, and its use must either be preceded by or accompanied with an effective prospectus. Informational material may, and should be, distributed to public investors already in the venture on a
periodic basis.

D. Sale of Venture Interests

1. Interests may be sold by sponsors and/or registered
broker-dealers and/or affiliates of the sponsors.
Officers and directors of the sponsors who sell interests must be licensed as broker-dealers when required by statute and may be paid no commissions,
either directly or indirectly, in any form in connection with the sale of the interests.

2. Compensation to broker-dealers shall be a one time
only cash commission. Indeterminate compensation
to broker-dealers is prohibited. In the absence
of a firm underwriting, warrants or options to
broker-dealers are prohibited.

3. The broker-dealer, or the sponsor in the case of direct sales, shall take all action reasonably required to assure that venture interests are sold only to purchasers for whom such interests are suitable.

Judgment of suitability of any particular venture interest for an individual investor shall be based on the financial capacity of the purchaser, including the purchaser's net worth and income tax bracket, after as reasonable inquiry into the purchaser's financial condition and other related and relevant factors as may be appropriate.

The broker-dealer or sponsor shall retain all records necessary to substantiate the fact that interests were sold only to purchasers for whom such securities were suitable. Securities administrators may require broker-dealers or sponsors to obtain from the purchaser a letter justifying the suitability of such investment.

4. Compensation to wholesale dealers must be a cash commission and such commission must be reasonable and fully disclosed.

III. Prospectus and Its Contents

A. Term of the Venture

The prospectus must clearly state the period of time for which the venture will operate. Such term may not initially exceed ten years in duration. If the sponsor retains the right to extend the period of the venture beyond the initial term, such right of continuance must be disclosed in the prospectus. No venture shall be formed with a contemplated term of less than three years.

B. History of Operations and Reporting Requirements

The sponsor's history of operation shall be fully disclosed, and all fees and remunerations, direct and indirect, received by the sponsor or an affiliate in each publicly-owned venture shall be scheduled. The prospectus must contain a schedule setting out, on an annual or other accounting period basis, the following information for the preceding three-year period or for such shorter period as the sponsor has been engaged in cattle feeding operations:

1. Average purchase weight of feeder cattle, by sex.
2. Average weight into the feed lot, by sex.
3. Average cost per head.
4. Buying commissions paid.
5. Average freight costs into the yard.
6. Average length of time on feed, by sex.
7. Average total cost of gain (per pound); specifying basis of computation of weight gain (pay weight to pay weight or in-weight to pay weight).

8. Average feed cost of gain (per pound); specifying basis of computation of weight gain (pay weight to pay weight or in-weight to pay weight).
9. Average interest rate on borrowed operating capital.
10. Other management or selling charges, if any.
11. Death loss (per cent).
12. Average sales weight, by sex (after 4% shrink at feed lot).
13. Average sales price per cwt, by sex.
14. Average profit or loss per head, by sex (estimated if not known).
15. Average equity investment per head, by sex (estimated if not known).

For ventures which engage in affiliate dealings, the prospectus must set out the above information, for each feed lot, for the following categories:

1. Custom feeding, to the extent such information is known.
2. Cattle fed for the account of the sponsor and/or all affiliates.

The above information shall also be furnished to the public investors in the venture on at least an annual basis.

C. Area of Operations

A general description of the areas in which it is anticipated that the venture's activities will be conducted shall be set out.

D. Maximum and Minimum

The prospectus shall indicate the maximum amount of subscriptions to be sought from the public and the minimum amount of subscriptions necessary to activate the venture. The minimum amount of funds to activate the venture shall be sufficient to accomplish the objectives of the venture, including "spreading the risk" and shall be set out in the prospectus. Any minimum less than $250,000 will be presumed to be inadequate to spread the risk of the public investors. Provision must be made for the return to public investors of 100% of paid subscriptions in the event that the established minimum to activate the venture is not reached.

E. Repurchase of Venture Interests

No representations shall be made that venture interests are readily marketable. Public investors must be allowed to withdraw from the venture on at least an annual basis, following the first full year of operation of the venture. The beginning redemption date for each year shall be specified in the prospectus, and public investors desiring to withdraw shall give written notice to the sponsor at least 30 days prior to such beginning redemption date. As to all cattle owned by the venture on the beginning redemption date, the withdrawing investor shall have a liquidating interest, and his account will be credited with his pro rata share of the proceeds of sales of all such cattle. As soon as practicable after the liquidation of all such cattle, the withdrawing investor shall be paid his pro rata share of such proceeds. A penalty, not to exceed ten per cent of the proceeds credited to his account, may be charged the investor who chooses to withdraw prior to the end of the venture. No penalty may be charged at the termination date of the venture, nor at any time thereafter if the termination date is extended, nor after the venture has been in existence for five years, whichever time is earlier. The ten per cent penalty for early withdrawal must be credited to the venture.

F. Tax Considerations

1. The sponsor of the venture must obtain an Internal Revenue Service ruling, or an opinion of qualified tax counsel (acceptable to the administrator) stating that the desired income tax treatment will be accorded the venture.

2. The prospectus must fully disclose all tax benefits and liabilities associated with investment in the venture. It shall be clearly disclosed in the prospectus that the venture is not a tax-shelter.

G. Use of Proceeds

The prospectus must clearly account for the use of the proceeds of the offering. Proposed use should be set out in dollar amounts as well as percentages of the total offering proceeds. 'Funds to be obtained through leveraging are also subject to these requirements.

H. The prospectus may contain, in summary form, a schedule setting forth examples of an investment in a cattle feeding venture. Such schedule must contain three examples: (1) Showing a loss on investment, (2) Showing a break-even on investment, and (3) Showing a profit on investment, commensurate with the loss shown in the first schedule.

I. Completeness

The prospectus must contain all material facts necessary for the public investor to make an investment decision and for the administrator to make a finding after examination as to the fairness of the proposed offering. Any disclosure required by these guidelines to be included in the prospectus, which disclosure is prohibited by the United State Securities and Exchange Commission, may be waived by the administrator.

STATEMENT OF POLICY REGARDING
REAL ESTATE PROGRAMS

I. INTRODUCTION

A. Application

1. The rules contained in these guidelines apply to qualifications
and registrations of real estate programs in the form of limited partnerships (herein sometimes called "programs" or "partnerships") and will be
applied by analogy to real estate programs in other forms. While
applications not conforming to the standards contained herein shall be
looked upon with disfavor, where good cause is shown certain guidelines
may be modified or waived by the Administrator.

2. Where the individual characteristics of specific programs
warrant modification from these standards they will be accommodated,
insofar as possible while still being consistent with the spirit of
these Rules.

3. Where these guidelines conflict with requirements of the
Securities and Exchange Commission, the guidelines will not apply.

B. Definitions

1. ACQUISITION FEE - the total of all fees and commissions paid
by any party in connection with the purchase or development of property
by a program, except a development fee paid to a person not affiliated
with a sponsor, in connection with the actual development of a project
after acquisition of the land by the program. Included in the
computation of such fees or commissions shall be any real estate
commission, acquisition fee, selection fee, development fee, nonrecurring
management fee, or any fee of a similar nature, however designated.

2. ADMINISTRATOR - the official or agency administering the
securities law of a state.

3. AFFILIATE - means (i) any person directly or indirectly
controlling, controlled by or under common control with another person,
(ii) any person owning or controlling 10% or more of the outstanding
voting securities of such other person (iii) any officer, director,
partner of such person and (iv) if such other person is an officer,
director or partner, any company for which such person acts in any such
capacity.

4. APPRAISED VALUE - value according to an appraisal made by
an independent qualified appraiser.

5. ASSESSMENTS - additional amounts of capital which may be
mandatorily required of or paid at the option of a participant beyond
his subscription commitment.

6. AUDITED FINANCIAL STATEMENTS - financial statements (balance
sheet, statement of income, statement of partners' equity, and statement of changes in financial position) prepared in accordance with
generally accepted accounting principles and accompanied by an auditor's
report containing an opinion acceptable to the Administrator of an
independent certified public accountant or independent public accountant.

7. CAPITAL CONTRIBUTION - the gross amount of investment in a
program by a participant, or all participants as the case may be.

8. CASH FLOW - program cash funds provided from operations,
including lease payments on net leases from builders and sellers,

without deduction for depreciation, but after deducting cash funds used to pay all other expenses, debt payments, capital improvements and replacements.

9. CASH AVAILABLE FOR DISTRIBUTION - cash flow less amount set aside for restoration or creation of reserves.

10. CONSTRUCTION FEE - a fee for acting as general contractor to construct improvements on a program's property either intially or at a later date.

11. DEVELOPMENT FEE - a fee for the packaging of a program's property, including negotiating and approving plans, and undertaking to assist in obtaining zoning and necessary variances and necessary financing for the specific property, either initially or at a later date.

12. NET WORTH - the excess of total assets over total liabilities as determined by generally accepted accounting principles, except that if any of such assets have been depreciated, then the amount of depreciation relative to any particular asset may be added to the depreciated cost of such asset to compute total assets, provided that the amount of depreciation may be added only to the extent that the amount resulting after adding such depreciation does not exceed the fair market value of such asset.

13. NON-SPECIFIED PROPERTY PROGRAM - a program where, at the time a securities registration is ordered effective, less than 75% of the net proceeds from the sale of program interests is allocable to the purchase, construction, or improvement of specific properties, or a program in which the proceeds from any sale or refinancing of properties may be reinvested. Reserves shall be included in the non-specified 25%.

14. ORGANIZATION AND OFFERING EXPENSES - those expenses incurred in connection with and in preparing a program for registration and subsequently offering and distributing it to the public, including sales commissions paid to broker-dealers in connection with the distribution of the program.

15. PARTICIPANT - the holder of a program interest.

16. PERSON - any natural person, partnership, corporation, association or other legal entity.

17. PROGRAM - a limited or general partnership, joint venture, unincorporated association or similar organization other than a corporation formed and operated for the primary purpose of investment in and the operation of or gain from an interest in real property.

18. PROGRAM INTEREST - the limited partnership unit or other indicia of ownership in a program.

19. PROGRAM MANAGEMENT FEE - a fee paid to the sponsor or other persons for management and administration of the program.

20. PROPERTY MANAGEMENT FEE - the fee paid for day to day professional property management services in connection with a program's real property projects.

21. PROSPECTUS - shall have the meaning given to that term by Section 2(10) of the Securities Act of 1933, including a preliminary prospectus; provided, however, that such term as used herein shall also include an offering circular as described in Rule 256 of the General Rules and Regulations under the Securities Act of 1933 or, in the case of an intrastate offering, any document by whatever name known, utilized for the purpose of offering and selling securities to the public.

22. PURCHASE PRICE OF PROPERTY - the price paid upon the purchase or sale of a particular property, including the amount of acquisition fees and all liens and mortgages on the property, but excluding points and prepaid interest.

23. SPONSOR - a "sponsor" is any person directly or indirectly instrumental in organizing, wholly or in part, a program or any person who will manage or participate in the management of a program, and any affiliate of any such person, but does not include a person whose only relation with the program is as that of an independent property manager, whose only compensation is as such. "Sponsor" does not include wholly independent third parties such as attorneys, accountants, and underwriters whose only compensation is for professional services rendered in connection with the offering of syndicate interests.

24. STANDARD REAL ESTATE COMMISSION - that real estate or brokerage commission paid for the purchase or sale of property which is reasonable, customary and competitive in light of the size, type and location of the property.

II. REQUIREMENTS OF SPONSORS

A. Experience. The sponsor and the general partner or their chief operating officers shall have at least two years relevant real estate or other experience demonstrating the knowledge and experience to acquire and manage the type of properties being acquired, and they or any affiliate providing services to the program shall have had not less than four years relevant experience in the kind of service being rendered or otherwise must demonstrate sufficient knowledge and experience to perform the services proposed.

B. Net Worth Requirement of General Partner. The financial condition of the general partner or general partners must be commensurate with any financial obligations assumed in the offering and in the operation of the program. As a minimum, the general partners shall have an aggregate financial net worth, exclusive of home, automobile and home furnishings, of the greater of either $50,000 or an amount at least equal to 5% of the gross amount of all offerings sold within the prior 12 months plus 5% of the gross amount of the current offering, to an aggregate maximum net worth of the general partners of one million dollars. In determining net worth for this purpose, evaluation will be made of contingent liabilities to determine the appropriateness of their inclusion in computation of net worth.

C. Reports to Administrator. The sponsor shall submit to the Administrator any information required to be filed with the Administrator, including, but not limited to, reports and statements required to be distributed to limited partners.

D. Liability. Sponsors shall not attempt to pass on to limited partners the general liability imposed on them by law except that the partnership agreement may provide that a general partner shall have no liability whatsoever to the partnership or to any limited partner for any loss suffered by the partnership which arises out of any action or inaction of the general partner, if the general partner, in good faith, determined that such course of conduct was in the best interest of the partnership, and such course of conduct did not constitute negligence of the general partner. The sponsor may be indemnified by the program against losses sustained in connection with the program, provided the losses were not the result of negligence or misconduct on the part of the sponsors.

III. SUITABILITY OF THE PARTICIPANT

A. Standards to be Imposed. Given the limited transferability, the relative lack of liquidity, and the specific tax orientation of many real estate Programs, the Sponsor and its selling representatives should be cautious concerning the Persons to whom such securities are marketed. Suitability standards for investors will, therefore, be imposed which are reasonable in view of the foregoing and of the type of Program to be offered. Sponsors will be required to set forth in the Prospectus the investment objectives as a program, a description of the type of person who could benefit from the program and the suitability standards to be applied in marketing it. The suitability standards proposed by the sponsor will be reviewed for fairness by the Administrator in processing the application. In determining how restrictive the standards must be, special attention will be given to the existence of such factors as high leverage, substantial prepaid interest, balloon payment financing, excessive investments in unimproved land, and uncertain or no cash flow from program property. As a general rule, programs structured to give deductible tax losses of 50% or more of the capital contribution of the participant in the year of investment should be sold only to persons in higher income tax brackets considering both state and federal income taxes. Programs which involve more than ordinary investor risk should emphasize suitability standards involving substantial net worth of the investor.

B. Sales to Appropriate Persons.

1. The sponsor and each person selling limited partnership interests on behalf of the sponsor or program shall make every reasonable effort to assure that those persons being offered or sold the limited partnership interests are appropriate in light of the suitability standards set forth as required above and are appropriate to the customers' investment objectives and financial situations.

2. The sponsor and/or his representatives shall ascertain that the investor can reasonably benefit from the program, and the following shall be evidence thereof:

a. The investor has the capacity of understanding the fundamental aspects of the Program, which capacity may be evidenced by the following:

(1) The nature of employment experience;
(2) Educational level achieved;
(3) Access to advice from qualified sources, such as, attorney, accountant and tax adviser;
(4) Prior experience with investments of a similar nature.

b. The sponsor and/or his representatives shall ascertain that the investor has apparent understanding;

(1) of the fundamental risks and possible financial hazards of the investment;
(2) of the lack of liquidity of this investment;
(3) that the investment will be directed and managed by the sponsor; and
(4) of the tax consequences of the investment.

c. The participant is able to bear the economic risk of the investment. For purposes of determining the ability to bear the economic risk, unless the Administrator approves a lower suitability standard, participants shall have a minimum annual gross income of $20,000 and a net worth of $20,000, or in the alternative, a net worth of $75,000. Net worth shall be determined exclusive of home, home furnishings and automobiles. In high risk or principally tax oriented offerings, higher suitability standards may be required. In the case of sales to fiduciary accounts, the suitability standards shall be met by the fiduciary or by the fiduciary account or by a donor who directly or indirectly supplies the funds to purchase the interest in the program.

C. Maintenance of Records. The sponsor shall maintain a record of the information obtained to indicate that a participant meets the suitability standards employed in connection with the offer and sale of its interests and a representation of the participant that he is purchasing for his own account or, in lieu of such representation, information indicating that the participants for whose account the purchase is made meet such suitability standards. Such information may be obtained from the participant through the use of a form which sets forth the prescribed suitability standards in full and which includes a statement to be signed by the participant in which he represents that he meets such suitability standards and is purchasing for his own account. However, where the offering is underwritten or sold by a broker-dealer, the sponsor shall obtain a commitment from the broker-dealer, to maintain the same record of information required of the sponsor.

D. Minimum Investment. A minimum initial cash purchase of $2,500 per investor shall be required. Subsequent transfers of such interests shall be limited to no less than a minimum unit equivalent to an initial minimum purchase, except for transfers by gifts, inheritance, intra-family transfers, family dissolutions, and transfers to affiliates.

IV. FEES - COMPENSATION - EXPENSES.

A. Fees, Compensation and Expenses to be Reasonable.

1. The total amount of consideration of all kinds which may be paid directly or indirectly to the sponsor or its affiliates shall be reasonable, considering all aspects of the syndication program and the investors. Such consideration may include, but is not limited to:

a. Organization and offering expenses
b. Compensation for acquisition services
c. Compensation for development and/or construction services
d. Compensation for program management
e. Additional compensation to the sponsor/subordinated interests and promotional interests.
f. Real estate brokerage commissions on resale of property
g. Property management fee

2. Except to the extent that a subordinated interest is permitted for promotional activities pursuant to Subdivision E, hereof, consideration may only be paid for reasonable and necessary goods, property or services.

3. The application for qualification or registration and the Prospectus must fully disclose and itemize all consideration which may be received from the program directly or indirectly by the sponsor, its affiliates and underwriters, what the consideration is for and how, and when it will be paid. This shall be set forth in one location in tabular form.

B. Organization and Offering Expenses. All Organization and Offering Expenses incurred in order to sell program interests shall be reasonable and shall comply with all statutes, rules and regulations imposed in connection with the offering of other securities in the state.

C. Compensation for Acquisition Services. Payment of an acquisition fee shall be reasonable and shall be payable only for services actually rendered and to be rendered directly or indirectly and subject to the following conditions:

1. The total of all such compensation paid to everyone involved in the transaction by the program and/or any other person shall be deemed to be presumptively reasonable if it does not exceed the lesser of such

compensation customarily charged in arm's length transactions by others rendering similar services as an ongoing public activity in the same geographical location and for comparable property or an amount equal to 18% of the gross proceeds of the offering. The acquisition fee to be paid to the sponsor shall be reduced to the extent that other real estate commissions, acquisition fees, finder's fees, or other similar fees or commissions are paid by any person in connection with the transaction. For purposes of this section, a standard real estate commission shall be based on the purchase price of the property.

2. The sponsor shall set forth on the face of the prospectus the amount of all acquisition fees which may be paid. This amount shall be expressed in both absolute dollars and as a percentage of the gross proceeds of the offering and may, in addition, be expressed as a percentage of the sum of the purchase price of the property, plus the acquisition fee.

3. The sum of the purchase price of the program's properties plus the acquisition fees paid shall not exceed the appraised value of the properties.

D. Program Management Fee.

1. A general partner of a Program owning unimproved land shall be entitled to annual compensation not exceeding 1/4 of 1% of the cost of such unimproved land for operating the Program until such time as the land is sold or improvement of the land commences by the limited partnership. In no event shall this fee exceed a cumulative total of 2% of the original cost of the land regardless of the number of years held.

2. A general partner of a Program holding property in government subsidized projects shall be entitled to annual compensation not exceeding 1/2 of 1% of the cost of such property for operating the Program until such time as the property is sold.

3. Program management fees other than as set forth above shall be prohibited.

E. Promotional Interest. An interest in the limited partnership will be allowed as a promotional interest and partnership management fee, provided the amount or percentage of such interest is reasonable. Such an interest will be considered presumptively reasonable if it is within the limitations expressed in either subparagraph 1 or 2 below:

1. An interest equal to 25% in the undistributed cash amounts remaining after payment to investors of an amount equal to 100% of capital contribution; or

2. An interest equal to:

(i) 10% of distributions from cash available for distribution; and

(ii) 15% of cash distributions to investors from the proceeds remaining from the sale or refinancing of properties after payment to investors of an amount equal to 100% of capital contributions, plus an amount equal to 6% of capital contributions per annum cumulative, less the sum of prior distributions to investors from cash available for distribution.

3. For purposes of this Section, the capital contribution of the investors shall only be reduced by a cash distribution to investors of the proceeds from the sale or refinancing of properties.

4. Dissolution and liquidation of the partnership. The distribu-

tion of assets upon dissolution and liquidation of the partnership shall conform to the applicable subordination provisions of subsections 1 and 2(ii) herein, and appropriate language shall be included in the partnership agreement.

F. Real Estate Brokerage Commissions on Resale of Property. Payment of all real estate commissions or similar fees to the sponsor on the resale of property by a program shall not exceed the lesser of 9% of the gross proceeds of the offering or 50% of the standard real estate commission. Such commission shall be paid only for services actually performed, and shall be subordinated as in E. 2. above. If the sponsor participates with an independent broker on resale, the subordination requirement shall apply only to the commission earned by the sponsor.

V. CONFLICTS OF INTEREST AND INVESTMENT RESTRICTIONS.

A. Sales, Leases and Loans

1. Sales and Leases to Program

A program shall not purchase or lease property in which a sponsor has an interest unless:

a. The transaction occurs at the formation of the program and is fully disclosed in its prospectus or offering circular, and

b. The property is sold upon terms fair to the program and at a price not in excess of its appraised value, and

c. The cost of the property and any improvements thereon to the sponsor is clearly established. If the sponsor's cost was less than the price to be paid by the program, the price to be paid by the program will not be deemed fair, regardless of the appraised value, unless some material change has occurred to the property which would increase the value since the sponsor acquired the property. Material factors may include the passage of a significant amount of time (but in no event less than 2 years), the assumption by the promoter of the risk of obtaining a re-zoning of the property and its subsequent re-zoning, or some other extraordinary event which in fact increases the value of the property.

d. The provisions of this subsection notwithstanding, the sponsor may purchase property in its own name (and assume loans in connection therewith) and temporarily hold title thereto for the purpose of facilitating the acquisition of such property or the borrowing of money or obtaining of financing for the program, or completion of construction of the property, or any other purpose related to the business of the program, provided that such property is purchased by the program for a price no greater than the cost of such property to the sponsor, except compensation in accordance with Section IV above of these Rules, and provided there is no difference in interest rates of the loans secured by the property at the time acquired by the sponsor and the time acquired by the program, nor any other benefit arising out of such transaction to the sponsor apart from compensation otherwise permitted by these Rules.

2. Sales and Leases to Sponsor. The program will not ordinarily be permitted to sell or lease property to the sponsor except that the program may lease property to the sponsor under a lease-back arrangement made at the outset and on terms no more favorable to the sponsor than those offered other persons and fully described in the prospectus.

3. Loans. No loans may be made by the program to the sponsor or affiliate.

4. Dealings with Related Programs. A program shall not acquire property from a program in which the sponsor has an interest.

B. Exchange of Limited Partnership Interests. The program may not acquire property in exchange for limited partnership interests, except for property which is described in the prospectus which will be exchanged immediately upon effectiveness. In addition, such exchange shall meet the following conditions:

1. A provision for such exchange must be set forth in the partnership agreement, and appropriate disclosure as to tax effects of such exchange are set forth in the prospectus;

2. The property to be acquired must come within the objectives of the program;

3. The purchase price assigned to the property shall be no higher than the value supported by an appraisal prepared by an independent, qualified appraiser;

4. Each limited partnership interest must be valued at no less than:

a. Market value if there is a market or if there is no market,

b. Fair market value of the program's assets as determined by an independent appraiser within the last 90 days, less its liabilities, divided by the number of interests outstanding;

5. No more than one-half of the interests issued by the program shall have been issued in exchange for property;

6. No securities sales or underwriting commissions shall be paid in connection with such exchange; and

7. Such exchange, however, is prohibited between the program and the sponsor.

C. Exclusive Agreement. A program shall not give a sponsor an exclusive right to sell or exclusive employment to sell property for the program.

D. Commissions on Reinvestment. A program shall not pay, directly or indirectly, a commission or fee to a sponsor in connection with the reinvestment of the proceeds of the resale, exchange, or refinancing of program property.

E. Services Rendered to the Program by the Sponsor.

1. Property Management Services. The sponsor or his affiliates may perform property management services for the program provided that the compensation to the sponsor therefor is competitive in price and terms with other non-affiliated persons rendering comparable services. All such self-dealing and the compensation paid therefor shall be fully disclosed in the prospectus or offering circular.

2. Other Services. Any other services performed by the sponsor. for the program will be allowed only in extraordinary circumstances fully justified to the Administrator. As a minimum, self-dealing arrangements must meet the following criteria:

a. the compensation, price or fee therefor must be comparable and competitive with the compensation, price or fee of any other person who is rendering comparable services or selling or leasing comparable goods which could reasonably be made available to the programs and shall be on competitive terms, and

b. the fees and other terms of the contract shall be fully disclosed in the prospectus, and

c. the sponsor must be previously engaged in the business of rendering such services or selling or leasing such goods, independently of the program and as an ordinary and ongoing business, and

d. all services or goods for which the sponsor is to receive compensation shall be embodied in a written contract which precisely describes the services to be rendered and all compensation to be paid, which contract may only be modified by a vote of the majority of the limited partners. Said contract shall contain a clause allowing termination without penalty on 60 days notice.

F. Rebates, Kickbacks and Reciprocal Arrangements.

1. No rebates or give-ups may be received by the sponsor nor may the sponsor participate in any reciprocal business arrangements which would circumvent these Rules. Furthermore the prospectus and program charter documents shall contain language prohibiting the above as well as language prohibiting reciprocal business arrangements which would circumvent the restrictions against dealing with affiliates or promoters.

2. No sponsor shall directly or indirectly pay or award any commissions or other compensation to any person engaged by a potential investor for investment advice as an inducement to such advisor to advise the purchaser of interests in a particular program; provided, however, that this clause shall not prohibit the normal sales commissions payable to a registered broker-dealer or other properly licensed person for selling program interests.

G. Commingling of Funds. The funds of a program shall not be commingled with the funds of any other person.

H. Expenses of Program. All expenses of the programs shall be billed directly to and paid by the program. Reimbursements (other than for organization and offering expenses) to any sponsor shall not be allowed, except for reimbursement of the actual cost to the sponsor of goods and materials used for or by the program. Expenses incurred by the sponsor or any affiliate in connection with his administration of the program, including but not limited to salaries, rent, travel expenses and such other items generally falling under the category of sponsor's overhead, shall not be charged to the program.

I. Investments in Other Programs. Investments in limited partnership interests of another program shall be prohibited; however, nothing herein shall preclude the investment in general partnerships or ventures which own and operate a particular property provided the program acquires a controlling interest in such other ventures or general partnerships. In such event, duplicate property management or other fees shall not be permitted. Such prohibitions shall not apply to programs under Sections 236 or 221(d)(3) of the National Housing Act or any similar programs that may be enacted, but unless prohibited by the applicable federal statute, such partnership (herein referred to as lower tier partnership) shall provide for its limited partners all of the rights and obligations required to be provided by the original program in Section VII of these Rules.

J. Lending Practices.

1. On financing made available to the program by the sponsor, the sponsor may not receive interest and other financing charges or fees in excess of the amounts which would be charged by unrelated lending institutions on comparable loans for the same purpose in the same locality of the property. No prepayment charge or penalty shall be required by the sponsor on a loan to the program secured by either a first or a junior or all-inclusive trust deed, mortgage or encumbrance on the property, except to the extent that such prepayment charge or penalty is attributable to the underlying encumbrance. Except as permitted by subsection 2. of this Section, the sponsor shall be prohibited from providing permanent financing for the program.

2. An "all-inclusive" or "wrap-around" note and deed of trust (the "all-inclusive note" herein) may be used to finance the purchase of property by the program only if the following conditions are complied with:

a. The sponsor under the all-inclusive note shall not receive interest on the amount of the underlying encumbrance included in the all-inclusive note in excess of that payable to the lender on that underlying encumbrance;

b. The program shall receive credit on its obligation under the all-inclusive note for payments made directly on the underlying encumbrance, and

c. A paying agent, ordinarily a bank, escrow company, or savings and loan, shall collect payments (other than any initial payment of prepaid interest or loan points not to be applied to the underlying encumbrance) on the all-inclusive note and make disbursements therefrom to the holder of the underlying encumbrance prior to making any disbursement to the holder of the all-inclusive note, subject to the requirements of subparagraph a. above, or, in the alternative, all payments on the all-inclusive and underlying note shall be made directly by the program.

K. Development or Construction Contract. The sponsor will not be permitted to construct or develop properties, or render any services in connection with such development or construction unless all of the following conditions are satisfied:
1. The transactions occur at the formation of the program.

2. The specific terms of the development and construction of identifiable properties are ascertainable and fully disclosed in the prospectus.

3. The purchase price to be paid by the program is based upon a firm contract price which in no event can exceed the sum of the cost of the land and the sponsor's cost of construction. For the purposes of this subdivision, cost of construction includes the contractor or construction fee customarily paid for services as a general contractor, provided, however, that any overhead of the general contractor is not charged to the program or included in the cost of construction.

4. In the case of construction, the only fees paid to the sponsor in connection with such project shall consist of a construction fee for acting as a general contractor, which fee must be comparable and competitive with the fee of disinterested persons rendering comparable services (excluding, however, any overhead of the contractor) and a real estate commission in connection with the acquisition of the land, if appropriate under the circumstances. Any such real estate commission shall be subject to the provisions of Section IV C. of these Rules.

5. The sponsor demonstrates the presence of extraordinary circumstances as required by subsection 2. of Section V.E. and otherwise complies with subdivisions b., c., and d. thereunder.

L. Completion Bond Requirement. The completion of property acquired which is under construction should be guaranteed at the price contracted by an adequate completion bond or other satisfactory arrangements.

M. Requirement for Real Property Appraisal. All real property acquisitions must be supported by an appraisal prepared by a competent, independent appraiser. The appraisal shall be maintained in the sponsor's records for at least five years, and shall be available for inspection and duplication by any participant. The prospectus shall contain notice of this right.

VI. NON-SPECIFIED PROPERTY PROGRAMS. The following special provisions shall apply to non-specified property programs:

A. Minimum Capitalization. A non-specified property program shall provide for a minimum gross proceeds from the offering of not less than $1,000,000.00 after payment of all marketing and organization expenses before it may commence business.

B. Experience of Sponsor. For non-specified property programs, the sponsor or at least one of its principals must establish that he has had the equivalent of not less than five years experience in the real estate business in an executive capacity and two years experience in the management and acquisition of the type of properties to be acquired or otherwise must demonstrate to the satisfaction of the Administrator that he has sufficient knowlege and experience to acquire and manage the type of properties proposed to be acquired by the non-specified property program.

C. Statement of Investment Objectives. A non-specified property program shall state types of properties in which it proposes to invest, such as first-user apartment projects, subsequent-user apartment projects, shopping centers, office buildings, unimproved land, etc., and the size and scope of such projects shall be consistent with the objectives of the program and the experience of the sponsors. As a minimum the following restrictions on investment objectives shall be observed:

1. Unimproved or non-income producing property shall not be acquired except in amounts and upon terms which can be financed by the program's proceeds or from cash flow;

2. Investments in junior trust deeds and other similar obligations shall be limited. Normally such investments shall not exceed 10% of the gross assets of the program.

3. The manner in which acquisitions will be financed, including the use of an all-inclusive note or wrap-around, and the leveraging to be employed shall all be fully set forth in the statement of investment objectives.

4. The Statement shall indicate whether the program will enter into joint venture arrangements and the projected extent thereof.

D. Period of Offering and Expenditure of Proceeds. No offering of securities in a non-specified property program may extend for more than one year from the date of effectiveness. While the proceeds of an offering are awaiting investment in real property, the proceeds may be temporarily invested in short-term highly liquid investments where there is appropriate safety of principal, such as U. S. Treasury Bonds or Bills. Any proceeds of the offering of securities not invested within two years from the date of effectiveness (except for necessary operating capital) shall be distributed pro rata to the partners as a return of capital.

E. Special Reports. At least quarterly, a "Special Report" of real property acquisitions within the prior quarter shall be sent to all participants until the proceeds are invested or returned to the partners as set forth in paragraph D above. Such notice shall describe the real properties, and include a description of the geographic locale and of the market upon which the sponsor is relying in projecting successful operation of the properties. All facts which reasonably appear to the sponsor to materially influence the value of the property should be disclosed. The "Special Report" shall include, by way of illustration and not of limitation, a statement of the date and amount of the appraised value, if applicable, a statement of the actual purchase price including terms of the purchase, a statement of the total amount of cash expended by the program to acquire each property, and a statement regarding the amount of proceeds in the program which remain unexpended or uncommitted. This unexpended or uncommitted amount shall be stated in terms of both dollar amount and percentage of the total amount of the offering of the program.

F. Assessments. Plans calling for assessments shall not be allowed.

G. Multiple Programs. Sponsors shall be discouraged from offering for sale more than one unspecified property program at any point in time unless the programs have different investment objectives. Similarly, the continuance of new offerings by the same sponsor shall not be looked upon with favor if that sponsor has not substantially committed or placed the funds raised from pre-existing unspecified property programs.

H. Allocation of Acquisition Fee. Sponsors of a non-specified property syndication shall not collect an acquisition fee until properties are acquired by the program and the purchase has closed. The acquisition fee shall be reasonable in light of the services performed; shall be based on the purchase price of the property; and shall not exceed, at any time, 18% of the gross proceeds of the offering, applied on the purchase of specific properties by the program.

VII. RIGHTS AND OBLIGATIONS OF PARTICIPANTS.

A. Meetings. Meetings of the limited partnership may be called by the general partner(s) or the limited partner(s) holding more than 10% of the then outstanding limited partnership interests, for any matters for which the partners may vote as set forth in the limited partnership agreement. A list of the names and addresses of all limited partners shall be maintained as part of the books and records of the limited partnership and shall be made available on request to any limited partner or his representative at his cost. Upon receipt of a written request either in person or by registered mail stating the purpose(s) of the meeting, the general partner shall provide all partners, within ten days after receipt of said request, written notice (either in person or by registered mail) of a meeting and the purpose of such meeting to be held on a date not less than fifteen nor more than sixty days after receipt of said request, at a time and place convenient to participants.

B. Voting Rights of Limited Partners. To the extent the law of the state in question is not inconsistent, the limited partnership agreement must provide that a majority of the then outstanding limited partnership interests may, without the necessity for concurrence by the general partner, vote to (1) amend the limited partnership agreement, (2) dissolve the program, (3) remove the general partner and elect a new general partner, and (4) approve or disapprove the sale of all or substantially all of the assets of the program. The agreement should provide for a method of valuation of the general partner's interest, upon removal of the general partner, that would not be unfair to the participants. The agreement should also provide for a successor general partner where the only general partner of the program is an individual.

C. Reports to Holders of Limited Partnership Interests. The partnership agreement shall provide that the sponsor shall cause to be prepared and distributed to the holders of program interests during each year the following reports:

1. In the case of a program registered under Section 12(g) of the Securities Exchange Act of 1934, within sixty days after the end of each quarter of the program, a report containing:

(i) a balance sheet, which may be unaudited,
(ii) a statement of income for the quarter then ended, which may be unaudited, and

(iii) a cash flow statement for the quarter then ended, which may be unaudited, and

(iv) other pertinent information regarding the program and its activities during the quarter covered by the report;

2. In the case of all other programs in addition to the annual report required by paragraph 4 hereof, within sixty days after the end of the program's first six-month period, a semiannual report containing the same information as to the proceding six-month period as that required in quarterly reports under paragraph 1 hereof;

3. In the case of all programs, within 75 days after the end of each program's fiscal year, all information necessary for the preparation of the limited partners' federal income tax returns;

4. In the case of all programs, within 120 days after the end of each program's fiscal year, an annual report containing (i) a balance sheet as of the end of its fiscal year and statements of income, partners' equity, and changes in financial position and a cash flow statement, for the year then ended, all of which, except the cash flow statement, shall be prepared in accordance with generally accepted accounting principles and accompanied by an auditor's report containing an opinion of an independent certified public accountant or independent public accountant, (ii) a report of the activities of the program during the period covered by the report, and (iii) where projections have been provided to the holders of limited partnership interests, a table comparing the projections previously provided with the actual results during the period covered by the report. Such report shall set forth distributions to limited partners for the period covered thereby and shall separately identify distributions from (a) cash flow from operations during the period, (b) cash flow from operations during a prior period which had been held as reserves, (c) proceeds from disposition of property and investments, (d) lease payments on net leases with builders and sellers, and (e) reserves from the gross proceeds of the offering originally obtained from the limited partners.

5. Where assessments have been made during any period covered by any report required by paragraphs 1, 2 and 4 hereof, then such report shall contain a detailed statement of such assessments and the application of the proceeds derived from such assessments; and

6. Where any sponsor receives fees for services, including acquisition fees from the program, then he shall, within 60 days of the end of each quarter wherein such fees were received, send to each limited partner a detailed statement setting forth the services rendered, or to be rendered by such sponsor and the amount of the fees received. This requirement may not be circumvented by lump-sum payments to management companies or other entities who then disburse the funds.

D. Access to Records. The limited partners and their designated representatives shall be permitted access to all records of the program at all reasonable times.

E. Admission of Participants. Admission of participants to the program shall be subject to the following:

1. Admission of original participants. Upon the original sale of partnership units by the program, the purchasers should be admitted as limited partners not later than 15 days after the release from impound of the purchaser's funds to the program, and thereafter purchasers should be admitted into the program not later than the last day of the calendar month following the date their subscription was accepted by the program. Subscriptions shall be accepted or rejected by the program within 30 days of their receipt; if rejected, all subscription monies should be returned to the subscriber forthwith.

2. Admission of substituted limited partners and recognition of assignees. The program shall amend the certificate of limited partnership at least once each calendar quarter to effect the substitution of substituted participants, although the sponsor may elect to do so more frequently. In the case of assignments, where the assignee does not become a substituted limited partner, the program shall recognize the assignment not later than the last day of the calendar month following receipt of notice of assignment and required documentation.

F. Redemption of Program Interests. Ordinarily, the program and the sponsor may not be mandatorily obligated to redeem or repurchase any of its program interests, although the program and the sponsor may not be precluded from purchasing such outstanding interests if such purchase does not impair the capital or the operation of the program. Notwithstanding the foregoing, a real estate program may provide for mandatory redemption rights under the following necessitous circumstances:

1. death or legal incapacity of the owner, or

2. a substantial reduction in the owner's net worth or income provided that (i) the program has sufficient cash to make the purchase, (ii) the purchase will not be in violation of applicable legal requirements and (iii) not more than 15% of the outstanding units are purchased in any year.

G. Transferability of Program Interests. Restrictions on assignment of limited partnership interests will not be allowed. Restrictions on the substitution of a limited partner are generally disfavored and will be allowed only to the extent necessary to preserve the tax status of the partnership and any restriction must be supported by opinion of counsel.

H. Assessability. Except as provided in Section VI F, herein in the case of non-specified property programs, if the anticipated income cash flow from property (after payment of debt service and all operating expenses) is not sufficient to pay taxes and/or special assessments imposed by governmental or quasi-governmental units, the program agreement may include a provision for assessability to meet such deficiencies, including those obligations of a defaulting particpant. Assessability must be limited to the foregoing obligations, and all amounts derived from such assessments must be applied only to satisfaction of said obligations.

I. Defaults. In the event of a default in the payment of assessments by a limited partner, his interests shall not be subject to forfeiture, but may be subject to a reasonable penalty for failure to meet his commitment. Provided that the arrangements are fair, this may take the form of reducing his proportionate interest in the program, subordinating his interest to that of nondefaulting partners, a forced sale complying with applicable procedures for notice and sale, the lending of the amount necessary to meet his commitment by the other participants or a fixing of the value of his interest by independent appraisal or other suitable formula with provision for a delayed payment to him for his interest not beyond a reasonable period, but a debt security issued for such interest should not have a claim prior to that of the other investors in the event of liquidation.

VIII. DISCLOSURE AND MARKETING REQUIREMENTS.

A. Sales Promotional Efforts.

1. Sales Literature. Sales literature, sales presentations (including prepared presentations to prospective investors at group meetings) and advertising used in the offer or sale of partnership interests shall conform in all applicable respects to requirements of

filing, disclosure and adequacy currently imposed on sales literature, sales presentations and advertising used in the sale of corporate securities.

2. Group Meetings. All advertisements of and oral or written invitations to "seminars" or other group meetings at which program interests are to be described, offered or sold shall clearly indicate that the purpose of such meeting is to offer such program interests for sale, the minimum purchase price thereof, and the name of the sponsor, underwriter or selling agent. No cash, merchandise or other item of value shall be offered as an inducement to any prospective participants to attend any such meeting. In connection with the offer or sale of program interests, no general offer shall be made of "free" or "bargain price" trips to visit property in which the program or proposed program has invested or intends to invest. All written or prepared audio-visual presentations (including scripts prepared in advance for oral presentations) to be made at such meetings must be submitted in advance to the Administrator not less than three business days prior to the first use thereof. The foregoing paragraphs 1 and 2 shall not apply to meetings consisting only of representatives of securities broker-dealers.

B. Offerings Registered With the Securities and Exchange Commission ("SEC"). With respect to offerings registered with the Securities and Exchange Commission under the Securities Act of 1933, as amended, and qualified with the Administrator by coordination, a Prospectus which is part of a Registration Statement which has been declared effective by said Commission shall be deemed to comply with all requirements as to form of this Rule; provided, however, that the Administrator reserves the right to require additional disclosure of substance in his discretion

C. Contents of Prospectus. The following information shall be included in the prospectus of the program:

1. Information on Cover Page. There should be set forth briefly on the cover page of the Prospectus a summary which should include the following:

The title and general nature of the securities (interests in the proposed program) being offered; the maximum aggregate amount of the offering; the minimum amount of net proceeds; the minimum subscription price; the period of the offering; the maximum amount of any sales or underwriting commissions to be paid (or if none, or if such commissions are paid by the sponsor), the maximum acquisition fee, or development and/or construction fee; the estimated amount of organization and offering expenses.

2. Definitions. Technical terms used in the Prospectus should be defined either in a glossary or as they appear in the Prospectus.

3. Risk Factors. The investor should be advised in a carefully organized series of short, concise paragraphs, under subcaptions where appropriate, of the risks to be considered before making an investment in the program. These paragraphs should include a cross-reference to further information in the Prospectus. Possible disadvantageous tax consequences such as potential inability to deduct prepaid interest in the year paid, tax liability for potential depreciation recapture, depreciation recapture greater than cash distributions and tax liability in the event of foreclosure shall be disclosed.

4. Business Experience. The business experience of the sponsor(s) general partner(s), principal officers of a corporate general partner (Chairman of the Board, President, Vice-President, Treasurer, Secretary or any person having similar authority or performing like functions) and other managers of the program, shall be prominently disclosed in the Prospectus, such disclosure indicating their business experience for the

past ten years. The lack of experience or limited experience of the sponsor, general partner, principal officer of a corporate general partner, or other manager of a real estate program shall be prominently disclosed in the Prospectus.

5. Compensation. All indirect and direct compensation which may be paid by the program to the sponsor of every type and from every source shall be summarized in tabular form in one location in the forepart of the Prospectus.

6. Use of Proceeds. State the purposes for which the net proceeds to the program are intended to be used and the approximate amount intended to be used for each such purpose. Also state the minimum aggregate amount necessary to initiate the program and the disposition of the funds raised if they are not sufficient for that purpose.

7. Deferred Payments Schedule. If deferred payments are called for or allowed, the schedule for same shall be set forth.

8. Assessments. If provisions for assessment of the limited partners are allowed, the method of assessment and the penalty for default shall be prominently set forth.

9. Investment Objectives and Policies. Describe the investment objectives and policies of the program (indicating whether they may be changed by the general partner without a vote of the limited partners) and, if and to the extent that the sponsor is able to do so, the approximate percentage of assets which the program may invest in any one type of investment.

10. Description of Real Estate and Proposed Method of Financing. State the location and describe the general character of all materially important real properties now held or presently intended to be acquired by or leased to the program. Include information as to the present or proposed use of such properties and their suitability and adequacy for such use. Describe terms of any material lease affecting the property. Describe the proposed method of financing, including estimated down payment, leverage ratio, prepaid interest, balloon payment(s), prepayment penalties, due-on-sale or encumbrance clauses and possible adverse effects thereof and similar details of the proposed financing plan. A statement that title insurance and any required construction, permanent or other financing, and performance bonds or other assurances with respect to builders have been or will be obtained on all properties acquired shall be set forth.

11. "Track Records" when required or permitted by the Administrator, shall contain the following information:

a. The previous syndication experience of the sponsor and other relevant parties shall be disclosed in the prospectus for all programs during the past five years which:

1. involved a public offering registered under state or federal securities laws,
2. involved a private or limited offering, the results of which are material to an informed investment decision by the investor.

b. The Administrator may require information on previous programs including, but not limited to, the following:

1. Identification of the program, including the name and location.
2. The effective date of the offering, the date it commenced operations and the date of dissolution or termination or, if it is continuing, that fact.

3. The total amount of interests offered, the gross amount of capital raised by the program, and the number of participants.

4. The types of property acquired, by general classification, and cost separately stating the aggregate cash payment for non-capital items, such as prepaid interest, points, prepaid management fees, etc. whether new or used and depreciation rate used; date of purchase by program; the initial encumbrance, amount of reduction thereof, and whether fully amortized by equal payments over term or whether balloon payments or maturity will occur during contemplated holding period; the ratio of the sponsor's projected net operating income before debt service to the total purchase price for the property; and, if the properties have been sold, the date and results of sale in terms of whether the property was sold at a gain or loss taking into account recapture of depreciation and in terms of type of consideration received and the terms thereof.

5. Total dollar amounts of federal tax deductible items passed on to investors.

6. Cash distributions to participants segregated as to payments to participants from cash available for distribution, proceeds from sale and refinancing, reserves from the gross amount of investment in the program, lease payments on net leasebacks and other sources.

7. Compensation to the sponsor, segregated as to type, to be received on disposition of the property.

8. Disclosure of any foreclosure or sale or conveyance in lieu of foreclosure of any prior program.

9. A comparison between all projected and actual results.

10. Such additional or different disclosures of the success or failure of the programs as may be permitted or required by the Administrator.

11. The following caveat should be prominently featured in the presentation of the foregoing information: "It should not be assumed that investors in the offering covered by this prospectus will experience returns, if any, comparable to those experienced by investors in prior programs."

c. Information required to be set forth in subparagraphs (5), (6), and (7) of subsection "b" above shall be supported in the application for qualification by an affidavit of the sponsor that the performance summary is a fair representation of the information contained in the audited financial statements or the federal income tax returns of the program.

12. Operating Data - furnish appropriate operating data with respect to each improved property which is separtely described in answer to subsection 10 of Section VIIIC.

13. The Partnership.

    a. Date of Formation
    b. Place of Formation
    c. General Partners
    d. Initial Partners
    e. Address and telephone number of partnership and general partner.
    f. Duration.
    g. Information called for in items "a through f" hereof shal be given for any other programs, such as local programs operating property in which the public program invests.

14. Summary of Terms of the Partnership

    a. Powers of the Sponsor
    b. Rights and Liabilities of the Participants
    c. Allocation of Distributions
    d. Provisions for Replacement and Maintenance Reserves
    e. Termination and Dissolution
    f. Meetings and Reports

g. Amendment of Agreement
h. Provision for Additional Assessments
i. Other Pertinent Matter

15. Federal Tax Consequences

a. A summary of an opinion of tax counsel acceptable to
the Administrator and/or a ruling from the Internal Revenue Service
covering major tax questions relative to the program, which may be
based on reasonable assumptions such as those described in Section
IX F. below. To the extent the opinion of counsel or Internal Revenue
Service ruling is based on the maintenance of or compliance with certain
requirements or conditions by the issuer or sponsor(s), the Prospectus
shall to the extent practicable, contain representations that such
requirements or conditions have been met and that the sponsors shall use
their best efforts to continue to meet such requirements or conditions.
b. Tax treatment of the program
c. Tax treatment of the participants
d. Allocation of depreciation, investment, credit
construction interest, points, etc.
e. Method of depreciation, useful life, applicable recapture
provisions and consequences thereof.
f. Method of allocation of losses or profits and cash
distribution upon transfer of a partnership interest or the right to
income.
g. Any other pertinent information applicable to the tax
shelter aspects of the investment.
h. Possibility of requirement for filing tax returns with
states in which properties are held.

16. Limited Partnership Interests

a. Amount
b. Minimum purchase
c. Assessability
d. Transferability
e. Voting rights

17. Plan of Distribution

a. Discounts and commissions
b. Estimated fees and expenses paid or reimbursed by program
c. Indemnification provisions
d. Terms of payment
e. Identity of underwriter, managing dealer or selling agent
f. Type of underwriting - best efforts or firm commitment
g. Minimum and Maximum Sales
h. Escrow Provisions
i. Material Relationship of Underwriter to program, if any.

18. Pending Legal Proceedings - Briefly describe any pending
legal proceedings to which the program or the sponsor is a party which
is material to the program and any material legal proceedings between
sponsor and participants in any prior program of the sponsor and describe
any material legal proceedings to which any of the program's property
is subject.

19. Transactions with Affiliates - Describe fully any transaction
which have been in the past five years or which may be entered into between
the program and any affiliate of the sponsor. Include a description of
the material terms of any agreement between the program and any such
affiliate. Where the sponsor sponsors other programs, describe the
equitable principles which will apply in resolving any conflict between
the programs.

20. Interest of Affiliates in Program Property. If within the last five years any affiliate had a material interest in any transaction with the sponsor or was previously in the chain of title or had a beneficial interest in any property to be acquired, this fact must be disclosed.

21. Interest of Counsel and Experts in the Sponsor or Program. Where counsel for the selling representatives or the sponsor are named in the Prospectus as having passed upon the legality of the securities being registered or upon other legal matters in connection with the registration or offering of such securities, there should be disclosed in the Prospectus the nature and amount of any direct or indirect interest of any such counsel, other than legal fees to be received by such counsel, in the sponsor. Any such interest received or to be received in connection with the registration or offering of the securities being registered, including the ownership or receipt by counsel, or by members of the firm participating in the matter, of securities of the sponsor or the program for services shall be disclosed. Employment by the sponsor, other than retainer as legal counsel, should be disclosed in the prospectus.

22. Financial Statements and Projections. As provided elsewhere in these regulations.

23. Summary of Agreement of Limited Partnership.

24. Investment Company Act of 1940. Where beneficial interests of a limited partnership are to be sold, treatment under the Investment Company Act of 1940 must be disclosed.

25. Additional Information. Any additional information which may be material should be included; further, in furnishing the information requested in the paragraphs listed above, the instructions for completing Form S-11 for filing under the Securities Act of 1933 should be referred to as a guide for the information to be furnished.

D. Projections

1. Use of Projections. The presentation of predicted future results of operations ("projections") of real estate programs shall be permitted but not required. Such projections shall be included in the prospectus, offering circular or sales material of the partnership only if they comply with the following requirements:

a. General. Projections shall be realistic in their predictions and shall clearly identify the assumptions made with respect to all material features of the presentation. Projections should be prepared by a qualified person or firm and that person or firm should be identified in the prospectus or offering circular as being responsible for the preparation of the projections. No projections shall be permitted in any sales literature which does not appear in the prospectus or offering circular. If any projections are included in the sales literature, all projections must be presented.

b. Material Information. Projections shall include all the following information:

(1) Annual predicted revenue by source; including the occupancy rate used in predicting rental revenue;
(2) Annual predicted expenses;
(3) Mortgage obligation - annual payments for principal and interest, points and financing fees; shown as dollars, not percentages.
(4) The required occupancy rate in order to meet debt service and all expenses; rental revenue shall also be predicted based on occupancy rates 10% below the break-even occupancy rate;
(5) Predicted annual cash flow; stating assumed occupancy rate;

(6) Predicted annual depreciation and amortization with full description of methods to be used;

(7) Predicted annual taxable income or loss and a simplified explanation of the tax treatment of such results; assumed tax brackets may not be used;

(8) Predicted construction costs - including disclosure regarding contracts;

(9) Accounting policies - e.g. with respect to points, financing costs and depreciation.

c. Presentation

(1) Caveat. Projections shall prominently display a statement to the effect that they represent a mere prediction of future events based on assumptions which may or may not occur and may not be relied upon to indicate the actual results which will be obtained.

(2) Format. The presentation of projections proposed in accordance with these standards shall be coupled with a summary of predicted results in the event of a material adverse change in one or more significant economic factors, e.g., the effect on partnership cash flow and rate of return of revenues of rental projects at rates 10% to 15% less than expected and in addition the effect of a level of operating expenses 10% to 15% greater than anticipated in the primary projections. A break-even point insofar as occupancy and expenses should be disclosed as should other relevant financial ratios.

(3) Additional Guidelines. Explanatory notes describing assumptions made and referring to risk factors should be integrated with tabular and numerical information.

(4) Sale-leasebacks. When a sale-leaseback is employed, the statement that the seller is assuming the operating risk and consequently may have charged a higher price for the property must be included.

d. Additional Disclosures and Limitations.

(1) Projections shall be for a period at least equivalent to the anticipated holding period for the property, or 10 years, whichever is shorter, but they shall defintely project a resale occurrence, including depreciation recapture, if applicable. The projected resale price must be reasonable.

(2) Adequate disclosure shall be made of the changing economic effects upon the limited partners resulting principally from federal income tax consequences over the life of the partnership property, e.g., substantial tax losses in early years followed by increasing amounts of taxable income in later years.

(3) Projections shall disclose all possible undesirable tax consequences of an early sale of the program property (such as, depreciation, recapture or the failure to sell the property at a price which would return sufficient cash to meet resulting tax liabilities of the participants.

(4) In computing the return to investors, no appreciation, so-called "equity buildup", or any other benefits from unrealized gains or value shall be shown or included.

2. Projections shall not be allowed for unimproved land. Instead, a table of deferred payments specifying the various holding costs, i.e., interest, taxes, and insurance shall be inserted. However, where the program intends to develop and sell the land as its primary business, a detailed cash flow statement showing the timing of expenditures and anticipated revenues shall be required. Additionally, the consequences of a delayed selling program shall be shown.

IX. MISCELLANEOUS PROVISIONS.

A. Fiduciary Duty. The program agreement shall provide that the sponsor shall have fiduciary responsibility for the safekeeping and use of all funds and assets of the program, whether or not in his immediate possession or control, and that he shall not employ, or permit another to employ such funds or assets in any manner except for the exclusive benefit of the program.

B. Deferred Payments. Arrangements for deferred payments on account of the purchase price of program interests may be allowed when warranted by the investment objectives of the partnership, but in any event such arrangements shall be subject to the following conditions:

1. The period of deferred payments shall coincide with the anticipated cash needs of the program.

2. Selling commissions paid upon deferred payments are collectible when payment is made on the note.

3. Deferred payments shall be evidenced by a promissory note of the investor. Such notes shall be with recourse and shall not be negotiable and shall be assignable only subject to defenses of the maker. Such notes shall not contain a provision authorizing a confession of judgment.

4. The program shall not sell or assign the deferred obligation notes at a discount to meet financing needs of the program.

C. Reserves. Provision should be made for adequate reserves in the future by retention of a reasonable percentage of proceeds from the offering and regular receipts for normal repairs, replacements and contingencies. Normally, not less than 5% of the offering proceeds will be considered adequate.

D. Reinvestment of Cash Flow and Proceeds on Disposition of Property. Reinvestment of Cash Flow (excluding proceeds resulting from a disposition or refinancing of property) shall not be allowed. The partnership agreement and the Prospectus shall set forth that reinvestment of proceeds resulting from a disposition or refinancing will not take place unless sufficient cash will be distributed to pay any state or federal income tax (assuming investors are in a specified tax bracket) created by the disposition or refinancing of property. Such a prohibition must be contained in the Prospectus.

5. Statements of Income for Corporate Sponsors. A statement of income for the last fiscal year of any corporate sponsor (or for the life of the corporate sponsor, if less), prepared in accordance with generally accepted accounting principles and accompanied by an auditor's report containing an unqualified opinion of an independent certified public accountant or independent public accountant, and an unaudited statement for any interim period ending not more than ninety days prior to the date of filing an application. The inclusion of such statements in the prospectus shall be at the discretion of the Administrator.

6. Filing of Other Statements. Upon request by an applicant, the Administrator may, where consistent with the protection of investors, permit the omission of one or more of the statements required by these regulations of the filing, in substitution thereof, of appropriate statements verifying financial information having comparable relevance to an investor in determining whether he should invest in the program.

F. Opinions of Counsel.

The application for qualification and registration shall contain a favorable ruling from the Internal Revenue Service or an opinion of counsel to the effect that the issuer will be taxed as a "partnership" and not as an "association" for federal income tax purposes. An opinion of counsel shall be in form and substance satisfactory to the Administrator and shall be unqualified except to the extent permitted by the Administrator

However, an opinion of counsel may be based on reasonable assumptions, such as: (1) facts or proposed operations as set forth in the offering circular or prospectus and organizational documents; (2) the absence of future changes in applicable laws; (3) the securities offered are paid for; (4) compliance with certain procedures such as the execution and delivery of certain documents and the filing of a certificate of limited partnership or an amended certificate; and (5) the continued maintenance of or compliance with certain financial, ownership, or other requirements by the issuer or general partner(s). The Administrator may request from counsel as supplemental information such supporting legal memoranda and an analysis as he shall deem appropriate under the circumstances. To the extent the opinion of counsel or Internal Revenue Service ruling is based on the maintenance of or compliance with certain requirements or conditions by the issuer or general partner(s), the offering circular or prospectus shall contain representations that such requirements or conditions will be met and the partnership agreement shall, to the extent practicable, contain provisions requiring such compliance.

There shall be included also an opinion of counsel to the effect that the securities being offered are duly authorized or created and validly issued interests in the issuer, and that the liability of the public investors will be limited to their respective total agreed upon investment in the issuer.

E. Financial Information Required on Application. In any offering of interests by a real estate program, the program shall provide as an exhibit to the application or where indicated below shall provide as part of the Prospectus, the following financial information and financial statements:

1. Cash Flow Statement of Program. As part of the prospectus, if the program has been formed and owns assets, a cash flow statement, which may be unaudited, for the program for each of the last three fiscal years of the program (or for life of the program, if less) and unaudited statements for any interim period between the end of the latest fiscal year and the date of the balance sheet furnished, and for the corresponding interim period of the preceding years.

2. Balance Sheet of Program. As part of the prospectus, a balance sheet of the program as of the end of its most recent fiscal year, prepared in accordance with generally accepted accounting principles and accompanied by an auditor's report containing an unqualified opinion of an independent certified public accountant, and an unaudited balance sheet as of a date not more than ninety days prior to the date of filing.

3. Statements of Income, Partners' Equity, and Changes in Financial Position of Program. As part of the prospectus, if the program has been formed and owns assets, statements of income, statements of partners' equity, and statements of changes in financial position for the program for each of the last three fiscal years of the program (or for the life of the program, if less), all of which statements shall be prepared in accordance with generally accepted accounting principles and accompanied by an auditor's report containing an unqualified opinion of an independent certified public accountant or independent public accountant, and unaudited statements for any interim period ending not more than ninety days prior to the date of filing an application.

4. Balance Sheet of Sponsor.

(i) Corporate Sponsor. A balance sheet of any corporate sponsors as of the end of their most recent fiscal years, prepared in accordance with generally accepted accounting principles and accompanied by an auditor's report containing an unqualified opinion of an independent certified public accountant or independent public accountant, and an unaudited balance sheet as of a date not more than ninety days prior to the date of filing. Such statements shall be included in the prospectus.

(ii) Other Sponsors. A balance sheet for each non-corporate general partner (including individual partners or individual joint venturers of a sponsor) as of a time not more than ninety days prior to date of filing an application; such balance sheet, which may be unaudited, should conform to generally accepted accounting principles, shall be signed and sworn to by such sponsors and prepared by a certified public accountant. A representation of the amount of such net worth must be included in the prospectus, or in the alternative, a representation that such sponsors meet the net worth requirements of Section II B.

G. Provisions of Partnership Agreement. The requirements and/or provisions of appropriate portions of the following sections shall be included in a partnership agreement: II.C; IV.D.; IV.E.; IV.F.; V.A.; V.B.; V.C.; V.D.; V.E.; V.F.; V.G.; V.H.; V.I.; V.J.; V.M.; VI.C.; VI.D.; VI.E.; VI.F.; VII.A.; VII.B.; VII.C.; VII.D.: VII.E.; VII.F.; VII.H.; VII.I.; IX.A.; IX.B.4.; IX.C; and IX.D.

GUIDELINES FOR THE REGISTRATION
OF OIL AND GAS PROGRAMS

Adopted by the

NORTH AMERICAN SECURITIES ADMINISTRATORS ASSOCIATION

on September 22, 1976

PREFACE

The guidelines set forth, following this preface, were adopted by the Association in executive session on September 22, 1976, to be effective on publication in CCH Blue Sky Law Reporter or November 1, 1976, whichever is earlier.

The earlier guidelines, related to drilling programs only, adopted on October 7, 1971 by the Association, are superseded by the new guidelines.

It is to be noted that in these guidelines no reference is being made at this time to the matter of voting rights under Section VIII entitled "Rights and Obligations of Participants" and likewise no specific standards are included under Subsection V.B. entitled "Compensation", for drilling programs in which the sponsor receives a subordinated or reversionary working interest. This is a temporary approach and results from two schools of thought, each with substantial support, on both of these items.

In connection with the matter of voting rights for limited partners, one position is that the guidelines should not include any provision whatsoever requiring that limited partners be accorded certain specified voting rights. The contrary position is that the guidelines should contain a provision substantially as follows:

> "To the extent the law of the state of organization is not inconsistent, the limited partnership agreement must provide that holders of a majority of the then outstanding units may, without the necessity for concurrence by the general partner, vote to (a) amend the limited partnership agreement or charter document, (b) dissolve the program, (c) remove the general partner and elect a new general partner, (d) elect a new general partner if the general partner elects to withdraw from the program, (e) approve or disapprove the sale of all or substantially all of the assets of the program, and (f) cancel any contract for services with the sponsor or any affiliate without penalty upon sixty days notice."

and should contain a further provision requiring that the limited partnership agreement contain a detailed provision, in connection with the removal of a general partner, for the substitution of a new general partner in an appropriate and equitable manner.

On the matter of the proper compensation arrangement for a drilling program, in which the sponsor receives a subordinated or reversionary working interest, one position is that such a compensation arrangement should be described and provided for through the use of the following language:

"As an alternative to sharing revenues on a basis related to costs paid, it will be considered reasonable for a sponsor of a drilling program to receive a promotional interest in the form of a subordinated percentage of the working interest. The holder of a subordinated working interest shall be entitled to receive his share of revenues only after payout is reached, determined on either a prospect or total program basis, and when such promotional interest is entitled to receive distribution, it shall bear costs in the same ratio as it participates in revenues. As used in this subsection, the term "payout", as applied to a prospect, is defined as the time at which the participants' share of revenues from production and other items credited to a prospect equal the sum of the cost of acquisition, the cost of drilling and development incurred, all operating costs for the prospect, and an appropriately allocated portion of all other program expenses, including organization and offering expenses. As applied on a program basis, the term "payout" is defined as the time at which the revenues of the program equal all the expenses of the program. Said promotional interest shall not exceed 33-1/3 percent if determined on a total program basis, and 25 percent if determined on a prospect basis."

whereas the opposite view is that the following approach should be required:

"As an alternative to sharing revenues on a basis related to costs paid, it will be considered reasonable for a sponsor of a drilling program to receive a promotional interest in the form of a subordinated percentage of the working interest. A subordinated interest shall provide for the return from production to the participants in cash of 100% of their capital contribution, determined on a prospect or total program basis, before the holder of the subordinated working interest may receive a share of revenues, and shall provide that, when such promotional interest is entitled to receive distribution, it will bear costs in the same ratio as it participates in revenues. Such subordinated interest shall not exceed 33-1/3 percent if determined on a total program basis and 25 percent if determined on a prospect basis."

The NASAA Oil and Gas Interests Committee will continue with all due diligence its efforts to resolve the issues on these two separate matters. In the interim, individual states may be using varied approaches on these two matters, with individual states in many cases continuing to follow approaches previouly used, which may embrace one or the other of those above described. As soon as the committee, within itself, settles on the approach it will recommend, on either of the two matters, for adoption at the 1977 annual NASAA conference, appropriate information will be distributed to the association's members.

A. M. Swarthout
Chairman
Oil and Gas Interests Committee

I. INTRODUCTION

A. Application

1. These guidelines apply to the registration and qualification of oil and gas programs in the form of limited partnerships (herein sometimes called "programs" or "partnerships"), and will be applied by analogy to oil and gas programs in other forms, including general partnerships formed solely to invest as a limited partner in an affiliated program. While applications not conforming to the standards contained herein shall be looked upon with disfavor, where good cause is shown, certain guidelines may be modified or waived by the Administrator.

2. Where the individual characteristics of specific programs warrant modification from these standards, they will be accommodated, insofar as possible while still being consistent with the spirit of these guidelines.

B. Definitions. As used in the guidelines, the following terms mean:

1. Administrator - The official or agency administering the securities laws of a state.

2. Affiliate - An affiliate of another person means (a) any person directly or indirectly owning, controlling, or holding with power to vote 10 per centum or more of the outstanding voting securities of such other person; (b) any person 10 per centum or more of whose outstanding voting securities are directly or indirectly owned, controlled, or held with power to vote, by such other person; (c) any person directly or indirectly controlling, controlled by, or under common control with such other person; (d) any officer, director or partner of such other person, and (e) if such other person is an officer, director or partner, any company for which such person acts in any such capacity.

3. Assessments - Additional amounts of capital which may be mandatorily required of or paid voluntarily by a participant beyond his subscription commitment.

4. Capital Contributions - The total investment, including the original investment, assessments and amounts reinvested, in a program by a participant or by all participants, as the case may be.

5. Capital Expenditures - Those costs which are generally accepted as capital expenditures pursuant to the provisions of the Internal Revenue Code.

6. Cost - When used with respect to property in Section VI means (1) the sum of the prices paid by the seller for such property, including bonuses; (2) title insurance or examinations costs, brokers' commissions, filing fees, recording costs, transfer taxes, if any, and like charges in connection with the acquisition of such property; and (3) rentals and ad valorem taxes paid by the seller with respect to such property to the date of its transfer to the buyer, interests on funds used to acquire or maintain such property, and such portion of the seller's reasonable, necessary and actual expenses for geological, geophysical, seismic, land engineering, drafting, accounting, legal and other like services allocated to the property in accordance with generally accepted industry practices, except for expenses in connection with the past drilling of wells which are not producers of sufficient quantities of oil or gas to make commercially reasonable their continued operations, and provided that such expenses shall have been incurred not more than 36 months prior to the purchase by the program; provided that such period may be extended, at the discretion of the Administrator, upon proper justification. When used with respect to services, "cost" means the reasonable, necessary and actual expense incurred by the seller on behalf of the program in providing such services, determined in accordance with presently existing generally accepted accounting principles. As used elsewhere, "cost" means the price paid by the seller in an arm's-length transaction.

7. Development Well - A well drilled as an additional well to the same reservoir as other producing wells on a lease, or drilled on an offset lease

usually not more than one location away from a well producing from the same reservoir.

8. Exploratory Well - A well drilled either (a) in search of a new and as yet undiscovered pool of oil or gas, or (b) with the hope of greatly extending the limits of a pool already developed.

9. General and Administrative Overhead - All customary and routine legal, accounting, geological, engineering, well supervision fee, travel, office rent, telephone, secretarial, salaries, and other incidental reasonable expenses necessary to the conduct of the partnership business, and generated by the sponsor.

10. Landowner's Royalty Interest - An interest in production, or the proceeds therefrom, to be received free and clear of all costs of development, operation, or maintenance, reserved by a landowner upon the creation of an oil and gas lease.

11. Non-Capital Expenditures - Expenditures that under present law are generally accepted as fully deductible currently for federal income tax purposes.

12. Operating Costs - Expenditures made and costs incurred in producing and marketing oil or gas from completed wells, including, in addition to labor, fuel, repairs, hauling, materials, supplies, utility charges and other costs incident to or therefrom, ad valorem and severance taxes, insurance and casualty loss expense, and compensation to well operators or others for services rendered in conducting such operations.

13. Organization and Offering Expenses - All costs of organizing and selling the offering including, but not limited to, total underwriting and brokerage discounts and commissions (including fees of the underwriters' attorneys), expenses for printing, engraving, mailing, salaries of employees while engaged in sales activity, charges of transfer agents, registrars, trustees, escrow holders, depositaries, engineers and other experts, expenses of qualification of the sale of the securities under federal and state law, including taxes and fees, accountants' and attorneys' fees.

14. Overriding Royalty Interest - An interest in the oil and gas produced pursuant to a specified oil and gas lease or leases, or the proceeds from the sale thereof, carved out of the working interest, to be received free and clear of all costs of development, operation, or maintenance.

15. Participant - The purchaser of a unit in the oil and gas program.

16. Program - As used in these guidelines, the term "program" refers to a single partnership. (This does not mean that a Prospectus may not offer a series of partnerships, with individual partnerships being formed in sequence as the minimum amount necessary to form a partnership is obtained.)

17. Prospect - A geographic or stratigraphic area in which the program owns or intends to own one or more oil and gas interests, which is geographically defined on the basis of geological data by the sponsor of such programs and which is reasonably anticipated by the sponsor to contain at least one reservoir. Such area shall be enlarged or contracted on the basis of geological data to define the productive limit of such reservoir and must include all of the territory encompassed by any such reservoir; provided, however, that the program shall not be required to expend additional funds for acquisition of property unless such acquisition can be made from the initial capitalization of the program or from borrowed funds which the sponsor believes are prudent to borrow for the purpose of acquiring such additional property.

18. Proved Reserves - Those quantities of crude oil, natural gas, and natural gas liquids which, upon analysis of geologic and engineering data, appear with reasonable certainty to be recoverable in the future from known oil and gas reservoirs under existing economic and operating conditions. Proved reserves are limited to those quantities of oil and gas which can be expected, with little

doubt, to be recoverable commercially at current prices and costs, under existing regulatory practices and with existing conventional equipment and operating methods. Depending upon their status of development, such proved reserves shall be subdivided into the following classifications:

(a) Proved Developed Reserves. These are proved reserves which can be expected to be recovered through existing wells with existing equipment and operating methods. This classification shall include:

(1) Proved Developed Producing Reserves. These are proved developed reserves which are expected to be produced from existing completion interval(s) now open for production in existing wells; and

(2) Proved Developed Non-Producing Reserves. These are proved developed reserves which exist behind the casing of existing wells, or at minor depths below the present bottom of such wells, which are expected to be produced through these wells in the predictable future, where the cost of making such oil and gas available for production should be relatively small compared to the cost of a new well.

Additional oil and gas expected to be obtained through the application of fluid injection or other improved recovery techniques for supplementing the natural forces and mechanisms of primary recovery should be included as "Proved Developed Reserves" only after testing by a pilot project or after the operation of an installed program has confirmed through production response that increased recovery will be achieved.

(b) Proved Undeveloped Reserves.. These are proved reserves which are expected to be recovered from new wells on undrilled acreage, or from existing wells where a relatively major expenditure is required for recompletion. Reserves. on undrilled acreage shall be limited to those drilling units offsetting productive units, which are virtually certain of production when drilled. Proved reserves for other undrilled units can be claimed only where it can be demonstrated with certainty that there is continuity of production from the existing productive formation.

Under no circumstances should estimates for proved undeveloped reserves be attributable to any acreage for which an application of fluid injection or other improved recovery technique is contemplated, unless such techniques have been proved effective by actual tests in the area and in the same reservoir. If warranted, however, a narrative discussion can be provided to point out those areas where future drilling or other operations may develop oil and gas production which at the time of filing is considered too uncertain to be expressed as numerical estimates for proved reserves.

19. Sponsor - Any person directly or indirectly instrumental in organizing a program or any person who will manage or participate in the management of a program, including the general partner(s) and any other person who, pursuant to a contract with the program, regularly performs or selects the person who performs 25% or more of the exploratory, developmental or producing activities of the program, or segment thereof. "Sponsor" does not include wholly independent third parties such as attorneys, accountants, and underwriters whose only compensation is for professional services rendered in connection with the offering of units. Whenever the context of these guidelines so requires, the term "sponsor" shall be deemed to include its affiliates.

20. Working Interest - An interest in an oil and gas leasehold which is subject to some portion of the expense of development, operation, or maintenance.

II. REQUIREMENTS OF SPONSOR

A. Experience

The general partner or its chief operating officers shall have at least three years relevant oil and gas experience demonstrating the knowledge and experience to carry out the stated program policies and to manage the program operations. Additionally, the general partner or any affiliate providing services to the program shall have had not less than four years relevant experience in the kind of service being rendered or otherwise must demonstrate sufficient knowledge and experience to perform the services proposed. If any managerial responsibility for the program is to be rendered by persons other than the general partner, then such persons must be identified in the Prospectus, their experience must be similar to that required of a general partner and must be set out in the Prospectus, and a contract setting forth the basis of their relationship with the program must be filed with and not disapproved by the Administrator.

B. Net Worth

1. The financial condition of the general partner must be commensurate with any financial obligations assumed by it. The general partner must specifically have a minimum aggregate net worth at all times equal to 5% of participants' capital in all existing programs organized by the general partner plus 5% of total subscriptions in the program being offered, but such minimum required net worth shall in no case be less than $100,000 nor shall net worth in excess of $1,000,000 be required. An individual general partner's net worth shall be determined exclusive of home, home furnishings and automobiles. Audited balance sheets of sponsors shall be furnished, except that in the event that an individual is a general partner, an unaudited balance sheet prepared by a certified public accountant and signed and sworn to by such individual general partner may be accepted for the purpose of determining said required net worth, in the discretion of the Administrator, and such unaudited statement will be carefully scrutinized.

2. In determining a general partner's net worth, the discounted value of proved reserves, as determined by an independent petroleum appraiser, of oil, gas and other minerals owned by a general partner may be used. Notes and accounts receivables from all programs, interests in all programs, and all contingent liabilities will be scrutinized carefully to determine the appropriateness of their inclusion in the net worth computation. If an individual general partner's net worth is used in complying with the above requirements, a statement as to such net worth shall be included in the Prospectus.

3. If more than one person acts or serves as general partner of a program, the net worth requirements may be met by aggregating the net worth of all such persons. In addition, the net worth of any guarantor of the general partner's obligations to or for the program may be included in the net worth computation, but only if the guarantor's liability is coextensive with that of the general partner.

C. Tax Ruling or Opinion

The sponsor must have a tax ruling from the Internal Revenue Service or an opinion of qualified tax counsel in a form acceptable to the Administrator concerning the flow-through tax benefits and the other tax consequences to the public investor.

D. Investment in Program

In appropriate cases, the Administrator may require that the sponsor purchase for cash a minimum amount of participation units.

E. Reports

The sponsor shall agree to file with the Administrator, if he so requests it, concurrently with their transmittal to participants, a copy of each report made pursuant to Section VIII.C. of these guidelines.

F. Liability and Indemnification

Sponsors shall not attempt to pass on to limited partners the general liability imposed on them by law except that the program agreement may provide for indemnification of the general partner under the following circumstances and in the manner and to the extent indicated:

1. In any threatened, pending or completed action, suit or proceeding to which the general partner was or is a party or is threatened to be made a party by reason of the fact that he is or was the general partner of the partnership (other than an action by or in the right of the partnership), the partnership may indemnify such general partner against expenses, including attorneys' fees, judgments and amounts paid in settlement actually and reasonably incurred by him in connection with such action, suit or proceeding if he acted in good faith and in a manner he reasonably believed to be in or not opposed to the best interests of the partnership. The termination of any action, suit or proceeding by judgment, order or settlement shall not, of itself, create a presumption that the general partner did not act in good faith and in a manner which he reasonably believed to be in or not opposed to the best interests of the partnership.

2. In any threatened, pending or completed action or suit by or in the right of the partnership, to which the general partner was or is a party or is threatened to be made a party, the partnership may indemnify such general partner against expenses, including attorneys' fees, actually and reasonably incurred by him in connection with the defense or settlement of such action or suit if he acted in good faith and in a manner he reasonably believed to be in or not opposed to the best interests of the partnership, except that no indemnification shall be made in respect of any claim, issue or matter as to which such person shall have been adjudged to be liable for negligence, misconduct, or breach of fiduciary obligation in the performance of his duty to the partnership unless and only to the extent that the court in which such action or suit was brought shall determine upon application, that, despite the adjudication of liability but in view of all circumstances of the case, such person is fairly and reasonably entitled to indemnity for such expenses which such court shall deem proper.

3. To the extent that a general partner has been successful on the merits or otherwise in defense of any action, suit or proceeding referred to in subparagraph (1) or (2) above, or in defense of any claim, issue or matter therein, the partnership shall indemnify him against the expenses, including attorneys' fee, actually and reasonably incurred by him in connection therewith.

4. Any indemnification under subparagraph (1) or (2) above, unless ordered by a court, shall be made by the partnership only as authorized in the specific case and only upon a determination by independent legal counsel in a written opinion that indemnification of the general partner is proper ·in the circumstances because he has met the applicable standard of conduct set forth in subparagraph (1) or (2) above.

III. SELLING OF UNITS AND SALES MATERIAL

A. Sale of Units

1. Compensation to broker-dealers shall be a cash commission. Indetermina compensation to broker-dealers, such as overriding interests and net profit interests, for example, is prohibited. In the absence of a firm underwriting, warrants or options to broker-dealers are prohibited.

2. Compensation to wholesale dealers must be a cash commission, must be reasonable and must be fully disclosed.

3. Sales commissions based on assessment of units are prohibited.

B. Sales Material

Supplementary materials (including prepared presentations for group meetings) must be submitted to the Administrator in advance of use, and its use must either be preceded by or accompanied with an effective Prospectus.

IV. SUITABILITY OF THE PARTICIPANT

A. Standards to be Imposed

In view of the limited transferability, the relative lack of liquidity, the high risk of loss or the specific tax orientation of many oil and gas programs, suitability standards which are reasonably related to the risks to be undertaken, will be required for the participants, and they must be set forth both in the Prospectus and in a written instrument to be executed by each participant.

B. Sales to Appropriate Persons

1. The sponsor and each person selling limited partnership interests on behalf of the sponsor or program shall make every reasonable effort to assure that those persons being offered or sold the limited partnership interests are appropriate in light of the suitability standards set forth as required above and are appropriate to the customers' investment objectives and financial situations.

2. The sponsor and/or his representatives shall make every reasonable effort to ascertain that the participant can reasonably benefit from the program, and the following shall be evidence thereof:

(a) The participant has the capacity of understanding the fundamental aspects of the program, which capacity may be evidenced by the following:

(1) The nature of employment experience;

(2) Educational level achieved;

(3) Access to advice from qualified sources, such as, attorney, accountant and tax adviser; and

(4) Prior experience with investments of a similar nature.

(b) The participant has apparent understanding:

(1) of the fundamental risks and possible financial hazards of the investment; and

(2) the lack of liquidity of the investment.

(c) The participant is able to bear the economic risk of the investment and can reasonably benefit from the program, on the basis of his net worth and taxable income. For purposes of determining the ability to bear the economic risk and to reasonably benefit from the program, unless circumstances warrant and the Administrator allows another standard, a participant shall have:

(1) a net worth of $200,000 or more (exclusive of home, furnishings and automobiles), or

(2) a net worth of $50,000 or more (exclusive of home, furnishings and automobiles) and had during the last tax year, or estimates that he will have during the current tax year, "taxable income" as defined in Section 63 of the Internal Revenue Code of 1954, as amended, some portion of which was or will be subject to federal income tax at a rate of 50% or more, without regard to the investment in the program.

C. Suitability Standards for Production Purchase Program

1. In the case of programs engaged primarily in investing in income producing properties (production purchase program) the Administrator may allow lower suitability standards than those described in subsection B.2.(c). Subject to a satisfactory showing as to the plan of business of the program, the following suitability standards will be deemed reasonable:

(a) the participant has a net worth of $75,000 or more (exclusive of home, furnishings and automobiles), or

(b) the participant has a net worth of $20,000 or more (exclusive of home, furnishings and automobiles) and an annual income of $20,000 or more.

D. Minimum Investment

For a drilling program, the minimum purchase shall not be less than $5,000 and the initial investment by a participant not less than $5,000, and for an income or production purchase program, the minimum purchase shall not be less than $2,500 and the initial investment not less than $2,500. All of the aforesaid minimums must be paid within 12 months from the date the program commences. Assignability of the unit must be limited so that no assignee (transferee) or assignor (transferor) may hold less than the prescribed minimums except by gifts or by operation of law.

E. Maintenance of Suitability Records

The broker-dealer or sponsor shall retain for at least five years all records necessary to substantiate the fact that program interests were sold only to purchasers for whom such securities were suitable. Administrators may require broker-dealers or sponsors to obtain from the purchaser a letter justifying the suitability of such investment.

V. FEES, COMPENSATION AND EXPENSES

A. Organization and Offering Expenses, and Management Fees

1. All organization and offering expenses incurred in order to sell program units shall be reasonable, and the total of those organization and offering expenses, which may be charged to the program, plus any management fee, which may be charged by the sponsor, shall not exceed 15% of the initial subscriptions.

2. Commissions payable on the sale of program units shall be paid in cash solely on the amount of initial subscriptions. Payment of commissions in the form of overriding royalties, net profit interests or other interests in production will not be approved, except that no objection will be raised to the payment of commissions in the form of interests in the program, provided the amount does not exceed that purchasable by applying the aggregate cash commission allowable to the unit offering price.

3. All items of compensation to underwriters or dealers, including, but not limited to, selling commissions, expenses, rights of first refusal, consulting fees, finders' fees and all other items of compensation of any kind or description paid by the program, directly or indirectly, shall be taken into consideration in computing the amount of allowable selling commissions.

B. Compensation

The participation in program revenues by the sponsor and any affiliate shall be reasonable taking into account all relevant factors. Overriding royalty interests will be looked upon with disfavor. Sponsors' interests in revenues will be considered reasonable if they meet the standards set forth below. Any other combination of fees, working or net profits interests, or interests subordinated to payout to the public investors, which are justified, in light of the entire offering, may be considered reasonable by the Administrator. References in this subsection B to a percent of revenues refer to that percent of program revenues, and references to a percent working interest refer to that percent of the working interest owned by a program in a prospect, if the program does not own the total working interest.

1. Drilling Programs - Functional Allocation

(a) Where the sponsor agrees to pay all capital expenditures of the program, but in any case at least 10% of the total program's capital contribution, his share of revenue will be determined by the following formula:

(1) if the agreement is to pay all capital expenditures but in any case a sum of not less than 10% of the capital contribution of the program, the sponsor is entitled to receive 35% of program revenues; and

(2) the sponsor's revenue sharing may be increased in additional increments of 5% for each additional 5% increase in the percentage of capital contribution agreed to be paid by him up to a maximum of 50% of revenues subject to sponsor's agreement to pay in any case all capital expenditures.

(b) As one alternative to subdivision (a), the sponsor may elect to receive 15% of revenues and an additional percentage of revenues determined by computing the sponsor's capital expenditures as compared to total costs associated with obtaining production, on a prospect basis, until such time as the sponsor shall have received from such additional percentage of revenues an amount equal to his capital expenditures; after which, revenues shall be distributed as follows: 15% of revenues to the sponsor and 85% of revenues to the participants until the participants shall have received on a program basis a return of their capital contributions and then, 15% plus the additional percentage of revenues shall be paid to the sponsor and the remainder to the participants.

(c) In connection with other possible alternatives that may be submitted to the above subdivision (a), a promotional interest in excess of 25% on a program basis will not be permitted, and a minimum commitment by the sponsor to pay at least 10% of the total program's contributions will be required.

(d) The aforesaid arrangement to pay capital expenditures refers to and includes all capital expenditures for the drilling and completing of wells during the life of the program, but does not include capital expenditures for facilities downstream of a wellhead. If the sponsor should enter into farm-out or other arrangements through which only he is relieved of his obligations to pay for such capital expenditures, then the sponsor's share of revenue shall be proportionately reduced, the amount to be determined on an individual basis.

(e) In order to elect a sharing arrangement as above provided, the sponsor must have a net worth of $300,000 or 10% of the total contributions to the program by the participants, whichever is greater, and must be under a contractual obligation to pay his share of expenses as such expenses are paid by the program and to complete his minimum financial commitment to the program by the payment of cash by the end of the third fiscal year succeeding the fiscal year in which the program commenced operations.

(f) For the purposes of this subsection, if a well is not abandoned within 60 days following the commencement of production, then it shall be deemed to be a commercial well insofar as the program is concerned and the sponsor may not recapture its capital expenditures from the program, which otherwise would be treated as non-capital expenditures upon abandonment. As used herein, production shall refer to the commencement of the commercial marketing of oil or gas, and shall not include any spot sales of oil or gas produced as a result of testing procedures. All revenues from a well abandoned under this subsection shall be allocated pro rata to those persons bearing the costs of such well.

(g) The sharing arrangement set forth in this subsection shall not be considered presumptively reasonable (1) for a sponsor who does not actively participate in obtaining a significant portion of the program's prospects and who does not assume management responsibility for drilling, completing, equipping and operating a significant portion of a program's wells, unless such sponsor shall satisfactorily demonstrate that his compensation together with the costs of procuring such services for the program from third parties does not exceed the permissible compensation to the sponsor set forth in this subsection, (2) in the case of sharing arrangements in which the sponsor pays all development costs and exploratory wells are drilled on prospects which cannot reasonably be expected to require developmental drilling if the exploratory drilling is successful, or (3) in the case of sharing arrangements where the sponsor does not pay his share or category of costs on a current basis.

2. Income or Production Purchase Programs

(a) Where a major portion of the sponsor's management and operating responsibilities are performed by third parties, the cost of which is paid by the program, the sponsor may take a 3% working interest convertible to not more than a 5% working interest after the return from production to the investors of 100% of their capital contribution, computed on a total program basis.

(b) Where the sponsor maintains the operating capabilities and techinal staff so as to be in a position to, and in fact does, provide the program with a major part of the management and operating responsibilities of the program, the sponsor may take no more than a 15% working interest.

Where the individual characteristics of specific programs warrant modification from the above two approaches to production purchase programs, they will be accommodated, insofar as possible, while still being consistent with the aforesaid compensation arrangements.

The sponsor's interest in a program or in properties owned by a program shall bear a pro rata share of all costs, expenses and obligations of the program including, but not limited to, costs of operations, general and administrative expenses, debt service and any other items of expense chargeable to the operation of the program.

C. Program Expenses

1. All actual and necessary expenses incurred by the program may be paid by the sponsor out of capital contributions and out of program revenues.

2. A sponsor may be reimbursed out of capital contributions and program revenues for all actual and necessary direct expenses paid or incurred by it in connection with its operation of a program, and for an allocable portion of its general and administrative overhead, computed on a cost basis. All overhead costs shall be determined in accordance with generally accepted accounting principles, subject to annual independent audit. Administrative and similar charges for services must be fully supportable as to the necessity thereof and the reasonableness of the amount charged. The Prospectus shall disclose in tabular form an estimate of such expenses to be charged to the program showing direct expenses and general and administrative overhead separately, and the sponsor must demonstrate that it has a reasonable basis for such estimates. The estimate of general and administrative overhead shall be broken down into the various types of services and costs, with a separate breakdown for salaries to officers, directors and other principals of the sponsor and any affiliate of the sponsor; a summary of the manner in which such expenses are allocated shall be included. In addition, the Prospectus shall disclose in tabular form for each program formed in the last three years the dollar amount of the expenses so charged and allocated, and the percentage of subscriptions raised reflected thereby. The sponsor shall bear a percentage of general and administrative overhead equal to its percentage of revenue participation. A subordinated interest shall bear its percentage of general and administrative overhead from the time that the sponsor participates in program revenues.

VI. TRANSACTIONS WITH AFFILIATES AND CONFLICTS OF INTEREST

A. Sales and Purchases of Properties

1. Neither the sponsor of a drilling program nor any affiliated person shall sell, transfer or convey any property to or purchase any property from the

program, directly or indirectly, except pursuant to transactions that are fair
and reasonable to the participants of the program and then subject to the following conditions:

(a)   In the case of a sale, transfer or conveyance to a program;

(1)   The Prospectus discloses the fact that the sponsor will
sell, transfer or convey property to the program and whether or not the property
will be sold from the sponsor's existing inventory.

(2)   The property is sold, transferred or conveyed to the
program at the cost of the sponsor, unless the seller has reasonable grounds to
believe that cost is materially more than the fair market value of such property,
in which case such sale should be made for a price not in excess of its fair
market value.

(3)   If the sponsor sells, transfers or conveys any oil, gas
or other mineral interests or property to the program, he must, at the same time,
sell to the program an equal proportionate interest in all his other property in
the same prospect. If the sponsor or any affiliate subsequently proposes to acquire an interest in a prospect in which the program possesses an interest or in
a prospect abandoned by the program within one year preceding such proposed acquisition, the sponsor shall offer such interest to the program; and, if cash or
financing is not available to the program to enable it to consummate a purchase
of an equivalent interest in such property, neither the sponsor nor any of its
affiliates shall acquire such interest or property. The term "abandon" for the
purpose of this subsection shall mean the termination, either voluntarily or by
operation of the lease or otherwise, of all of the program's interest in the prospect. The provisions of this subsection shall not apply after the lapse of 5
years from the date of formation of the program. For the purpose of this subsection, the terms "sponsor" and "affiliate" shall not include another program
where the interest of the sponsor is identical to, or less than, his interest in
the subject program.

(4)   A sale, transfer or conveyance of less than all of the
ownership of the sponsor in any interest or property is prohibited unless the
interest retained by the sponsor is a proportionate working interest, the respective obligations of the sponsor and the program are substantially the same
after the sale of the interest by the sponsor and his interest in revenues does
not exceed the amount proportionate to his retained working interest. The sponsor
may not retain any overrides or other burdens on the interest conveyed to the
program and may not enter into any farm-out arrangements with respect to his
retained interest, except to nonaffiliated third parties or other programs managed
by the sponsor.

(b)   In the case of a transfer of nonproducing property from a program, the transfer is made at a price which is the higher of the fair market
value or the cost of such property.

(c)   The sponsor, or affiliates other than other public programs,
shall not be permitted to purchase producing property from a program.

2.   Neither the sponsor of a production purchase program nor any affiliated person shall sell, transfer or convey any property to or purchase any
property from the program, directly or indirectly, except pursuant to transactions that are fair and reasonable to the participants of the program and then
subject to the following conditions:

(a)   In the case of a purchase from or sale to a program;

(1)   The Prospectus discloses the fact that the sponsor may sell
property to the program and whether or not the property will be sold from the
sponsor's existing inventory.

(2)   The purchase from or sale to the program is at cost as
adjusted for intervening operations, unless the sponsor has reasonable grounds to
believe that cost is materially more than or less than the fair market value of
such property, in which case such sale or purchase should be made for a price not

in excess of its fair market value, as determined by an independent petroleum reservoir engineer.

(b) Any such transaction must be consistent with the objectives of the program.

3. The program shall not purchase properties from nor sell properties to any program in which its sponsor or any affiliated person has an interest. This subsection shall not apply to transactions among programs for whom the same person acts as sponsor by which property is transferred from one to another in exchange for the transferee's obligation to conduct drilling activities on such property or to joint ventures among such programs, provided that the respective obligations and revenue sharing of all parties to the transactions are substantially the same and provided further that the compensation arrangement or any other interest or right of the sponsor and any affiliated person of such sponsor is the same in each program, or, if different, the aggregate compensation of the sponsor does not exceed the lower of the compensation he would have received in any one of the programs.

B. Restricted and Prohibited Transactions

1. Neither the sponsor nor any affiliate (excluding another program in which the sponsor is a general partner) shall enter into any farm-out or other agreement with the program where in consideration for services to be rendered, an interest in production is payable to such sponsor or affiliate.

2. During the existence of a program and before it has ceased operations, neither the sponsor nor any affiliate (excluding another program where the interest of the sponsor is identical to or less than his interest in the first program) shall acquire, retain, or drill for its own account any oil and gas interest on any prospect upon which such program possesses an interest, except for sales or lease transactions which comply with Section VI.A.1(a)(4) of these guidelines. In the event the program abandons its interest in the prospect, this restriction shall continue until two years following the abandonment. If the geological limits of a prospect are enlarged to encompass any interest held by such sponsor or affiliate (excluding another program where the interest of the sponsor is identical to or less than his interest in the first program), such interest shall be sold to such program in accordance with the provisions of Section VI.A.1(a)(3) of these guidelines and any net income previously received by the sponsor or affiliate shall be paid over to such program. If within this period, the sponsor acquires additional acreage or interest in a prospect of the program, he must sell such to the program and is prohibited from retaining any such interest, except as may be permitted by Section VI.A.1. of these guidelines.

3. The sponsor shall not take any action with respect to the assets or property of the program which does not benefit primarily the program, including among other things:

(a) the utilization of funds of the program as compensating balances for his own benefit, and

(b) future commitments of production.

4. All benefits from marketing arrangements or other relationships affecting property of the sponsor and the program shall be fairly and equitably apportioned according to the respective interests of each.

5. Any agreements or arrangements which bind the program must be fully disclosed in the Prospectus.

6. Anything to the contrary notwithstanding, a sponsor may never profit by drilling in contravention of his fiduciary obligation to the participants.

7. Neither the sponsor nor any affiliate shall render to the program any oil field, equippage or drilling services nor sell or lease to the program any equipment or related supplies unless:

(a) such person is engaged, independently of the program and as an ordinary and ongoing part of his business, in the business of rendering such services or selling or leasing such equipment and supplies to a substantial extent to other persons in the oil and gas industry in addition to programs in which he has an interest,

(b) the compensation, price or rental therefor is competitive with the compensation, price or rental of other persons in the area engaged in the business of rendering comparable services or selling or leasing comparable equipment and supplies which could reasonably be made available to the program, and

(c) provided, that, if such person is not engaged in a business within the meaning of subdivision (a), then such compensation, price or rental shall be the cost of such services, equipment or supplies to such person or the competitive rate which could be obtained in the area whichever is less.

8. With the exception of compensation authorized by Section V. of these guidelines, all services for which the sponsor and any affiliated person is to receive compensation shall be embodied in a written contract which precisely describes the services to be rendered and all compensation to be paid.

9. No loans may be made by the program to the sponsor.

10. On loans made available to the program by the sponsor, the sponsor may not receive interest in excess of its interest costs, nor may the sponsor receive interest in excess of the amounts which would be charged the program (without reference to the sponsor's financial abilities or guaranties) by unrelated banks on comparable loans for the same purpose and the sponsor shall not receive points or other financing charges or fees regardless of the amount.

C. Custody of Program Funds and Properties

1. Funds of a program must not be commingled with funds of any other entity; the Prospectus must clearly prohibit any such commingling. Advance payments to the sponsor or its affiliates should be prohibited, except where necessary to secure tax benefits of prepaid drilling costs. Advance payments should not include nonrefundable payments for completion costs prior to the time that a decision is made that the well or wells warrant a completion attempt.

2. Program properties may be held in the names of nominees temporarily to facilitate the acquisition of properties and for similar valid purposes. On a permanent basis, program properties may be held in the name of a special nominee partnership organized by the general partner provided the nominee's sole purpose is the holding of record title for oil and gas properties and it engages in no other business and incurs no other liabilities.

VII. FARM-OUTS

A. Definition

1. As used in these guidelines, the term "farm-out" means an agreement whereby the owner of the leasehold or working interest agrees to assign his interest in certain specific acreage to the assignees, retaining some interest such as an overriding royalty interest, an oil and gas payment, offset acreage or other type of interest, subject to the drilling of one or more specific wells or other performance as a condition of the assignment.

2. The Prospectus shall contain the definition of farm-out and no other term shall be used to describe a farm-out transaction.

B. Disclosure

1. The Prospectus shall state the circumstances under which the sponsor may farm-out a prospect or lease, the ability to farm-out to other public programs of the sponsor or its affiliates and any limitations on the ability to farm-out to such public programs.

2. The Prospectus shall state that neither the sponsor nor any affiliate (except other programs of the sponsor or an affiliate) shall enter into any farm-out or other agreement with the program where in consideration for services to be rendered, an interest in production is payable to such sponsor or affiliate.

3. The Prospectus shall state that:

Program leases will not be farmed out, sold, or otherwise disposed of unless the sponsor exercising the standard of a prudent operator, determines:

(a) The program lacks sufficient funds to drill on the leases and cannot obtain suitable alternative financing for such drilling;

(b) The leases have been downgraded by events occurring after assignment to the program to the point that drilling would no longer be desirable to the program, or

(c) Drilling on the leases would result in an excessive concentration of program funds in one location creating in the opinion of the sponsor undue risk to the program.

4. In any event, where program leases are farmed out, sold or otherwise disposed of, the program will obtain and/or retain such economic interests and concessions as a reasonable prudent operator would or could obtain or retain under the circumstances.

C. Conflict of Interest

1. The Prospectus shall state that the decision with respect to making a farm-out and the terms of a farm-out to a program involve conflicts of interest, as the sponsor may benefit from cost savings and reduction of risk, and in the event of a farm-out to an affiliated public program, the sponsor will represent both partnerships.

2. The Prospectus shall contain a statement regarding farm-outs from a drilling or combination program to another such program meeting the requirements of Section VI.A.3.

3. Except as required by Section VI.A.1(a)(3), the Prospectus shall state that the program shall acquire only those leases that are reasonably acquired for the stated purpose of the program and no leases shall be acquired for the purpose of subsequent sale or farm-out, unless the acquisition of such leases by the program is made after a well has been drilled to a depth sufficient to indicate that such an acquisition is believed to be in the best interests of the program.

4. The Prospectus shall state that the sponsor shall not farm-out a lease for the primary purpose of avoiding payment of sponsor's costs relating to drilling a lease or prospect.

D. Reporting

The semi-annual report shall contain a description of all farm-outs including sponsors justification, location, time, to whom, and general description of terms.

VIII. RIGHTS AND OBLIGATIONS OF PARTICIPANTS

A. Meetings

Meetings of the participants may be called by the general partner(s) or by participants holding more than 10% of the then outstanding units for any matters for which the participants may vote as set forth in the limited partership agreement or charter document. Such call for a meeting shall be deemed to have been made upon receipt by the general partner of a written request from holders of the requisite percentage of units stating the purpose(s) of the meeting. The general partner shall deposit in the United States mails within fifteen days after receipt of said request, written notice to all participants of the meeting and the purpose of such meeting, which shall be held on a date not less than thirty nor more than sixty days after the date of mailing of said notice, at a reasonable time and place.

B. Annual and Periodic Reports

1. The partnership agreement or charter document shall provide for the transmittal to each participant of an annual report within 120 days after the close of the fiscal year, and commencing with the year following investment of substantially all the program subscriptions, a report within 75 days after the end of the first six months of its fiscal year, containing, except as otherwise indicated, at least the following information:

(a) Financial statements, including a balance sheet and statements of income, partners' equity and changes in financial position prepared in accordance with generally accepted accounting principles and accompanied by a report of an independent certified public accountant or independent public accountant stating that his examination was made in accordance with generally accepted auditing standards and that in his opinion such financial statements present fairly the financial position, results of operations and the changes in financial position in accordance with generally accepted accounting principles consistently applied, except that semiannual reports need not be audited. Along with such financial statements shall be a summary itemization, by type and/or classification of the total fees and compensation, including any overhead reimbursements, paid by the program, or indirectly on behalf of the program, to the sponsor and affiliates of the sponsor. If compensation is paid on a subordinated interest, a reconciliation of all such payments to the conditions precedent and limitations thereto.

(b) A description of each geological prospect in which the program owns an interest, except succeeding reports need contain only material changes, if any, regarding such geological prospects.

(c) A list of the wells drilled by such program (indicating whether each of such wells has or has not been completed), and a statement of the cost of each well completed or abandoned. Justification shall be included for wells abandoned after production has commenced.

(d) With respect to a program which compensates the sponsor on a basis related to certain costs paid by the sponsor, (1) a schedule reflecting the total program costs, and where applicable, the costs pertaining to each prospect, the costs paid by the sponsor and the costs paid by the participants, (2) the total program revenues, the revenues received or credited to the sponsor and the revenues received or credited to the participants, and (3) a reconciliation of such expenses and revenues to the limitations prescribed.

(e) Annually, beginning with the fiscal year succeeding the fiscal year in which the program commenced operations, a computation of the total oil and gas proven reserves of the program and dollar value thereof at then existing prices and of each participant's interest in such reserve value. The reserve computations shall be based upon engineering reports prepared by qualified independent petroleum consultants. In addition, there shall be included an estimate of the time required for the extraction of such reserves and the present worth of such reserves, with a statement that because of the time period required to extract such reserves the present value of revenues to be obtained in the future is less than if immediately receivable. In addition to the annual computation and estimate required, as soon as possible, and in no event more than 90 days after the occurrence of an event leading to a reduction of such reserves of the program of more than 10%, excluding reduction as a result of normal production, a computation and estimate shall be sent to each participant.

2. By March 15 of each year, the general partner must furnish a report to each participant containing such information as is pertinent for tax purposes.

3.   Production purchase programs that are subject to the continuing reporting requirements of the Securities Exchange Act of 1934 and agree to make all such reports available to participants on request, will not be required to transmit to participants reports other than the annual reports required under subsection 1 above, and the reports for tax purposes required by subsection 2 above.

C. Access to Program Records

1.   The general partner shall maintain a list of the names and addresses of all participants at the principal office of the partnership. Such list shall be made available for the review of any participant or his representative at reasonable times, and upon request either in person or by mail the general partner shall furnish a copy of such list to any participant or his representative for the cost of reproduction and mailing.

2.   The participants and/or their accredited representatives shall be permitted access to all records of the program, after adequate notice, at any reasonable time. The sponsor shall maintain and preserve during the term of the program and for four (4) years thereafter all accounts, books, and other relevant program documents. Notwithstanding the foregoing, the sponsor may keep logs, well reports and other drilling data confidential for a reasonable period of time.

D. Transferability of Program Interests

Restrictions on assignment of units will be looked upon with disfavor. Restrictions on the substitution of a limited partner are generally disfavored and will be allowed only to the extent necessary to preserve the tax status of the partnership and any restriction must be supported by opinion of counsel as to its legal necessity.

E. Assessability and Defaults

1.   In appropriate cases there may be a provision for assessability; provided, however, that the maximum amount which may be assessed for a voluntary assessment shall not exceed 100% of the initial subscription and for a mandatory assessment shall not exceed 25% of the initial subscription, and provided further, that in no case shall the total of all assessments exceed 100% of the initial subscription. All such assessments shall be solely for the purpose of drilling or completing a development well or wells or for acquiring additional interests or leases related to a prospect already owned by the program. In such cases, the aggregate offering price of the units as set forth in the application for qualification shall include and show separately the basic unit offering price and the maximum amount of the assessment.
2.   In the event of a default in all or a portion of the payment of assessments, the participant's percentage interest in the program represented by his unit should not be subject to forfeiture, but may be subject to a reasonable reduction for the failure of the particinant to meet his commitment. Provisions which conform to the following will be considered reasonable.

(a) For voluntary assessments,

(1)   A proportionate reduction of the participant's percentage interest in revenues derived from future development based on the ratio of his unpaid assessment to all capital contributions and assessments used for such future development, or

(2)   A subordination of the defaulting participant's right to receive revenues from future development until those nondefaulting participants who have paid the defaulting participant's assessment have received an amount of revenues from revenues of the program from future development equal to 300% of the proportionate amount of the defaulted assessment which they paid.

(b) For mandatory assessments,

(1)   A proportionate reduction of the participant's percentage interest in program revenues based on the ratio of his unpaid assessment to all capital contributions and assessments, or,

(2)   A subordination of the defaulting participant's right to receive revenues from the program until those nondefaulting participants who have paid the defaulting participant's assessment have received an amount of revenues from all revenues of the program equal to 300% of the proportionate amount of the defaulted assessment which they paid.

(c)   In order to make any assessment, the sponsor shall include with the call for such assessment a statement of the purpose and intended use of the proceeds from such assessment, a statement of the reduction to be imposed for failure of the participant to meet the assessment, and to the extent practicable, a summary of pertinent geological data on the relevant properties to which the assessments relate.

(d)   The above alternatives, set forth in (a) and (b), are not exclusive and other provisions demonstrated to be essentially equivalent to these alternatives may be permitted by the Administrator.

IX. MISCELLANEOUS PROVISIONS

A. Minimum Program Capital

The minimum amount of funds to activate a partnership shall be sufficient to accomplish the objectives of the program, including "spreading the risk". Any minimum less than $500,000, after deduction of all front end charges, will be presumed to be inadequate to spread the risk of the public investors. In those instances were it appears unlikely that the stated objectives of the program can be achieved with the minimum subscriptions, the Administrator may require a greater amount or a reduction of the stated objectives of the program. Provision must be made for the return to public investors of one hundred percent (100%) of paid subscriptions in the event that the established minimum to activate the program is not reached. All funds received prior to activation of the program must be deposited with an independent custodian, trustee, or escrow agent whose name and address shall be disclosed in the Prospectus.

B. Temporary Investment of Proceeds and Return of Unused Proceeds

1.   Until proceeds from the public offering are invested in the program's operations, such proceeds may be temporarily invested in short-term highly liquid investments, where there is appropriate safety of principal, such as U.S. Treasury Bills.

2.   Any proceeds of the public offering of a drilling program not used, or committed for use, in the program's operations within one year of the closing of the offering, except for necessary operating capital, must be distributed pro rata to the participants as a return of capital, and without any deductions for selling and offering expenses.

3.   If a production purchase program sponsor has not used, or committed for use, an amount equal to 80% of the proceeds of the public offering which are available for property acquisitions within one year of the closing of the offering, such sponsor shall not be permitted to continue offering interests in subsequent programs of a similar nature, until such time as the requirement has been met. If the production purchase program sponsor has not used, or committed for use, an amount equal to 100% of the proceeds of the public offering which are available for property acquisitions within two years of the closing of the offering, any excess proceeds, except for necessary operating capital, must be distributed pro rata to the participants as a return of capital, and without any charges for selling or offering expenses being allocable to the return of capital.

C. Deferred Payments

Arrangements for deferred payments on account of the purchase price of program interests may be allowed when warranted by the investment objectives of the partnership, but in any event such arrangements shall be subject to the following conditions:

1. The period of deferred payments shall coincide with the anticipated cash needs of the program, but the full amount of the purchase price shall be paid within nine (9) months of the date on which the program commences operations.

2. Selling commissions paid upon deferred payments are collectible when such payment is made.

3. The program shall not sell or assign the deferred payments.

In the event of a default in the payment of any deferred payment when due, the participant's percentage interests in the program shall not be subject to forfeiture but may be subject to a reasonable reduction for failure of the participant to meet his commitment. Reduction provisions will be considered reasonable if they conform to the reduction provisions provided for in Section VIII.F.2(b) of these guidelines, relating to defaults of mandatory assessments.

D. Cash Redemption Values

When cash redemption values of units are computed, such value must be clearly based on appraisal of properties by qualified independent petroleum consultants. Any evaluation by company personnel must be based on such independent appraisals. Any redemption must be for cash. No redemption shall be considered effective until after cash payments have been paid to the participants.

E. Future Exchanges and Reinvestment of Revenues

1. No sponsor or any affiliates shall make or cause to be made any offer to a participant to exchange his units for a security of any company, unless:

(a) such offer is made after the expiration of two years after such program commenced operations;

(b) such offer is made to all participants;

(c) such offer, if made by a third party to the sponsor or principal underwriter, or any affiliate of such sponsor or principal underwriter, is on a basis not more advantageous to such sponsor, principal underwriter or affiliate than to participants;

(d) the value of the security or other consideration offered is at least equivalent to the value of the units;

(e) the value of any reserves used in computing the exchange ratio is supported by an appraisal prepared by an independent petroleum consultant within 120 days of the date such exchange is to be made; the value of any undeveloped acreage used in computing the exchange ratio is at cost unless fair market value, as evidenced by supporting data, is higher; and the value of other assets used in computing the exchange ratio is based upon audited financial statements prepared in accordance with generally accepted accounting principles consistently applied, and

(f) the offer is made pursuant to all registration requirements under both federal and state laws.

For the purposes of this subsection, an "offer of exchange" includes any security of a program which is convertible into a security issued by the sponsor or another issuer.

2. No offering will be approved by the Administrator that includes a provision which requires that the participant reinvest his share of distributable cash distributions. Subject to compliance with applicable securities laws, a program may make available to its participants a voluntary plan for systematic reinvestments in such program or in any other program. No sales commissions may be charged the participants, however, for effecting such reinvestment.

F. Distribution of Revenues

From time to time and not less often than quarterly, the sponsor will review the program's accounts to determine whether cash distributions are appropriate. The program will distribute pro rata to the participants funds received by the program and allocated to their accounts which the sponsor deems unnecessary to retain in the program. The determination to make cash distributions and the percentage calculation thereof from the program to the sponsor will be made on the same basis.

X. PROSPECTUS AND DISCLOSURE AND MARKETING REQUIREMENTS

A. Sales Materials and Marketing Restrictions

1. Sales Literature. Sales literature, including without limitation, books, pamphlets, movies, slides, article reprints, and television and radio commercials, sales presentations (including prepared presentations to prospective participants at group meetings) and all other advertising used in the offer or sale of units shall conform in all applicable respects to filing, disclosure and adequacy requirements currently imposed on the sale of corporate securities under these guidelines. When periodic or other reports, except those required by and filed with the Securities and Exchange Commission, furnished to participants in prior programs are furnished to prospective participants in a program not yet sold, such reports will be treated as sales literature subject to the above requirements. Sales literature shall not be so excessive in size or amount as to detract from the Prospectus, nor shall any sales literature be used by securities broker-dealers or agents unless such literature has been approved by the sponsor in writing.

2. Group Meetings. All advertisements of, and oral or written invitations to "seminars" or other group meetings at which units are to be described, offered or sold shall clearly indicate that the purpose of such meeting is to offer such units for sale, the minimum purchase price thereof, the suitability standards to be employed, and the name of the person selling the units. No cash, merchandise or other items of value shall be offered as an inducement to any prospective participants to attend any such meeting. All written or prepared audi-visual presentations (including scripts prepared in advance for oral presentations) to be made at such meetings must be submitted to the Administrator within the prescribed review period. The provisions of this section shall not apply to meetings consisting only of representatives of securities broker-dealers.

B. Offerings Registered with the Securities and Exchange Commission "SEC"

With respect to offerings registered with the Securities and Exchange Commission under the Securities Act of 1933, as amended, and registered or qualified with the Administrator, a Prospectus which is part of a registration statement which has been declared effective by said Commission shall be deemed to comply with all requirements as to form of these guidelines; provided, however, that the Administrator reserves the right to require additional disclosure of substance in his discretion.

C. Contents of Prospectus

1. The following information shall be included in the Prospectus of each program:

(a) Initial Information:

(1) Information on Cover Page. There should be set forth briefly on the cover page of the Prospectus a summary which should include the following: The title and general nature of the units being offered; the maximum aggregate amount of the offering; the minimum amount of net proceeds; the minimum subscription price; the period of the offering; the maximum amount of any sales or underwriting commissions to be paid (or, if none, or if such commissions are paid by the sponsor); the nature of any sharing arrangement and fees; the estimated amount to be paid during the first twelve (12) months following commencement of operations for administrative and similar services.

(2) Sales to Appropriate Persons. There should be set forth in the second page of the Prospectus, the suitability requirements for participants as set forth in Section IV of these guidelines.

(b) Definitions. Technical terms used in the Prospectus should be defined either in a glossary or as they appear in the Prospectus.

(c) Risk Factors. Offerees should be advised in a carefully organized series of short, concise paragraphs, under subcaptions where appropriate, of the risks to be considered before making an investment in the program. These paragraphs should include a cross-reference to further information in the Prospectus. In particular, in those cases where the sponsor has elected the compensation arrangement described in Section V.B.1., there should be set forth the fact that there is a conflict where the sponsor must decide whether to complete a well which is anticipated to have a marginal return since the tangible costs he would incur would not appear to warrant his investment, although completion of the well would be in the best interests of the participants.

(d) Business Experience. The business experience of the sponsor(s), including general partner(s), principal officers of a corporate general partner (chairman of the board, president, vice president, treasurer, secretary or any person having similar authority or performing like function) and others responsible for the program, shall be prominently disclosed in the Prospectus, such disclosure indicating their business experience for the past ten years. The lack of experience or limited experience of the sponsor, or other person supplying services to the program, shall be prominently disclosed in the Prospectus.

(e) Compensation. All indirect and direct compensation which may be paid by the program to the sponsor or any affiliate of every type and from every source shall be summarized in tabular form and in narrative where appropriate to fully disclose material information, in one location, in the forepart of the Prospectus. Also include estimates of all actual and necessary direct expenses paid or incurred or to be paid or incurred by the sponsor for a period of three years in connection with its operations of a program for which the sponsor is to be reimbursed out of capital contributions and program revenues. Such table shall also include administrative and similar charges for services.

(f) Use of Proceeds. State the purposes for which the net proceeds to the program are intended to be used and the approximate amount and percentages intended to be used for each such purpose. Also state the minimum aggregate amount necessary to initiate the program and the disposition of the funds raised if they are not sufficient for that purpose.

(g) Deferred Payment Schedule. If deferred payments are called for or allowed, the schedule of payment shall be set forth.

(h) Assessments. If provisions for assessments are provided, the method of assessment and the penalty for default shall be prominently set forth.

(i) Investment Objectives and Policies. Describe the investment objectives and policies of the program (indicating whether they may be changed by the general partner without a vote of the limited partners) and, if and to the extent that the sponsor is able to do so, the approximate percentage of assets which the program may invest in any one type of investment. State the approximate percentage of exploratory and developmental drilling to be done by the program, the method of acquisition of leases, including information as to possible farmouts, and the approximate percentage of development drilling to be done through acquisition of offsetting leases as opposed to development of drilling sites acquired in the exploratory state. State also the expected percentage of leases where the program will not have control of drilling and operation.

(j) Description of Oil and Gas Interests. State the location and describe the general character of all materially important oil and gas interests now held or presently intended to be acquired by the program.

(k) "Performance", when required or permitted by the Administrator, shall contain the following information:

(1)   The previous program experience of the sponsor and other relevant parties shall be disclosed in the Prospectus for all programs during the past five years which:

(i)   Involved a public offering registered under state or federal securities laws;

(ii)   Involved a private or limited offering, the results of which are material to an informed investment decision by the offeree.

(2)   Information on previous programs shall include, but not be limited to, the following:

(i)   Name of the program, including the type of legal entity and state of incorporation or organization;

(ii)   The effective date of the offering, the date it commenced operations and the date of dissolution or termination, or if it is continuing;

(iii)   The total amount of units, the gross amount of capital raised by the program, the number of participants, and the amount of investment of the sponsor, if applicable;

(iv)   The drilling results of the program, including the number of gross and net wells drilled, both oil and gas, both exploratory and developmental, and both successful and unsuccessful;

(v)   Total dollar amounts of federal tax deductible items passed on to participants;

(vi)   Income credited and cash distributed to participants and the sponsor;

(vii)   Compensation and fees to the sponsor and its affiliates, segregated as to type;

(viii) Disclosure of any development wells drilled which did not or have not returned the investment therein within four years;

(ix)   Such additional or different disclosures of the success or failure of the programs as may be permitted or required by the Administrator.

(3)   All of the foregoing information shall be set forth on a cumulative basis for each program, and in tabular form wherever possible.

(4)   The following caveat should be prominently featured in the presentation of the foregoing information: "It should not be assumed that participants in the offering covered by this Prospectus will experience returns, if any, comparable to those experienced by investors in prior programs".

(5)   The foregoing information shall be supported in the application by an affidavit of the sponsor that the performance summary is a fair representation of the information contained in the audited financial statement or the federal income tax returns of the program or in other reports or data of the program or sponsor.

(1)   Operating Data. Include appropriate data with respect to each property which is separately described in answer to paragraph (j) above.

(m)   The Program:

(1)   Date of formation.

(2)   Place of formation.

(3)   Sponsor.

(4)   Address and telephone number of the program and the sponsor.

(5)   Duration.

(6)   Information called for in items (1) through (5) hereof shall be given for any other programs in which the program invests.

(n)   Summary of Terms of the Program:

(1)   Powers of the sponsor.

(2)   Rights and liabilities of the participants.

(3)   Allocation of costs and revenues.

(4)   Termination and dissolution.

(5)   Meetings and reports.

(6)   Indemnification to sponsor.

(7)   Amendment of partnership agreement.

(8)   Provision for additional assessments.

(9)   Other pertinent matters.

(o)   Federal Tax Consequences:

(1)   A summary of an opinion of tax counsel acceptable to the Administrator and/or a ruling from the IRS covering federal tax questions relative to the program, which may be based on reasonable assumptions described in the opinion letter. To the extent the opinion of counsel or IRS ruling is based on the maintenance of or compliance with certain requirements or conditions by the sponsor(s), the Prospectus shall to the extent practicable contain representations that such requirements or conditions have been met and that the sponsors shall use their best efforts to continue to meet such requirements or conditions.

(2)   Tax treatment of the program.

(3)   Tax treatment of the participants.

(4)   Allocation of intangible drilling deductions, depreciation, depletion allowances, etc.

(5)   Method of allocation of losses or profits and cash distributions upon transfer of a unit or the rights to income or revenues.

(6)   Any other pertinent information applicable to the tax shelter aspects of the investment.

(7)   Possibility of requirement for filing tax returns with states in which prospects are located.

(p)   Units:

(1)   Amount.

(2)   Minimum purchase.

(3)   Assessability.

(4)   Transferability.

(5)   Voting rights.

(6)   Redemption provisions, including the basis for appraisal.

(q) Plan of Distribution:

    (1) Discounts and commissions.

    (2) Estimated fees and expenses paid or reimbursed by the program.

    (3) Indemnification and hold harmless provisions.

    (4) Terms of payment.

    (5) Identity of underwriter, managing dealer and/or principal selling agent.

    (6) Type of underwriting - best efforts or firm commitment.

    (7) Minimum and maximum sales.

    (8) Escrow provisions.

    (9) Material relationship of underwriter to the program, if any.

(r) Pending Legal Proceedings. Briefly describe any legal proceedings to which the program or the sponsor is a party which is material to the program and any material legal proceedings between sponsor and participants in any prior program of the sponsor. Also, describe any material legal proceedings to which any of the program's or sponsor's property is subject.

(s) Conflicts of Interest and Transactions with Affiliates. Describe fully any transactions and the dollar amount thereof which may be entered into between the program and the sponsor or any affiliate. Include a full description of the material terms of any agreement and the dollar amount thereof between the program and the sponsor or any affiliate. Where the sponsor originates or promotes other programs, describe the equitable principles which will apply in resolving any conflict between the programs. In the case where the program has been in existence, include all transactions and contracts of the program with the sponsor or any affiliate during the period of such existence. All conflicts shall be set forth in one section and shall be denominated with the title of this subsection.

(t) Interest of Affiliates in Program Property. If within the past five years the sponsor or any affiliate has been in the chain of title or had a beneficial interest in any property to be acquired by the program this fact must be disclosed.

(u) Interest of Counsel and Experts in the Sponsor or Program. Where counsel for the selling representatives or the sponsor are named in the Prospectus as having passed upon the legality of the units being registered or upon other legal matters in connection with the registration or offering of such units, there should be disclosed in the conflict of interest section in the Prospectus the nature and amount of any direct or indirect material interest of any such counsel, other than legal fees to be received by such counsel, in the sponsor or any affiliate. Any such interest received or to be received in connection with the registration or offering of the units being registered, including the ownership or receipt by counsel, or by members of the firm participating in the matter, of securities of the sponsor or any affiliate of the program, for services shall be disclosed. Employment by the sponsor, other than retainer as legal counsel, should be disclosed in the Prospectus.

(v) Investment Company Act of 1940. Where beneficial interests of a program are to be sold, treatment under the Investment Company Act of 1940 must be disclosed.

(w) Financial Statements. As provided in subsection D below.

(x) Additional Information. Any additional information which is material should be included.

D. Financial Information Required on Application

The sponsor or the program shall provide as an exhibit to the application or where indicated below shall provide as part of the Prospectus, the following financial information and financial statements:

1. Balance Sheet of General Partner

(a) Corporate General Partner. A balance sheet of any corporate general partners as of the end of their most recent fiscal year, prepared in accordance with generally accepted accounting principles and accompanied by an auditor's report containing an unqualified opinion of an independent certified public accountant or independent public accountant, and an unaudited balance sheet as of a date not more than ninety days prior to the date of filing. Such statements shall be included in the Prospectus.

(b) Other General Partners. A balance sheet for each non-corporate general partner (including individual partners or individual joint venturers of a sponsor) as of a time not more than ninety days prior to the date of filing an application; such balance sheet, which may be unaudited, should conform to generally accepted accounting principles and shall be signed and sworn to by such general partners. A representation of the amount of such net worth must be included in the Prospectus.

2. Statement of Income for Corporate General Partners

A statement of income for the last fiscal year of any corporate general partner (or for the life of the corporate general partner, if less) prepared in accordance with generally accepted accounting principles and accompanied by an auditor's report containing an unqualified opinion of an independent certified public accountant or independent public accountant, and an unaudited statement for any interim period ending not more than ninety days prior to the date of filing an application.

3. Balance Sheet of Program

As part of the Prospectus, a balance sheet of the program as of the end of its most recent fiscal year prepared in accordance with generally accepted accounting principles and accompanied by an auditor's report containing an unqualified opinion of an independent certified public accountant or independent public accountant, and an unaudited balance sheet as of a date not more than ninety days prior to the date of filing.

4. Statements of Income, Partner's Equity, and Changes in Financial Position of Program.

As part of the Prospectus, if the program has been formed and owns assets, statements of income, statements of partner's equity, and statements of changes in financial position for the program for each of the last three fiscal years of the program (or for the life of the program, if less), all of which statements shall be prepared in accordance with generally accepted accounting principles and accompanied by an auditor's report containing an unqualified opinion of an independent certified public accountant or independent public accountant, and unaudited statements for any interim period ending not more than ninety days prior to the date of filing an application.

5. Cash Flow Statement of Program

As part of the Prospectus, if the program has been formed and owns assets, a cash flow statement, which may be unaudited, for the program for each of the last three fiscal years of the program (or for the life of the program, if less) and unaudited statements for any interim period between the end of the latest fiscal year and the date of the balance sheet furnished, and for the corresponding interim period of the preceding years.

6. Filing of Other Statements

Upon request by an applicant, the Administrator may, where consistent with the protection of investors, permit the omission of one or more of the statements required under this section and the filing, in substitution thereof, of appropriate statements verifying financial information having comparable relevance to an investor in determining whether he should invest in the program.

E. Opinions of Counsel

The application for qualification shall contain a favorable ruling from the IRS or an opinion of counsel to the effect that the program will be treated as a "partnership" and not as an "association taxable as a corporation" for federal   income tax purposes. An opinion of counsel shall be in form satisfactory to the Administrator and shall be unqualified except to the extent permitted by the Administrator. However, an opinion of counsel may be based on reasonable assumptions, such as (a) facts or proposed operations as set forth in the Prospectus and organization document; (b) the absence of future changes in applicable laws; (c) compliance with certain procedures such as the execution and delivery of certain documents and the filing of a certificate of limited partnership or an amended certificate, and (d) the continued maintenance of or compliance with certain financial, ownership or other requirements by the sponsor or general partner. The Administrator may request from counsel as supplemental information such supporting legal memoranda and an analysis as he shall deem appropriate under the circumstances. To the extent the opinion of counsel or IRS ruling is based on the maintenance of or compliance with certain requirements or conditions by the sponsor or general partner, the Prospectus shall contain representations that such requirements or conditions will be met and the partnership agreement shall, to the extent practicable, contain provisions requiring such compliance.

There shall be included also an opinion of counsel to the effect that the units being offered will be duly authorized or created and validly issued interests in the program, and that the liability of the participants will be limited to their respective capital contributions, except as set forth in the Prospectus.

AMENDMENTS TO
NASAA GUIDELINES FOR THE REGISTRATION
OF OIL AND GAS PROGRAMS

I.B.17.

PROSPECT - An area in which the program owns or intends to own one or more oil and gas interests, which is geographically defined on the basis of geological data by the sponsor of such program and which is reasonably anticipated by the sponsor to contain at least one reservoir.

II.F. Liability and Indemnification

The sponsors shall not attempt to pass on to participants the unlimited liability imposed upon them by law except that the program agreement may provide for indemnification of the sponsor(s) under the following circumstances and in the manner and to the extent indicated:

1. In any threatened, pending or completed action, suit or proceeding to which the sponsor was or is a party or is threatened to be made a party by reason of the fact that he is or was the sponsor of the program (other than an action by or in the right of the program) involving an alleged cause of action for damages arising from the performance of oil and gas activities including exploration, development, completion, or operation or other activities relative to management and disposition of oil and gas properties or production from such properties, the program may indemnify such sponsor against expenses, including attorneys' fees, judgments and amounts paid in settlement actually and reasonably incurred by him in connection with such action, suit or proceeding if the sponsor acted in good faith and in a manner he reasonably believed to be in or not opposed to the best interests of the program, and provided that his conduct does not constitute gross negligence, wilful or wanton misconduct, or a breach of his fiduciary obligations to the participants. The termination of any action, suit or proceeding by judgment, order or settlement shall not, of itself, create a presumption that the sponsor did not act in good faith and in a manner which he reasonably believed to be in or not opposed to the best interests of the program.

2. In any threatened, pending or completed action or suit by or in the right of the program, to which the sponsor was or is a party or is threatened to be made a party, involving an alleged cause of action by a participant or participants for damages arising from the activities of the sponsor in the performance of management of the internal affairs of the program as prescribed by the program agreement or by the law of the state of organization, or both, the program may indemnify such sponsor against expenses, including attorneys' fees, actually and reasonably incurred by him in connection with the defense or settlement of such action or suit if he acted in good faith and in a manner he reasonably believed to be in or not opposed to the best interests of the program as specified in this Subsection 2, except that no indemnification shall be made in respect of any claim, issue or matter as to which the sponsor shall have been adjudged to be liable for negligence, misconduct, or breach of fiduciary obligation in the performance of his duty to the program as specified in this Subsection 2, unless and only to the extent that the court in which such action or suit was brought shall determine upon application, that, despite the adjudication of liability but in view of all circumstances of the case, such person is fairly and reasonably entitled to indemnity for such expenses which such court shall deem proper.

3. To the extent that a sponsor has been successful on the merits or otherwise in defense of any action, suit or proceeding referred to in subparagraph (1) or (2) above, or in defense of any claim, issue or matter therein, the program shall indemnify him against the expenses, including attorneys' fees, actually and reasonably incurred by him in connection therewith.

4. Any indemnification under subparagraph (1) or (2) above, unless ordered by a court, shall be made by the program only as authorized in the specific case and only upon a determination by independent legal counsel in a written opinion that indemnification of the sponsor is proper in the circumstances because he has met the applicable standard of conduct set forth in subparagraph (1) or (2) above.

V.B.1(a)

(a)   Where the sponsor agrees to pay all capital expenditures of the program, but in any case at least 10% of the capital contributions to the program (excluding any capital contributions from the sponsor or any of his affiliates), his share of revenues will be determined by the following formula:

(1) if the agreement is to pay all capital expenditures but in any case a sum of not less than 10% of the capital contributions to the program (excluding any capital contributions from the sponsor or any of his affiliates), the sponsor will be entitled to receive 35% of program revenues;

(2)   the sponsor's revenue sharing may be increased in additional increments of 5% for each additional 5% increase in the percentage of capital contributions to the program (excluding any capital contributions from the sponsor or any of his affiliates) agreed to be paid by him up to a maximum of 50% of revenues subject to sponsor's agreement to pay in any case all capital expenditures.

V.B.2.   (New Material)

2.   Drilling Programs - Subordinated or Reversionary Working Interest

As an alternative to sharing revenues on a basis related to costs paid, it will be considered reasonable for a sponsor of a drilling program to receive a promotional interest in the form of a subordinated percentage of the working interest.   The holder of a subordinated working interest shall be entitled to receive his share of revenues only after the participants have had allocated to their respective accounts an amount determined in accordance with either one of the following alternative formulas: (1) an amount which reflects that the participants' share of revenues from production and other items credited to a prospect equal the sum of the costs of acquisition, drilling and development, all costs of operating the leases underlying the prospect, and an appropriately allocated portion of all other program expenses, including organizational and offering expenses; or (2) an amount which reflects that the revenues of the program equal all the expenses of the program.

If the sponsor elects to use the first formula, his subordinated working interest shall entitle him to receive 25% of program revenues and if he chooses the second formula his interest shall equal 33-1/3% of program revenues.

At such time as the sponsor is entitled to receive his promotional interest, he shall also bear program costs in the same ratio as he participates in program revenues.

V.B.3.   (same as original V.B.2. but renumbered)

VI.A.1(a)(3)

(3)   If the sponsor sells, transfers or conveys any oil, gas or other mineral interests or property to the program, he must, at the same time, sell to the program an equal proportionate interest in all his other property in the same prospect.   If the sponsor or any affiliate subsequently proposes to acquire an interest in a prospect in which the program possesses an interest or in a prospect abandoned by the program within one year preceding such proposed acquisition, the sponsor shall offer an equivalent interest therein to the program; and, if cash or financing is not available to the program to enable it to consummate a purchase of an equivalent interest in such property, neither the sponsor nor any of its affiliates shall acquire such interest or property.   The term "abandon" for the purpose of this subsection shall mean the termination, either voluntarily or by operation of the lease or otherwise, of all of the program's interest in the prospect.   The provisions of this subsection shall not apply after the lapse of 5 years from the date of formation of the program.   For the purpose of this subsection, the terms "sponsor" and "affiliate" shall not include another program where the interests of the sponsor is identical to, or less than, his interest in the subject program.

VI.B.   Restricted and Prohibited Transactions

1.   During the existence of a program and before it has ceased operations, neither the sponsor nor any affiliate (excluding another program where the interest of the sponsor is identical to or less than his interest in the first program) shall acquire, retain, or drill for its own account any oil and gas interest in any prospect upon which such program possesses an interest, except for transactions which comply with Section VI.A.1(a)(4) of these guidelines. In the event the program abandons its interest in a prospect, this restriction shall continue for one year following abandonment. The geological limits of a prospect shall be enlarged or contracted on the basis of subsequently acquired geological data to define the productive limits of a reservoir, and must include all of the acreage determined by the subsequent data to be encompassed by such reservoir; provided, however, that the program shall not be required to expend additional funds unless they are available from the initial capitalization of the program or if the sponsor believes it is prudent to borrow for the purpose of acquiring such additional acreage. If the geological limits of a prospect as so enlarged encompass any interest held by a sponsor or affiliate, that interest shall be sold to the program in accordance with the provisions of Section VI.A.1(A)(3) of these guidelines if the interest held by the sponsor at the time of the prospect's enlargement has been proved up the the program.

2.   A sponsor shall not take any action with respect to the assets or property of the program which does not primarily benefit the program, including among other things:

(a)   the utilization of program funds as compensating balances for its own benefit, and

(b)   the commitment of future production.

3. through 9.   (same as original 4 through 10 but renumbered)

VI.C.2.

2.   Program properties may be held in the names of nominees temporarily to facilitate the acquisition of properties and for similar valid purposes. On a permanent basis, program properties may be held in the name of a special nominee entity organized by the general partner provided the nominee's sole purpose is the holding of record title for oil and gas properties and it engages in no other business and incurs no other liabilities.

VII.B.2.

2.   If the sponsor or any of its affiliates enters into a farmout or other similar agreement with its program all such transactions must be in accordance with these guidelines and subject to the following conditions:

(a)   The sponsor, exercising the standard of a prudent operator shall determine that the farmout is in the best interests of the program, and

(b)   The terms of the farmout are consistent with and in any case no less favorable than those utilized in the geographic area for similar arrangements.

VII.B.3.

3.   No program lease will be farmed out, sold or otherwise disposed of unless the sponsor, exercising the standard of a prudent operator, determines:

(a)   The program lacks sufficient funds to drill on the leases and cannot obtain suitable alternative financing for such drilling; or

(b)   The leases have been downgraded by events occurring after assignment to the program so that drilling would no longer be desirable for the program; or

APPENDIX FIFTEEN
TAX SHELTERS AT A GLANCE
TAX FEATURES

Type of Investment	Minimum Investment	Type of Shelter	Potential for First-Year Excess Write-Off	Income Sheltered	Capital Gains	Allowable Depreciation Methods	Investment Tax Credit	Recapture	Phantom Income	Tax Preference Items**	Investment Interest**	Cash Flow	Appreciation	Liquidity	Degree of Economic Risk
5. Other Farming:															
a. Agricultural	$10,000 to 25,000	Mix of Long Term Deferral and Deep Shelter	Yes, subject to "at risk" limitations	Varies with program	Yes	Various	Yes	Most Depreciation Pre-1976 EDA Balance Special Rules as Items of to Some Expenditure	Possible	Excess Depreciation on Improvements	No	Speculative (Delayed)	Good but Speculative	Low	High
b. Timber	$10,000 to 25,000	Little Initial Shelter	Usually Not	Partial under special depletion rules	Yes, under Special Rules	None	No	No (unless EDA applicable)	No	None	No	Delayed	Speculative (Delayed)	Low to Moderate	Moderate to High
6. Exotics:															
a. Movies	$10,000 to 25,000	Long Term Deferral (High Risk)	Yes, subject to "at risk" limitations	Yes, until Crossover	Seldom Sold	Accelerated (High Risk)	Accelerated special rules	All Depreciation Investment Tax Credit rules Assured Phantom Income	High	None	Possible	Speculative and High Risk	Seldom Sold	Low	High
b. Equipment Leasing	$25,000 to 50,000	Mix of Long Term Deferral and Deep Shelter	Yes, for Corporate Lessors	Yes, until Crossover	Yes, if Residual Value Exceeds Cost	Accelerated	Yes, subject to stringent limitations on non-Corporate Lessors	All Depreciation Investment Tax Credit rules	Yes	Excess Depreciation	Possible	Moderate	Depends Upon Potential Residual Value of Equipment	Low	Depends Upon Quality of Lessee and Potential Obsolescence of Equipment
c. Records & Books	$10,000 to 25,000	Long Term Deferral (High Risk)	Yes	Yes, until Crossover	Seldom Sold	Accelerated (High Risk)	Yes (Risk of Disallowance)	All Depreciation Investment Tax Credit rules Assured Phantom Income	High	None	Possible	Speculative and High Risk	Seldom Sold	Low	High
d. Coal	$10,000 to 25,000	Mix of Long Term Deferral and Deep Shelter	Yes, subject to "partnership borrowing" restrictions	Partial	Yes	Only on Equipment Method Varies	Only on Equipment	Investment Tax Credit rules Assured Phantom Income	Yes	Excess Percentage Depletion	No	Speculative	Speculative	Low	High

* Not including capital gains on sale, or effects of converting personal service to non-personal service income.
** Not applicable to Corporations.
*** Limited to purchased animals.

For your convenience, a large-size reproduction of this chart, "Tax Shelters at a Glance," has been inserted in the pocket at the end of this book.

INDEX

All references are to paragraph ¶ numbers.

—A—